# NATIONAL GEOGRAPHIC
# Reach™
## Language • Literacy • Content

**Program Authors**

Nancy Frey

Lada Kratky

Nonie K. Lesaux

Sylvia Linan-Thompson

Deborah J. Short

Jennifer D. Turner

 NATIONAL GEOGRAPHIC LEARNING |  CENGAGE Learning

## Literature Reviewers

Carmen Agra Deedy, Grace Lin, Jonda C. McNair, Anastasia Suen

## Grade 5 Teacher Reviewers

**Terrie Armstrong**
*Bilingual/ESL Program Team Leader*
Houston Independent School District
Houston, TX

**Irma Bravo-Lawrence**
*Director II, District and English Learner*
*Support Services*
*Stanislaus County Office of Education*
Turlock, CA

**Julie Folkert**
*Language Arts Coordinator*
Farmington Public Schools
Farmington Hills, MI

**Norma Godina-Silva, Ph.D**
*Bilingual Education/ESL/*
*Title III Consultant*
ESL-BilingualResources.com
El Paso, TX

**Keely Krueger**
*Director of Bilingual Education*
Woodstock Community Unit School 200
Woodstock, IL

**Myra Junyk**
*Literacy Consultant*
Toronto, ON, Canada

**Lore Levene**
*Coordinator of Language Arts and Literacy*
Community Consolidated School District 59
Mt. Prospect, IL

**Estee Lopez**
*Professor of Literacy Education*
*and ELL Specialist*
College of New Rochelle
New Rochelle, NY

**Christine Kay Williams**
*ESOL Teacher*
Baltimore County Public Schools
Baltimore, MD

**Acknowledgments**
Grateful acknowledgment is given to the authors, artists, photographers, museums, publishers, and agents for permission to reprint copyrighted material. Every effort has been made to secure the appropriate permission. If any omissions have been made or if corrections are required, please contact the Publisher.

**Illustrator Credits:**
**Front Cover:** Joel Sotelo

Acknowledgments and credits continue on page 694.

For product information and technology assistance, contact us at
**Customer & Sales Support, 888-915-3276**

For permission to use material from this text or product, submit
all requests online at **www.cengage.com/permissions**
Further permissions questions can be emailed to
**permissionrequest@cengage.com**

**National Geographic Learning | Cengage Learning**
1 Lower Ragsdale Drive
Building 1, Suite 200
Monterey, CA 93940

Cengage Learning is a leading provider of customized learning solutions with office locations around the globe, including Singapore, the United Kingdom, Australia, Mexico, Brazil, and Japan. Locate your local office at **www.cengage.com/global**.

Cengage Learning products are represented in Canada by Nelson Education, Ltd.

Visit National Geographic Learning online at **NGL.Cengage.com**
Visit our corporate website at **www.cengage.com**

Printed in the USA.
Quad Graphics, Versailles, KY, USA

ISBN: 978-13054-93537
ISBN (CA): 978-13054-94596

Printed in the United States of America

18 19 20 21 22 23 24

13 12 11 10 9 8 7 6

# Contents at a Glance

# Table of Contents

# Crossing Between Cultures

**(?) BIG QUESTION**

How can where you are change who you are?

## Read More

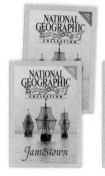

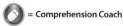 = Comprehension Coach     = Interactive Whiteboard     = NGReach.com

# Unit **1**

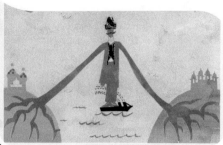

## SOCIAL STUDIES
▸ U. S. Immigration

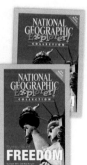

v

# Table of Contents

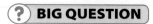 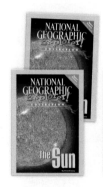
**Read More**

 = Comprehension Coach     = Interactive Whiteboard     = NGReach.com

## SCIENCE
▸ **The Sun's Energy**

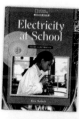
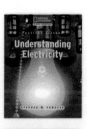

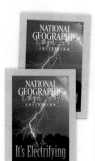

# Table of Contents

# Nature's Network

**Read More**

 = Comprehension Coach   = Interactive Whiteboard  = NGReach.com

# Unit **3**

## SCIENCE

▸ **Food Webs**
▸ **Ecosystems**

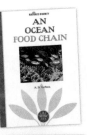
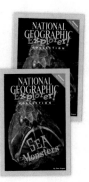

# Table of Contents

# Justice

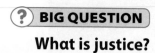 **BIG QUESTION**
**What is justice?**

## Read More

 = Comprehension Coach     = Interactive Whiteboard     = NGReach.com

# Unit 4

## SOCIAL STUDIES

▸ U. S. History:
  Human Rights

# Table of Contents

# Every Drop

**? BIG QUESTION**

**Why is water so important?**

## Read More

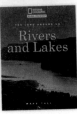

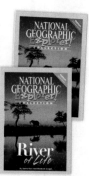

 = Comprehension Coach  = Interactive Whiteboard  = NGReach.com

# Unit 5

## SCIENCE

▸ Water Cycle
▸ Weather and Climate

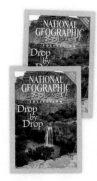

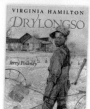

# Table of Contents

# The Wild West

**?** **BIG QUESTION**

**What does it take to settle a new land?**

## Read More

 = Comprehension Coach    = Interactive Whiteboard    = NGReach.com

# Unit 6

## SOCIAL STUDIES

▸ U. S. History: Westward Expansion

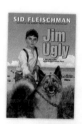

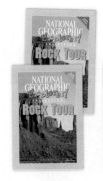
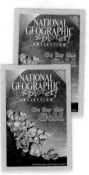

# Table of Contents

# Talking About Trash

(?) **BIG QUESTION**

**Why should we care about garbage?**

**Unit Launch** **Build Background Interactive Resource** . . . . . . . . **456**
Read Aloud: from *Earth's Garbage Crisis* CloseReading

**Skills**

Author's
Viewpoint

Synthesize

## Part 1

## Read More

 = Comprehension Coach     = Interactive Whiteboard    = NGReach.com

xvi

## SCIENCE

▸ Renewable and Nonrenewable Resources

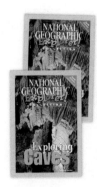

# Table of Contents

# One Idea

**?** **BIG QUESTION**

How can one idea change your future?

## Read More

 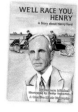  

 = Comprehension Coach     = Interactive Whiteboard     = NGReach.com

# Unit 8

## SOCIAL STUDIES
▸ Economics

# Genres at a Glance

= Interactive Whiteboard     = NGReach.com

# Crossing
# Between Cultures

How can where you are change who you are?

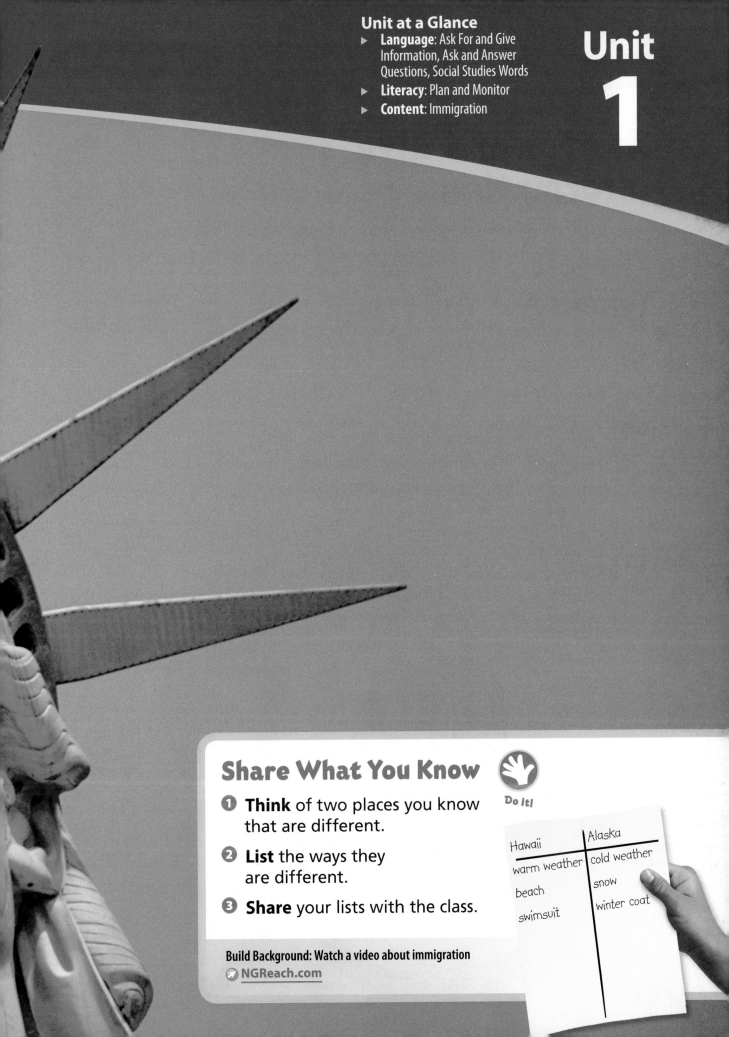

**Unit at a Glance**
▸ **Language**: Ask For and Give Information, Ask and Answer Questions, Social Studies Words
▸ **Literacy**: Plan and Monitor
▸ **Content**: Immigration

**Unit**
**1**

## Share What You Know

**Do It!**

❶ **Think** of two places you know that are different.

❷ **List** the ways they are different.

❸ **Share** your lists with the class.

| Hawaii | Alaska |
|---|---|
| warm weather | cold weather |
| beach | snow |
| swimsuit | winter coat |

**Build Background: Watch a video about immigration**
**NGReach.com**

## Ask For and Give Information

Listen to Lulu and Ricky's song. Then use **Language Frames** to ask for and give information about places you and your friends have lived.

## Where Are You From? *Song* ((( MP3 )))

 Where does your family come from?
Can you explain to me?

 I am from a sunny island in the Caribbean Sea.
We lived in Puerto Rico till I was eight years old.
Now I live in Texas, where winters can be cold.
Where does your family come from?
I'd really like to know.

 I grew up in Indonesia, where I never saw the snow.
We lived close to the ocean, and swam all winter long.
Now I live in Texas, where I feel I belong.

Tune: "Yellow Rose of Texas"

Welcome to Amarillo Texas!

**Key Words**

country
culture
education
employment
immigration

# Key Words

Look at the photographs. Use **Key Words** and other words to talk about moving to a new **country**.

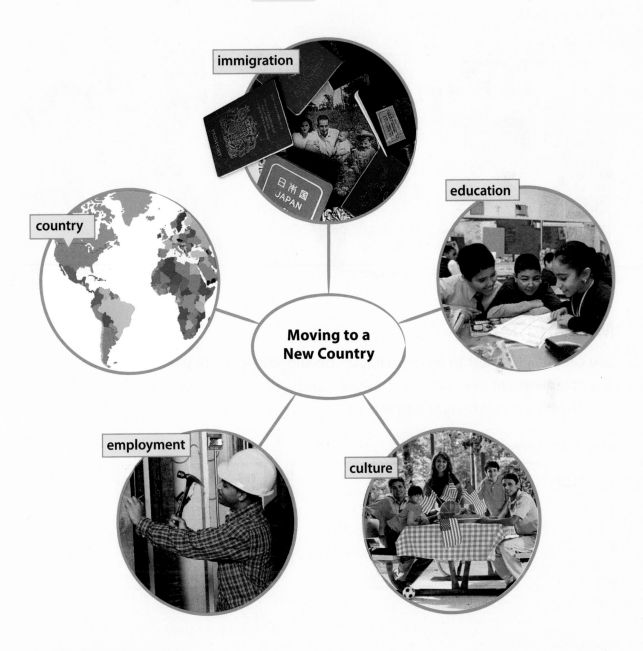

immigration

education

country

**Moving to a New Country**

employment

culture

**Talk Together**

How can moving to a new place change your life? With a partner, try to use **Language Frames** from page 4 and **Key Words** to ask for and give information.

5

# Character Development

Story characters grow and change, just like you. When you understand **character development**, or how a character changes, you can understand the story better.

## Map and Talk

You can make a chart to show character development. Write what the character is like at the beginning, middle, and end of the story. Notice how the character changes and think about why.

**Character Development Chart**

| Beginning | Middle | End |
|---|---|---|
| Lulu is with her big family. She enjoys the warm weather and the beach. | Lulu misses her big family. She feels lonely. Cold weather is strange to her. | Lulu meets a friend and feels less lonely. She enjoys school. |

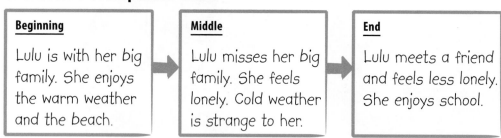

**Talk Together**

Talk with a partner about a story in which the character changed. Tell how the character changed and why. Have your partner make a character development chart.

# More Key Words

Use these words to talk about "My Diary from Here to There" and "I Was Dreaming to Come to America."

### opportunity
(ah-pur-**tü**-nu-tē)  *noun*

An **opportunity** is a good chance to do something. There is a job **opportunty** here.

### refuge
(**re**-fyūj)  *noun*

A **refuge** is a place where people go to be safe or to find shelter.

### symbol
(**sim**-bul)  *noun*

A **symbol** is something that stands for something else. A heart shape is a **symbol** for love.

### transition
(tran-**zi**-shun)  *noun*

A **transition** is a change from one situation to another. Moving to a new city is a big **transition**.

### translate
(**trans**-lāt)  *verb*

When you **translate**, you change words and ideas from one language to another.

### Talk Together

Use a Key Word to ask a question. Your partner answers using another Key Word.

> When do you have an opportunity to use two languages?

> when I translate English words into Spanish

**Add words to My Vocabulary Notebook.**
NGReach.com

# Learn to Plan and Monitor

Look at the cartoon. The text does not say why Lulu and Ricky are at the store, but you can look for details in the picture. This is how you **preview**. Then you can make a guess about, or **predict**, what will happen next.

When you get ready to read, you **preview** and **predict**, too.

## How to Preview and Predict

| | | | |
|---|---|---|---|
| 👁 | **1.** | Read the title. Look at the pictures. | *I read _____.*<br>*I see _____.* |
| ☁ | **2.** | Begin to read. Stop and make predictions. | *I predict _____.* |
| 📖 | **3.** | Read on to check whether your predictions are correct or incorrect. Confirm your prediction or make a new one. | *My prediction _____.* |

**Talk Together**

Read Lulu's blog entries. Read the sample prediction. Then use **Language Frames** to tell a partner about your prediction.

Blog

LULU'S Blog

◀ ▶ C ✕ 🏠 http://ngreach.com 🔍

# Lulu's Blog

HOME | ABOUT THIS BLOG | PICTURES

**April 5 | Author:** <u>Lulu</u>

Today a new student came to our class. She is from Puerto Rico, too! :) Ms. Keller made me her buddy. She said I could **translate** for her until she learned more English. This is a great **opportunity** for me to help Ana feel comfortable. I know how scared I felt when I started school! I want Ana's **transition** to American culture to be easier.

**April 20 | Author:** <u>Lulu</u>

As usual, Ricky, Ana, and I sat together at lunch. We had fun planning my birthday party. Ana understands why I miss my family so much. She says she has a special surprise for me that will make us both less homesick for Puerto Rico. ◀

**May 10 | Author:** <u>Lulu</u>

My party was so fun! I could not believe that Ana asked her cousins to come and play Puerto Rican music at the party. Since we had *arroz con gandules y pernil* (rice and beans with pork), too, I really felt like our home was a **refuge** today for all of us who miss Puerto Rico. Still, I love the United States. I wore red, white, and blue as a **symbol** of my happiness here. Now I am looking forward to our next party on the Fourth of July! ◀

"I read that a new girl has moved from Puerto Rico.

I see a smiley face in Lulu's diary entry.

I predict that Lulu and Ana will become good friends.

My prediction was correct!"

◀ = A good place to make a prediction

# Read a Story

## Genre

A diary is a record of a person's thoughts, feelings, and experiences. This **story** is a fictional diary. It is a record of a *character's* thoughts, feelings, and experiences.

## Narrator

In fiction, the narrator is the person who tells the story. The narrator can be a character in the story, or just a voice describing the events. In "My Diary from Here to There," the narrator is a character named Amada, who tells the story by writing in her diary.

Dear Diary,

    I know I should be asleep already, but I just can't sleep. If I don't write this all down, **I'll burst**!

# My Diary from Here to There

by Amada Irma Pérez

illustrated by Maya Christina Gonzalez

 Comprehension Coach

▶ **Set a Purpose**
Amada discovers that her family
is moving. Find out why.

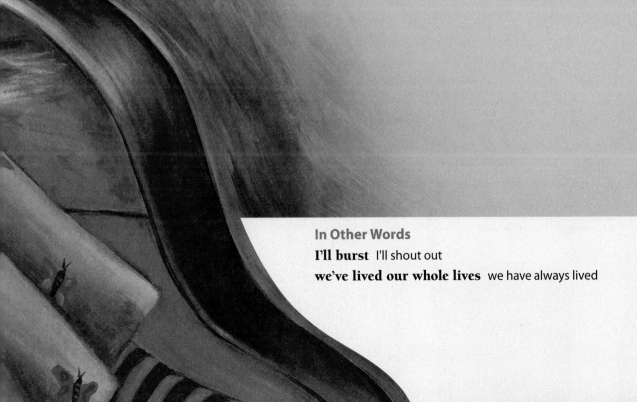

Dear Diary,

   I know I should be asleep already, but I just can't sleep. If I don't write this all down, **I'll burst**! Tonight after my brothers—Mario, Víctor, Héctor, Raúl, and Sergio—and I all climbed into bed, I overheard Mamá and Papá whispering. They were talking about leaving our little house in Juárez, Mexico, where **we've lived our whole lives**, and moving to Los Angeles in the United States. But why? How can I sleep knowing we might leave Mexico forever?

**In Other Words**
**I'll burst** I'll shout out
**we've lived our whole lives** we have always lived

Today at breakfast, Mamá explained everything. She said, "Papá lost his job. There's no work here, no jobs at all. We know moving will be hard, but we want **the best for all of you**. Try to understand." I thought the boys would be upset, but instead they got really excited about moving to the **States**.

Am I the only one who is scared of leaving our home, our beautiful country, and all the people we might never see again?

**In Other Words**
**the best for all of you** you to have a better life
**States** United States

14

My best friend Michi and I walked to the park today. There, we braided each other's hair and promised never to forget each other. We each **picked out** a smooth, heart-shaped stone to remind us always of our friendship. I've known Michi since we were little, and I don't think I'll ever find a friend like her in California.

"You're lucky your family will stay together," Michi said. Her sisters and father work in the U.S. I can't imagine **leaving anyone in our family behind**.

**In Other Words**

**picked out** found and kept

**leaving anyone in our family behind** going to California without everyone in my family

15

OK, Diary, here's the plan—in two weeks we leave for my grandparents' house in Mexicali, right across **the border from** California. We'll stay with them while Papá goes to Los Angeles to look for work.

The boys play and act like nothing bothers them. Mamá and Papá keep talking about all the **opportunities** we'll have in California. But what if we're not allowed to speak Spanish? What if I can't learn English? Will I ever see Michi again? What if we never come back?

While we were packing, Papá **pulled me aside**. He said, "Amada, *m'ija*, I can see how worried you've been. Don't be scared. Everything will be all right."

"But how do you know?" I said.

He smiled. "*M'ija*, I was born in Arizona, in the States. When I was six—not a big kid like you—my family moved back to Mexico. It was a big change, but we **got through it**. I know you will, too. You are stronger than you think." I hope he's right, because we leave tomorrow!

**In Other Words**
**the border from** from where Mexico meets
**pulled me aside** talked to me alone
*m'ija* my dear daughter (in Spanish)
**got through it** adjusted

▶ **Before You Move On**
1. **Explain** Why is Amada moving to a new **country**?
2. **Character** How does Amada feel about leaving her home? Find evidence in the text to support your answer.

▶ **Predict**
What will happen on the first part of the journey?

Our trip was long and hard. At night the desert was so cold we had to **huddle** together to keep warm. We drove right along the border, across from New Mexico and Arizona. Mexico and the U.S. are two different **countries,** but they look exactly the same on both sides of the border, with giant **saguaros** pointing up at the pink-orange sky. I made a wish on the first star I saw. Our little house in Juárez already seems so far away.

**In Other Words**
**huddle** move closer
◀ **saguaros** desert plants

We arrived in Mexicali late at night and my grandparents Nana and Tata, and all our aunts, uncles, and cousins (there must be fifty of them!) welcomed us with a **feast** of *tamales*, beans, *pan dulce*, and hot chocolate with cinnamon sticks. It's so good to see them all! Everyone gathered around us and told stories late into the night. But, Diary, I can't sleep. I keep thinking about Papá leaving tomorrow.

**In Other Words**
**feast** huge meal
*tamales* cornmeal and meat in corn husks ▶
*pan dulce* sweet rolls ▶

Papá left for Los Angeles this morning. Nana comforted Mamá, saying that Papá is a U.S. citizen, so he won't have a problem getting our "green cards" from the U.S. government. Papá told us that we each need a green card to live in the States, because we weren't born there.

I can't believe Papá's gone. **Tío** Tito keeps trying to make us laugh instead of cry, and *Tío* Chato pulled a silver coin out of my ear. Today it feels good to laugh.

**In Other Words**
*Tío* Uncle (in Spanish)

FINALLY! Papá sent our green cards—we're going to **cross the border** this weekend! The whole family is making a big **farewell dinner** for us tonight.

The boys have been causing a lot of trouble lately. Nana got mad when they used her pots and pans to make "music." Still, I think everyone is sad to see us go. Nana even gave me a new journal. She said, "Never forget who you are and where you are from. Keep your language and **culture** alive in your diary and in your heart."

**In Other Words**
**cross the border** go from Mexico to California
**farewell dinner** party

▶ **Before You Move On**

1. **Character** What happens on the first part of the journey? How does this make Amada feel?

2. **Clarify** Why does Amada's father leave before the rest of the family?

▶ **Predict**

How will Amada feel in the **transition** to her new life?

It's my first time writing in the U.S.A.! Crossing the border in Tijuana was crazy. Everyone was pushing and shoving, there were babies crying, and there were people fighting to be first in line. We held hands the whole way. When we finally got across, Mario had only one shoe on. I counted everyone and I still had five brothers. **Whew!**

**In Other Words**
**Whew!** I felt relieved!

Papá was waiting for us at the bus station in Los Angeles, just like he promised. We all jumped into his arms and laughed, and Mamá even cried a little. Papá's hugs felt so much better than when he left us in Mexicali!

Well, Diary, I finally found a place where I can sit and think and write. It may not be the little park in Juárez, but it's pretty. You know, just because I'm far away from Juárez and Michi and my family in Mexicali, it doesn't mean they're not here with me. They're inside my little rock; they're here in your pages, and in the language that I speak. And they're in my memories and my heart. Papá was right. I AM stronger than I think—in Mexico, in the States, anywhere. ❖

▶ **Before You Move On**

1. **Character** How does Amada feel about where she lives now?
2. **Draw Conclusions** Why are Amada's rock and diary important to her?

## Meet the Author

# Amada Irma Pérez

Do you ever feel that no one else understands your life? Amada Irma Pérez felt that way, and she didn't like it. So she decided to tell her story.

Amada moved to the United States from Mexico when she was a child. In school, she wondered why there were no books about children like her. Then, on her eleventh birthday, Amada's mother gave her a diary. "Wow!" thought Amada. "A whole book for me to fill up!"

Amada filled that diary, and many others like it, with her stories. When Amada grew up, some of those stories became books.

◀ Author Amada Irma Pérez, as a girl.

## Writer's Craft ✏

The author includes details about how things look and feel to Amada, including the color of the sky and the cold at night. Imagine that you are Amada. Write a new diary entry about your journey to the U.S. Include sensory details, such as how things look, smell, taste, sound, or feel.

25

## Key Words

| | |
|---|---|
| country | opportunity |
| culture | refuge |
| education | symbol |
| employment | transition |
| immigration | translate |

# Talk About It

1. What do **diary entries** tell you about the character who wrote them? Use examples from Amada's diary to explain your answer.

   Diary entries tell you what the character _____ .
   Amada's diary entries tell readers what she _____ .

2. What **information** might Amada give about herself to her new friends in the United States?

3. How can Amada keep her Mexican **culture** alive as she makes the **transition** to life in the United States?

Learn test-taking strategies.
NGReach.com

# Write About It

What exciting **opportunities** do you think Amada and her family will find in the United States? Write three sentences. Use **Key Words** to explain your ideas.

They will have an **opportunity** to _____ .

# Character Development

Use a character development chart to show how Amada changed during "My Diary from Here to There." Think about how Amada feels as she makes the move to Los Angeles.

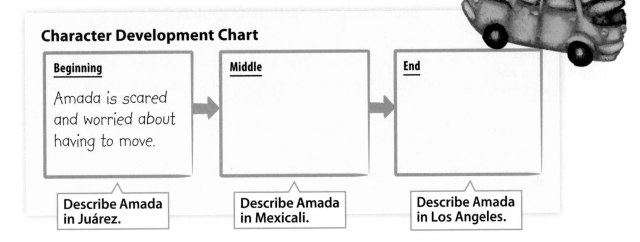

**Character Development Chart**

| Beginning | Middle | End |
|---|---|---|
| Amada is scared and worried about having to move. | | |

Describe Amada in Juárez.  Describe Amada in Mexicali.  Describe Amada in Los Angeles.

Now use your character development chart as you retell the story to a partner. Be sure to explain how Amada changes throughout the story. Use **Key Words** in your retelling.

> In the beginning of the story, Amada _____.
> In the middle of the story, Amada _____.
> By the end of the story, Amada _____.

# Fluency  Comprehension Coach

Use the Comprehension Coach to practice reading with expression. Rate your reading.

**Talk Together**

How does the move change Amada? Write a song or chant about Amada's move. Include **Key Words**. Share your song or chant with the class.

# Use a Dictionary

When you come to a word you don't know, use a **dictionary** to find the word's meaning and more information about it.

> These **symbols** show how to pronounce a word and how to break it into syllables.

> The word *promise* can be used as a **noun** and as a **verb**.

¹**promise** \ **pro-mus** \ **noun** 1: a statement that you will do something 2: a reason for hope or success *Her work shows great promise.* 3: something you say you will do [Middle English, from Latin *prōmissum*, past participle of *prōmittere* to send forth, to project, to promise, from *prō-* forth and *mittere* to send.]

²**promise** \pro-mus\ **verb** to say you will do something *I promise to write to you.*

## Try It Together

Read the dictionary entry. Then answer the questions.

¹**country** \kun-trē\ **noun 1**: an area of land with its own government *Every country has Its own flag.* **2**: a place that is not close to a city or town *He lives in the country.* [Middle English, from Old French *contree*, from Medieval Latin *contrāta* "lying opposite" (used of a land or region). Ultimately from Latin *contrā* facing, opposite.]

1. **How many meanings does the dictionary give for country?**

   A one

   B two

   C three

   D four

2. **How many syllables are there in country?**

   A one

   B two

   C three

   D four

Connect Across Texts You read the story of Amada's **immigration**. Now read about other immigrants' journeys.

Genre An **oral history** is a record of what a person says about the past.

# I Was Dreaming to Come to America

written and illustrated by
**Veronica Lawlor**

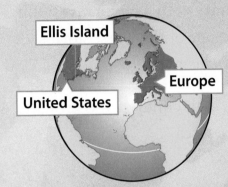

In the year 1900, most people who moved to the United States came from Europe. They traveled by ship across the Atlantic Ocean, in search of better lives. Many of these immigrants had to stop at Ellis Island, a tiny island near New York City, before they were allowed to officially enter the United States. For many of them, Ellis Island was a **symbol** of both a long journey and a new life.

Here, four immigrants describe their arrival at Ellis Island.

**In Other Words**
**to Come** of Coming

▶ **Before You Move On**

1. **Explain** Why was Ellis Island a **symbol** for immigrants from Europe?
2. **Predict** How do you think a variety of viewpoints will help you understand what it was like to arrive at Ellis Island?

"My first impressions of the new world
will always **remain etched** in my memory,
particularly that hazy October morning
when I first saw Ellis Island.

The **steamer** Florida,
14 days out of Naples,
**filled to capacity** with 1,600 natives of Italy,
had weathered one of the worst storms
in our captain's memory.

Glad we were, both children and grown-ups,
to leave the open sea
and come at last
through the narrows into the bay.

My mother, my stepfather, my brother Giuseppe,
and my two sisters, Liberta and Helvetia,
all of us together,
happy that we had come through the storm safely,
**clustered on the foredeck**
for fear of separation
and looked with wonder
on this miraculous land of our dreams."

Edward Corsi
Italy
Arrived in 1907 • Age 10

foredeck

**In Other Words**
**remain etched** stay
◀ **steamer** ship named
**filled to capacity** completely filled
**clustered on the foredeck** stood together
     at the front of the ship

▶ **Before You Move On**

1. **Analyze** How do you know that the text on page 30 represents the words of Edward Corsi?

2. **Interpret** What does the picture show about Edward Corsi's journey to the U.S.?

31

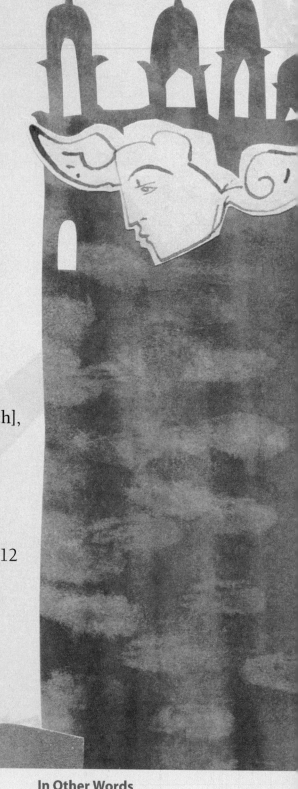

"I never saw such a big building [Ellis Island]—
the size of it. I think the size of it **got to me**.
**According** to the houses I left in my town,
this was like a whole city in one,
in one building.

It was an enormous thing to see, I tell you.
I almost felt smaller than I am
to see that beautiful [building],
it looked beautiful.

My basket, my little basket,
that's all I had with me.
**There was hardly any things.**

My mother gave me the *sorrah* [a kind of sandwich],
and I had one change of clothes.
That's what I brought from Europe."

Celia Adler
Russia
Arrived in 1914 • Age 12

**In Other Words**

**got to me**  surprised me

**According**  Compared

**There was hardly any things.**
    I did not have much in my basket.

"I feel like I had two lives.
You plant something in the ground,
it has its roots,
and then you **transplant** it
where it stays permanently.

That's what happened to me.
You put an end . . .
and forget about your childhood;
I became a man here.

**All of a sudden**, I started life new,
amongst people whose language
I didn't understand. . . .

[It was a] different life;
everything was different . . .
but **I never despaired**,
I was optimistic.

And this is the only **country**
where you're not a stranger,
because we are all strangers.
It's **only a matter of time**
who got here first."

Lazarus Salamon
Hungary
Arrived in 1920 • Age 16

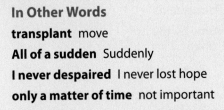

**In Other Words**

transplant move
**All of a sudden** Suddenly
**I never despaired** I never lost hope
**only a matter of time** not important

▶ **Before You Move On**

1. **Clarify** Why did Celia Adler feel so small when she got to Ellis Island?

2. **Figurative Language** What comparison does Lazarus Salamon make to help you understand his **transition**?

33

## ORAL HISTORY #4

"The language was a problem of course,
but it was **overcome**
**by the use of interpreters**.
We had interpreters on the island
who spoke **practically** every language.

**In Other Words**

**overcome by the use of interpreters**
        helped by people who could **translate**

**practically** almost; nearly

It would happen sometimes
that these interpreters—some of them—
were really **softhearted** people
and hated to see people being **deported**,
and they would, at times,
help the **aliens** by interpreting
in such a manner
as to **benefit** the alien
and not the government.

Unless you saw it,
you couldn't visualize
the misery of these people
who came to the United States from Europe. . . .

They were tired;
they had gone through
an awful lot of hardships.

It's impossible for anyone
who had not gone through the experience
to imagine what it was." ❖

Edward Ferro
Inspector, Ellis Island
Italy
Arrived in 1906 • Age 12

**In Other Words**
**softhearted** kind; caring
**deported** sent back to their **countries**
**aliens** people from other **countries**
**benefit** help

▶ **Before You Move On**
1. **Clarify** In what ways did the interpreters help the immigrants?
2. **Use Text Features** What is Edward Ferro's job? How do you know?

# Compare Genres

Key Words

| country | opportunity |
|---------|-------------|
| culture | refuge |
| education | symbol |
| employment | transition |
| immigration | translate |

Fiction and nonfiction are different forms of writing, or genres. How are the two genres the same? How are they different? Work with a partner to complete the Venn diagram.

**Venn Diagram**

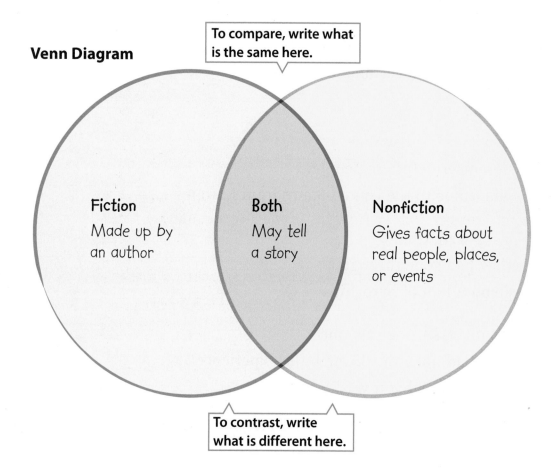

To compare, write what is the same here.

**Fiction**
Made up by an author

**Both**
May tell a story

**Nonfiction**
Gives facts about real people, places, or events

To contrast, write what is different here.

**Talk Together**

Can where you are change who you are? Think about Amada's diary and the oral history project about immigration. Use **Key Words** to talk about your ideas.

# Complete Sentences

A sentence tells a complete thought. A sentence starts with a capital letter and has an end mark. A **complete sentence** has two main parts.

| | |
|---|---|
| Our little house in Juárez | seems so far away. |

**subject :** what or whom the sentence is about

**predicate :** what the subject is, does, or has

## Grammar Rules  Parts of a Complete Sentence

| | |
|---|---|
| The **complete subject** includes all the words that tell about the subject. The **simple subject** is the most important noun. | **My friend Juanita** arrived in America a month ago. |
| The **complete predicate** includes the verb and all the other words in the predicate. The **simple predicate** is the verb. | My friend Juanita **arrived in America a month ago**. |

## Read Complete Sentences

Read this passage based on "My Diary from Here to There." What is the complete subject and predicate in each sentence?

The whole family jumped into his arms and laughed.
My mamá even cried a little.

## Write Complete Sentences

Write a sentence about one of the pictures in "I Was Dreaming to Come to America." Be sure that the sentence has a complete subject and complete predicate. Read your sentence aloud and compare it with a partner's.

**Language Frames**

• Can you _____ ?
• Yes, I can. I _____ .
• Do you like _____ ?
• Yes I do. I _____ .

# Ask and Answer Questions

Listen to the dialogue between Joe and Grandpa Joseph. Then use **Language Frames** to ask and answer questions.

## Memories   *Dialogue*   ((MP3))

**Joe:** Grandpa, can you remember your farm in Hungary?

**Grandpa:** Yes, I can. I was your age when we left.

**Joe:** Was it fun to live on a farm?

**Grandpa:** Yes, it was. But I like big cities, too.

**Joe:** Do you like New York?

**Grandpa:** Yes, I do. I love New York!

# Social Studies Vocabulary

| Key Words |
| --- |
| citizenship |
| custom |
| ethnic |
| foreign |
| origin |

# Key Words

Look at the photographs. Use **Key Words** and other words to talk about people's **customs** and their countries of **origin**.

▲ Every day in the United States, immigrants arrive from **foreign** countries.

Many take the oath of **citizenship** to become United States citizens. ▶

◀ **Ethnic** foods, such as pizza, falafels , and spring rolls, were brought to the United States by immigrants.

## Talk Together

Do you have to change who you are to fit in? Why? Try to use **Language Frames** from page 38 and **Key Words** to ask and answer this question with a partner.

39

# Compare and Contrast

When you **compare and contrast**, you think about how two things are alike and how they are different.

▲ Joseph on Farm          ▲ Joseph in City

## Map and Talk

You can use a Venn diagram to show how two things are alike and different.

**Venn Diagram**

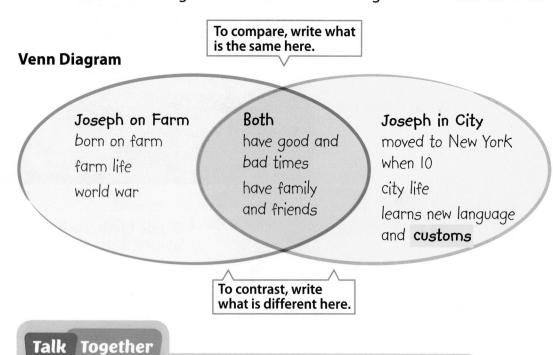

To compare, write what is the same here.

Joseph on Farm
born on farm
farm life
world war

Both
have good and
bad times
have family
and friends

Joseph in City
moved to New York
when 10
city life
learns new language
and **customs**

To contrast, write what is different here.

**Talk Together**

Talk with your partner about a day at school and a day at home.
Create a Venn diagram to compare and contrast these two days.

40

# More Key Words

Use these words to talk about "A Refugee Remembers" and "American Stories."

### adapt
(a-**dapt**) *verb*

If you **adapt,** you change. Visitors to Japan must **adapt** to a new way of eating.

### challenge
(**cha**-lunj) *noun*

A **challenge** is a difficult task or situation. Carrying all the books at once is a **challenge**.

### diversity
(dī-**ver**-se-tē) *noun*

The **diversity** of a group is how different the members of the group are.

### identity
(ī-**den**-tu-tē) *noun*

Your **identity** makes you who you are. Playing music is part of this boy's **identity**.

### society
(su-**sī**-u-tī) *noun*

A **society** is a group of people who share rules and customs. Our **society** has safety rules.

## Talk Together

Work with a partner. Make a Word Web of examples for each key word.

new school

new home

adapt to

new friends

new foods

**Add words to My Vocabulary Notebook.**
⊘ NGReach.com

# Learn to Plan and Monitor

Look at the movie poster. The picture does not tell you what the movie is about. But you can ask yourself a question about what you see. This is how you **monitor** your understanding. Then you can read more closely to find the answer, or to **clarify** your understanding.

When you read, you can **monitor** and **clarify**, too.

## How to Monitor and Clarify

| | | | |
|---|---|---|---|
|  | **1.** | When you do not understand the text, stop. Think about what the text means. | What does _____ mean? |
|  | **2.** | If you do not understand, reread the text. If the meaning is still not clear, read on. | I will _____ . |
|  | **3.** | Think about how the meaning has become clearer to you. | It means _____ . |

## Talk Together

Read the rest of Grandpa Joseph and Joe's discussion. Look at the sample. Then use **Language Frames** to tell a partner about how you monitor your reading.

Interview

# Grandpa Joseph's Move

**Joe:** It must have been a really big **challenge** for you to **adapt** to your new home in the United States.

**Grandpa Joseph:** It was very different here! In Hungary, almost everyone was the same. Here, people came from many countries. There was greater **ethnic diversity** than in Hungary. In our neighborhood, everyone was from someplace else.

**Joe:** Did you have to change to fit in?

**Grandpa Joseph:** We came from Hungary. My family did not want to forget our **origins**, so we kept some Hungarian **customs**. We still spoke our language at home, and Mama cooked the same foods. But we also added some American customs to our lives. ◀

**Joe:** So you became a Hungarian-American?

**Grandpa Joseph:** That's right! I became part of a new **society**. I got my American **citizenship** in 1965. I had a new **identity**. I was now a Hungarian-American. ◀

**Joe:** That's what I am, too!

> "What does ethnic diversity mean?
> I will read on to find out.
> It means people from many countries."

◀ = A good place to monitor and clarify your reading

43

# Read an Autobiography

## Genre

An **autobiography** is the story of a person's life, written by that person.

## Point of View

Point of view describes how a story is told. In first-person point of view, a narrator uses words like *I*, *me*, and *my* to tell the story as he or she sees it. Autobiographies are always told in first-person point of view.

The night the enemy soldiers came to my village, I remember that I had been feeling **tense all over**, as if my body were trying to tell me something.

# A Refugee Remembers

## The Autobiography of **John Bul Dau**

adapted from *God Grew Tired of Us*, by John Bul Dau

Comprehension Coach

▶ **Set a Purpose**
Find out how John Bul Dau's life
changed when he was twelve.

*In early 1987,* John Bul Dau was a happy twelve-year-old growing up in Duk Payuel, a Dinka community in southern Sudan. Like other Dinka boys, he had never had formal schooling. He had been raised for a life of cattle herding, farming, and close relationships with his family and community.

War changed everything. In 1987, soldiers from northern Sudan attacked John's village and many other villages like his. As villages across southern Sudan burned, thousands of boys and girls escaped into the wilderness. In search of a home, these "Lost Boys" and girls began a long, dangerous journey. John was one of them. This is his story, in his own words.

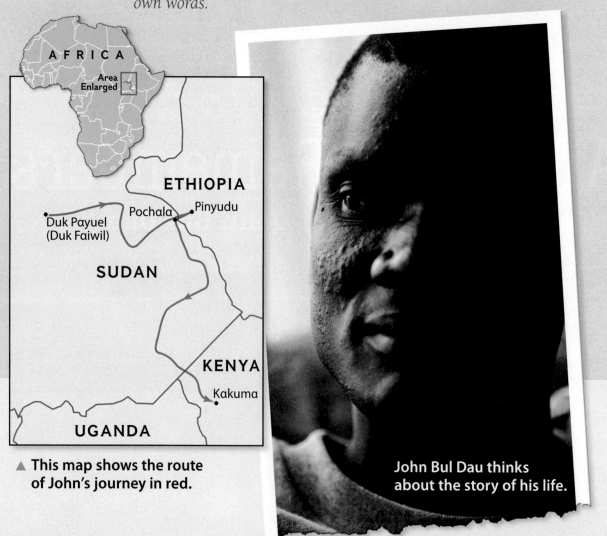

▲ This map shows the route of John's journey in red.

John Bul Dau thinks about the story of his life.

46

My family does not know the exact day of my birth, but we think it was in July 1974. It was the happiest of times in southern Sudan because we thought we would have peace forever. We lived in a row of **huts** next to our cattle and our garden. My father **tended** the garden for hours in the morning, before the heat of midday. "When you work, you get what you want," he always said.

◀ A Dinka boy plays outside the village where John was born.

**In Other Words**
**huts** houses
**tended** took care of

47

*On the night John's village was attacked, his life changed forever.*

The night the enemy soldiers came to my village, I remember that I had been feeling **tense all over**, as if my body were trying to tell me something.

My brothers and sisters and I stretched out on the ground inside a hut. I opened my eyes and stared toward the grass ceiling. It was as dark as the bottom of a well. Silence. Then, a whistle. Next came a sound like the cracking of some giant limb in the forest.

My village was being **shelled**.

I **sprang** up. I saw the man I thought was my father and raced after him into the tall grass.

**A Sudanese village at nightfall.**

48

▲ A Sudanese village after an attack.

All that night, as we waited in the grass for death or **daybreak**, I thought the man who pulled me to safety was my father. When the sun began to rise, I learned I was wrong. Abraham Deng Niop was my neighbor.

After about two hours the guns **fell** silent and we heard no more sounds from the village. Abraham told me we **ought to** move.

Every time we heard noises coming toward us, we **ducked** into the forest or the tall grass. Soldiers kept passing. When they disappeared, we started running again. East seemed a good direction; we heard no guns as we ran toward the rising sun.

**In Other Words**
**daybreak** the light of the sun
**fell** became
**ought to** should
**ducked** moved quickly

▶ **Before You Move On**
1. **Compare/Contrast** How did John's life change in a single night?
2. **Author's Style** What were John's feelings right before the attack?

*or four months,* John and Abraham traveled east. They carried no food or water. They had no weapons for protection. John didn't even have shoes. When they arrived at the Pinyudu refugee camp in Ethiopia, they were **starving**. They were among 265,000 other Sudanese—mostly men and boys—who had come to Ethiopia to seek refuge from the war.

John and Abraham stayed in Pinyudu for four years. Then a civil war in Ethiopia forced them to leave. First they went to the Pochala refugee camp in Sudan. Then bombing raids forced Abraham, John, and thousands of other "Lost Boys" to begin a long journey to Kenya. With the help of **international aid agencies**, the boys walked over 300 miles to Kakuma refugee camp. It was there John found new hope for the future.

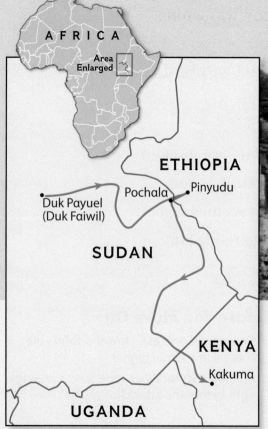

**Thousands of Lost Boys walk along a path in southern Sudan after leaving Ethiopia.** ▼

**In Other Words**

**starving** dying of hunger

**international aid agencies** organizations
from around the world

Like this Lost Boy, John wrote his lessons in the dirt of his camp.

I started first grade when I was 18 years old. I sat in the red dust of Kakuma refugee camp, **anticipating** my very first lesson from a real teacher. He was a Sudanese man, Atak. He told us he would read his **roster**, and he wanted each of us to respond when we heard our names by saying a **brand** new word. I heard Atak say the word, and got ready to use it when my turn came.

"John Bul Dau," Atak called out.

"Yes," I said.

It was a good word. Yes, I am here. Yes, I want to learn to read and write and discover the world and its rivers and cities and peoples . . . everything, everything. If I studied, I thought, I could do good things for myself and for my people. Yes, yes, yes.

In Other Words
**anticipating** waiting for
**roster** class list
**brand** completely

John studied hard. He awoke every morning **at dawn** and went to school. Every evening, he read as much as he could before it got dark. Over time, he passed each grade level, and completed high school.

One day, John heard that the United States government had approved the **resettlement** of some of the Kakuma refugees to the U.S. For the next few months, he and hundreds of other boys waited for letters **of acceptance or rejection**. One day, a letter came for John.

Some Kakuma camp residents view a soccer game from a tree. Many hoped to resettle in the United States.

**In Other Words**
**at dawn** when the sun came up
**resettlement** moving
**of acceptance or rejection** telling them if they were moving to the United States

▲ Kakuma residents look at a bulletin board in 2001. Names of resettlement candidates were posted on such boards.

News traveled to every corner of Kakuma when a new batch of letters arrived. **Resettlement candidates** ran to the post office. I ran, too. I looked for my letter but didn't see it in the mountain of mail. I pretended to be someone in charge and began sorting a pile of letters. I handed out letter after letter while **furiously scanning** the pile of envelopes for my name. Near the bottom I saw it: "John Bul Dau." I stopped pretending to be a postal worker and dropped everything to open my letter.

My eyes landed on four words: "You have been accepted."

**In Other Words**

**Resettlement candidates** Refugees hoping to move to the United States

**furiously scanning** looking closely at

▶ **Before You Move On**

1. **Clarify** Where did John find refuge from the wars in Sudan and Ethiopia?

2. **Figurative Language** Why do you think John compares the size of the pile of mail to a mountain?

$\mathcal{A}$**ccepted to the United States.** I was very, very happy.
I jumped and skipped as I ran home. I didn't know when I would
go, or what city I would fly to, but I didn't care. I put the letter
in a **prominent** place in my hut, so I could look at it again
and again.

A short time later, I began cultural orientation class to learn
about life in America. A woman from the U.S. came and talked.
It was a free country, she told us, and you will love having the
freedom to make choices about your life, choices you would not
have in Africa. But she didn't spend much time talking about the
basic laws. I don't think she even **mentioned** freedom of speech,
religion, or the press.

▲ John and his best friends drink **porridge** together after school.

**In Other Words**

**prominent** clearly visible
**mentioned** talked a little about
**porridge** a mixture of cornmeal
and water

54

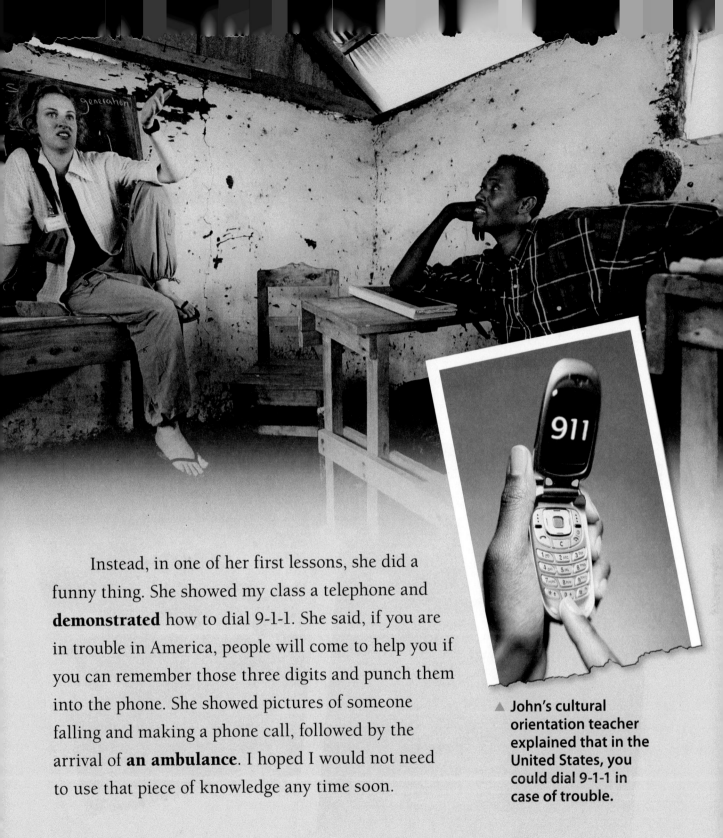

Instead, in one of her first lessons, she did a funny thing. She showed my class a telephone and **demonstrated** how to dial 9-1-1. She said, if you are in trouble in America, people will come to help you if you can remember those three digits and punch them into the phone. She showed pictures of someone falling and making a phone call, followed by the arrival of **an ambulance**. I hoped I would not need to use that piece of knowledge any time soon.

▲ John's cultural orientation teacher explained that in the United States, you could dial 9-1-1 in case of trouble.

**In Other Words**

**demonstrated** showed us

**an ambulance** a car that takes people to the hospital quickly

55

In a later class, a male teacher told us about cold weather. He reached into a box and pulled out something that looked like a piece of glass, only rounded like a river rock.

"Feel this," he said, and he placed it in my hand. It felt so cold, yet it seemed to burn.

"That is water. It gets so cold in America that water sometimes turns hard. We call this an 'ice cube.' Feel it, and feel the cold in America."

I was **amazed**. How could people live in a land where water turned to stone?

▲ John imagined a land where water turned to stone.

**The Lost Boys often danced and sang for each other in Kakuma camp.**

The eldest refugees in Kakuma helped prepare me for America by reminding me of my **heritage**. At **my send-off**, the elders began singing a song. You are going to a different world, they sang. You must have courage, just as if you were going to war. You must remember your **clan**.

After the song, the male elders told me and other Dinka boys more stories about America and how different it would be from anything we had ever seen. They told us not to fear, for we would succeed as long as we remembered who we were.

**In Other Words**

**heritage** Dinka background

**my send-off** the party they had for me before I left

**clan** family and community

▶ **Before You Move On**

1. **Clarify** How did John prepare for his life in America?

2. **Figurative Language** What comparisons does John make to describe what the ice cube looked like to him?

▶ **Predict**
What will John do with his new life
in the United States?

*In* **2001,** John moved to the city of Syracuse, New York. He **adapted** to life in the United States quickly. He found a job as a security guard at a local hospital. He even **enrolled in** college.

John went to work in another way, as well. He started several organizations to help Lost Boys living in the U.S. In addition, he created the American Care for Sudan Foundation. In 2007, the foundation, now called the John Dau Foundation, built a medical clinic in John's own village in Sudan.

As he makes his new life in the United States, John hopes to continue working to improve the lives of Lost Boys in both the U.S. and around the world.

▲ John (at right) and another former Lost Boy visit New York City.

▲ John visits his old village. In 2007, his foundation built a clinic there.

**In Other Words**
**enrolled in** started

58

In some ways, my story is like those of tens of thousands of boys who lost their homes, their families, and in many cases their lives in the war. In some ways, I represent the nearly 4,000 Sudanese refugees who found **haven** in the United States. But in other ways, my story is my own. I have a job, an apartment, and a wonderful new country to call home. I am studying **public policy** at a university, and I plan to use my education to make life better in Africa and in America. I know I have been **blessed** and that I have been kept alive for a purpose.

They call me a Lost Boy, but let me **assure** you, I am not lost anymore. ❖

---

**In Other Words**
**haven** refuge
**public policy** government
**blessed** very lucky
**assure** tell you for certain

▶ **Before You Move On**
1. **Clarify** In what ways does John contribute to American **society**?
2. **Compare/Contrast** How is John like other "Lost Boys"?

# Think and Respond

| Key Words | |
|---|---|
| adapt | ethnic |
| challenge | foreign |
| citizenship | identity |
| custom | origin |
| diversity | society |

# Talk About It

1. What do you think John Bul Dau is like, based on his **autobiography**? Provide evidence from the text.

2. Imagine that you can meet John Bul Dau. What **questions** would you **ask** him? What **answers** might he give?

3. What **challenge** does John set for himself on his first day of school at Kakuma? Does he achieve his goal? Explain.

**Learn test-taking strategies.**
**NGReach.com**

# Write About It

What do you think is the biggest **challenge** in **adapting** to life in a **foreign** country? Write a paragraph about your thoughts. Use **Key Words** to explain your thinking.

> I think _____ is challenging
> because _____ .

# Compare and Contrast

Compare and contrast John Bul Dau's life in Africa and his life in the United States.

**Venn Diagram**

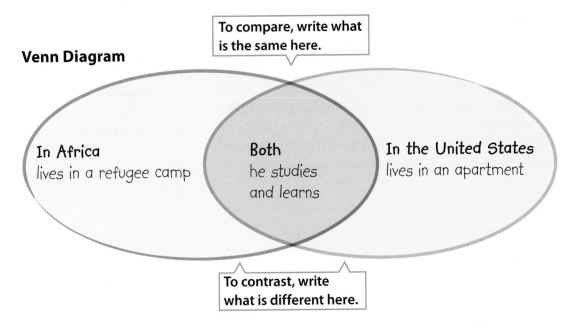

To compare, write what is the same here.

In Africa
lives in a refugee camp

Both
he studies
and learns

In the United States
lives in an apartment

To contrast, write what is different here.

Now use your diagram as you retell the story of John Bul Dau's life to a partner. Use as many **Key Words** as you can.

In Africa, John _____ . But in the United States, he _____ . In both places, John _____ .

# Fluency  Comprehension Coach

Use the Comprehension Coach to practice reading with expression. Rate your reading.

**Talk Together**

How did John Bul Dau have to change to fit in to life in the United States? Write a poem about John's move. Include **Key Words** in your poem. Share your poem with the class.

# Use a Thesaurus

A **thesaurus** lists synonyms and antonyms. Synonyms are words with almost the same meaning. Antonyms are words with opposite meanings.

Read this entry from a thesaurus.

> **challenge** noun **1.** *Judy thinks that Math is a real challenge for her.* DIFFICULTY, struggle, obstacle, trial **2.** *After Carla beat me at tennis, she accepted my challenge to a rematch.* DARE, contest, invitation,
> ▶ verb **1.** *After the game, we challenged them to a rematch.* DEMAND, dare, invite, confront, provoke  ANTONYM avoid

A **sample sentence** shows how to use the word. Then the **synonyms** are shown. Sometimes the first synonym is in capital letters.

**Antonyms** show an opposite meaning for the word.

## Try It Together

Read the thesaurus entry. Then answer the questions.

> **adapt** verb **1.** *It took me more than a year to adapt to living in the United States.* ADJUST, conform, change, fit in **2.** *The writer adapted the book to make it easier for children.* REWORK, modify, redo, edit
> ANTONYM stay the same, maintain

1. **Which word is an antonym for adapt?**

   **A** rework

   **B** maintain

   **C** easier

   **D** adjust

2. **Which words are synonyms?**

   **A** fit, rework

   **B** adapt, rework

   **C** adapt, maintain

   **D** adjust, comfortable

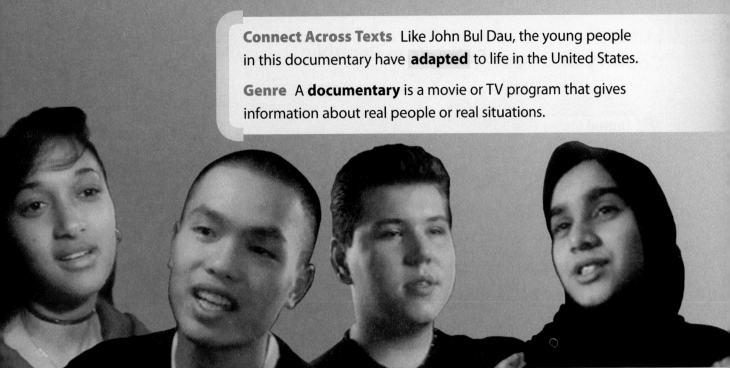

**Connect Across Texts** Like John Bul Dau, the young people in this documentary have **adapted** to life in the United States.

**Genre** A **documentary** is a movie or TV program that gives information about real people or real situations.

# American Stories

## adapted from the PBS series *In the Mix*

*Throughout history, the United States of America has been seen as the land of opportunity. In the past, millions of immigrants came to America. They left their countries for a new life, for **economic opportunity**, for political and religious freedom. Today, immigrants continue to come to this country. Many of them are young people, and they come from all parts of the world. Why do they come to America, what problems do they **face**, and how are they fitting in? The following **transcript** tells what four young immigrants think about their new lives in the United States.*

**In Other Words**
*economic opportunity* the chance to make money
*face* have
*transcript* written record

▶ **Before You Move On**

1. **Clarify** What will the young people in this documentary explain?
2. **Make Inferences** Why do many immigrants think America is a land of opportunity?

# Luincys
## Country of Origin: *Dominican Republic*

United States

Dominican Republic

"I came to America when I was eleven years old. The first time I went to school it was scary. My sister and I didn't know what to do. I wore clothes that were **out of fashion**. People could see that I was a **newcomer**.

"The first struggle was the language. I couldn't communicate with other people. It was frustrating because I am very friendly. The first six months in America I just listened. Then I started to write. In eighth grade I felt confident enough to speak."

Luincys enjoys life in America, but says she doesn't want to lose her "Dominican tradition."

**In Other Words**
**out of fashion** not popular
**newcomer** person who had just moved
to the United States

Michael enjoys playing music. He says, "In China, nobody expects you **to be a rocker**!"

## Michael
## Country of Origin: *China*

United States

China

"The reason my mom brought me to America was so that I could have a good future. When I got here, I changed my name from *Chen How* to *Michael*. You had to change yourself to **survive** here.

"I can't imagine going back to China. I really enjoy the way Americans do things. You can see that by the way I dress, the way I talk, and the music I listen to. Even though I want to be an American, I won't forget my own culture."

**In Other Words**
**to be a rocker** play rock music
**survive** fit in and succeed

▶ **Before You Move On**

1. **Clarify** What change did Michael make in order to fit into American culture?
2. **Use Text Features** How do you know whose words are quoted on each page?

65

## Anton
## Country of Origin: *Russia*

Anton says, "I like to be different. I want people to know I'm Russian."

United States

Russia

"I moved to the U.S. two years ago. Back home I used to wait in a line in the stores to get a meal, to get orange juice, to get bread. Sometimes there was no bread in the supermarket. So I would have to walk to another supermarket two miles away.

"I don't know if I want to live in America for the rest of my life. I like America, but I always dream about Russia and my friends there. It's important for me not to forget."

Fatima puts on lipstick. She says, "I definitely want to live here for the rest of my life."

## Fatima
## Country of Origin: *Tanzania*

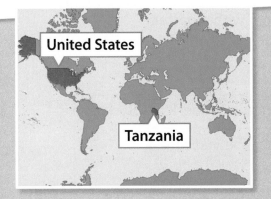

United States

Tanzania

"I moved to the United States when I was twelve. It was hard to make friends at first. People stared at me because I wear a **hijab**. In Africa, almost every Muslim girl wears a hijab. But in the United States, people don't understand.

"Just because I **have to do my Islamic duties** doesn't make me any different than any American. I go out to the movies. I go to the mall. I shop.

"I **consider myself** an African American Indian, because I was born in Africa, my ancestors are from India, and I'm living in America. I'm all three of them and I like it." ❖

**In Other Words**
◀ **hijab** scarf that covers my head and neck
**have to do my Islamic duties** am Muslim
**consider myself** think of myself as

▶ **Before You Move On**
1. **Clarify** In what ways is Fatima the same as "any American"?
2. **Generalize** What **challenges** do Anton and Fatima have as they try to fit into American **society**?

# Compare Literary Language

In "American Stories," the students tell about the experiences in a direct way. They describe things just as they happen. In a "A Refugee Remembers," John Bul Dau uses figurative language to describe his experiences. He uses similes and metaphors:

- A **simile** uses the word *like* or *as* to compare things.

- A **metaphor** compares two things without using *like* or *as*.

Compare how different narrators use language. Work with a partner to complete the chart.

**Comparison Chart**

| | John Bul Dau | Students in "American Stories" |
|---|---|---|
| Feelings | | Luincys: "The first time I went to school it was scary." |
| Sights | "It was as dark as the bottom of a well." | |
| Sounds | | |

**Talk  Together**

Think about John Bul Dau and the students in "American Stories." What do they think of life in the United States? Use **Key Words** to talk about your ideas.

# Compound Subjects

A **compound subject** has two or more simple subjects. The simple subjects are often joined by **and** or **or**. The <u>subject</u> and **verb** of a sentence must agree.

## Grammar Rules Compound Subjects

| Compound Subject | Subject-Verb Agreement |
|---|---|
| • Use a **plural verb** when **two** <u>subjects</u> are joined by *and*. | **American music** and **fashion** **feel** just right for me. |
| • If the subjects are joined by *or*, look at the last subject. | |
| • If the **last subject** is singular, use a **singular verb**. | More jobs or **a better way of** <u>life</u> **brings** people to America. |
| • If the **last subject** is plural, use a **plural verb**. | A better way of life or **more** <u>jobs</u> **bring** people to America. |

## Read Compound Subjects

Read this passage from "American Stories." Find the compound subject. Does it use a singular or plural verb?

> I may not live in America for the rest of my life. Russia and my friends there appear in my dreams night after night. I will not forget them.

## Write Compound Subjects

Choose two teens from "American Stories." Write two sentences about them. Use a compound subject in each sentence. Be sure that the subject and verb agree. Share your sentences with a partner.

# Write About Yourself

## Write a Personal Narrative 🖊

Tell about a time when you had to adjust to a new place or situation. Add your story to a class book about dealing with change.

## Study a Model

A personal narrative is a true story about something that happened to you.

### My First American Supermarket
#### by Eric Tran

My family moved to the U.S. from Vietnam. At first, everything in the U.S. seemed really strange, especially the supermarket!

**The beginning tells what the event is all about.**

In Vietnam, we shopped at the **market**. All the food was outdoors in stalls and carts. We bought rice noodles, farm-fresh vegetables, and fish from the rivers.

Our first trip to the **American supermarket** was a shock! All the food was on shelves inside a building. The fish was wrapped in plastic. The vegetables were canned or frozen.

**The writer compares two settings and gives plenty of examples to develop the main idea.**

I miss our old market. But, the American store has good food, too, such as pizza and yogurt. **So, I guess something can be different and still be really good**!

**The ending tells why the experience was important.**

GARDEN PEAS
IN WATER

## Prewrite

1. **Choose a Topic**  What experience will you write about? Talk with a partner to choose an event that was important to you.

| Language Frames | |
|---|---|
| **Tell Your Ideas** | **Respond to Ideas** |
| The biggest change I ever had was _____ . | Tell me why _____ was so important to you. |
| I remember when I _____ . | How did you feel about _____ ? |
| One thing that happened to me was _____ . | I'd like to read more about _____ because _____ . |

**Use sentences like these to help you decide about a topic.**

2. **Gather Information**  Collect details that tell where and when your event took place. Write down your feelings before and after. Tell how the experience affected you.

3. **Get Organized**  Use a T-Chart to help you organize your details.

**T-Chart**

| Vietnam | United States |
|---|---|
| -Vietnamese market | -U.S. supermarket |
| -outside | -inside a building |

## Draft

Use your T-Chart to write your draft. Tell what happened and how the experience affected you. Give plenty of examples to develop your ideas.

## Revise

1. **Read, Retell, Respond** Read your draft aloud to a partner. Your partner listens and then retells the story. Next, talk about ways to improve your writing.

<table>
<tr><td colspan="2" align="center">**Language Frames**</td></tr>
<tr><td>**Retell**</td><td>**Make Suggestions**</td></tr>
<tr><td>

• Your experience was mostly about _____ .

• At the beginning, you felt _____ . At the end, you felt _____ .

• The experience was important to you because _____ .

</td><td>

• I can't really picture_____ . Can you add more details?

• Why is _____ something you remember so well?

• Can you add more details about _____ ?

</td></tr>
</table>

Use sentences like these to respond to your partner's writing.

2. **Make Changes** Think about your draft and your partner's suggestions. Then use the Revising Marks on page 629 to mark your changes.

   • Did you develop your ideas with details and examples? Add more details if you need to.

   > All the food was stacked on shelves inside a building.
   > Our first trip to the American supermarket was a shock!∧

   • Did you include how the event affected you or changed your ideas? Replace or add words to make the change clear.

   > But, the American store has good food, too, such as pizza and yogurt. ∧I feel OK about that now.↵ So, I guess something can be different and still be really good!

## Edit and Proofread

Work with a partner to edit and proofread your personal narrative. Pay special attention to subject-verb agreement. Use the marks on page 629 to show your changes.

### Grammar Tip

For subjects connected by *or*, use a verb that agrees with the subject closest to it.

## Publish

**On Your Own**  Make a final copy of your personal narrative. Choose a way to share it with your classmates. You can read it aloud, or retell the story as though you were telling your younger brother or sister.

| Presentation Tips | |
|---|---|
| **If you are the speaker...** | **If you are the listener...** |
| For some parts of your story, change your voice to show how you were feeling. | Listen for details that help you picture what the speaker is describing. |
| Use gestures if they feel natural. | Make connections to similar experiences in your own life. |

**In a Group**  Collect all of the personal narratives from your class. Bind them into a book, and work together to think of a good title. You may want to add clip art or scan in a photograph to add interest to your own story.

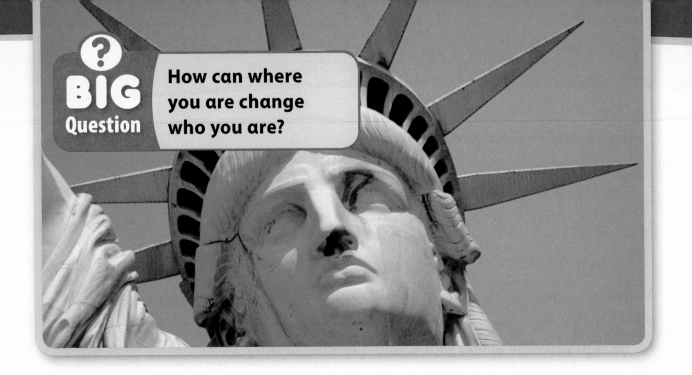

**Talk Together**

In this unit, you found lots of answers to the **Big Question**. Now, use your concept map to discuss the **Big Question** with the class.

**Concept Map**

What I eat

What I wear

How can where you are change who you are?

How I speak

How I see myself

Before I wore only dresses and skirts. Now I wear only jeans!

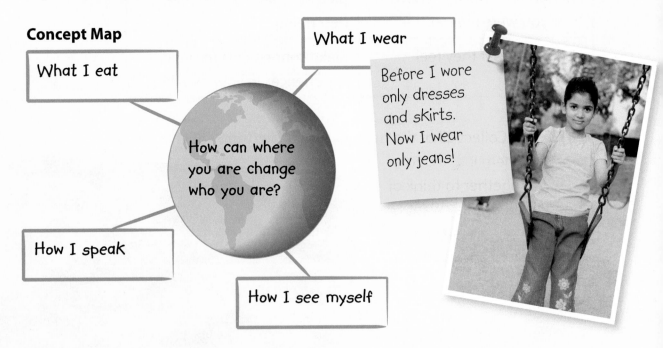

## Write a Diary Entry

Use your concept map to choose one change that happens to people when they move to a new place. Choose a person from this unit. Write a diary entry about how that person handled the change you have chosen.

# Share Your Ideas

Choose one of these ways to share your ideas about the **Big Question**.

## Write It!

### Write a Letter

Write a letter or an e-mail to a pen pal in a foreign country. Ask questions to find out what life is like in his or her country. Tell your pen pal about your life in the United States.

**Find a pen pal at** NGreach.com

## Talk About It!

### Create a Documentary

Choose a classmate to interview. Ask for information about his or her life. Use the information to sketch a simple story board showing important events. Then use those events to make a documentary about your classmate.

## Do It!

### Give a Tour

Pretend you and your classmates are tour guides. Make a list of places in your school that newcomers should know about. Write about that place. Then take your classmates on a tour of that place.

## Write It!

### Make a Collage

Make a collage that shows the different ways one of the people you read about changed and remained the same. Write a caption that names the person and explains why you chose the items.

# Catching THE LIGHT

**? BIG Question**

**What is the power of the sun?**

**Unit at a Glance**
▶ **Language:** Give and Carry Out Commands, Verify, Science Words
▶ **Literacy:** Ask Questions
▶ **Content:** Energy

# Unit
# 2

## Share What You Know

❶ **Think** of words that describe the sun. Make a list.

❷ **Choose a word** from your list and draw it.

❸ **Share your drawing** with the class.

Do It!

sunny
warm
bright

**Build Background:** Watch a video about the sun.
 NGReach.com

**Language Frames**

- Put _____ .
- Give _____ to
  _____ .

# Give and Carry Out Commands

Listen to Alfredo and Susana's song. Then use **Language Frames** to give commands to a partner. Have your partner restate the commands before doing them.

## Make Sun Tea  *Song* (((MP3)))

How I want some iced tea, Susana, Susana,
Will you make some for me, Susana my friend?

You can make tea with sunlight, Alfredo, Alfredo
In an hour it's done right, Alfredo my friend.

Put tea bags in water, Alfredo, Alfredo,
It gets hotter and hotter, Alfredo my friend.

Then you put in some fresh ice, Alfredo, Alfredo,
And the iced tea is quite nice, Alfredo my friend.

Give the pitcher to me, Susana, Susana,
And I'll make the iced tea, Susana my friend.

Tune: "There's a Hole in the Bucket"

pitcher

**Key Words**

absorb
heat
reflect
thermal
transmit

# Key Words

Look at this illustration. Use **Key Words** and other words to talk about how the sun **transmits** energy.

① The sun **transmits** energy, or sunlight.

② Plants, animals, and objects can **reflect** or **absorb** the sunlight.

③ Light that is absorbed can change into **thermal** energy, or **heat**.

④ Plants change sunlight into food.

**Talk Together**

How do plants and animals use the power of the sun? With a group, use **Key Words** to describe what a day in your life might be like without any sunshine at all.

# Character

When you think about the conflict, or problem, that **characters** in a story face, you often think about their roles, or parts they play, in the conflict. You also think about their functions, or what they do.

Look at these pictures of Alfredo and Susana.

## Map and Talk

You can use a character chart to describe characters' roles and functions in a conflict. Here's how you make one.

Write each character's role here.

Write each character's function here.

**Character Chart**

| Character | Role | Function | Conflict |
|---|---|---|---|
| Alfredo | learner | tries to get Susana to make tea for him | Susana wants Alfredo to make the tea. |
| Susana | teacher | tries to teach Alfredo to make sun tea | Alfredo wants Susana to make the tea |

Write each character's name here.

Write each character's conflict here.

**Talk Together**

With a partner, think of a story with a conflict. Use a character chart to show each character's role and function in the conflict.

# More Key Words

Use these words to talk about "Ten Suns" and "How the Fifth Sun Came to Be."

### assume
(a-**süm**) *verb*

When you **assume** something, you think it is true without checking the facts.

### event
(i-**vent**) *noun*

An **event** is something that happens. The street fair is a big **event**.

### explanation
(ek-splu-**nā**-shun) *noun*

An **explanation** gives a reason or makes something easy to understand.

### power
(**pow**-ur) *noun*

**Power** is strength or energy. This machine has the **power** to lift heavy things.

### theory
(**thē**-u-rē) *noun*

A **theory** is an idea that explains something. Her **theory** is that the dog did it.

## Talk Together

Work with a partner. Write a question using a **Key Word**. Answer the question using a different **Key Word**. Use all the words twice.

Question: What is a theory?

Answer: an explanation of something.

**Add words to My Vocabulary Notebook.**
⊘ NGReach.com

# Learn to Ask Questions

Look at the cartoon. When you wonder or get confused about something, you usually **ask a question** and then try to find the answer.

When you read, you can **ask questions**, too. The answers to some questions can be found **in the book**. Read to find the answers. This will help you understand the story better.

## How to Ask Questions

| | | |
|---|---|---|
| ? | **1.** As you read, ask a question. | I wonder _____ . |
| 👁 | **2.** Look for an answer in the text. You might find the answer right there in the text. Or you might have to think and search. | I read _____ .<br>So _____ . |
| 📖 | **3.** Think about the answer. Read on and ask more questions. | Now I wonder _____ . |

**Language Frames**

?    I wonder _____ .

👁    I read _____ .

       So _____ .

📖    Now I wonder

       _____ .

## Talk Together

Read Susana's story. Read the sample. Use **Language Frames** to ask questions. Tell a partner about them.

Science Fiction

# How the Sun Got Hot Again

Astronauts Sofie and Karl were ready to go into space. They were on a special mission. The sun had been growing colder every day. It was getting harder and harder to survive on Earth.

Sofie had an **explanation**. A **thermal** force deep inside the sun had stopped working. If her **theory** was right, setting off a huge explosion on the sun's surface should strengthen its **power**.

The spaceship took off. Before long, the sun was a huge ball right in front of them. It was as majestic as they had imagined it. "The **heat** shields on our spaceship are working," Sofie noted.

"We'd melt if they weren't," Karl said nervously. Soon it was time to send off the explosives. Sofie pressed a button. The little ship holding the explosives made its way to the sun.

Sofie turned the big ship around. They needed to get far from the sun before the explosion. KA-BOOM! The shock waves rocked the spaceship. Sofie spoke to Mission Control. "It worked!" she cried.

"Excellent!!" Karl exclaimed. "I **assume** that tomorrow's headlines will read: 'Astronauts Saved the Sun!' This **event** will go down in history!"

> "I wonder what is happening to the sun.
>
> I read that a thermal force has stopped working.
>
> So now I know what happened.
>
> Now I wonder if their mission will succeed."

◀ = a good place to stop and ask a question

# Read a Story

## Genre

A **myth** is a very old story. Its purpose is to explain something about the world. Myths often include gods and characters who have special powers, but who act in human ways.

## Point of View

Point of view describes who tells a story. In third-person point of view, a narrator outside of the story tells the story. The narrator uses words like *he*, *she*, or *they* to explain what characters experience, think, and feel.

But the **gratitude** of the earth's people and the importance of their work meant nothing to the boys. They **found their task** boring.

# Ten Suns

## A Chinese Myth

retold by **Eric A. Kimmel** • illustrated by **Marilee Heyer**

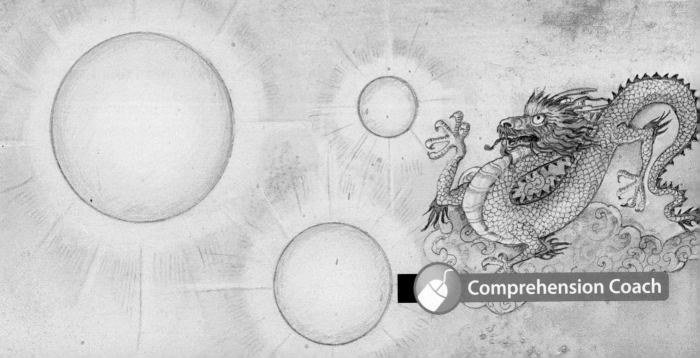

▶ **Set a Purpose**
Find out about an unusual family who lives in the sky.

Long ago, when the world was new, a giant mulberry tree grew on the far side of the sea, on the edge of the **eastern horizon**. Its roots plunged deep into the earth. Its branches scraped the sky.

Nestled in the topmost branches of this tree stood a **jade** palace. Hammered sheets of gold formed its roof. Its windows were made of the thinnest **panes of amethyst and lapis lazuli**. This was the palace of Di Jun (**dē jün**), the eastern emperor, the god who ruled the regions of the sky where the sun arises.

**In Other Words**
**eastern horizon** the land where the sun rises
**jade** green stone
◀ **panes of amethyst and lapis lazuli** purple and blue crystal

86

In those days there were ten suns: the children of Di Jun
and his wife, Xi He (**shē hoo**). They never walked across the sky
together. That would produce too much **heat** for the world to
**bear**. Instead, every morning before dawn, Xi He would awaken
one of her sons. They would climb into her dragon chariot and
drive to a point on the eastern horizon where Xi He's son would
begin his walk.

**In Other Words**
**bear** survive

Each day one of the suns would walk across the sky from east to west. When the people on Earth saw the sun crossing the heavens, bringing warmth and light, they offered thanks to Di Jun, Xi He, and their family.

But the **gratitude** of the earth's people and the importance of their work meant nothing to the boys. They **found their task** boring. Day after day, year after year, century after century, they followed the same path across the sky. There was no one to talk to, nothing new to see, nothing to do except follow that same **weary track** over and over again.

One night, as Di Jun's boys lay in bed, they began talking. Huo Feng Huang (**hwō fung hwang**), the oldest, said, "I would not mind walking the path so much if I **had some company**."

**In Other Words**
**gratitude** thankfulness
**found their task** thought their job was
**weary track** old path
**had some company** was not alone

"I feel the same way," Pi Li Xing (**pē lē shing**), the youngest, replied. "Tomorrow, let's do something different. Why don't we all get up early, take the dragon chariot, and walk across the sky together?"

The others agreed. "A splendid idea!"

In the dark of night, while their parents slept, the boys **arose**, put on their brightest **garments**, **hitched** the dragon to their mother's chariot, and rode across the star-swept sky to the eastern horizon. Laughing, chattering, with their arms around one another's shoulders, they began their walk.

**In Other Words**
**arose** got out of bed
**garments** clothes
**hitched** connected

▶ **Before You Move On**

1. **Ask Questions** Why are the children called both *suns* and *sons* in the story? Where can you find the answer?

2. **Character/Plot** What is the role of the sons in the story? What is their conflict?

▶ **Predict**
What will happen to Earth when the sons cross the sky together?

When dawn came, the people who lived on Earth were **astonished** to see ten suns appear above the horizon. The blazing heat of ten suns shining down at once was more than the world could bear. Crops **withered** in the fields. Forests caught fire. Lakes and rivers dried up. Mountains shattered to pieces. The sea began to boil. People and animals grew **faint**. They stretched themselves on the **scorching** ground and waited to die.

**In Other Words**
**astonished** very surprised
**withered** dried up and died
**faint** weak and dizzy
**scorching** burning hot

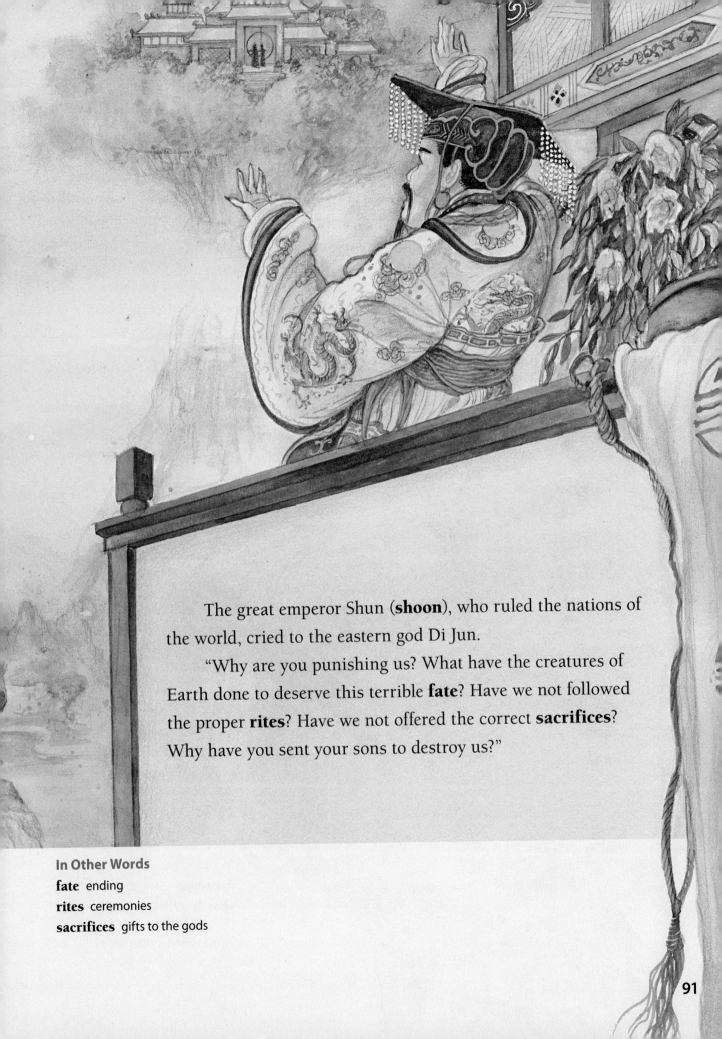

The great emperor Shun (**shoon**), who ruled the nations of the world, cried to the eastern god Di Jun.

"Why are you punishing us? What have the creatures of Earth done to deserve this terrible **fate**? Have we not followed the proper **rites**? Have we not offered the correct **sacrifices**? Why have you sent your sons to destroy us?"

**In Other Words**
**fate** ending
**rites** ceremonies
**sacrifices** gifts to the gods

The great emperor's cries woke Di Jun and Xi He. They looked out the window of the jade palace. In the distance, they saw their ten sons marching together across the sky. Di Jun and Xi He called to them, "Come back at once! Go no further!"

But the boys did not listen. Earth was far below. They could not see the damage they were causing. Higher and higher they climbed, until they reached the place where the sun stands at noon.

Di Jun could not allow the world to be destroyed. The **existence** of all living things depended on him. If his sons would not **abandon their reckless walk**, he would have to stop them. Di Jun **summoned** Hu Yi (**hü yē**), the Archer of Heaven.

**In Other Words**
**existence** survival
**abandon their reckless walk**
   stop walking across the sky
**summoned** called for

Hu Yi had once been a man. He introduced the science of archery to the world by inventing the bow and arrow. As a reward for his discovery, the gods placed him in the heavens among the **constellations**.

Di Jun presented Hu Yi with a magic bow and ten magic arrows. With tears filling his eyes, he told Hu Yi, "Shoot down the ten suns—my sons—who are burning up the earth."

---

**In Other Words**
**constellations** stars

▶ **Before You Move On**

1. **Ask Questions** Look at the picture of Hu Yi. What questions could you ask about him?

2. **Character/Plot** What conflict does Di Jun face? How does he work to solve it?

Hu Yi **refused**. "How can I harm your boys? They are like my children. I taught them to shoot with a bow and arrow. We both still love them, even when they **disobey**."

"I love the creatures of Earth, too. I must protect them," Di Jun told Hu Yi. "Do not be afraid. You will not harm the boys. My sons will not be hurt, but they will be changed. Never again will they cross the sky as suns. They will be gods no more. Hurry! Do as I command. **There is no time to spare**. Earth is dying."

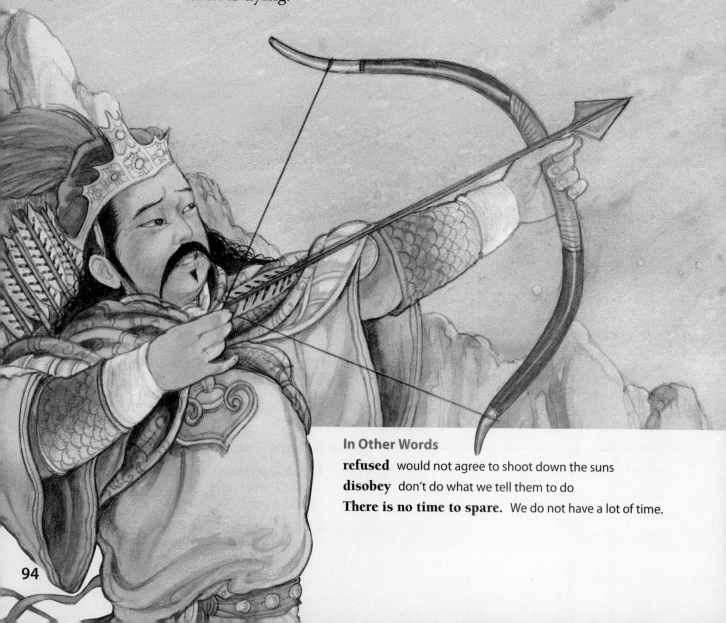

**In Other Words**
**refused** would not agree to shoot down the suns
**disobey** don't do what we tell them to do
**There is no time to spare.** We do not have a lot of time.

Hu Yi took Di Jun's bow and magic arrows. He rode the wind down to Earth. Taking his place on top of White Mountain, he planted his feet firmly and took careful aim. Hu Yi released the bowstring. The magic arrow **streaked** across the sky. It struck the first of the ten suns, shattering it to pieces.

One by one, Hu Yi's arrows **found their mark**. Each sun exploded, filling the sky with **blinding** light. The boys fell to Earth, but they did not die. Instead, they turned into black-feathered birds. They became crows.

**In Other Words**
**streaked** flew
**found their mark** hit their targets
**blinding** very bright

95

The emperor Shun watched the suns exploding in the sky. Suddenly he realized that if Hu Yi destroyed all the suns, there would be no heat or light. The earth would **be plunged into** icy darkness.

There was no time to **spare**. The emperor Shun summoned his fastest messenger.

"Go to the top of White Mountain. Find Hu Yi. Remove one arrow from his **quiver** to make sure he does not shoot down all the suns."

**In Other Words**
**be plunged into** suddenly become a place of
**spare** wait
◄ **quiver** bag of arrows

The messenger **mounted** his horse. He rode faster than he had ever ridden in his life, all the way to the top of White Mountain. There he saw Hu Yi. By now, only one sun remained in the sky. Shun's messenger **plucked** the last arrow from Hu Yi's quiver just as the Archer of Heaven reached for it. Finding no more magic arrows, Hu Yi **assumed** his work was done. He unstrung his bow and rode the wind back to the stars.

**In Other Words**
**mounted** climbed onto
**plucked** took

Since that day only one sun shines overhead. Every morning, the crows gather on White Mountain to greet the dawn. *"Gua! Gua!"* they call to their brother, the sun, as he begins his lonely walk across the sky.

For they remember that once they too were gods and hope for the day when their parents, Di Jun and Xi He, will forgive them. ❖

▶ **Before You Move On**

1. **Character/Plot**  Who saves Earth, and how does he or she save it?

2. **Genre**  What things in nature does this myth explain?

## Meet the Author

# Eric A. Kimmel

Eric A. Kimmel says that his greatest love is to share stories from different countries and cultures. It must be true, because he has retold over fifty tales from around the world! He often travels to different countries, and he is always looking for story ideas.

In China, Eric visited the Forbidden City, where Chinese emperors lived hundreds of years ago. There, the most important buildings face toward the east, to honor the sun.

◄ Eric Kimmel likes to travel the world in search of story ideas.

## Writer's Craft

The author doesn't just say that the suns were hot. Instead, he uses words like "blazing," "scorching," and "blinding" to describe them. Such vivid words make the myth more exciting for the reader. Write a description of the moon rising in the sky. Use vivid words to describe its light.

**Key Words**

| absorb | power |
|---|---|
| assume | reflect |
| event | theory |
| explanation | thermal |
| heat | transmit |

# Talk About It

1. Describe two elements of the story that make it a **myth**.

   I know "Ten Suns" is a myth because _____ .

2. Imagine that you are Di Jun. **Give commands** to a messenger. Say what he must do in order to save the world. Use your own words.

   Go _____ . Then _____ .

3. Tell a partner about a part of the story that you thought was hard to understand. Explain how you asked yourself questions to understand it better.

   I wondered _____ .
   I read _____ . So _____ .
   Then I wondered _____ .

**Learn test-taking strategies.**
**⊘ NGReach.com**

# Write About It

Do you think that Di Jun made the right decision about his sons? Write a paragraph that explains your answer. Include details from the myth in your **explanation**. Use Key Words.

I think that Di Jun _____ .
One reason I think that is
_____ . Another reason is
that _____ .

# Character

With a partner, discuss the characters and the conflict in "Ten Suns." Then make a character chart to tell about the characters' roles and functions in the conflict.

**Character Chart**

> Write the characters' roles here.

> Write the characters' functions here.

> Write the characters' roles in the conflict here.

| Character | Role | Function | Conflict |
|-----------|------|----------|----------|
| Di Jun | father | | sons want to light the sky all at once |
| ten sons | | | |

With your partner, use the chart to describe the characters and what happens to them. Use the sentence frames and **Key Words**. Record your retelling.

> Di Jun's conflict is with his sons. He wants _____ . But his sons want _____ .

# Fluency  Comprehension Coach

Use the Comprehension Coach to practice reading with intonation. Rate your reading.

**Talk Together**

How did the sons misuse their **power**? Draw a picture showing what happened. Use **Key Words** as labels. Share your picture with the class.

# Word Origins

Many English words include a **root** that came from another language. When you come to a word you don't know, look for a root to help you determine the meaning of the word.

This chart shows some common roots.

| Root | Origin | Meaning | Example |
|------|--------|---------|---------|
| graph | Greek | write | autograph, paragraph |
| cred | Latin | believe | credible, credit |
| wis, wit | Old English | know | wisdom, witness |

If *auto* means *self*, and the Greek root *graph* means *write*, what do you think the word *autograph* means?

## Try It Together

Read the paragraph. Then answer the questions. Use the chart to help you.

Characters in myths often possess great <u>wisdom</u>. Others can be reckless. Though it seems <u>incredible</u>, in the myth "Ten Suns," a father must sacrifice his sons to save the world from disaster.

1. **Look for the Old English root in the word *wisdom*. What do you think *wisdom* means?**

   **A** damaged

   **B** without care

   **C** knowledge

   **D** proved something to be true

2. **Look for the Latin root *cred*. What do you think *incredible* means?**

   **A** caused by heat

   **B** hard to believe

   **C** relating to three

   **D** stories or myths

**Connect Across Texts** You read a Chinese myth about the sun. Now read another myth from the Aztecs of Mexico.

**Genre** An **origin myth** is a very old story that explains how something in nature came to be. Most origin myths **reflect** the values of a particular culture.

# How the Fifth Sun Came to Be
## AN AZTEC MYTH

**retold by Lulu Delacre**
**illustrated by Rafael López**

*The Aztec people lived long ago in Mexico. Their culture was rich with traditional stories and myths. Aztec storytellers may have **passed down** these stories by chanting or singing them.*

**In Other Words**
***passed down*** taught

▶ **Before You Move On**

1. **Genre** What thing in nature do you think this myth will be about?
2. **Ask Questions** Based on the introduction, what questions do you have about Aztec storytellers?

103

**THE JAGUAR SUN**

**THE WIND SUN**

In the times before **the current era** there had been four worlds. Each time a new world was created, it was destroyed. The gods Tezcatlipoca (tez-cot-lē-**pō**-ko) and Quetzalcoatl (ket-sul-ku-**wo**-tul) were in constant battle to become the ruling sun of each world.

The first world was ruled by Tezcatlipoca, the **Jaguar** Sun. Under his rule, jaguars roamed the earth until they **devoured** all the people. This brought an end to the first world and let Quetzalcoatl become the second sun, the Wind Sun.

The Wind Sun ruled the second world and life on Earth returned. Then, wanting to rule again, Tezcatlipoca kicked Quetzalcoatl from the throne. Their conflict caused giant **hurricanes** to destroy the second world.

**In Other Words**
**the current era**  today's world
◀ **Jaguar**  Great Cat
**devoured**  ate
**hurricanes**  wind storms

THE RAIN SUN

THE WATER SUN

Quetzalcoatl returned and **selected** another god to become the third sun, the Rain Sun. Animals, plants, and humans again returned to the earth. But one day Quetzalcoatl, being jealous of the Rain Sun's successful rule, sent a rain of fire that poured over everything. Blazing fireballs **charred** every home, animal, and plant, leaving only blackness **in their wake**.

Quetzalcoatl then chose a new god to become the Water Sun, ruler of the fourth world. For a while, things went well. Then the sky fell to the earth and a great flood swept away all human life. **Thus** ended the fourth world.

**In Other Words**

**selected** chose
**charred** burned
**in their wake** wherever they had been
**Thus** That was what

▶ **Before You Move On**

1. **Generalize** How did the Aztecs explain natural disasters, such as floods and hurricanes? Give an example.
2. **Compare Characters** What roles do Quetzalcoatl and Tezcatlipoca play in the story? What is their conflict?

So it was that Quetzalcoatl **took it upon himself to** bring back the human race for the last time. He traveled far to find the way to populate the earth with men, women, and children once again. Once he brought back the people, he realized that the earth was still dark in an eternal night. A bitter cold enveloped it. No plants would grow without warmth and light, and animals and humans would go hungry.

Therefore, when the gods were called to a meeting in **sacred Teotihuacán**, Quetzalcoatl was first to arrive. There, surrounded by huge stone pyramids, burned the divine **hearth**. For a long time the spirits talked until they reached an agreement. They pointed to Nanahuatl (no-no-**wo**-tul), the most **humble** of the gods.

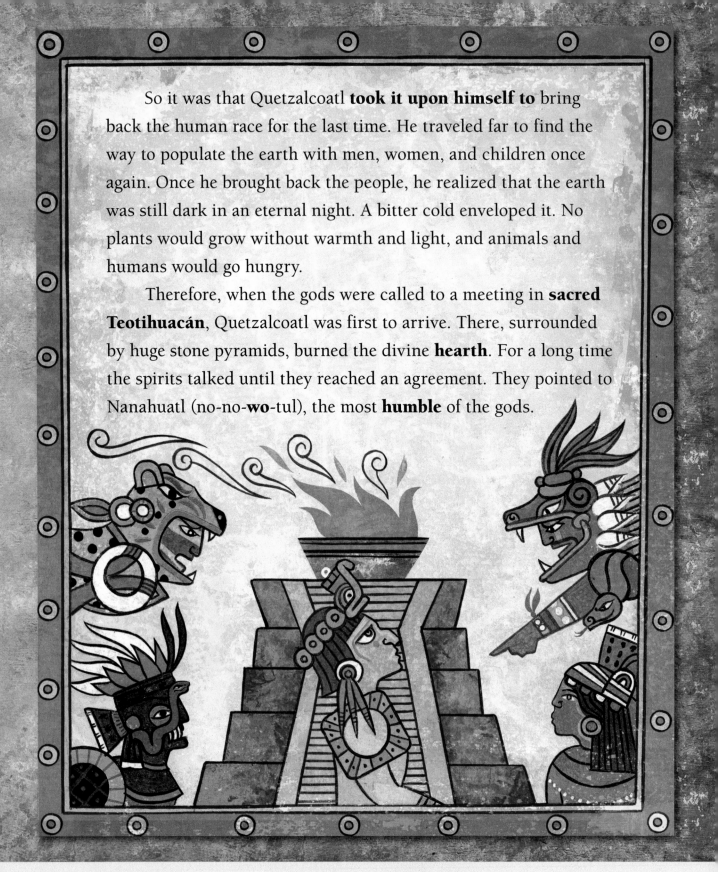

**In Other Words**
**took it upon himself to** decided that he would
**sacred Teotihuacán** the city of the gods
**hearth** fireplace
**humble** modest; respectful

"You, Nanahuatl," they spoke, "you must take care of
the sky and the earth. You must **sacrifice** yourself to become
the sun!"

So, Nanahuatl closed his eyes, **braced himself**, and leaped
into the blazing fire. The fire sputtered and flared, its flames
rising high into the sky.

Then, another spirit, who also **yearned** to be the sun,
followed Nanahuatl's steps and jumped into the center of the
swaying flames. When both spirits were gone, the gods sat down
to wait for Nanahuatl's appearance in the sky. They knew he
would become the fifth sun.

**In Other Words**
**sacrifice** give up
**braced himself** got ready
**yearned** wished

▶ **Before You Move On**

1. **Character** How does Quetzalcoatl's
role change?

2. **Make Inferences** Why do you think the
gods choose a humble god to become the
new sun?

They looked to the north and they looked to the south. They looked to the west and they looked to the east. But the sky remained as dark and the earth as cold as before. It was Quetzalcoatl who spoke next. "It will rise from the east," he said.

In an instant the whole sky became **crimson** and gold. The **spectacle** was so glorious that the gods believed the sun was rising from everywhere.

**As dawn defined itself**, they saw the new sun clearly rising from the east, blinding with its brilliance. Its rays reached farther and farther as it moved in its path, painting valleys and mountains, rivers and lakes, in its golden light. Then the gods noticed the second spirit who had jumped into the fire. He was now a faint moon, following the **majestic** sun.

**In Other Words**
**crimson** deep red
**spectacle** show of light
**As dawn defined itself** In the morning light
**majestic** marvelous and brilliant

It is said that the gods **knelt** at the sight of this spectacular fifth sun and gave praises to its **power**. They saw how its warmth affected seeds and made plants grow. They saw how its rays made water rise and pour back down in the form of light rain.

Now the people of the earth would live and **prosper**. And that was good.

According to the ancient Aztec calendar stone, we still live in the fifth world, ruled by the **Sun of Movement**. ❖

**Aztec Calendar Stone**

This is a drawing of the center part of the Aztec Calendar Stone, which was discovered in Mexico City in 1790. It shows the gods representing the five worlds. The fifth god is at the center.

**In Other Words**
**knelt**  got on their knees
**prosper**  do well
**Sun of Movement**  Fifth Sun

▶ **Before You Move On**

1. **Ask Questions**  What question do you have about the god who became the moon?

2. **Imagery**  How does the author's description of the new sun help you understand its **power**?

# Respond and Extend

**Key Words**

| | |
|---|---|
| absorb | power |
| assume | reflect |
| event | theory |
| explanation | thermal |
| heat | transmit |

# Compare Myths

"Ten Suns" and "How the Fifth Sun Came to Be" are **origin myths**. Work with a partner to fill in the chart below. Then talk about how the myths are alike and how they are different.

**Comparison Chart**

| | **"Ten Suns"** | **"How the Fifth Sun Came to Be"** |
|---|---|---|
| **Tell the type of myth.** | | Aztec |
| **Tell what the myth explains.** | | |
| **Setting** | | Mexico |
| **List the characters.** | Gods:<br>Heroes:<br>Other: | Gods:<br>Heroes:<br>Other: |
| **Tell what the story is about.** | Beginning:<br>Middle:<br>End: | Beginning:<br>Middle:<br>End: |
| **Tell the story's message.** | | |

**Talk Together**

Think about the two selections and the chart above. How do the two myths help you understand the importance of the sun? Use **Key Words** to discuss your ideas.

# Kinds of Sentences

There are **four kinds of sentences**.

| **Grammar Rules** Kinds of Sentences | |
|---|---|
| A **statement** tells something. | This myth is about gods and heroes. |
| A **command** tells you to do something. | Go quickly and take this message. |
| An **exclamation** shows strong feeling. | One sun is hot enough! |
| • A **question** asks something. You can *answer* some questions with *yes* or *no*. <br><br> • Other questions ask for more information. They begin with question words. | **Do** you like myths? Yes. <br><br> **Is** this myth from Mexico? No. It's from China. <br><br> **When**? **What**? **Why**? **Who**? **Where**? **How**? |

## Read Sentences

Read the passage. What kinds of sentences can you find?
What question words do you see? Work with a partner.

> The great emperor Shun cried out to Di Jun. "Why are you punishing us?" Shun's cries woke Di Jun and Xi He. They called to their sons. "Come back at once!"

## Write Sentences

Look at the illustration on pages 94–95. Write two sentences about what Hu Yi is doing. Include one question. Compare your sentences with a partner's.

# Verify

Listen to the song. Then use **Language Frames** to verify information of your own.

# Solar City

**Song** ((MP3))

We'll build a solar city.
That's powered by the sun.
We will check our progress,
Until our goal is won.

Solutions to pollution,
That is our final aim.
They said we couldn't do it,
But look at what we've gained!

Tune: "This World Is What We Make It"

# Key Words

Look at the diagram. Use **Key Words** and other words to talk about how **solar** electricity works.

| Key Words |
| --- |
| circuit |
| conduct |
| current |
| electrical |
| insulate |
| solar |
| volt |
| watt |

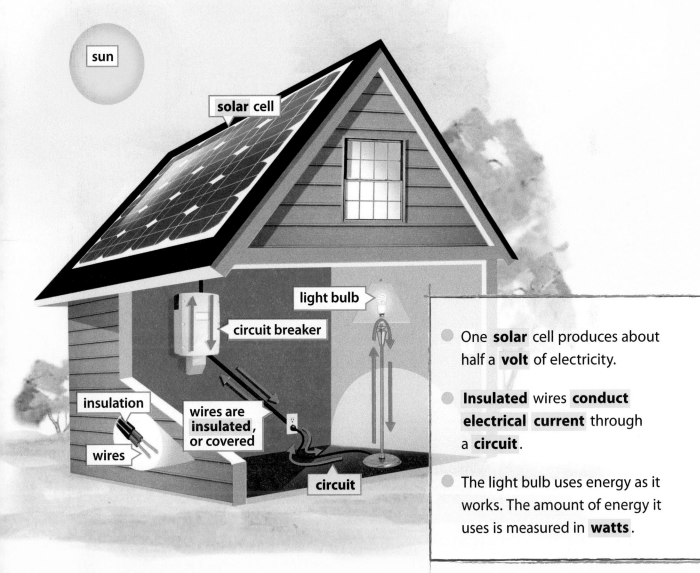

sun

solar cell

light bulb

circuit breaker

insulation

wires are insulated, or covered

wires

circuit

- One **solar** cell produces about half a **volt** of electricity.

- **Insulated** wires **conduct** **electrical** **current** through a **circuit**.

- The light bulb uses energy as it works. The amount of energy it uses is measured in **watts**.

## Talk Together

How do we capture the sun's power? Talk with a partner. Use **Language Frames** from page 112 and **Key Words** to verify how people use solar energy.

# Goal and Outcome

When you start a project, first you think about a **goal**, or what you want to happen. Sometimes during the project, you encounter problems, or obstacles. Then you use strategies to fix the problems. The **outcome** is the final result of the project.

Look at these pictures from the song "Solar City."

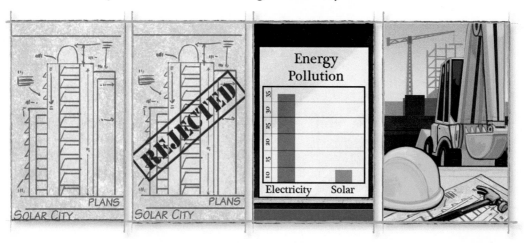

## Map and Talk

You can use a goal-and-outcome chart to talk about a project. Here's how you make one.

**Goal-and-Outcome Chart**

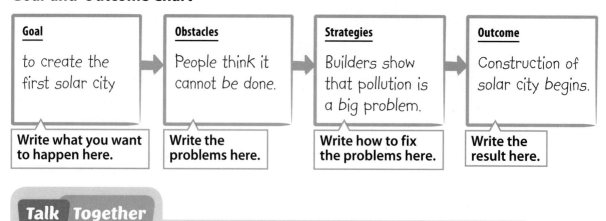

| Goal | Obstacles | Strategies | Outcome |
|------|-----------|------------|---------|
| to create the first solar city | People think it cannot be done. | Builders show that pollution is a big problem. | Construction of solar city begins. |
| Write what you want to happen here. | Write the problems here. | Write how to fix the problems here. | Write the result here. |

**Talk Together**

With a partner, think of a project in your school. Use a goal-and-outcome chart to show the possible goal, obstacles, strategies, and outcome.

# More Key Words

Use these words to talk about "Energy for the Future" and "How to Make a Solar Oven."

## alternate
(**awl**-tur-nut) *adjective*

**Alternate** means different. He must find an **alternate** location.

## decrease
(di-**krēs**) *verb*

To **decrease** means to become less or smaller. When I spend money, my savings **decrease**.

## energy
(**e**-nur-jē) *noun*

**Energy** is the power to do work. It takes a lot of **energy** to run a marathon.

## obstacle
(*ob-sti-kul*) *noun*

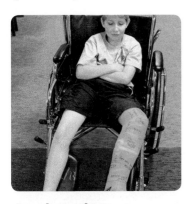

An **obstacle** is something that stops you from succeeding. A broken leg is an **obstacle** to biking.

## rely
(*ri-lī*) *verb*

If you **rely** on something, you need it. We **rely** on electricity in our home.

## Talk Together

With a partner, make an Expanded Meaning Map for each **Key Word**.

### Expanded Meaning Map

| Definition | Characteristics |
|---|---|
| source of power | powerful strong |
| *energy* | |
| **Examples** | **Non-examples** |
| electricity sunlight | rock pencil |

Add words to My Vocabulary Notebook.
NGReach.com

# Learn to Ask Questions

Look at the diagram. Sometimes when you see an image, you **ask questions** about it. You may have to look again or look more carefully to find the answers.

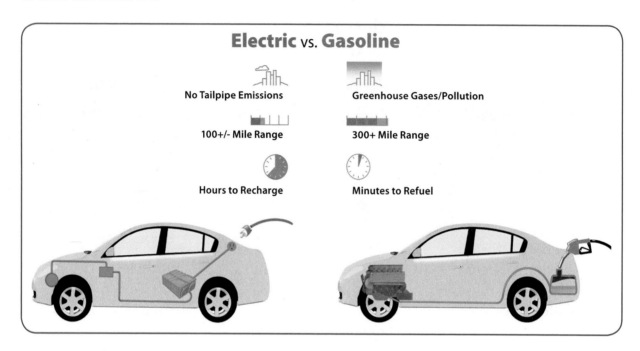

When you read, you can **ask questions**, too. The answers to some questions are **in your head**. Think to come up with answers. This will help you understand the text better.

## How to Ask Questions

| | | |
|---|---|---|
| ? | 1. As you read, ask yourself a question. | I wonder _____ . |
| ☁ | 2. Think about your experiences and what you know. | I think/know _____ . |
| 📖 | 3. Think about the answer. Read on and ask more questions. | Now I wonder _____ . |

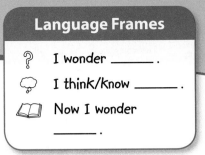
## Talk Together

Read the blog. Read the sample. Use **Language Frames** to ask questions. Tell a partner about them.

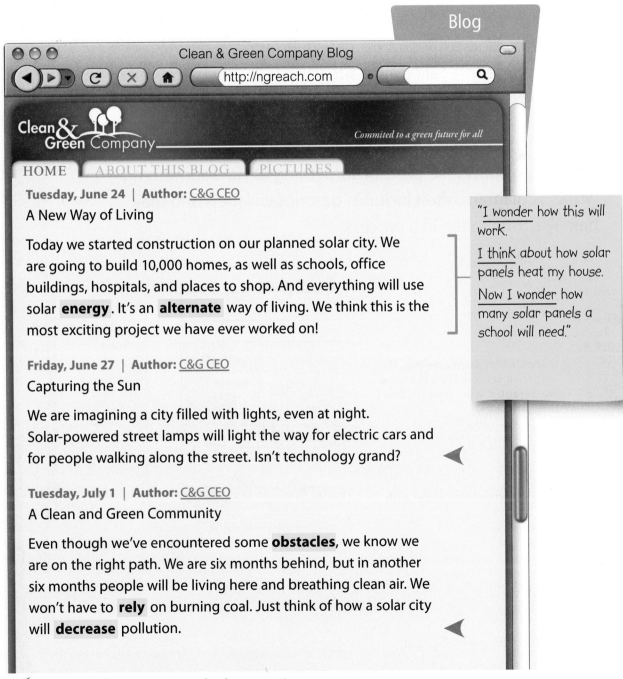

Blog

Clean & Green Company Blog

http://ngreach.com

**Clean & Green** Company _____     *Commited to a green future for all*

HOME    ABOUT THIS BLOG    PICTURES

**Tuesday, June 24** | **Author:** <u>C&G CEO</u>

A New Way of Living

Today we started construction on our planned solar city. We are going to build 10,000 homes, as well as schools, office buildings, hospitals, and places to shop. And everything will use solar **energy** . It's an **alternate** way of living. We think this is the most exciting project we have ever worked on!

**Friday, June 27** | **Author:** <u>C&G CEO</u>

Capturing the Sun

We are imagining a city filled with lights, even at night. Solar-powered street lamps will light the way for electric cars and for people walking along the street. Isn't technology grand? ◄

**Tuesday, July 1** | **Author:** <u>C&G CEO</u>

A Clean and Green Community

Even though we've encountered some **obstacles**, we know we are on the right path. We are six months behind, but in another six months people will be living here and breathing clean air. We won't have to **rely** on burning coal. Just think of how a solar city will **decrease** pollution. ◄

"<u>I wonder</u> how this will work.

<u>I think</u> about how solar panels heat my house.

<u>Now I wonder</u> how many solar panels a school will need."

◄ = a good place to stop and ask a question

117

ALTERNATIVE ENERGY

# Read a Blog

## Genre

A **blog** is a site on the Internet where someone posts his or her writing. Blog entries, or *posts*, usually appear in time order. In the past, people called such sites *web logs*. The name was later shortened to *blogs*.

## Text Feature

A **diagram** shows the parts of something or how something works. A diagram often includes descriptive labels and may help illustrate a step in a process.

**Step 2**
Compare two thermometers. Wait until their sensors show the same temperature. Write it down. Don't touch the bulbs!

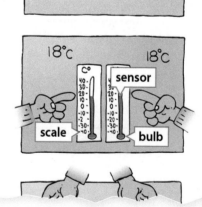

**Step 3**
Slide a thermometer under each

# ENERGY
# for the
# FUTURE

by **Thomas Taha Rassam Culhane**

 **Comprehension Coach**

▶ **Set a Purpose**
Find out how we use the
sun's **energy**.

Solar CITIES Blog

http://ngreach.com

HOME | BLOG | ABOUT THIS BLOG | PICTURES | CREATE A BLOG

# GREETINGS!

You have reached the **Solar** CITIES blog. Wait! Don't **click away**. If you want information about solar **energy**, you came to the right place.

First, let me introduce myself. I am Thomas Culhane, co-founder of Solar CITIES. My organization teaches about the most important source of energy in the world. Can you guess what it is? Hint: It's large, round, and fiery.

It's the sun! The sun's energy is all around us, yet few people really **take advantage of** its power. My goal is to change that. I want to show people around the world how easy it is to **capture** the sun's energy for themselves. Click here or on the BLOG menu above to find out what Solar CITIES is **up to** lately.

▲ **My goal is to teach people how they can use the sun's energy.**

**In Other Words**
**click away**  leave this Web site
**take advantage of**  make good use of
**capture**  use
**up to**  doing

HOME | BLOG | ABOUT THIS BLOG | PICTURES | CREATE A BLOG

Search All Posts

[GO!]

BLOG ARCHIVE
January
Februray
March

POSTS BY CATEGORY
Cairo, Egypt
What Is Energy?
Chemical Energy
Electrical Energy
Light Energy
Thermal Energy
Putting It Together
Finding Solutions
We Did It!

**April**
| S | M | T | W | T | F | S |
|---|---|---|---|---|---|---|
|  |  |  |  | 1 | 2 | 3 |
| 4 | 5 | 6 | 7 | 8 | 9 | 10 |
| 11 | 12 | 13 | 14 | 15 | 16 | 17 |
| 18 | 19 | 20 | 21 | 22 | 23 | 24 |
| 25 | 26 | 27 | 28 | 29 | 30 |  |

‹‹March

Category: Cairo, Egypt | Date: Monday, April 5, 2010

# Welcome to the City of the Sun

This week I am in Cairo, Egypt. I am here to teach a group of students how to use the sun's energy to heat water for their school. At our first meeting, I held up a large black **panel**. "We'll use something like this to heat the water," I told them. The students were confused. "Where is the **flame**?" they asked.

▲ **I tell the kids they are going to become energy experts.**

Over the next two weeks, the students will learn that to create heat energy, they don't always need a flame. In fact, they will become energy experts. I will post our lessons on this blog,

Cairo

▲ **Cairo was known by ancient Egyptians as "The City of the Sun."**

along with updates on our progress. Our goal is to have their solar water heater **in place** by April 16th.

POSTED BY: Thomas Culhane

2 COMMENTS    LINKS TO THIS POST

---

**In Other Words**
**panel** board
**flame** fire
**in place** ready to use

▶ **Before You Move On**

1. **Goal/Outcome** What two goals are stated in the blog?
2. **Analyze** Look at the headings and images. Does this blog seem informal? Why or why not?

# What Is Energy?

Today I gave the students their first lesson in **energy** . I explained that energy is the ability to do work. Work isn't just what students do to get good grades, however. In science, work is what causes objects to move and change—including **human objects**. So when you move your body, even a little, you're doing work.

You don't have to be alive to do work, however. Objects can do work, too. Say you put a burrito in the microwave. As soon as you press *On*, the **microwave** heats the burrito. That change in temperature takes work.

All work requires energy. Luckily, energy comes in many different forms, and it can even change forms.

▲ **Everybody in this picture is using energy to do work.**

**In Other Words**
**human objects** people
**microwave** oven

122

# Chemical Energy

One form of energy is chemical energy. You can find lots of it at the grocery store. That's because food is a form of chemical energy. When you eat food, chemical **reactions** inside your body break it down, giving you the energy you need to move and grow.

▲ Food, such as fruit, provides chemical energy.

**Batteries** also contain chemical energy. They power everything from watches, to cameras, to cell phones. They can even store energy to be used at another time.

▲ Batteries like these power a variety of portable devices.

Chemical energy **fuels** cars, too. The chemical energy in gasoline is what allows most buses, trains, and cars to get you where you need to go.

POSTED BY: Thomas Culhane

2 COMMENTS      LINKS TO THIS POST

**In Other Words**

**reactions** responses; actions
**Batteries** Objects that store **energy**
**fuels** powers
**portable** movable

▶ **Before You Move On**

1. **Clarify** Reread the first paragraph on this page. How are chemical **energy** and work connected?
2. **Paraphrase** Use your own words to explain what **energy** is.

123

# Electrical Energy

Today I told the students about something truly "**shocking**"— **electrical energy**. For many people in the world, electrical energy, or electricity, makes life a lot easier. It makes lights glow, computers hum, water hot, and toast, well . . . toast! Electrical energy does work for people, so they can use their own energy for other things.

Most of the electrical energy in the world comes from power plants. A power plant is a place where machines called generators **transform** other forms of energy into electrical energy. Most power plants in the world get their energy from some form of chemical energy, like coal, oil, or natural gas.

▲ **The electricity you use probably comes from an electrical power plant like this one.**

**In Other Words**
**shocking** both amazing and charged with electricity
**transform** change

Have you ever boiled water on a stove? If so, then you understand how a fuel-based power plant works. Inside, burning fuel heats a large pool of water. At 100° **C** (212° **F**), the water boils, and steam rises from it. The energy contained in the steam turns a giant magnet surrounded by a **coil**. When the magnet spins, tiny, invisible **particles** inside the coil start to move. These particles are called electrons. Their movement creates electrical energy that flows through wires on poles to homes, businesses, and anywhere people need to plug something in.

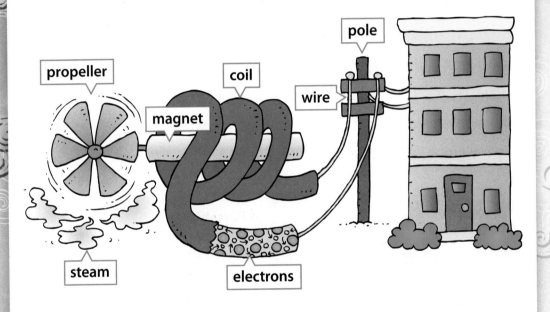

▲ **In a power plant, steam turns a magnet to produce electricity.**

POSTED BY: Thomas Culhane

7 COMMENTS     LINKS TO THIS POST

**In Other Words**

° **C** degrees Celsius

° **F** degrees Farenheit

**coil** large piece of wire wrapped into a roll

**particles** bits; pieces

▶ **Before You Move On**

1. **Ask Questions** What questions about power plants does the blog answer? What other questions do you have?

2. **Use Text Features** What is inside the coil wrapped around the magnet? What does the coil connect to?

# Light Energy

I came to class today carrying my **electric** guitar. "Today I am going to teach you about my favorite form of **energy**," I told the students. "Light!"

What does an electric guitar have to do with light energy, you ask?

▲ **Solar cells turn light energy into electrical energy for my guitar.**

Well, thanks to **solar** cell technology, we can now use light energy directly, to create electricity. That means that I don't need to plug in to **an outlet** to play the electric guitar. I can just point my cells at the sun, plug in my guitar, and make beautiful music.

◀ **Portable solar panels let me plug in my guitar wherever there is sunlight. That means I can play musical chairs outdoors.**

**In Other Words**
**an outlet** place in the wall where you put a plug

Here is how solar cells work. You know that moving electrons create electricity. These electrons are held by larger particles, called atoms. Everything on Earth is made of atoms, and all atoms carry electrons. But some atoms are different than others. The atoms inside a solar cell, for example, are made to hold their electrons very loosely. When sunlight hits the cell, the atoms release their electrons easily. The freed electrons have electricity. That electricity goes by wire into a battery, or directly to a **circuit**.

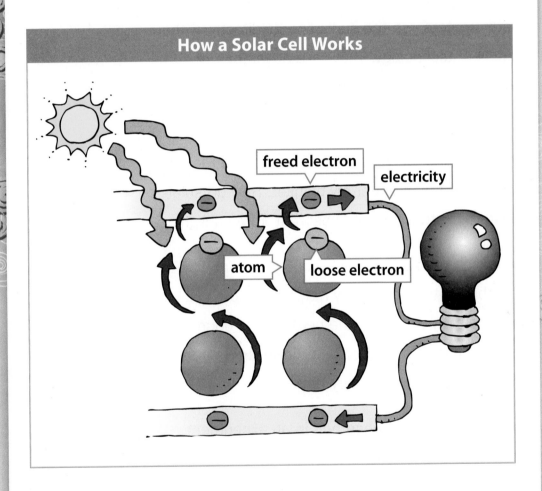

**How a Solar Cell Works**

POSTED BY: Thomas Culhane

4 COMMENTS        LINKS TO THIS POST

▶ **Before You Move On**

1. **Ask Questions** What question could you ask the author about **solar** cells?

2. **Analyze** How does the informal tone of this blog help you understand the information better?

# Thermal Energy

I'm happy to say that **solar** cell technology is improving all the time. Soon, people may not have to **rely** on **distant** power plants for their electrical energy. But solar cells are still **relatively expensive**. There's an even easier way for people to use the power of the sun, and it's free!

Solar-powered water heaters use the sun's energy directly, without any special materials or technology. They take advantage of another important form of **energy**—thermal energy, or the energy of heat.

Thermal energy is all around us. Today, my students and I felt it in the warm air. Tonight, I feel it under my blanket. How do solar-powered water heaters capture it? They absorb it from sunlight.

The sun's light **produces** both visible light and heat energy. When light hits an object, its heat energy may be reflected or absorbed. If it is completely reflected, the heat energy bounces back into space. If it is completely absorbed, however, its heat energy stays. And it can make things very hot!

Today, the students and I became **absorbed in** an experiment that tests heat absorption. Try it and see the power of absorption for yourself.

**In Other Words**
**distant** faraway
**relatively expensive** more expensive than other power sources
**produces** makes
**absorbed in** very interested in

# Reflection and Absorption: An Experiment

## Step 1
Place one black and one white piece of paper in the sun.

## Step 2
Compare two thermometers. Wait until their sensors show the same temperature. Write it down. Don't touch the bulbs!

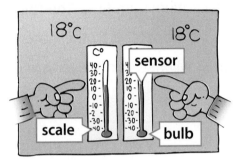

## Step 3
Slide a thermometer under each piece of paper. Leave them in the sun for an hour.

## Step 4
Compare the thermometers. Have the temperatures changed? Why?

POSTED BY: Thomas Culhane

5 COMMENTS     LINKS TO THIS POST

## ▶ Before You Move On

1. **Interpret** What do the results of the experiment show about the color black?

2. **Use Text Features** How do the sensor and scale work together to show the temperature?

Today, I held up the same black panel that I showed the students at our first meeting. This time, they knew exactly what it was for. "To absorb the sun's thermal **energy**!" they shouted.

The students and I will use our **knowledge** of heat and light energy as we build our water heater. The heater will contain water pipes lined with black aluminum fins. The fins will absorb the sun's heat energy and transfer it to the water in the pipes. As the water gets warmer, it will rise and move through the pipes into a storage **tank**.

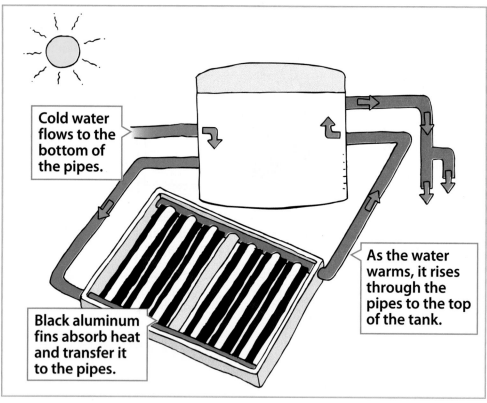

Cold water flows to the bottom of the pipes.

As the water warms, it rises through the pipes to the top of the tank.

Black aluminum fins absorb heat and transfer it to the pipes.

▲ As the sun heats the water, it rises through the pipes and into a storage tank.

**In Other Words**
**knowledge** understanding
**tank** container

130

Our first task is to build another solar panel. Solar panels are large, thin boxes with glass lids. They can be made out of **aluminum**, plastic, wood, or any other material you can shape into a box. The students and I will build our panel using aluminum. We're lucky because aluminum is **light** and easy to carry to a rooftop!

Next, we will **line** the box with **insulation**, and place our aluminum-lined water pipes inside. The students know that the last step is also the most important: paint. The color black absorbs the most heat. So to make sure the pipes get really hot, we need to paint them, and their aluminum fins, black.

▲ **Aluminum boxes are easy to make and carry.**

▲ **Water pipes can be made of any common metal. Ours are made of copper.**

▲ **With a little black paint, the solar panel is finished.**

POSTED BY: Thomas Culhane

8 COMMENTS      LINKS TO THIS POST

**In Other Words**
**aluminum**  metal
**light**  not heavy
**line**  cover the inside of

▶ **Before You Move On**
1. **Goal/Outcome**  What actions are the students taking to reach their goal?
2. **Ask Questions**  What questions could you ask the author about how the water heater will work?

Today we had a problem. We tested our metal storage tank. It leaked! Then one student had an idea. He took me to a place where plastic barrels from a shampoo factory were being re-sold. The barrels were **inexpensive**, and perfect for our hot water heaters.

▲ **We have found a perfect hot water tank.**

When we returned, the students cheered. "But how will the water in the tank stay hot?" asked one student. "Maybe it just needs a blanket," said another.

▲ **With insulation, the water tank will not lose its heat as fast.**

Clearly, the students have become energy problem-solvers. At the end of the day today, we **insulated** our tank with a "blanket" of **fiberglass insulation**, and then gave each other high-fives.

POSTED BY: Thomas Culhane

9 COMMENTS    LINKS TO THIS POST

**In Other Words**
**inexpensive**  not high-priced
**fiberglass insulation**  cloth made from glass

Category: We Did It! | Date: Friday, April 16, 2010

Today we finally reached our goal. The students cheered as I carefully placed the tank on a stand above the **solar** panels and filled it with cold water. We waited for most of the day as the cold water made its way through the pipes inside the panels. At the end of the day, we opened the pipe that carries hot water down to the schoolyard.

It worked! Hot water flowed from the pipe. It was even hot enough for a shower. The students were amazed at how easy it was to use the sun's **energy**. "This is just the beginning," I told them. "The real power is what you have learned about energy. One day, your knowledge will help you change the world!" ❖

POSTED BY: Thomas Culhane

▲ **Pipes inside our solar panels heat the water.**

▲ **The hot water is stored in our tank.**

▲ **The water is hot enough for a shower!**

14 COMMENTS     LINKS TO THIS POST

NEWER POSTS »

▶ **Before You Move On**

1. **Goal/Outcome** What two **obstacles** did Culhane and the students face on Thursday?

2. **Explain** How are the students **energy** problem-solvers?

## Talk About It

1. What kind of information does Thomas Culhane post on his **blog**? Give two specific examples.

2. Imagine that you and a partner are writing a report on **solar** technology. You need to collect facts and **verify** them. Talk to your partner about what you know from this blog and what you need to verify. Use your own words.

   According to Mr. Culhane, solar technology _____ . I will check _____ to verify that _____ .

3. Think about the four types of **energy** discussed in this **blog**. Explain one of them and how you **rely** on it in your own life.

**Learn test-taking strategies.**
🌐 NGReach.com

## Write About It

A person who writes a **blog** often invites readers to ask questions. Write three questions about **solar energy** that you would like to post on Thomas Culhane's blog. Use **Key Words** and questions that start with *how, why, where*.

Why _____ ?
How _____ ?
Where _____ ?

# Goal and Outcome

Make a goal-and-outcome chart to talk about what happened in "Energy for the Future."

**Goal-and-Outcome Chart**

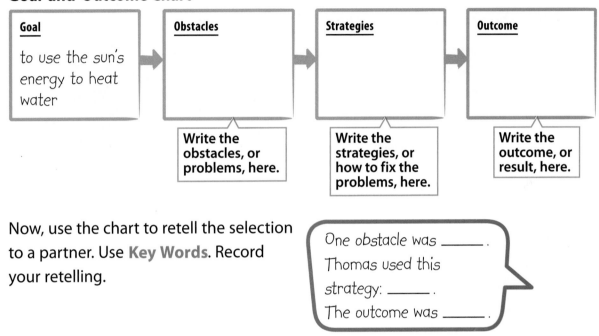

| Goal | Obstacles | Strategies | Outcome |
|---|---|---|---|
| to use the sun's energy to heat water | | | |

Write the obstacles, or problems, here.

Write the strategies, or how to fix the problems, here.

Write the outcome, or result, here.

Now, use the chart to retell the selection to a partner. Use **Key Words**. Record your retelling.

> One obstacle was _____ .
> Thomas used this strategy: _____ .
> The outcome was _____ .

# Fluency  Comprehension Coach

Use the Comprehension Coach to practice reading with phrasing. Rate your reading.

**Talk Together**

Work together as a class. Describe how Thomas Culhane captures sunlight to heat water. Have one student draw a diagram on the board. Use **Key Words** as labels.

# More Word Origins

Many English words contain a **root** that came from another language. Knowing the meaning of a word's root can help you determine the meaning of the word.

This chart shows some common roots.

| Root | Origin | Meaning | Example |
|------|--------|---------|---------|
| meter | Greek | measure | thermometer , speedometer |
| port | Latin | carry | report , transport |
| tru | Old English | faithful | true, truth, truthful |

The Old English root *tru* means *faithful*. What do you think the word *truly* means?

## Try It Together

Read the paragraph. Then answer the questions. Use the chart to help you.

Solar panels can be made from plastic, wood, or aluminum. Some people use aluminum because it is <u>portable</u> and not heavy. When you make a solar panel, be sure the <u>perimeter</u> of the glass lid will fit the perimeter of the box.

1. Look for the Latin root in the word *portable*. What do you think **portable** means?

   A furniture

   B able to carry

   C a type of table

   D parts of a whole

2. Look for the Greek root *meter*. What do you think **perimeter** means?

   A wooden box

   B huge and heavy

   C measurement around

   D light and breakable

NATIONAL
GEOGRAPHIC

**Connect Across Texts** Find out how the sun's **energy** can be used to heat food.

**Genre** A **how-to article** is a procedural text that gives instructions on how to do something. It may be in print or online. How-to articles are often written by an author or a contributor, who is an expert in the subject.

How To Make A Solar Oven

File   Edit   View   History   Bookmarks   Tools   Help

http://www.ngreachhowto.com

# NGReachHowTo.com
Your online source for learning how to do things

Search ▶

- ▶ Arts and Crafts
- ▶ Business
- ▶ Computers
- ▼ Environment
  - Solar Oven
  - Compost Bin
  - Tin Can Garden
- ▶ Food
- ▶ Hobbies and Games
- ▶ Home and Garden
- ▶ Pets
- ▶ Relationships and Family
- ▶ Sports and Fitness
- ▶ Travel

About NGReachHowTo

Contact NGReachHowTo

Contribute to NGReachHowTo

## How to Make a Solar Oven
by Solargirl, *contributor*

The following directions will show you how to make your own **solar** oven. Solar ovens work like **concentrating solar power generators**. They reflect sunlight from a large area onto a small area, or focal point. The focal point absorbs the light, and can get very hot.

▲ solar oven

▲ concentrating solar power generator

NEXT »

**In Other Words**

**contributor** person who writes the article for free

**concentrating solar power generators** machines that focus sunlight to make power

▶ **Before You Move On**

1. **Use Text Features** Compare the pictures. How is light reflected into the oven and onto the generator?
2. **Analyze** What makes this how-to article formal?

137

NGReachHowTo.com
Your online source for learning how to do things

Search ▶

▶ Arts and Crafts
▶ Business
▶ Computers
▼ Environment
  Solar Oven
  Compost Bin
  Tin Can Garden
▶ Food
▶ Hobbies and Games
▶ Home and Garden
▶ Pets
▶ Relationships and Family
▶ Sports and Fitness
▶ Travel
About NGReachHowTo
Contact NGReachHowTo
Contribute to NGReachHowTo

## Things You Will Need

To make your **solar** oven, you will need these tools and materials:

- one large pizza box
- a pen or pencil
- scissors
- aluminum foil

- clear plastic wrap
- tape
- black construction paper
- two long straws

 Follow instructions carefully. Use materials and oven as instructed in the article.

## Steps You Will Take

To make your solar oven, follow these steps:

**Step 1**

Draw a square on the lid of a pizza box. The square should measure about one inch from all four sides of the lid.

**Step 2**

Cut the square's sides and front. Do not cut the back edge of the square.

**Step 3**

Fold up along the uncut line to form a flap. This is your oven's "solar **panel**."

« PREVIOUS | NEXT »

ds
collector

▶ **Before You Move On**

1. **Make Inferences** What do you think is the purpose of the oven's "**solar** panel"?
2. **Steps in a Process** Which tools and materials do you use in the first three steps? What will you use next?

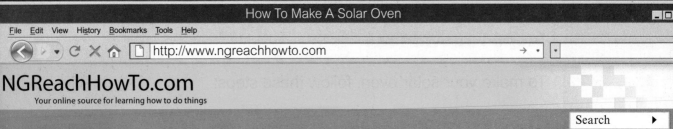

File    Edit    View    History    Bookmarks    Tools    Help

http://www.ngreachhowto.com

# NGReachHowTo.com
Your online source for learning how to do things

Search ▶

- ▶ Arts and Crafts
- ▶ Business
- ▶ Computers
- ▼ Environment
    - Solar Oven
    - Compost Bin
    - Tin Can Garden
- ▶ Food
- ▶ Hobbies and Games
- ▶ Home and Garden
- ▶ Pets
- ▶ Relationships and Family
- ▶ Sports and Fitness
- ▶ Travel

About NGReachHowTo

Contact NGReachHowTo

Contribute to NGReachHowTo

« PREVIOUS | NEXT »

## Step 4

Cut a piece of aluminum foil to fit the underside of the flap. Tape it in place. The foil will help reflect the sun's light into the box.

## Step 5

Cut a piece of clear plastic wrap slightly bigger than the flap. Open the flap. Tape the plastic to the lid's underside, covering the opening.

## Step 6

Tape a square of aluminum foil to the inside bottom of the box. This will help **insulate** it. Tape black construction paper over the foil. The paper will absorb the sun's thermal **energy**.

## Step 7

Place food on the construction paper. Solar ovens work best for cooking things like nachos* at low temperatures. Close the lid and prop open the flap with straws. Tape the straws in place.

## Step 8

Turn the oven toward the sun. Depending on the sun's **intensity**, your oven could reach 65° C (150° F) or more. Leave your oven in the sun until your food is warm.

## Step 9

### Solargirl's Cook Test Comparisons Table

| Food | Solar Oven on a 30° C (86° F) Day | Regular Oven at 150° C (300° F) |
|------|-----------------------------------|---------------------------------|
| nachos | cheese melted in 1 hour | cheese melted in 12 minutes |
| soup | turned warm but did not boil | boiled in 3 minutes |
| marshmallow | melted in 15 minutes | melted in 1 minute |

\* Tell a teacher or other adult before using a solar oven.

While your food is heating, think about how you can improve the design of your oven. Is there a better way to concentrate the sun's energy onto your box? Can you insulate it better? Finally, sit down and enjoy your food. You've **earned** it!

« PREVIOUS

**Note:** Solar ovens should only be used to heat up food that has already been cooked, such as nachos. Solar ovens should not be used to heat meat or eggs.

**In Other Words**

**intensity** strength

**earned** worked hard for

▶ **Before You Move On**

1. **Paraphrase** In your own words, explain the last six steps in order.

2. **Use Text Features** What can you conclude about **solar** ovens, based on Solargirl's cook test comparisons?

# Compare Online Documents

**Key Words**

| alternate | insulate |
|-----------|----------|
| circuit | obstacle |
| conduct | rely |
| current | solar |
| decrease | volt |
| electrical | watt |
| energy | |

You read two **online documents**. How are they alike? How are they different? Work with a partner to analyze and compare the online documents.

**Comparison Chart**

| | "How to Make a Solar Oven" | "Energy for the Future" |
|---|---|---|
| **Genre** | | |
| **Point of View** | Choose one:<br>• first person<br>• second person<br>• third person | Choose one:<br>• first person<br>• second person<br>• third person |
| **Formal or Informal**<br><br>Did the writer use:<br>• slang<br>• exclamation points<br>• abbreviations<br>• questions<br>• conversational<br>• voice | Choose one:<br>• formal<br>• informal | Choose one:<br>• formal<br>• informal |

Analyze the writing. If the writer used three or more of these writing styles, then the writing is informal.

**Talk Together**

Think about the two selections and the chart above. Use these resources and **Key Words** to discuss how people can use the sun's power.

# Compound and Complex Sentences

A **compound sentence** has two independent clauses, or sentences. A **complex sentence** has an independent clause and a dependent clause.

## Grammar Rules — Compound and Complex Sentences

| For **Compound Sentences**: Use a **comma** plus a **conjunction** to join two independent clauses. | Plants use light energy**, and** people rely on it. |
| | The sun's energy is all around us**, but** few people take advantage of it. |
| | Machines can run on electrical energy**, or** they can use solar energy. |
| For **complex sentences**: If the **dependent clause** comes first, put a **comma** after it. | **Since the beginning of time**, the sun has been a powerful force. |
| Do not use a comma if the **independent clause** comes first. | **The sun has been a powerful force** since the beginning of time. |

## Read Compound and Complex Sentences

Read the passage. What compound and complex sentences can you find?

We feel heat on a hot day because thermal energy is all around us. It comes from the movement of atoms. When they move quickly, they give off heat.

## Write Compound and Complex Sentences

Write one compound sentence and one complex sentence describing light energy. Compare your sentences with the sentences of a partner.

# Write As a Storyteller

## Write a Myth ✏️

Write a myth that explains how something in nature came to be. You and your classmates will share your myths with a group of younger students.

## Study a Model

A myth is a story that explains something about the world. It usually has gods or other non-human beings that act in human ways. Read Ted's myth about why there are earthquakes.

---

### What Makes the Earth Quake?
#### by Ted Walzcak

Before there were people in the world, there were **giants**. They were the ones who cared for the Earth. They planted forests. They built mountains. They made places for rivers to flow.

After a few thousand years, **some of the giants got pretty tired** of working. They wanted to have fun! So they started ripping up the trees and knocking down mountains. They even blocked rivers to make the land flood!

The gods were upset. What could they do? Finally, they decided to put the troublemakers in big caves deep inside the earth. That would stop the mischief!

Well, the trapped giants weren't very happy. When they pound on the walls of their caves, the ground above shakes and cracks. That's why we have earthquakes!

The story begins by introducing the **characters**.

The writer tells about the **conflict**, or problem.

The writer uses **different kinds of sentences** to make the story interesting.

---

# Prewrite

1. **Choose a Topic**  What thing in nature could you use a myth to explain? Talk with a partner to choose an idea that would be fun to write about.

2. **Gather Information**  What will happen in your story? Write down the details you will use to develop the characters and events.

3. **Get Organized**  Use a chart to help you organize your details.

**Character Chart**

| Character | Role | Function | Conflict |
|-----------|------|----------|----------|
| giants | | | want to have fun by destroying things |
| gods | | | |

# Draft

Use your chart and details to write your draft.

- Your title should tell what the myth will be about.

- In the first paragraph, introduce your characters and setting.

- Next, tell what the conflict is and how the characters react.

# Revise

1. **Read, Retell, Respond** Read your draft aloud to a partner. Your partner listens and then retells the myth. Next, talk about ways to improve your writing.

<table>
<tr><td colspan="2" align="center">**Language Frames**</td></tr>
<tr>
<td>

**Retell**

• Your myth explains _____ .

• Your characters are _____ , and your setting is _____ .

• First, _____ . Then, _____ . Finally, _____ .

</td>
<td>

**Make Suggestions**

• I couldn't picture your characters. You could add details about _____ .

• I didn't understand why _____ .

</td>
</tr>
</table>

2. **Make Changes** Think about your draft and your partner's suggestions. Then use the Revising Marks on page 629 to mark your changes.

   • Do all of your details help develop your idea? Remove any that don't.

   > Finally, they decided to put the troublemakers in big caves deep inside the Earth. ~~Each one was the size of Mammoth Cave! The giants figured~~ that would stop the mischief!

   • Different types of sentences will make your writing more interesting. Turn some simple sentences into compound and complex sentences.

   > When
   > They pound on the walls of their caves, The ground above shakes and cracks.

146

## Edit and Proofread

Work with a partner to edit and proofread your myth. Make sure you've punctuated compound and complex sentences correctly. Also check that you have used the correct end mark for each sentence. Use the marks on page 629 to show your changes.

Use the marks on page 629 to show your changes.

### Punctuation Tip

In a compound sentence, add a comma before the conjunction that connects the two parts.

## Publish

**On Your Own**  Make a final copy of your myth. Choose a way to share your work with your classmates. You can read it aloud, or act it out.

| Presentation Tips | |
|---|---|
| **If you are the speaker…** | **If you are the listener…** |
| Make sure you change your tone to show questions and exclamations. | Listen for details that tell you what the writer is trying to explain or teach. |
| Make eye contact with your listeners to help them stay connected. | Smile or nod to show the speaker that you are enjoying the story. |

**In a Group**  Myths were usually passed on by storytellers. Arrange to visit a class of younger children, and share your myths with them. Afterwards, ask them to draw pictures to go with your story. Later, you can post your myths on your school's Web site.

## Talk Together

In this unit, you found lots of answers to the **Big Question**. Now, use the concept map to discuss the **Big Question** with the class.

**Concept Map**

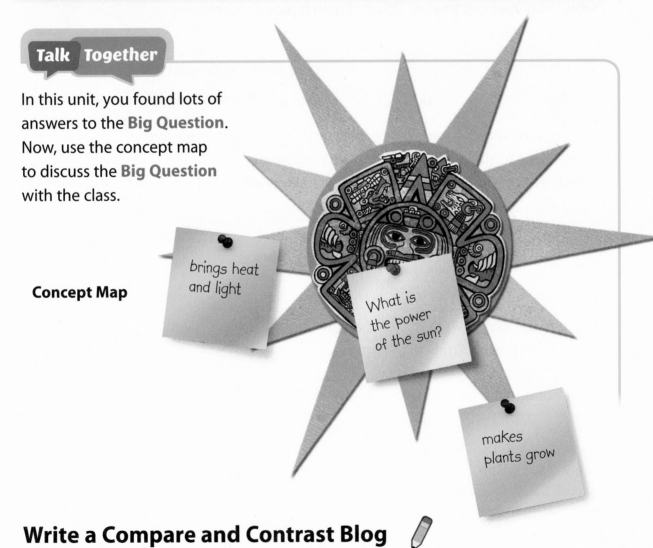

brings heat and light

What is the power of the sun?

makes plants grow

## Write a Compare and Contrast Blog

Use the concept map to write a blog that tells how the power of the sun affects people and nature.

# Share Your Ideas

Choose one of these ways to share your ideas about the **Big Question**.

## Write It!

### Write to an Astronaut

Write a letter to an astronaut. Include a question you would like to ask about the sun. Use the Internet to search the NASA Web site for the address where you should send the letter.

> Dear NASA Astronaut,
> I heard that the view of the sun from space is amazing! I have a question about the sun.

## Talk About It!

### Hold a Press Conference

With a partner hold a "press conference" about the first solar oven at your school. First, prepare interesting facts and details. Tell this information to an audience of "reporters" (your classmates). Then invite the reporters to ask questions.

## Do It!

### Perform a Myth

Choose a myth from the unit. Work with a group of classmates to perform it as a play. Decide who will play each part. Then talk about how you will perform the key events. Create some props and costumes. Rehearse the play several times and then perform it for the class.

## Write It!

### Write a Song or Chant

Work with a partner to write a song or chant to introduce one of the selections. The song or chant should match the mood or feeling of the selection. Perform the song or chant for the class.

# Nature's Network

**? BIG Question**

What is nature's network?

**Unit at a Glance**
▶ **Language**: Tell an Original Story,
Engage in Conversation, Science Words
▶ **Literacy**: Determine Importance
▶ **Content**: Food Webs

# Unit
# 3

## Share What You Know

*Do It!*

❶ **Think** about what animals eat.

❷ **Draw** an animal on
a note card and **label** it.

❸ **Tell** the class what plant
or animal your animal eats.

fish

**Build Background: Use the interactive resource to learn
about connections in nature.**
🌐 **NGReach.com**

# Tell an Original Story

Listen to Melissa's song, which tells a story about a hawk and a squirrel.

## The Hawk and the Squirrel  *Song* (((MP3)))

The story happens out in my backyard,
Where lots of squirrels like to play.
One day a big hawk comes to my backyard.
The story is about that day.

A baby squirrel is out in the open,
When I see a hawk outside.
The squirrel's problem is he is out there
With nowhere good for him to hide.

I see the hawk dive. I have to think fast.
The baby squirrel depends on me.
I make a big noise. The hawk is frightened.
The squirrel runs safely up a tree.

Tune: "La Cucaracha"

# Key Words

**Key Words**

carnivore
consumer
food chain
herbivore
omnivore
producer

Look at this diagram. Use **Key Words** and other words to talk about the relationship between plants and animals in a **food chain**.

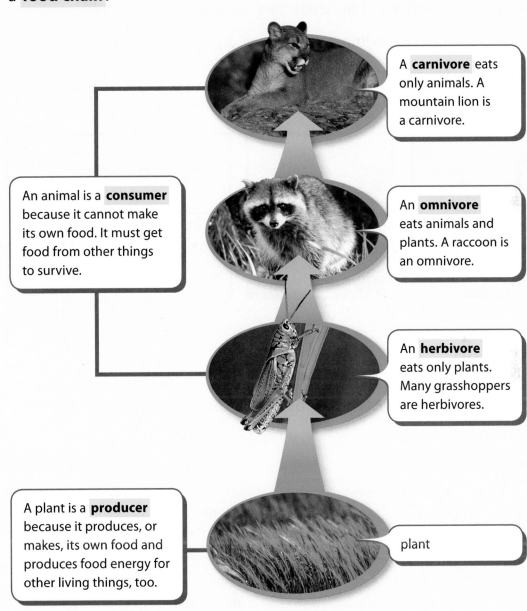

A **carnivore** eats only animals. A mountain lion is a carnivore.

An animal is a **consumer** because it cannot make its own food. It must get food from other things to survive.

An **omnivore** eats animals and plants. A raccoon is an omnivore.

An **herbivore** eats only plants. Many grasshoppers are herbivores.

A plant is a **producer** because it produces, or makes, its own food and produces food energy for other living things, too.

plant

**Talk Together**

How are living things in nature connected? With a partner, use the **Key Words** to answer this question.

# Plot

**Plot** is what happens in a story. Plots are built around a problem that the main character faces.

- The events happen because of the characters' actions.
- The turning point is when an important change occurs.
- The resolution is the event that solves the problem.

Look at the pictures. They show what happens in Melissa's story.

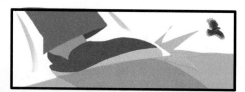

## Map and Talk

You can use a plot diagram to keep track of parts in a story. First, tell what the problem is. Then, tell the events in the order they happen. Next, tell the turning point. Last, tell the resolution.

**Plot Diagram**

**Problem:** The baby squirrel is in danger from the hawk.

**Events:** The hawk flies down toward the baby squirrel. Melissa sees it.

**Turning Point:** When Melissa makes noise, the hawk flies away.

**Resolution:** The baby squirrel climbs up the tree to safety.

Talk Together

Work with your partner to retell an animal story you know or have experienced. Use a plot diagram to help you retell the story.

# More Key Words

Use these words to talk about "Coyote and Badger" and "Living Links."

## cooperate
(kō-**o**-pu-rāt) *verb*

When you **cooperate**, you work together. We **cooperated** to clean up our messy room.

## essential
(i-**sen**-shul) *adjective*

**Essential** means important and necessary. Water is **essential** for our survival.

## partnership
(**pahrt**-nur-ship) *noun*

Individuals in a **partnership** work together and share the results of their work.

## store
(stōr) *verb*

When you **store** something, you keep it somewhere until it is needed.

## transfer
(**trans**-fur) *verb*

**Transfer** means to move from one place to another. She **transfers** the food to the plate.

### Talk Together

Make a Vocabulary Example Chart for each **Key Word**. Then compare your chart to a partner's.

| Word | Definition | Example from My Life |
|------|-----------|----------------------|
| store | keep | old games in my closet |

**Add words to My Vocabulary Notebook.**
NGReach.com

155

# Learn to Determine Importance

To determine what's important, you focus on what matters. One way to determine what's important is to **summarize**, or tell only the most important information.

Look for the most important details in the picture to help you summarize Melissa's day with her friends.

When you read, you can look for important details to help you **summarize**, too.

## How to Summarize

**1.** Identify the topic. Ask, "What is the paragraph mostly about?"

> The topic is _____.

**2.** Look for the important details.

> Detail #1 is _____.
> Detail #2 is _____.

**3.** Tell about the topic and the most important ideas.

> The paragraph is about _____.

Language Frames

?    The topic is _____.

👁    Detail #1 is _____.
      Detail #2 is _____.

✎    The paragraph
      is about _____.

## Talk Together

Read Melissa's personal narrative. Read the sample.
Then use **Language Frames** to summarize the narrative
to a partner.

Personal Narrative

# The Oak Tree

My brother and I love to explore the woods behind my
family's house. Lots of different plants and animals live in this
forest. My favorite place is the big oak tree. It is an **essential**
place for the animals. It gives them food and a home. Red
squirrels gather nuts from the tree and **store** them there for
the winter. Birds build their nests in the oak tree.

Last week, there was a terrible storm. Lightning hit the oak
tree, and it caught fire. By the time the fire was out, most of
the tree was gone. The squirrels and birds lost their home, but
we're happy that they weren't harmed in the fire. The squirrels
lost their food, too. Without their winter supply of nuts, they
were in real trouble.

We had to do something. My brother and I formed a
**partnership** to help the squirrels. We gathered many nuts
and seeds for them. Then we put them at the edge of the woods
for the squirrels to find. The squirrels were able to **transfer**
our nuts and seeds to their new home in another tree. When
my brother and I **cooperate**, we
can do anything!

"The topic is the oak
tree in the woods.

Detail #1 is the oak tree
provides food and a
home for the squirrels.

Detail #2 is birds live in
the oak tree.

The paragraph is about
the importance of the
oak tree."

◄ = a good place to stop and summarize

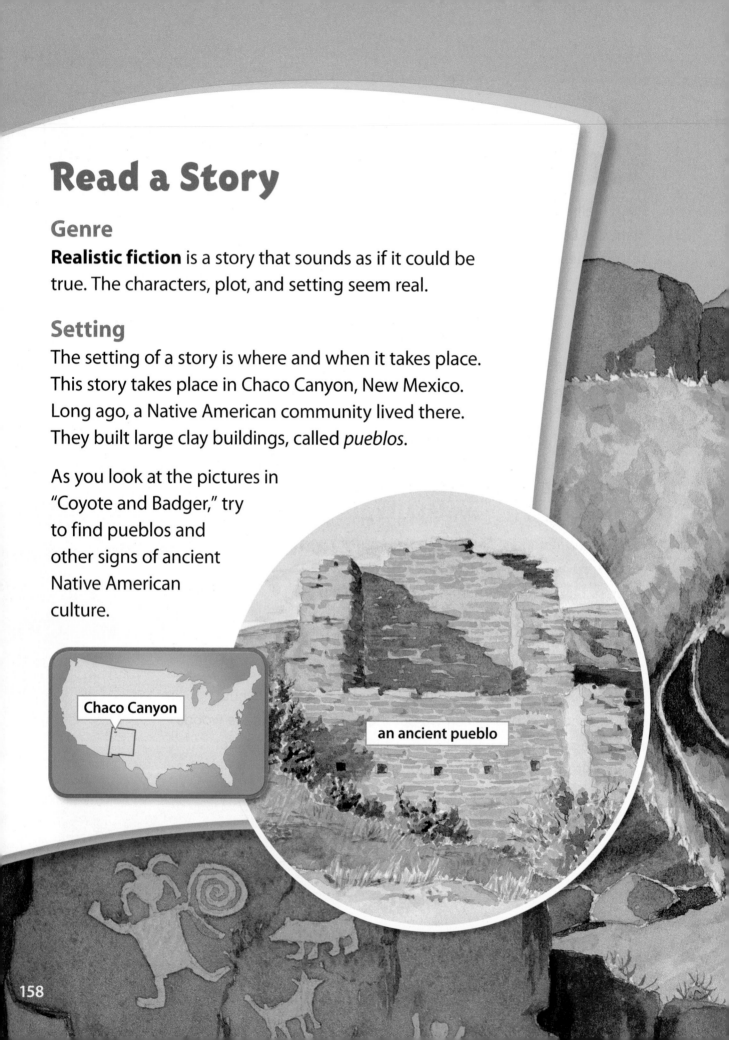

# Read a Story

## Genre

**Realistic fiction** is a story that sounds as if it could be true. The characters, plot, and setting seem real.

## Setting

The setting of a story is where and when it takes place. This story takes place in Chaco Canyon, New Mexico. Long ago, a Native American community lived there. They built large clay buildings, called *pueblos*.

As you look at the pictures in "Coyote and Badger," try to find pueblos and other signs of ancient Native American culture.

Chaco Canyon

an ancient pueblo

# COYOTE
# AND BADGER

written and illustrated by
**Bruce Hiscock**

▶ **Set a Purpose**
The animals of Chaco Canyon
have a problem. What is it?

Coyote woke up hungry, again. He stretched and looked out at the desert. **The sun was going down**, but the air was still hot. Coyote hoped to **spy** a rabbit, or even a mouse, since he hadn't eaten in two days.

These were hard times for all the animals of Chaco Canyon. No rain had fallen that spring, and there were no fresh leaves for the small animals to feed on.

And so Coyote, the hunter, often went hungry, too. Now he trotted silently up the canyon to **try his luck** once more.

**In Other Words**
**The sun was going down** It was nearly night
**spy** find
**try his luck** try to find food

Across the **arroyo**, Coyote scared up a rabbit, and a dizzy chase began. The rabbit **streaked** through the saltbush, with Coyote snapping at its heels. For a moment, it looked as though **Old Hunter** might eat well. But the **cottontail** was too quick and squeezed between some rocks by the canyon wall. Coyote scratched around the hiding place awhile and then went to look for something slower, or maybe something dead, to eat.

**In Other Words**
**arroyo** dry stream
**streaked** ran quickly
**Old Hunter** Coyote
**cottontail** rabbit

Farther up the canyon, Badger **emerged from her den**. She left her two pups safely underground and **waddled off** as the air began to cool. Badger was a night hunter, too, but she **seldom chased rabbits**. She was a digger, not a runner.

When Badger found the hole of an antelope squirrel, she tore into the hard soil with her long claws. The dirt flew, and **in a wink** she was underground following a dark tunnel. No animal can dig as fast as a badger, but the squirrel raced ahead and escaped.

**In Other Words**
**emerged from her den** came out of her home
**waddled off** walked away
**seldom chased rabbits** didn't hunt rabbits often
**in a wink** soon

Badger dug many holes that night before she came home with meat for the pups. **Prey was scarce** now, especially around the den. It was time to move her family to a new hunting ground.

As the sun rose, Badger led the way down the canyon with her little ones close behind. Few animals ever **messed with** Badger, for she was a fierce fighter. But **the open desert** is a dangerous place for pups. Overhead, in the clear morning air, an eagle watched them closely.

**In Other Words**
**Prey was scarce** Food was hard to find
**messed with** tried to attack
**the open desert** land with no place to hide

▶ **Before You Move On**

1. **Plot** Why is the dry weather a problem for Coyote and Badger? How do you think it will affect them in the future?
2. **Make Inferences** Why is the eagle watching Badger and her pups so closely?

▶ **Predict**
How will Coyote and Badger find
enough food to survive?

**A**t last they reached one
of Badger's other **burrows** by
an old pueblo. She checked
the tunnel for rattlesnakes,
as the pups scurried into
their new home.

Not far from there,
Coyote settled down to sleep
for the day. He was still
terribly hungry.

When evening came,
Badger began hunting.
Coyote heard the sound
of her digging. Quietly,
carefully, he **stole** closer.

Suddenly a kangaroo rat, **fleeing** from
Badger, hopped from a tunnel. A quick **pounce**
and Coyote had food. Another rat, about to leave
its burrow, saw Coyote and fled back down the
tunnel. That rat became Badger's dinner.

**In Other Words**
**burrows** homes
**stole** moved
**fleeing** running
**pounce** attack

164

When Badger **scrambled** back to the surface, she found Coyote waiting. Instantly she backed away, showing her powerful teeth. For a moment the two animals faced each other, hissing, growling, their fur standing **on end**. Then a curious thing happened. As they sniffed each other's scent, they relaxed a little.

Coyote came forward. He **took in** Badger's musky odor, while she could almost smell the hunger on his fur. And as they circled one another, the ancient and mysterious bond between coyotes and badgers **took hold**.

**In Other Words**
**scrambled** climbed quickly
**on end** straight up
**took in** smelled
**took hold** returned

They began hunting together that very night. Coyote, the **swift** runner, led the way to a prairie dogs' den as Badger shuffled behind.

Then Badger, **the master** digger, went to work. With Coyote **standing guard**, there was no safe place for the prairie dogs above ground or below. Soon each partner had a full belly, and Badger was headed home, carrying meat for the pups.

In the nights that followed, Coyote and Badger became a **fearsome** team. Not every hunt was successful, but it was much better than hunting alone.

**In Other Words**
**swift** fast
**the master** who was a very good
**standing guard** watching and waiting
**fearsome** strong

1. **Plot** How do Coyote and Badger solve their problem? What do you think will happen in the future, as a result?
2. **Summarize** Summarize the most important story events so far.

▶ **Predict**
Will Coyote and Badger keep
hunting together?

The **drought** grew worse as summer arrived. Each cactus, once **swollen with** water, **shrank** as it waited for the rains to begin.

Coyote and Badger often traveled far in search of prey, resting side by side when they grew tired. But they seldom went hungry, and Badger always took meat back to her pups.

The pups were getting big now. Badger let them play and dig little holes by the burrow when she was home. They were so full of energy and life.

**In Other Words**
**drought** dry weather
**swollen with** full of
**shrank** got smaller

Then one morning, Badger returned from a long hunt with Coyote to find only one pup in the den. She looked for the missing youngster at his favorite digging spot, but there was no sign of him. Badger searched everywhere. Then, behind the pueblo, she found **shreds** of fur, some blood, and an eagle feather. Badger, mother of many pups, knew this one would never return.

When Coyote looked for Badger that evening, she was gone. He found Badger's trail, but he did not follow it. **The time of parting had come**.

**In Other Words**
shreds  pieces
**The time of parting had come.**
   It was time to hunt separately again.

169

Coyote went back to hunting by himself. Even mice were hard to find now, for the rains still had not come. Through the dark nights, Coyote searched for food, and **when the sun burned down**, he slept.

One night as Coyote **prowled** near **the ruins of an ancient kiva**, the Old Hunter threw back his head and let out a long yip and howl. From around the canyon other coyotes joined in. The song echoed off the dark walls and floated up toward the river of stars in the sky.

**In Other Words**
**when the sun burned down** during the day
**prowled** hunted
**the ruins of an ancient kiva** an old Native American meeting room

Late the next afternoon, Coyote woke to the rumble of distant thunder. Wind rippled through the dry grass, and Coyote caught the **scent** of rain.

In her den, Badger felt a tingle as lightning **split** the sky. The summer rains were here at last. Now the desert would be green again, and for a time there would be more food for all the animals.

Badger listened as the rain **swept up** the canyon. And deep in the storm she heard something strange, yet familiar. It sounded like Coyote, howling in the wind. ❖

**In Other Words**
**scent** smell
**split** flashed through the middle of
**swept up** moved quickly into

▶ **Before You Move On**

1. **Plot** What did Badger do after her pup was killed? Why do you think she did it?
2. **Explain** The phrase "caught the scent" is an idiom. What do you think it means?

# PREDATOR PARTNERS

For hundreds of years, people have told stories about coyotes and badgers hunting together. In the mid-1980s, scientists saw this strange event many times in Wyoming's National Elk Refuge. When coyotes were hunting squirrels above ground, badgers looked for squirrels below ground, in burrows. Some coyotes would wait for the badgers to **flush out squirrels** from the burrows. If a coyote didn't catch a squirrel, sometimes the badger would get it. Scientists found that coyotes who hunted with badgers caught more squirrels than those who hunted alone!

Badgers like this one sometimes hunt with coyotes. ▼

**In Other Words**
**flush out squirrels**
chase the squirrels out

## Meet the Author and Illustrator

# BRUCE HISCOCK

Bruce Hiscock loves to draw—and he believes that anyone can learn how. He says, "Practice is the only way to improve."

Bruce has been practicing for a long time. When he was a child, he spent a lot of time outdoors. When he grew up, he became a scientist, and then an author and illustrator.

Bruce has explored natural places in the United States and Canada. He always travels with a sketchbook and a journal. He visited Chaco Canyon three times while working on this book.

**This is how Bruce draws a mouse. Follow his steps and draw your own.** ▼

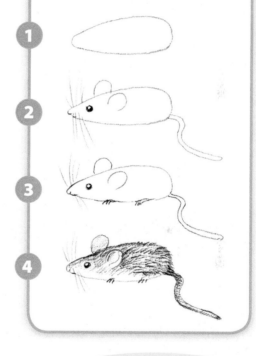

1
2
3
4

▲ Bruce Hiscock likes to spend time in his studio, where he works on his writing and drawing.

## Writer's Craft ✏️

The author uses precise words, such as "raced," "pounced," and "scrambled" to help the reader imagine how his characters hunt. Write your own description of a predator chasing its prey using precise words.

# Talk About It

1. What seems **realistic** about this **fiction** story?

   _____ could really happen in the desert.
   Coyotes _____ in real life.
   Badgers _____ in real life.

2. Imagine that Coyote and Badger meet again. **Tell an original story** about what they do.

   The story happens in _____ .
   The story is about _____ .
   This time Coyote and Badger's problem is _____ .
   This is how the characters solve the problem: _____ .

3. Think about the **partnership** Coyote and Badger have. What surprises you about it, based on what you know about these animals?

Learn test-taking strategies.
 NGReach.com

# Write About It

Do you think the desert ecosystem is a difficult place for animals to survive? Write a paragraph. Use **Key Words** to explain why or why not.

   I think the desert ecosystem _____ .
   One reason is _____ .

# Plot

Make a plot diagram for "Coyote and Badger."

**Plot Diagram**

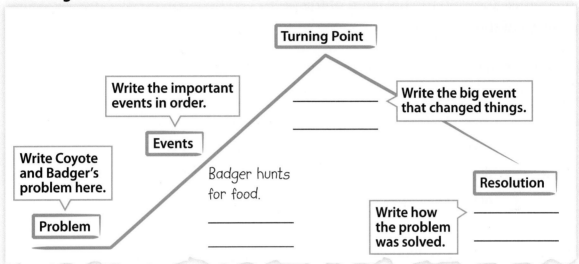

Turning Point

Write the important events in order.

Write the big event that changed things.

Events

Write Coyote and Badger's problem here.

Badger hunts for food.

Resolution

Problem

Write how the problem was solved.

Now use your plot diagram as you retell the story to a partner. Use **Key Words** in your retelling.

The problem is _____ .
Coyote and Badger _____ .
The turning point happens when _____ .

# Fluency  Comprehension Coach

Use the Comprehension Coach to practice reading with intonation. Rate your reading.

**Talk Together**

The illustration on pages 166–167 shows how Coyote and Badger work together. Use **Key Words** to tell a partner what the illustration shows about how living things are connected.

# Prefixes

Many long words begin with a **prefix**, or a short word part, like *dis-* and *un-*. Many of these English prefixes came from Latin, Greek, or Old English. Sometimes knowing the meaning of the prefix can help you predict the meaning of the word.

This chart shows some common prefixes.

| Prefix | Origin | Meaning | Example |
|--------|--------|---------|---------|
| in- | Latin | not | indirect, incapable |
| micro- | Greek | small | microculture |
| mis- | Old English | wrongly | misuse, mistake |

The prefix *mis-* means *wrongly*. What do you think the word *misjudge* means?

## Try It Together

Read the sentences. Then answer the questions. Use the chart to help you.

> Some people have studied the microculture of coyotes and badgers and have evidence that they sometimes work together to find food. Others think this is inaccurate. They believe coyotes and badgers wouldn't work together since they are natural enemies.

1. **Look for the Greek prefix in the word *microculture*. What do you think microculture means?**

   **A** animal culture

   **B** life in forests

   **C** culture of small groups

   **D** behavior of large groups

2. **Look for the Latin prefix *in-*. What do you think inaccurate means?**

   **A** true

   **B** not accurate

   **C** wrongly support

   **D** the opposite of hungry

# Living Links

## by **Diane Salisian**

**Connect Across Texts** Learn another way that living things depend on each other to survive.

**Genre** **Expository nonfiction** is any text that gives facts and information about a topic.

As the desert sun sets, a bat flies out of her cave. It's time for dinner. She lands on a nearby cactus and begins to dine on its fruit. Suddenly, an owl **snatches her**. It's time for the owl to eat, too!

The cactus, the bat, and the owl are parts, or links, in one desert **food chain**. In a food chain, each living thing **transfers** its energy to the living thing that eats it.

## A Desert Food Chain

1. A saguaro cactus uses the sun's energy to make food.

2. The saguaro flower's pollen is food for the Mexican long-tongued bat.

3. The bat is food for the desert great horned owl.

**In Other Words**
**Links** Connections
**snatches her** takes her away

▶ **Before You Move On**

1. **Summarize** In your own words, explain how a **food chain** works, beginning with the sun.

2. **Use Text Features** How does a bat get energy and pass it along?

# Desert Producers

Plants are an important link in any food chain. Through the process of photosynthesis, they take in energy from the sun and **transform** it into food. They use this food to grow roots, stems, leaves, and flowers.

Plants are like living **energy storage lockers**. When a plant is eaten, all the energy it contains comes out of storage. The plant then transfers that energy to the animal that eats it. That's why plants are called **producers**. They produce, or make, not only their own food, but also the food energy that other living things need for life.

Plants store another thing—water! The shape of these cacti helps them store as much water as possible.

**In Other Words**
**transform** change
**energy storage lockers** places that **store** energy

# Desert Consumers

**Consumers** are everywhere in the desert. Just listen for their **chirps**, rattles, growls, and **squeals**. Consumers are the animals that call the desert home. Unlike producers, they cannot make their own food. They must eat other things in order to survive.

Consumers are grouped by the kind of food they eat. **Herbivores** are animals that eat plants. In the desert, they may nibble on seeds, flowers, roots, and grasses. Some herbivores get most of their water from the plants they eat.

**Carnivores** are animals that eat other animals. Eagles, snakes, and bobcats are desert carnivores. **Omnivores**, on the other hand, are not picky. They may eat any plant or animal that looks appetizing, including eggs, fruits, and insects. Consumers **form** another important link in any food chain.

herbivore

carnivore

omnivore

---

**In Other Words**
**chirps** quiet noises
**squeals** loud noises
**form** make

▶ **Before You Move On**

1. **Main Idea** How do **producers** get energy? How do **consumers** get energy?
2. **Analyze** How does the author organize her ideas? How does this organization help you understand the text?

# Desert Decomposers

When a plant or an animal dies, the energy stored in its body does not go away. Instead, it is transformed once again. This time decomposers, such as fungi (including mushrooms) and bacteria, do the work.

Decomposers help break down dead plants and animals. As they dine, they return **essential nutrients** to the soil. Plants need these nutrients in order to survive.

◄ Bacteria are decomposers that live in the desert soil.

The sun, producers, consumers, and decomposers are all linked. In ecosystems like the desert, they form networks of food chains, called food webs. By studying food webs, we can better understand how all living things are connected. ❖

**In Other Words**
**essential nutrients**
what plants need to grow

# A Desert Food Web

Food chains show a single path of energy. Food *webs* are made up of many different food chains. In food web diagrams, the arrows show where the energy goes.

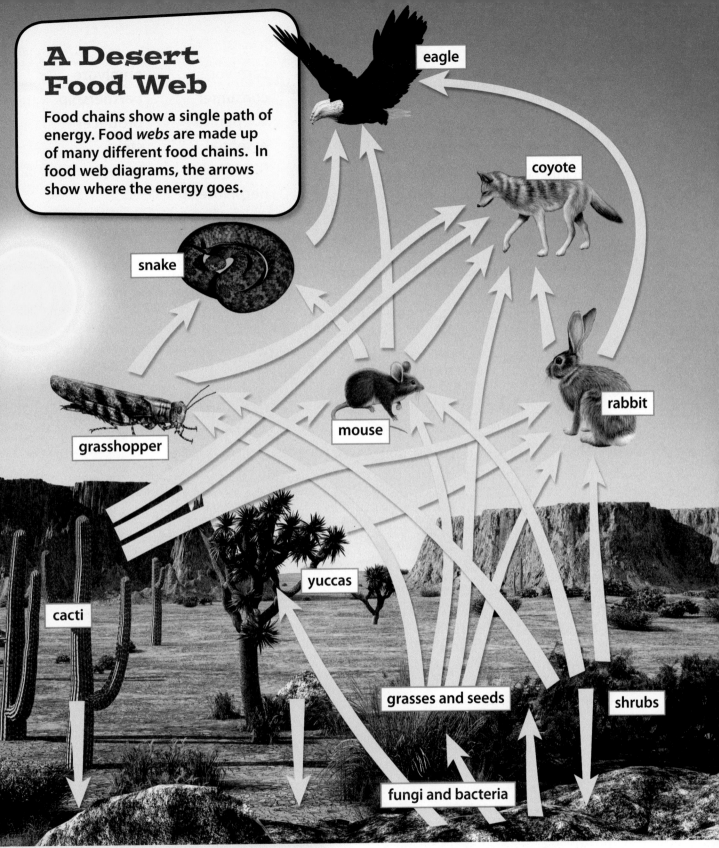

eagle

coyote

snake

rabbit

grasshopper

mouse

yuccas

cacti

grasses and seeds

shrubs

fungi and bacteria

▶ **Before You Move On**

1. **Details** What is the role of decomposers in an ecosystem?

2. **Use Text Features** Find one **food chain** in the food web diagram. Explain how energy flows through it.

# Compare Content

In "Living Links" you learned how plants and animals are connected in a food web. Where do the plants and animals from "Coyote and Badger" belong in a food web? With a partner, make a food web like the one below. Write each plant and animal name where it fits in the web.

**Food Web**

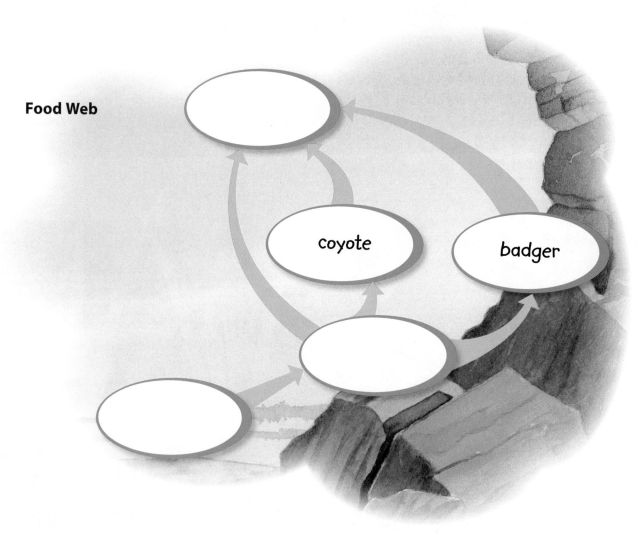

coyote

badger

**Talk Together**

How are the animals and plants in this food web connected? Use **Key Words** to talk about your ideas.

182

# Plural Nouns

A **noun** names a person, place, thing, or idea. A **singular noun** shows "one." A **plural noun** shows "more than one."

## Grammar Rules  Plural Nouns

|  | singular nouns | plural nouns |
|---|---|---|
| • Add **–s** to most nouns to show more than one. | tunnel | tunnel**s** |
| • Add **–es** to nouns that end in **x**, **ch**, **sh**, **ss**, **z**, and sometimes **o**. | fox <br><br> echo → | fox**es** <br><br> echo**es** |
| • For most nouns that end in **y**, change the **y** to **i** and then add **–es**. BUT for nouns that end with a vowel and **y**, just add **–s**. | community → <br><br> day → | communit**ies** <br><br> day**s** |
| • For most nouns that end in **f** or **fe**, change the **f** to **v** and add **–es**. For some nouns that end in **f**, just add **–s**. | leaf <br><br> cliff → | lea**ves** <br><br> cliff**s** |

## Read Plural Nouns

Read aloud this passage. Talk to a partner about the plural nouns you find.

> Herbivores are animals that eat plants. In the desert, they may nibble on seeds, flowers, roots, leaves, and grasses.

## Write Plural Nouns

Talk to a partner about what you see on pages 162 and 163. Write a sentence. Include two plural nouns. Compare your sentence with your partner's.

**Language Frames**

- Why do you feel
  _____ ?
- What do you think
  _____ ?

# Engage in Conversation

Listen to Jaime and Josie's conversation. Then use
**Language Frames** to talk with a partner about the importance
of small things in nature.

## Why Are Bees Special? *Dialogue* ((MP3))

**Jaime:** You have so many bees! Where do they all live?

**Josie:** I build beehives for them. We can move closer to see one.

**Jaime:** I think I'll stay here. Why do you feel it's important to work
with bees?

**Josie:** Bees are important to the food web. They help plants grow.

**Jaime:** How do bees do that?

**Josie:** They spread pollen from plant to plant as they look for
food inside flowers. Plants need pollen to make seeds.

**Jaime:** What do you think is the most interesting thing about bees?

**Josie:** They communicate by dancing. I like to watch them do
a waggle dance.

**Jaime:** When do they do that dance?

**Josie:** They do a waggle dance to show each other how to get
to a good source of food.

**Jaime:** Who makes sure they have enough food?

**Josie:** Bees don't need help with that. They can start a hive
wherever there are flowering plants nearby.

beehive

**Key Words**

chlorophyll

magnify

microscope

nutrients

photosynthesis

# Key Words

The sun helps plants, including those in the ocean, make food. This is called **photosynthesis**. **Chlorophyll** in plants changes the sun's energy into food. Look at this diagram. Use **Key Words** and other words to talk about an ocean food chain.

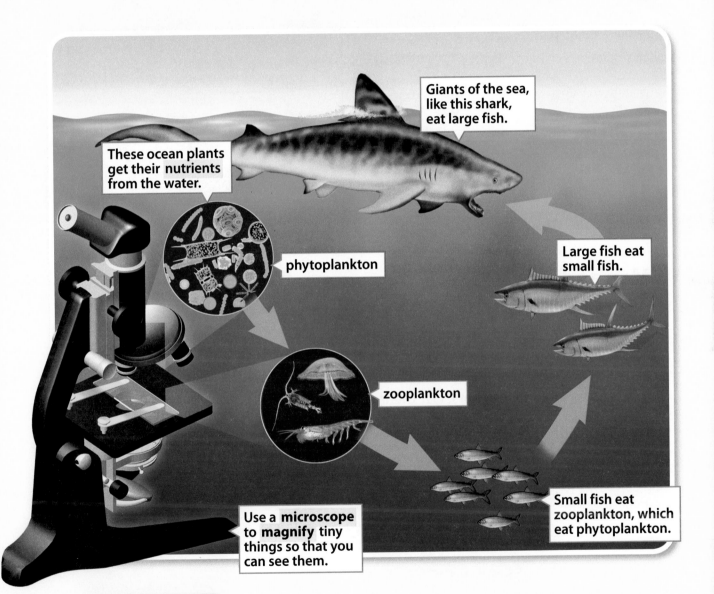

These ocean plants get their **nutrients** from the water.

Giants of the sea, like this shark, eat large fish.

phytoplankton

Large fish eat small fish.

zooplankton

Use a **microscope** to **magnify** tiny things so that you can see them.

Small fish eat zooplankton, which eat phytoplankton.

**Talk Together**

How do tiny things fit into nature's network? With a partner, try to use **Language Frames** and **Key Words** to have a conversation about this question.

# Main Idea and Details

When someone gives you information, they sometimes give you the big idea, or main idea. Then you ask questions to get the details.

## Map and Talk

You can use a tree diagram to keep track of the main idea and details in a conversation. Here's how you build one.

Start with the main point, or main idea, of the section. Write it next to the page where it appears. List the important details.

### Tree Diagram

| Page 184 | How do bees help plants grow? | They spread pollen from plant to plant as they look for food. |
| | | Plants need pollen to make seeds. |

**Talk Together**

Interview your partner about a small plant or animal he or she thinks is important. Use a tree diagram to keep track of the main idea and details.

# More Key Words

Use these words to talk about "Fish of the Future" and "Phyto-Power!"

### classify
(kla-si-fī) *verb*

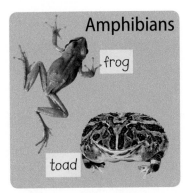

Amphibians
frog
toad

When you **classify** things, you put them into groups based on their similarities.

### investigate
(in-**ves**-te-gāt) *verb*

When you **investigate** something, you try to find out more about it.

### observe
(ub-**zerv**) *verb*

**Observe** means to watch someone or something closely. The hikers **observe** birds in the tree.

### propose
(pru-**pōz**) *verb*

**Propose** means to suggest something, such as an idea or plan. He **proposes** the blue one.

### specialize
(**spe**-shu-līz) *verb*

To **specialize** is to learn or know a lot about one thing. He **specializes** in fixing bicycles.

## Talk Together

Use a **Key Word** to write a question. Your partner uses a different **Key Word** to answer the question. Use each **Key Word** twice.

| Questions | Answers |
|---|---|
| What animals would you like to investigate? | I propose that we learn more about ocean organisms. |

**Add words to My Vocabulary Notebook.**
NGReach.com

# Learn to Determine Importance

To determine what's important, focus on what matters. One way to do this is to find the **main idea**, or what something is mostly about.

Look at the picture of the store window. What is the main idea of the picture? Look for **details** to support your main idea.

When you read, you can identify the **main idea and details**, too.

## How to Identify Main Idea and Details

 **1.** Think about the title. Turn the title into a question.

 **2.** Look for information that answers your question. These are the details.

 **3.** Think about how the details answer your question. The answer is your main idea.

My question is _____ .

Detail #1 is _____ .
Detail #2 is _____ .

The main idea is _____ .

## Talk Together

Read Jaime's interview. Read the sample. Then use **Language Frames** to tell a partner about other main ideas and details.

Interview

# All About Bee-Eaters

**Jaime:** I know you are a bird expert. What can you tell me about the bee-eater?

**Dr. Amos:** Bee-eaters are birds. They are easy to see. Males and females are all brightly colored.

**Jaime:** Where does the bee-eater live?

**Dr. Amos:** All the different kinds of bee-eaters make their homes in different areas. They are found in Europe, Asia, Africa, and Australia.

**Jaime:** I think I know why the bird is called the "bee-eater." Does it eat bees?

**Dr. Amos:** Of course! It also gets **nutrients** from eating wasps and other bugs.

**Jaime:** How do you know so much about bee-eaters?

**Dr. Amos:** I **specialize** in bee-eaters. I **investigate** them by **observing** them in the places where they live. First, I **classify** them, and then I write about them.

"My question is, 'What is the bee-eater?'

Detail #1 is the bee-eater is a bird.

Detail #2 is it is brightly colored.

The main idea is the bee-eater is a brightly colored bird."

◀ = A good place to ask a question about a main idea

189

# Read an Interview

## Genre

An **interview** gives information and opinions. In an interview, one person asks questions and another person answers them.

## Text Features

**Charts** and **tables** are used to organize information. A chart may take the form of a table, graph, diagram, or picture.
A table is a specific kind of chart that shows facts and figures in rows and columns.

title

| Sunfish Size Comparisons | | |
|---|---|---|
| **Animal** | **Average Length** | **Average Weight** |
| sea lion | 2.7 m (9 ft) | 566 kg (1,248 lbs) |
| sunfish | 1.8 m (6 ft) | 999 kg (2,202 lbs) |
| great white shark | 4.6 m (15 ft) | 2,268 kg (5,000 lbs) |
| blue whale | 29.9 m (98 ft) | 99,800 kg (220,021 lbs) |

row

column

# FISH OF THE
# Future

## by **Cheryl Block**

 **Comprehension Coach**

▶ **Set a Purpose**
Learn about a unique fish that
is part of the ocean ecosystem.

When you think of large predators, you may think of **fierce** lions in the jungle or giant grizzly bears in the forest. In the ocean, you may think of **streamlined** sharks and powerful killer whales. But who would think of this funny-looking sunfish, or Mola mola, as an important predator in the ocean food web? Dr. Tierney Thys certainly does.

**Sunfish are predators, but they will not harm humans if approached gently.**

**In Other Words**
**fierce** dangerous
**streamlined** smooth, fast

192

# Understanding the Ocean Ecosystem

Dr. Tierney Thys is a marine biologist who has made it her life's work to learn more about the ocean ecosystem. She has focused her research on the sunfish, a unique fish that most people have never even heard about. She uses a variety of technologies, including satellite tracking, to study this giant fish.

▲ **Dr. Tierney Thys has been interested in the ocean since she was a girl.**

Tierney has two goals—to better understand the ocean sunfish and to increase public awareness of ocean conservation. "We need to learn as much as we can about our ocean in order to conserve its great resources for the future. Understanding the **connectedness of** the ocean environment is critical to its health and our survival." In the following interview, Tierney explains her reasons for thinking this way.

**In Other Words**

**connectedness of** close relationships between living things in

▶ **Before You Move On**

1. **Use Text Features** Reread the photo captions on pages 192 and 193. What do you think this interview is about?

2. **Compare** How is a sunfish different from animals that most people picture when they think of fierce predators?

# What's Special About the Sunfish?

**Q:** Why did you decide to study the sunfish?

**A:** I've always been interested in how an animal's shape relates to how it uses its body. Why do animals look the way they do? How does their shape help them? You can see that a tuna's streamlined body is built for speed. I wanted to **investigate** why the sunfish has such an odd body shape.

| Basic Body Shapes of Fish | | |
|---|---|---|
| **Type** | **Body Shape** | **Fish** |
| torpedo (fusiform) | rounded body that **tapers** | |
| compressed | tall body with flat sides | |
| depressed | flat body | |
| eel-like | thin, snake-like body | |

◄ This tuna's tapered body is built for speed.

**In Other Words**
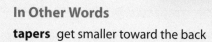
**tapers** get smaller toward the back

## Parts of a Sunfish

dorsal fin

pectoral fin

caudal area (clavus)

open, beak-like mouth

anal fin

For example, most fish use pectoral and/or caudal fins to propel them through water. In contrast, the sunfish barely uses its small pectoral fins, and does not have a true caudal fin.

Yet this strange shape does not **hinder** the sunfish. By moving its dorsal and anal fins in opposite directions, it swims quite well. It can dive deep in the water many times a day looking for food. Some dives are as deep as 800 meters (2,625 feet).

Another interesting part of the sunfish is its hard, beak-like mouth. Its main food is **jellies**. To eat them, the sunfish simply sucks them in and out of its mouth until they break into easy-to-swallow chunks.

**In Other Words**
**hinder**  hold back
**jellies**  jellyfish

▶ **Before You Move On**

1. **Main Idea**  What is unique about the sunfish's body shape?
2. **Use Text Features**  Which of the four basic body shapes of fish does the sunfish have?

**Q:** What else can you tell us about the sunfish?

**A:** It gets its common name from its habit of lying on its side at the ocean's surface, as if it is sunning itself.

The sunfish is a floating buffet. It is covered with parasites, which feed on its body. These parasites are food for other animals, such as cleaner fish, and sea birds.

The sunfish holds three world records! As it grows, it increases in weight more than any other **vertebrate**—up to 60 million times its size at **hatching**. If you grew that much, you'd be as big as 30 thousand school buses!

Second, it is the world's heaviest bony fish. The heaviest sunfish ever recorded weighed more than 2,300 kilograms (over 5,000 pounds). That's as heavy as ten grand pianos, or five large cows!

Third, the sunfish produces more eggs at one time than any other vertebrate. Scientists found one mother sunfish carrying **an estimated** 300 million eggs.

**Seagulls like this one like to dine on parasites that cover the sunfish.** ▶

**In Other Words**
**vertebrate**  animal with a backbone
**hatching**  birth
**an estimated**  what they calculated were

cleaner fish

## Sunfish Size Comparisons

| Animal | Average Length | Average Weight |
|---|---|---|
| sea lion | 2.7 m (9 ft) | 566 kg (1,248 lbs) |
| sunfish | 1.8 m (6 ft) | 999 kg (2,202 lbs) |
| great white shark | 4.6 m (15 ft) | 2,268 kg (5,000 lbs) |
| blue whale | 29.9 m (98 ft) | 99,800 kg (220,021 lbs) |

▲ The sunfish can be compared to some of the largest animals in the ocean.

▶ **Before You Move On**

1. **Details** How does the sunfish help birds and other animals?
2. **Use Text Features** About how many sea lions would equal the weight of one sunfish?

# The Sunfish and the Ocean Food Web

**Q:** How does the sunfish fit into the ocean food web?

**A:** The sunfish is a carnivorous predator. Its main food is jellies, which eat plankton. It may also eat fish and squid.

The sunfish can also be prey. Smaller, younger sunfish are prey to sea lions, sharks, and killer whales. However, the adult sunfish's huge size helps protect it from most predators, except humans.

Right now, many things are changing the ocean food web. One major factor is our overfishing. We catch and consume too many large predators, like tuna and sharks, as well as their food supply.

## Sunfish Food Chain

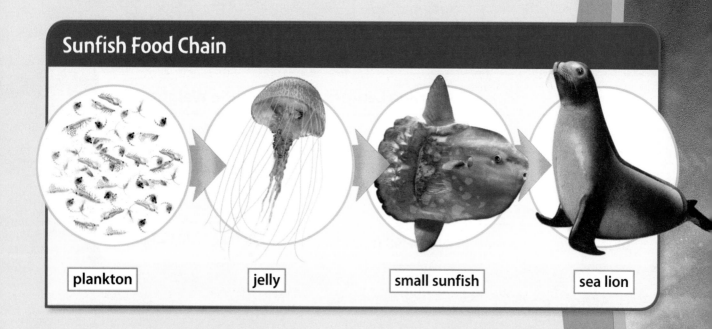

| plankton | jelly | small sunfish | sea lion |

**Q:** How does overfishing affect the food web?

**A:** When too many large predators and their prey are caught, jellies can move into their empty **niches**. When jelly populations grow too large, they can compete with other sea creatures for food.

The good news is that the sunfish **specializes** in eating jellies.

These photos show some different jelly **species**.

**In Other Words**
**niches** places in the ocean food web
**species** types

▶ **Before You Move On**
1. **Summarize** How does overfishing affect the ocean food web?
2. **Draw Conclusions** Why could the sunfish become even more important as a carnivore?

**Q:** Why is it important to us that sunfish eat jellies?

**A:** To answer this question, we need to understand that jellies are near the bottom of ocean food webs. They eat producers, such as algae, and plant plankton, or phytoplankton.

They also eat zooplankton, or animal plankton. This includes the **larvae** of many different kinds of animals such as fish, crabs, and sponges.

An increase in jellies could mean a decrease in zooplankton. This, in turn, could mean a decrease in many other animals, including the fish that people eat.

By slurping up jellies, the sunfish **has the potential** to keep jelly populations from getting out of control.

**In Other Words**
**larvae** babies
**has the potential** may be able

# An Ocean Food Web

killer whale

tuna

sea lion

sunfish

sardines

jelly

zooplankton

Jellies eat zooplankton, which include the larvae of many animals. Fortunately, sunfish eat jellies.

phytoplankton

▶ **Before You Move On**

1. **Main Idea** What could result from an increase in jellies in the ocean?

2. **Use Text Features** Study the diagram. Explain how a sunfish depends on phytoplankton.

# Technology Rules!

**Q:** How do you study the ocean sunfish?

**A:** We track the sunfish using pop-up satellite tags. These tags are attached to the animal with a dart. The tag contains sensors and a mini-computer that help us track the animal's movement for up to two years. Then the tag releases from the animal's body, floats to the surface, and **uploads data** to a satellite. The data are then downloaded to our computers.

**Q:** What have you learned from tagging?

**A:** Tagging lets us see the ocean through the eyes of the fish. We have learned that sunfish make repeated deep dives into **cold** waters but spend most of their time in **warmer** waters. We're also learning about their home ranges and **migration routes**.

pop-up satellite tag

▲ Tierney (right) and fellow scientist, Dr. Dewar, use satellite tags to gather information about the sunfish.

**In Other Words**

**uploads data** sends information

**cold** 1-2° Celsius (34-35° Fahrenheit)

**warmer** 13-19° Celsius (55-66° Fahrenheit)

**migration routes** where they go when they leave their home ranges

# How to Track a Sunfish

Follow the steps below to learn how Tierney and her team track a sunfish using information from a satellite tag.

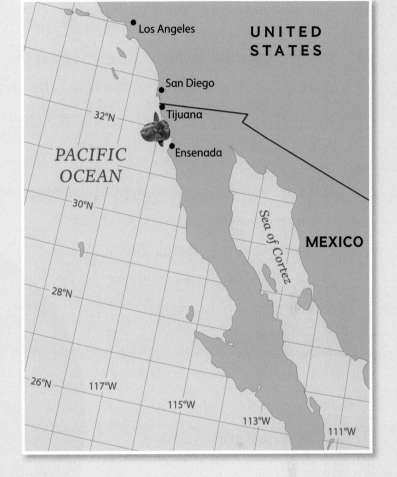

1. Look at the geographical coordinates, or numbers, in the first row of the list below.

## Geographical Coordinates

N 32, W 117

N 30, W 117

N 28, W 117

2. Find the horizontal line on the map labeled 32° N.

3. Find the vertical line labeled 117° W.

4. With your fingers, follow both lines until they meet. Notice the sunfish **icon**. This is the first location from which the tag sent data.

5. Look at the next two rows of geographical coordinates. You can use them to find the next two locations from which the tag sent data.

**In Other Words**

**icon** symbol

▶ **Before You Move On**

1. **Summarize** Explain in logical order the process of tracking a sunfish.

2. **Use Text Features** Find where the next two icons belong on the map. In which direction is the sunfish moving?

# Fish of the Future

**Q:** Will you continue to study the sunfish?

**A:** Yes. We still have so much to learn about the sunfish. Are there different species of sunfish? Are the numbers of sunfish increasing or decreasing? How does a sunfish find food? Where do females release their eggs?

As I said before, the sunfish plays an important role in the ocean food web. As a large carnivore that specializes in eating jellies, the sunfish has a unique part to play in our rapidly changing ocean.

**Scientists still have many questions about the sunfish.** ▶

**Q:** What do you hope your research will accomplish?

**A:** I see the sunfish as **an ambassador** for understanding the ocean. Finding answers to our questions will help us learn the best ways to protect it. We also hope to protect the sunfish by making the public and the fishing industry aware of it and its importance to the ocean ecosystem.

In fact, the sunfish might just be the fish of the future. It shows us that all creatures in nature have a part to play, and that it's important to keep all parts of the ocean environment **intact**. ❖

Every ocean creature has a part to play in keeping the ocean environment healthy.

**In Other Words**
**an ambassador** a messenger
**intact** together

▶ **Before You Move On**

1. **Paraphrase** In your own words, explain how Tierney helps to protect the sunfish.

2. **Synthesize** Do you think there will be more sunfish in the future? Why or why not?

205

# Talk About It

**Key Words**

| | |
|---|---|
| chlorophyll | nutrients |
| classify | observe |
| investigate | photosynthesis |
| magnify | propose |
| microscope | specialize |

1. What is Tierney Thys like, based on her **interview**?

2. With a partner, have a **conversation** about the work that Tierney Thys does and what it might be like to have her job, based on what you read. Think of questions you might ask her to start your conversation.

   Tierney probably spends a lot of time _____.

   I would/would not enjoy _____.

3. Compare the role of the ocean sunfish to the role of jellies in the ocean food web.

Learn test-taking strategies.
🌐 NGReach.com

# Write About It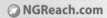

Write a paragraph that describes the kind of scientist you would most like to be. What would you like to **investigate**?

   If I were a scientist, I would specialize in _____ . I would investigate _____ .

   I think _____ .

# Main Idea and Details

Use a tree diagram to keep track of the main idea and details of each section of the interview. Each section begins with a heading.

**Tree Diagram**

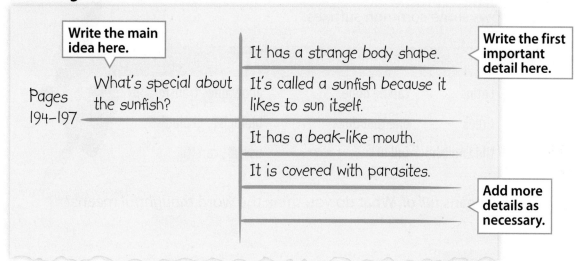

Now use your tree diagram to summarize the interview to a partner.

The interview is mainly about _____ .

# Fluency  Comprehension Coach

Use the Comprehension Coach to practice reading with expression. Rate your reading.

**Talk Together**

Why should we care about the small things in nature? Write a poem that praises something small in nature. Include **Key Words** in your poem. Share your poem with the class.

# Suffixes

Many English words end with a **suffix**, or a short word part. Many of these English suffixes came from Latin, Greek, or Old English. Sometimes knowing the meaning of the suffix can help you predict the meaning of the word.

This chart shows some common suffixes.

| Suffix | Origin | Meaning | Example |
|--------|--------|---------|---------|
| -able | Latin | can be done | allowable , transferable |
| -ist | Greek | one that does | biologist , geologist |
| -ful | Old English | full of | useful , careful |

The suffix *-ful* means *full of*. What do you think the word *thoughtful* means?

## Try It Together

Read the sentences. Then answer the questions. Use the chart to help you.

Marine botanists study plant life in the ocean—from spiky sea urchins, to bountiful seaweed. They think studying plants is enjoyable and useful work.

1. **Look for the Latin suffix in the word *enjoyable*. What do you think enjoyable means?**

   A  not enjoyable

   B  one who enjoys things

   C  a fun object

   D  can be enjoyed

2. **Look for the Greek suffix *-ist*. What do you think botanist means?**

   A  an ocean plant

   B  one that studies botany

   C  the study of plant life

   D  a male scientist

# Phyto-Power!

### by Mary M. Cerullo

Imagine that you are going on an undersea **voyage** to meet the most important creatures on Earth. You step into your submarine. Then you shrink, becoming smaller than the period at the end of this sentence. You look through your porthole and see strange, amazing life forms: phytoplankton. These tiny creatures are responsible for all other life in the sea. They also help make the oxygen we breathe.

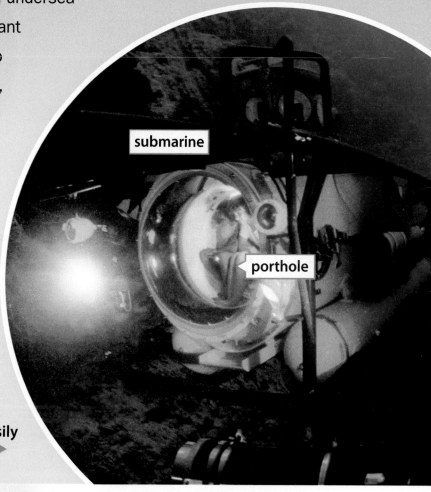

submarine

porthole

In this submarine, people can easily **observe** the underwater world. ▶

**In Other Words**
**voyage** journey; trip

▶ **Before You Move On**

1. **Main Idea**  Why are phytoplankton important?
2. **Synthesize**  To what can you compare the size of phytoplankton? What are they smaller than, according to the text?

**209**

# Tiny Drifters

Phytoplankton are tiny, microscopic, plant-like organisms. They don't look like the plants on land. They have no roots, stems, or leaves. Instead, phytoplankton resemble spiky balls, links on a bracelet, spaceships, and other oddly-shaped objects.

Phytoplankton are incredibly small. One spoonful of sea water can hold a million phytoplankton.

Phytoplankton need light in order to grow, so they are usually found near the surface of the water. Most of them drift through the ocean on **currents**, waves, and **tides**.

**Phytoplankton come in many different shapes. These photographs show phytoplankton magnified by a microscope.** ▶

210

# Food and Oxygen Factories

At the surface of the ocean, where phytoplankton live, there is sunlight, water, and carbon dioxide. These three things allow phytoplankton to make their own food.

Like plants, phytoplankton have a chemical called **chlorophyll**. Chlorophyll **captures** sunlight and changes it into **sugars and starches**. This chemical reaction is called **photosynthesis**. Photosynthesis also **produces** oxygen and releases it into the water and air.

## Phytoplankton Photosynthesis

energy from the sun

carbon dioxide from the air

oxygen into the air

carbon dioxide from the water

oxygen into the water

phytoplankton

**In Other Words**

**captures** takes in
**sugars and starches** food
**produces** makes

## ▶ Before You Move On

1. **Make Comparisons** How are phytoplankton and land plants the same? How are they different?
2. **Use Text Features** Where do phytoplankton get the carbon dioxide they need for photosynthesis?

# Feeding the Ocean Food Chain

Directly or indirectly, phytoplankton feed everything else in the ocean, even whales. Here's how this happens. Tiny animals called zooplankton eat phytoplankton. Zooplankton, in turn, may be eaten by small fishes. These small fishes are eaten by bigger fishes. Big fishes are eaten by sharks, some kinds of whales, and other large ocean predators.

In order to feel full, an adult killer whale may need to eat over 135 kilograms (300 pounds) of fish a day. These fish have eaten zooplankton. Each zooplankter (single zooplankton) has fed on as many as 130 thousand phytoplankton. Therefore, one meal for a killer whale may represent more than 400 billion phytoplankton!

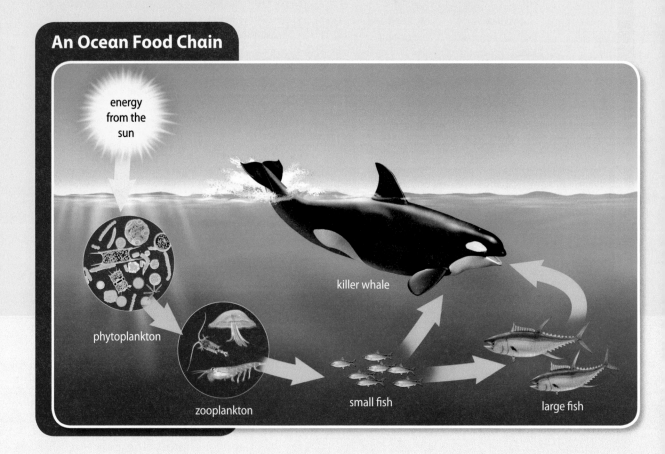

**An Ocean Food Chain**

energy from the sun

phytoplankton

zooplankton

small fish

killer whale

large fish

# Have You Thanked Phytoplankton Today?

Perhaps most important of all, phytoplankton help us breathe. About half of the world's oxygen may come from phytoplankton. That means every other breath you take is probably because of the work of phytoplankton.

So the next time you are amazed by a giant killer whale, are impressed by the beautiful green ocean, or take a breath of fresh, oxygen-rich air, don't forget to thank phytoplankton. They helped make all these things possible! ❖

**All forms of ocean life depend on phytoplankton, including this killer whale.** ▶

▶ **Before You Move On**
1. **Main Idea** How do phytoplankton help people?
2. **Details** What organisms connect phytoplankton to whales?

# Respond and Extend

**Key Words**

| | |
|---|---|
| chlorophyll | nutrients |
| classify | observe |
| investigate | photosynthesis |
| magnify | propose |
| microscope | specialize |

# Compare Genres

"Phyto-Power!" is a **science article**. "Fish of the Future" is an **interview**. How are the two selections alike? How are they different? Make a chart to compare the two selections. Think about each selection's purpose, text structure, and text features.

**Comparison Chart**

| | Science Article | Interview |
|---|---|---|
| **Purpose**<br>Is the purpose to inform, entertain, persuade, or tell readers how to do something? | | |
| **Text Structure** | Main Idea and Details | Questions and Answers |
| **Text Feature** | Photos<br>Yes<br>Tables<br><br>Charts<br><br>Illustrations<br><br>Headings<br><br>Maps<br><br>Diagrams | Photos<br>Yes<br>Tables<br><br>Charts<br><br>Illustrations<br><br>Headings<br><br>Maps<br><br>Diagrams |

**Talk Together**

How are humans connected to ocean life? Think about the science article and the interview with Tierney Thys. Use **Key Words** to talk about your ideas.

# More Plural Nouns

There are different ways to form **plural nouns**.

## Grammar Rules  More Plural Nouns

| | |
|---|---|
| • Some nouns use the same form for "one" and "more than one." | sheep ➜ sheep |
| • Some nouns have special spellings for "more than one." | tooth ➜ teeth<br><br>child ➜ children<br><br>woman ➜ women |
| • **Collective nouns** name groups of people, animals, or things. | groups of people: **class**, **family**, **team**<br><br>groups of animals: **school**, **litter**, **pack**<br><br>groups of things: **mail**, **money**, **trash** |

## Read Plural Nouns

Read this passage based on "Phyto-Power!" Find three nouns that have the same form for "one" and "more than one."

> Think of the thin layer of water at the surface of the ocean. Here there is sunlight, water, and carbon dioxide.

## Write Plural Nouns

Write two sentences about the photographs on page 210. Compare your sentences to a partner's.

# Write As a Reporter
## Write an Interview ✏️

Interview someone who has expert knowledge of animals and nature. Write an article to share what you learn.

## Study a Model

In an interview, you gather information by asking another person questions. Read the results of Rachel's interview with an animal control officer.

### Pam Marks, Animal Control
#### by Rachel Grant

<u>Pam Marks is an animal control officer for the city</u>. I asked her about the coyote problem we've been having.

**Q. Why have coyotes come to the city?**
**A. In a way, we've invited them!** As cities grow, the coyotes' habitats get smaller. So they come to the city, where they have easy access to food, water, and shelter.

**Q. How dangerous are coyotes?**
**A. They can be very dangerous.** They'll steal small pets, but they will also attack larger animals and even people. Sometimes they bring disease.

**Q. What can we do to keep them away?**
A. Keep garbage cans sealed. Make sure small animals are inside at night, when coyotes like to hunt. In other words, **don't make the coyotes want to visit you!**

**The title and first paragraph** introduce the person who was interviewed.

Rachel's **questions** flow naturally.

**The answers** are the person's exact words.

## Prewrite

1. **Choose a Topic**  What questions do you have about animals and how they live? Work with a partner to choose a good topic and person to interview.

---

**Language Frames**

| Tell Your Ideas | Respond to Ideas |
|---|---|
| • I want to Know about _____ . | • Who would Know about _____ ? |
| • I've always wondered how animals live in _____ . | • I'm curious about _____ , too. Can you also ask about _____ ? |
| • _____ seem like interesting animals. I'd like to find out more about them. | • _____ doesn't sound like a good interview topic. Do you have other ideas? |

---

2. **Gather Information**  Use a chart to help you prepare your interview questions ahead of time. Then take notes or record the interview.

| Who? | Pam Marks |
|---|---|
| What? | What can we do to Keep coyotes away? |
| Where? | |
| When? | |
| Why? | Why do they come to the city? |
| How? | How dangerous are coyotes? |

3. **Get Organized**  Review your notes or recording. Choose the most important or interesting questions and answers.

## Draft

Use the questions and answers you chose to write your article. Introduce the person you interviewed first, and then write the questions and answers in a logical order.

## Revise

1. **Read, Retell, Respond**  Read your draft aloud to a partner. Use the words *question* and *answer* so your partner will understand which parts you are reading. Then you can both talk about your article and how to improve it.

<table>
<tr><td colspan="2">Language Frames</td></tr>
<tr>
<td>

**Retell**

- You interviewed _____ .
- Some of the things you asked about were _____ .
- The most interesting information I heard was _____ .

</td>
<td>

**Make Suggestions**

- I didn't understand _____ . Is that exactly what the person said?
- The questions might flow better if you moved _____ to _____ .

</td>
</tr>
</table>

2. **Make Changes**  Think about your draft and your partner's suggestions. Use the Revising Marks on page 629 to mark your changes.

   - Are your questions in a logical order?  Would a different order make more sense?

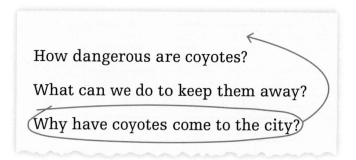

How dangerous are coyotes?

What can we do to keep them away?

Why have coyotes come to the city?

## Edit and Proofread

Work with a partner to edit and proofread your interview. Pay special attention to plural nouns. Be sure to start sentences with capital letters and end them with periods.

## Publish

**On Your Own**  Make a final copy of your interview. Read it aloud to your classmates. You could also invite the person you interviewed to visit and answer additional questions.

| Presentation Tips | |
|---|---|
| **If you are the speaker…** | **If you are the listener…** |
| Pause between questions and answers. Speak clearly. | What did you learn that you didn't know? Take notes on new information. |
| Show pictures of the animal you asked about. | Keep track of anything you didn't understand. Then ask questions. |

**With a Group**  Use the results of your interviews to create a special-edition newspaper. Add pictures and other articles related to your topics. Print copies of your newspaper to share around school.

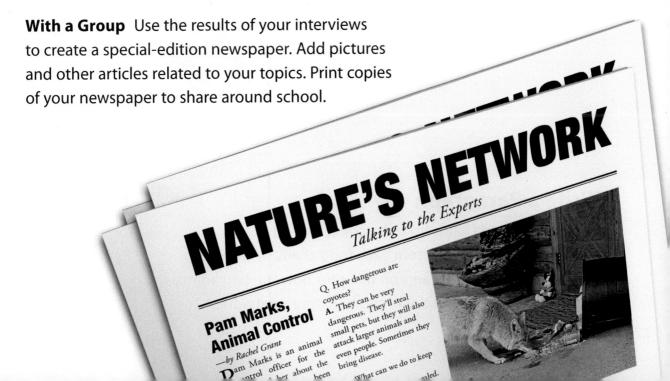

**NATURE'S NETWORK**
*Talking to the Experts*

**Pam Marks, Animal Control**
—by Rachel Grant

Pam Marks is an animal control officer for the ... her about the ... been ...

Q. How dangerous are coyotes?
A. They can be very dangerous. They'll steal small pets, but they will also attack larger animals and even people. Sometimes they bring disease.

What can we do to keep ... aled.

## Talk Together

In this unit, you found lots of answers to the **Big Question**. Now, use your concept map to discuss the **Big Question** with the class.

**Concept Map**

Pond Food Chain

What is nature's network?

Desert Food Chain

## Write a Paragraph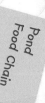

Choose two food chains from the concept map. Then choose one animal from each food chain. Write a comparison-contrast paragraph that tells how the two animals are alike and different in their roles in nature's network.

# Share Your Ideas

Choose one of these ways to share your ideas about the **Big Question**.

## Write It!

### Make a Food Chain

Research other plants and animals that live in the desert or the ocean. Make a new food chain. Find or draw pictures of the plants and animals in your food chain. Write captions to go with the pictures.

The Top of the Ocean Food Chain

## Talk About It!

### Perform a Play

With a small group, talk about how you could turn "Coyote and Badger" into a play. Work together to rewrite part of the story as a play. Then perform it for the class.

## Do It!

### Act Out a Food Web

Make a food web card for each student. Give a ball of string to the person who has the "Sun" card. Pass the string from the sun to each producer. Then pass the string between the producers and the herbivores. Finally, pass the string between the herbivores and the carnivores. Watch the food web grow.

## Write It!

### Write an Ode

An ode is a short poem written to praise its subject. Choose your favorite animal from this unit, and write an ode in praise of this animal. Tell what is great about the animal and why it is important to the world. Read your ode aloud to the class.

221

# Justice

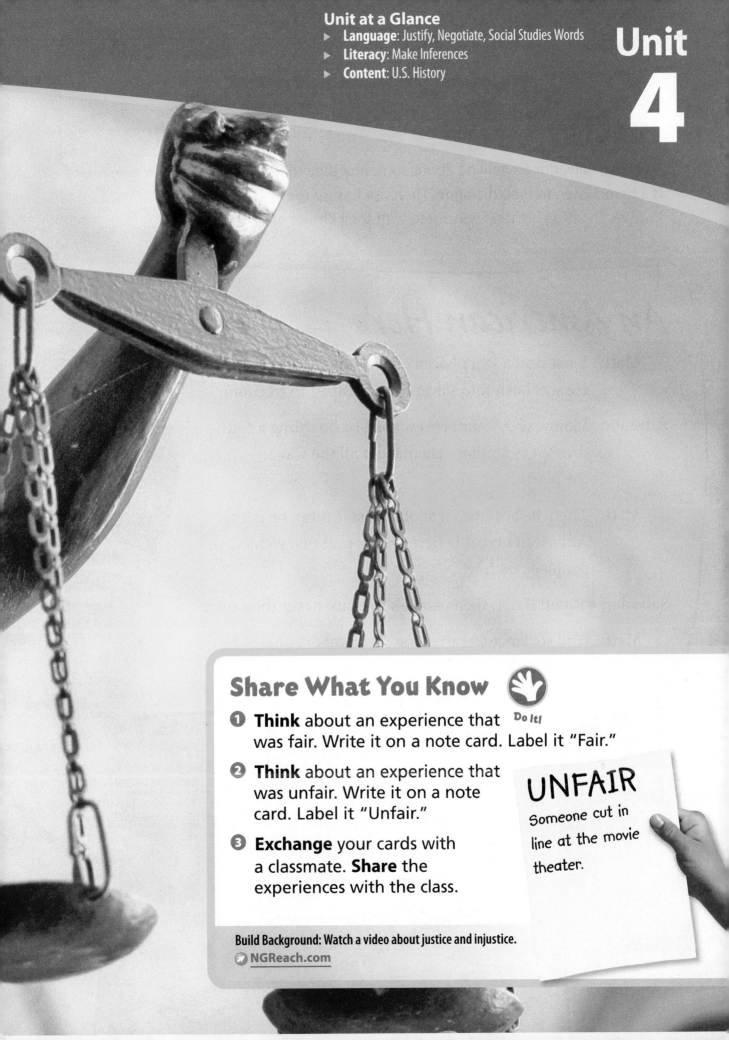

# Unit
# 4

## Share What You Know

❶ **Think** about an experience that was fair. Write it on a note card. Label it "Fair."

❷ **Think** about an experience that was unfair. Write it on a note card. Label it "Unfair."

❸ **Exchange** your cards with a classmate. **Share** the experiences with the class.

Do It!

UNFAIR
Someone cut in line at the movie theater.

**Build Background:** Watch a video about justice and injustice.
🌐 NGReach.com

# Justify

Matt and Salvador are talking about someone they think is a hero. Listen to their dialogue. Then use **Language Frames** to tell a partner if you agree with their choice and why.

## An American Hero  *Dialogue* (((**MP3**)))

**Matt:** I just read a story based on the life of Frederick Douglass. He was born into slavery and escaped to freedom.

**Salvador:** I know about him! He escaped by boarding a train dressed as a sailor. He made it all the way to the North.

**Matt:** Then, he became an abolitionist. I think he is an American hero. I believe this because he wanted all people to be free.

**Salvador:** Right! If not, then people's lives are never their own.

**Matt:** And so, I'm going to do my book report on Frederick Douglass.

Frederick Douglass

# Social Studies Vocabulary

**Key Words**

abolish

emancipation

escape

law

plantation

slavery

# Key Words

Look at the pictures. Use **Key Words** and other words to talk about slavery in the United States.

During **slavery** many Africans were forced to work on **plantations**. The work was hard. They were not paid.

Before **emancipation** some enslaved people **escaped** from, or left, the plantation.

Many enslaved people used secret paths to travel North, where slavery was against the **law**. Along the way, people helped them.

Later, the Thirteenth Amendment to the Constitution **abolished**, or ended, slavery.

## Talk Together

Some enslaved people risked their lives for freedom. What would you risk for freedom? With a group, use **Language Frames** from page 224 and the **Key Words** to justify your answer.

# Theme

The main message of a story is its **theme**. To identify theme, think about all the parts of a story. Then think about the message the author wants you to learn or discover.

Look at the pictures from the story that Matt read. The title is *Frederick Douglass' Civil War*.

Douglass speaks out against **slavery**.

Douglass writes about the war.

The 54th Regiment goes to war.

## Map and Talk

You can use a theme chart to help you discover the theme of a story. First, write down clues you find from the title. Then write clues from the characters, the setting, and the plot. Finally, use the clues to find the **theme**.

**Theme Chart**

| Clues from the Title | Clues from the Characters |
|---|---|
| Douglass plays an important part in the Civil War. | Douglass and abolitionists are against slavery. |
| **Theme** People fight for justice in many different ways. | |
| Clues from the Setting set at the time of the Civil War | Clues from the Plot Douglass writes about the war. He wants African Americans to fight, too. |

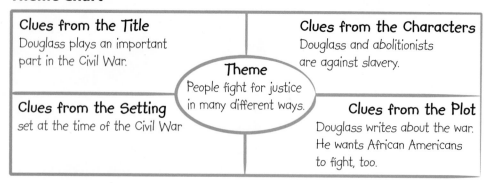

**Talk Together**

Talk with your partner about a television show you have seen about a hero. Your partner can make a theme chart. Use the chart to find the theme of the TV Show.

# More Key Words

Use these words to talk about "Crossing Bok Chitto: A Choctaw Tale of Friendship and Freedom" and "Journey To Freedom."

## distinguish
(di-**stin**-gwish) *verb*

**Distinguish** means to tell the difference between two things. It's hard to **distinguish** Chris from his twin Joe.

## equality
(ē-**kwo**-lu-tē) *noun*

When people have **equality,** they all have the same rights. **Equality** makes things even.

## freedom
(**frē**-dum) *noun*

**Freedom** is being able to say, think, and do what you want. A bird has the **freedom** to fly.

## risk
(risk) *verb*

When you **risk** something, you are in danger of losing or harming it.

## route
(rüt) *noun*

A **route** is a path to get from one place to another. Use a map to find a **route** to the ocean.

## Talk Together

Work with a partner. Role-play a scene in which two people risk something for justice. Use at least two **Key Words** in the scene.

> Enslaved people **risked** their lives in order to reach **freedom**.

**Add words to My Vocabulary Notebook.**
NGReach.com

# Learn to Make Inferences

Look at the cartoon of Matt and Salvador. Think about the details you see in the picture and what you already know about the library. Figure out, or **make an inference** about, what will happen next.

When you read, you can **make inferences**, too.

## How to Make Inferences

| | | |
|---|---|---|
| 👁 | **1.** Look for details in the text. | *I read* _____ . |
| ☁ | **2.** Think about what you already know about the details and the topic. | *I know* _____ . |
| 🧩 | **3.** Put your ideas together. What else can you figure out about the text? | *And so* _____ . |

## Talk Together

Read Matt's personal narrative about standing up for justice. Read the sample. Then use **Language Frames** to tell a partner about your inferences.

Personal Narrative

# My Grandfather, My Hero

The other day, I read about a man who stood up for what was right. That made me think of my grandfather. He stood up for justice fifty years ago and even helped to change the **law** . Back then some schools were separate and not equal. My grandfather marched with many other Americans. He spoke out for **equality** between African-American and Caucasian students.

My grandfather said that **emancipation** from **slavery** happened more than one hundred years ago. But, even in the 1950s and 1960s, African Americans still were not free. We still had to speak up for our **freedom** . He showed me pictures of things that happened when African Americans would **risk** trying to ride at the front of a bus, or eat at a "Whites only" lunch counter. Grandpa got very quiet, and tears were in his eyes.

He showed me a picture of Al, an African American student from the North who helped his mother vote for the first time. He was one of many people who came from the North. They traveled many **routes** through the south to help African Americans vote. They risked their lives and were so brave. Al taught Grandpa to **distinguish** between right and wrong, and to stand up for what is right. I can see how important that lesson is even today!

"I read that schools were not equal.

I know that 'equality' means being treated equally.

And so African Americans and Caucasians were not treated equally."

◄ = a good place to stop and make an inference

229

# Read a Story

## Genre

A **tale** is a story that is told over and over again before it is written down. This tale is based on historical events.

## Characters and Setting

Characters are the people in a story. The setting of a story is *when* and *where* it takes place. This story takes place before the Civil War, near a **plantation** in Mississippi.

Little Mo

Martha Tom

# Crossing Bok Chitto

## A Choctaw Tale of Friendship and Freedom

by **Tim Tingle**

illustrated by **Jeanne Rorex Bridges**

▶ **Set a Purpose**
Martha Tom and Little Mo are
from different cultures. How do
they meet?

There is a river called Bok Chitto that flows through Mississippi. In the days before the **War Between the States**, in the days before the **Trail of Tears**, Bok Chitto was a boundary. On one side of the river lived the Choctaws, a nation of **Indian** people. On the other side lived the **plantation** owners and the people they had enslaved. If an enslaved person **escaped** and made his way across Bok Chitto, that person was free. That was the **law**.

One Sunday morning during this time, a Choctaw momma woke her daughter.

"Martha Tom, get up! I have a wedding to cook for today. Take this basket and fill it with blackberries."

But Martha Tom couldn't find any blackberries on the Choctaw side of the river, so she did something she'd been told never to do—she went **crossing** Bok Chitto. The only way to cross Bok Chitto in those days was a stone path just beneath the surface of the river. Only the Choctaws knew it was there, for the Choctaws had built it.

**In Other Words**

**War Between the States**  Civil War

**Trail of Tears**  Native Americans in the South
      were forced to leave their homes

**Indian**  Native American

**crossing**  across

Martha Tom found a patch of blackberries on the plantation side of the river. She filled her basket and started for home, but she soon realized that she was lost. She tried to find the river, but instead she walked deeper into the woods.

stone path ▶

She came upon a clearing filled with logs that looked like benches. A skinny, dark-skinned man with a cane stepped out of the trees. He climbed onto a stump and called out, "We are **bound for the Promised Land**! Oh, who will go with me?"

What happened next would change Martha Tom's life forever.

A group of enslaved people stepped from behind the trees where they were hiding. "We will go with you," they replied.

"We are bound for the Promised Land!"

It was the calling together of the forbidden church, deep in those Mississippi woods. The people began to sing. Martha Tom had never heard music like this before, but it **touched her deeply**.

**In Other Words**

**bound for the Promised Land** going to a place where we will be free

**touched her deeply** filled her with strong feelings

Then something else touched her—on the shoulder. She looked up to see the biggest man she had ever seen.

"You're lost, little girl?" he said in a **deep** voice. "You're Choctaw, from across Bok Chitto?"

Martha Tom nodded.

"What is your name?"

"Martha Tom."

"Well, Martha Tom, I'll get my son to take you back to the river. Little Mo!" he called.

A boy appeared. "Little Mo, this girl is lost. She is Choctaw from across Bok Chitto. Take her to the **riverbank** and she can get home from there."

"Daddy, I **better not**," Little Mo said. "The men from the **plantation** house told us to stay away from the river."

**In Other Words**
**deep** low
**riverbank** side of the river
**better not** don't think I should do that

▶ **Before You Move On**

1. **Summarize** How do Martha Tom and Little Mo meet?

2. **Make Inferences** Why do you think the **plantation** owners want the people they had enslaved to stay away from the river?

235

▶ **Predict**
Do you think Little Mo will take
Martha Tom to the river? Explain.

His father **knelt down** and said, "Son, there is a way to move amongst them where they won't even notice you. It's like **you're invisible**. You move not too fast, not too slow, eyes to the ground, away you go! Now give it a try and get this little girl home!"

So Little Mo took Martha Tom by the hand and off they went, not too fast, not too slow, eyes to the ground, away you go!

They walked right in front of the **plantation** house porch, where the owners were sitting. But no one **paid them any mind**.

**In Other Words**
**knelt down**  got on his knees
**you're invisible**  no one can see you
**paid them any mind**  noticed them

236

When they arrived at the river, Martha Tom took Little Mo by the hand and the two of them went crossing Bok Chitto to the Choctaw side.

Even before they stepped from the stones to the earth, Little Mo heard the sound of chanting. He thought it must be the heartbeat of the earth itself. It was the old men calling the Choctaws to the wedding ceremony.

"Way, hey ya hey ya
You a hey you ay
A hey ya a hey ya!

Way, hey ya hey ya
You a hey you ay
A hey ya a hey ya!"

Little Mo had never heard music like this before, but it touched him deeply.

Then something else touched them both—on the shoulder. It was Martha Tom's mother!

"Little girl, you have been crossing Bok Chitto! You take him to the river and come right back!"

Martha Tom knew her mother could **cackle** like a crow on the outside, while inside she would **coo** like a dove with love for her daughter. She took Little Mo to the river and showed him how to cross **on his own**. And so began a friendship that would last for years.

Every Sunday morning Martha Tom would cross Bok Chitto. She sat with Little Mo's family in church. She sang the songs in English, and then she sang them in Choctaw on her way home.

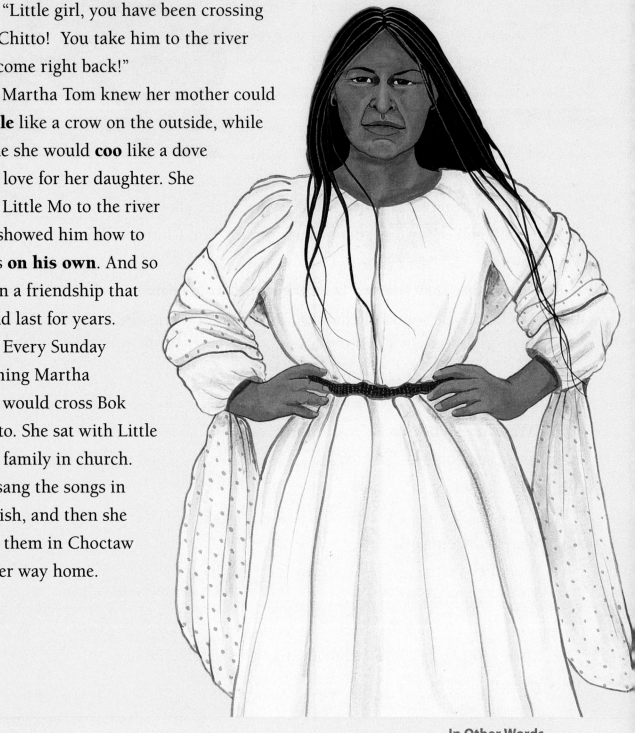

**In Other Words**
**cackle** shout; yell
**coo** sing
**on his own** by himself

Then one day **trouble came**. Twenty enslaved people were going to be sold. The men were called together to listen to the names being read. Little Mo's mother was on that list.

Little Mo's father wondered how to tell his family.

After supper, he motioned for them to be still. Feeling his knees grow weak, he said, "Your mother has been sold."

"Nooo!" she cried. The children began to cry, too.

"This is our last evening together!" he said. "Stop your crying. I want every one of you to find something small and **precious** to give your mother to remember you by."

No one moved.

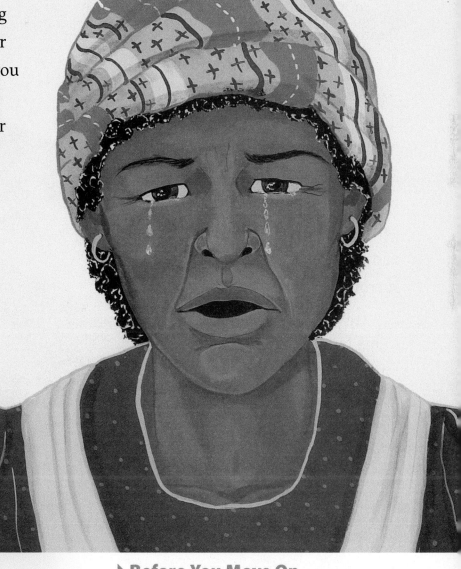

**In Other Words**
**trouble came** there was a big problem
**precious** special

▶ **Before You Move On**

1. **Paraphrase** How did Little Mo get Martha Tom home? In your own words, explain the advice his father gave him and how it helped.

2. **Theme** What is the effect of **slavery** on Little Mo's family at this point in the story?

▶ **Predict**
What might Little Mo's family do
to solve their problem?

Then Little Mo said, "Daddy, there is a way we can stay together. We can go crossing Bok Chitto."

"Son, they'll have the dogs guarding the river."

"Daddy, we can go like you taught me—not too fast, not too slow, eyes to the ground, away you go! Daddy, we have to try."

Hope filled the father's heart. "You are right, son. We have to try."

They packed quickly, but they were not quick enough.

The men in the **plantation** house saw them working late. They called for the guards with the dogs and the **lanterns** and the guns, and they surrounded that little house.

Little Mo's daddy said to his family, "This night's journey is about **faith**. It is about **freedom**. We will go out the front door."

**In Other Words**
**lanterns** lights
**faith** believing we will be OK

240

And so they did—not too fast, not too slow, eyes to the ground, away you go!

Then something remarkable happened. They walked into the **circle of lanterns**, but even the dogs did not know they were there. It was like they were invisible.

Soon they stood on the banks of Bok Chitto. Little Mo said, "Daddy, I've never been here at night. I can't get us across!"

His father said, "Son, we call you Little Mo. But you know that your real name is Moses. Now, Moses, get us across that water!"

**In Other Words**
**circle of lanterns** light

Little Mo dipped his arms into the chilly waters till he found the stone path. Quick as a bird, he **flew** across the stones and **burst** into Martha Tom's home.

"We are trying to cross the river," he said. "The **plantation** men are **after us**. Can you help us?"

Martha Tom's mother jumped out of bed.

"Son, hide your family in the bushes near the river. You'll know when to come across. Go! I have work to do!"

She went to every home in that village and called inside, "Women! Put on your white dresses! Bring a candle and meet me at the river."

And this is what happened.

**In Other Words**
**flew** ran
**burst** entered without knocking
**after us** trying to catch us

242

The guards stood on the plantation side of the river with their dogs and lanterns and guns. Suddenly, they saw **emerging from** the white fog on the Choctaw side a group of women dressed in white. The Choctaw women carried candles that **cast a glow around** their faces.

Rising from the bushes, the guards saw seven people escaping. They lifted their guns to **fire**.

They never shot their guns that night, for stepping out of the group of women they saw the most beautiful little girl. Her right hand held a candle, her left hand was outstretched, and it looked like she was walking on the water!

**In Other Words**
**emerging from** coming out of
**cast a glow around** shined light on
**fire** shoot

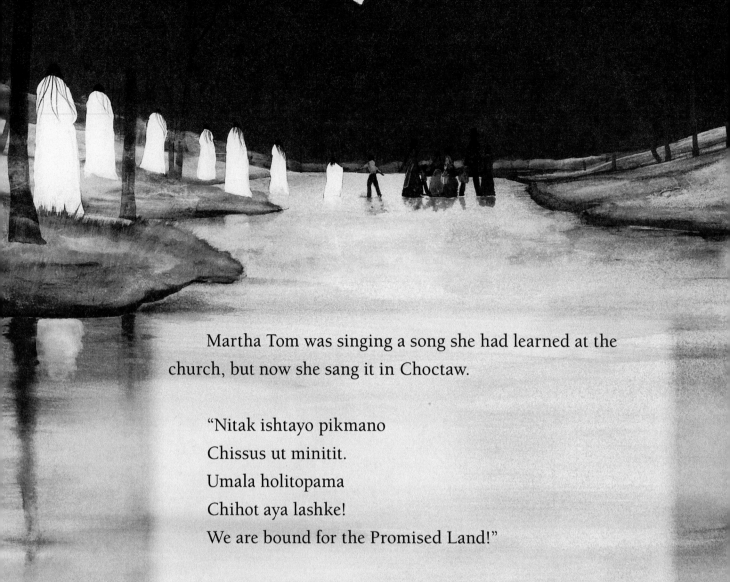

Martha Tom was singing a song she had learned at the church, but now she sang it in Choctaw.

"Nitak ishtayo pikmano
Chissus ut minitit.
Umala holitopama
Chihot aya lashke!
We are bound for the Promised Land!"

Then Martha Tom led Little Mo and his family across Bok Chitto. The family was never seen on the **plantation** side again.

The **descendants** of those people still talk about that night. The Choctaws talk about the bravery of that little girl, Martha Tom. The dark-skinned people talk about the faith of that little boy, Moses. But maybe the white people tell it best. They talk about the night their **forefathers** witnessed seven enslaved people, walking on the water—to **freedom**! ❖

**In Other Words**
**descendants** grandchildren and great-grandchildren
**forefathers** grandparents and great-grandparents

▶ **Before You Move On**

1. **Confirm Prediction** What do the guards think the family is doing? How is the family really crossing Bok Chitto?

2. **Theme** What lesson can you learn from Martha Tom and Little Mo's experience?

## Meet the Author

# Tim Tingle

AWARD WINNER

Tim Tingle is a member of the Choctaw Nation of Oklahoma. He wrote "Crossing Bok Chitto" to honor all the Native Americans who helped enslaved people **escape**.

Tim got the idea for the story when he visited a Choctaw elder in Mississippi. The wise old man told Tim about a family who helped people escape from **slavery**.

Tim turned the elder's words into a story that he hopes others will pass along. In this way, an important piece of Choctaw history will not be forgotten.

*"As long as our stories are told, we can be Choctaw forever."*

—Tim Tingle

## Writer's Craft

The narrator uses old-fashioned language like "went crossing," "no one paid them any mind," and "trouble came," to help set the time, place, and mood, or feeling, of the story. Write the first part of a story you know. Use language that helps the reader envision the setting and feel the mood.

# Talk About It

1. What details in this **tale** do you think are real? Which are not? How do you know?

2. What did Little Mo and his family **risk** when they decided to cross Bok Chitto? Do you think it was a good idea? **Justify** your answer.

3. What did the Choctaw people believe about **slavery** and **emancipation**? Use details from the story to explain how you know.

   I read _____ . I know _____ . And so_____ .

Learn test-taking strategies.
NGReach.com

# Write About It

What might Little Mo say to Martha Tom after his family **escapes** to **freedom**? Write a letter from Little Mo to Martha Tom. Use **Key Words** to thank her for her help.

_____ , 1820

Dear Martha Tom,

  Now my family and I are _____ .
Thank you for _____ .
  We will never forget _____ .

  Your friend,
  Little Mo

# Theme

Use the theme chart to find the theme of "Crossing Bok Chitto."

**Theme Chart**

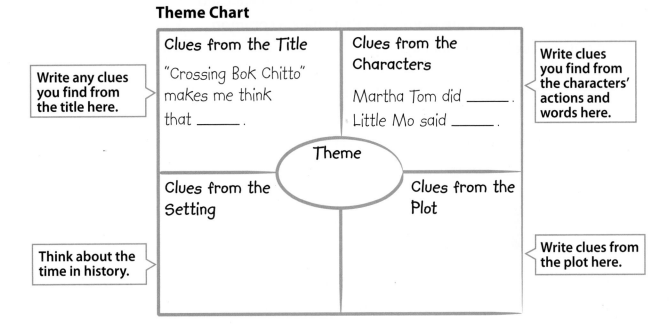

Write any clues you find from the title here.

**Clues from the Title**

"Crossing Bok Chitto" makes me think that _____ .

**Clues from the Characters**

Martha Tom did _____ .
Little Mo said _____ .

Write clues you find from the characters' actions and words here.

Theme

**Clues from the Setting**

Think about the time in history.

**Clues from the Plot**

Write clues from the plot here.

Now use your theme chart as you retell the story to a partner. Tell what the theme is and explain how you identified it. Use **Key Words** in your retelling.

The theme for this story is _____ .

# Fluency  Comprehension Coach

Use the Comprehension Coach to practice reading with expression. Rate your reading.

 **Talk Together**

What did Martha Tom risk for justice? Write about a person you know who experienced injustice. What did they do about it? Use **Key Words** in your paragraph. Share the paragraph with the class.

# Antonyms

**Antonyms** are words with opposite meanings. The word pair *slavery, freedom* are antonyms. Sometimes antonyms are used in analogies. Analogies are word pairs that share a common relationship. Look at this analogy.

These words are antonyms.

These words are antonyms.

[ <u>dry</u> is to <u>wet</u> ]    as    [ <u>cold</u> is to <u>hot</u> ]

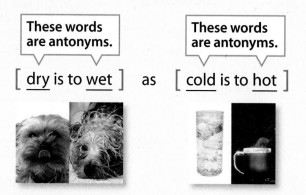

A word analogy shows how two words relate to each other. When you see word analogies on a test, it is your job to figure out the relationship between the sets of word pairs. How would you complete this analogy?

[ <u>abolish</u> is to <u>start</u> ]    as    [ <u>sadness</u> is to _____ ]

## Try It Together

Read each item. Choose the word that best completes the analogy.

1. **<u>enslaved</u> is to <u>free</u> as**
   **<u>safe</u> is to _____**
   A  challenging
   B  dangerous
   C  comfortable
   D  unfriendly

2. **<u>sharp</u> is to <u>dull</u> as**
   **<u>decrease</u> is to _____**
   A  plain
   B  evident
   C  increase
   D  slavery

NATIONAL GEOGRAPHIC

**Connect Across Texts** Learn about real people who took **risks** for **freedom**.

**Genre** A **history article** is nonfiction. It can tell about people, places, and events in the past.

# Journey to Freedom

by **Peter Winkler**

Before the Civil War, **slavery** was **legal** in southern states. It was not legal in the northern states, Canada, or Mexico. So enslaved people who were running away often traveled hundreds of miles to reach **freedom**. Many used a **network** called the Underground Railroad.

▲ This group of people escaping slavery worked together to find freedom.

**In Other Words**
**legal** allowed by **law**
**network** group of people

▶ **Before You Move On**

1. **Make Inferences** Why do you think people **escaping slavery** had to use a special network to get away?
2. **Summarize** Why did most enslaved people travel north to find **freedom**?

# Underground Railroad

The Underground Railroad did not have trains or **railway tracks**. It was a group of free people who helped those who were enslaved. As they traveled the hundreds of miles to reach **freedom**, people escaping **slavery** would stop at safe homes or other buildings called "stations." There, people welcomed them with a meal and a place to rest. As the runaways moved from one station to the next, they were accompanied by a "**conductor**" who made sure they arrived safely at the next **destination**. At the end of their journey, the formerly enslaved people started new lives as free people.

Runaways faced great dangers when they **escaped**. They could be **captured** and sent back to slavery. The people who helped them faced great dangers, too. They **risked** prison and even death to help people escape.

▲ Horace Alfred Ford was a conductor on the Underground Railroad. He helped hide runaways in "stations" like this house in Canesto, New York.

**In Other Words**
**railway tracks**  roads for trains
**conductor**  guide
**destination**  stopping place
**captured**  caught

Free State

Slave State

Territory

Arrows show major avenues of escape. Widths indicate relative numbers of runaway slaves.

Some runaways traveled through Texas to Mexico, where slavery was **illegal**. Others **fled** by boat to the islands of the Caribbean. Most followed the Underground Railroad to northern states or Canada, where slavery was also outlawed.

**In Other Words**

**illegal** not allowed by **law**

**fled** left

▶ **Before You Move On**

1. **Explain** Was a conductor's job on the Underground Railroad dangerous? Explain.

2. **Use Text Features** Why do the arrows on the map point both north and south?

251

# Underground Heroes

Who were the heroes of the Underground Railroad? They were ordinary people. Some were formerly enslaved people who were freed or had **escaped**. Some belonged to religious groups. Some were from the North, and others were from the South. The members of the Underground Railroad had different reasons for helping people escape **slavery**. Yet they all shared the belief that people should not have to live in slavery.

Helping people escape was dangerous work. According to the **law**, people could be punished for **aiding** an enslaved person. The greatest danger, however, was from supporters of slavery. They sometimes **injured** or killed people who helped enslaved people escape.

▲ These twenty men were **arrested** for helping just one enslaved person escape.

**In Other Words**
**aiding** helping
**injured** hurt
**arrested** put in jail

◀ Rhoda Jones was a member of the Underground Railroad in Ohio.

# The Gift of Freedom

Members of the Underground Railroad knew the work was dangerous, but they **accepted** the **risks**. Rhoda Jones was one example. She lived in Ohio. Some people in that state had been killed for their work on the Underground Railroad. Still, Jones opened her home to people escaping slavery.

Rhoda Jones was just one of the thousands who risked great danger to help others. The members of the Underground Railroad didn't get money for their work. Most never became famous. Yet they were all willing to put their lives at risk to help others find **freedom**. ❖

**In Other Words**
**accepted** took

▶ **Before You Move On**

1. **Paraphrase** In your own words, explain what kinds of people belonged to the Underground Railroad.
2. **Make Inferences** How do you think those people felt about their work?

# Compare Figurative Language

**Key Words**

| abolish | law |
| distinguish | plantation |
| emancipation | risk |
| equality | route |
| escape | slavery |
| freedom | |

Authors use **figurative language**, such as similes or metaphors, to help you to create pictures in your mind. The pictures help you see, hear, feel, and understand what the authors are writing about.

Work with a partner. Find figurative language from the selection to complete the chart below.

**Comparison Chart**

| "Journey to Freedom" | "Crossing Bok Chitto" |
|---|---|
| Enslaved people who were running away often traveled hundreds of miles to **reach** freedom.<br><br>*In my mind, I can see the people arriving at a safe place.* | **Quick as a bird**, Little Mo flew across the stones.<br><br>*In my mind, I can see Little Mo hopping quickly across the stones.* |
| | |

**Talk  Together**

Both selections tell about what people **risked** to help others find justice and **freedom**. How does each author use figurative language to make the people and events come to life? Use **Key Words** to talk about your ideas.

# Present-Tense Action Verbs

A **present-tense action verb** tells about an action that is happening now.
The verb must agree with the subject.

| **Grammar Rules** Present-Tense Action Verbs | |
|---|---|
| • Use **-s** at the end of an action verb if the subject is **he**, **she**, or **it**. <br> 👤 **he** <br> 👤 **she** <br> 📖 **it** | Duncan learn**s** about slavery. <br><br> **He** learn**s** about slavery. <br><br> Peggy visit**s** a plantation. <br><br> **She** visit**s** a plantation. <br><br> History remind**s** us about our past. <br><br> **It** remind**s** us about our past. |
| • Do not use **-s** for **I**, **you**, **we**, or **they**. <br> 👥👥👥👥 | **I** write about history. <br><br> **You** listen to the speech. <br><br> **We** learn about Civil Rights struggles. <br><br> **They** read about women's rights. |

## Read Present-Tense Action Verbs

Read the passage. Work with a partner to find present-tense action verbs.

> Every Sunday morning Martha Tom crosses Bok Chitto. She
> sits with Little Mo's family in church. She sings the songs in
> English, and then she sings them in Choctaw on her way home.

## Write Present-Tense Action Verbs

Look at the illustrations on pages 236–237. Write two sentences
that describe what you see. Use a present-tense action verb in each
sentence. Be sure the subject and verb agree. Compare your sentences
with a partner's.

# Negotiate

Listen to Carmen and Rachel's song. Then use **Language Frames** to talk to a partner about ways to achieve justice through negotiation.

## THE MURAL    *Song* ((MP3))

**Carmen:** Let's discuss the school mural.

**Rachel:** Yes. The problem is clear.

I want to paint lots of animals.

You want to paint the best school volunteers.

**Carmen:** Maybe we could put them together—

There's no need for regrets.

How about we paint volunteers

with their favorite pets?

Tune: "Take Me Out to the Ballgame"

# Social Studies Vocabulary

**Key Words**

conditions

demands

labor

nonviolence

protest

strike

# Key Words

Look at these photograph. Use **Key Words** and other words to talk about how some workers **protest** unfair treatment.

striker

Workers go on strike. A **strike** is a way to protest with **nonviolence**.

César Chávez

Workers often strike for better **labor**, or work, **conditions**.

demands

Strikers make signs to express their **demands**.

## Talk Together

How can you achieve justice through **nonviolence**? With a partner, use the **Key Words** and **Language Frames** from page 256 to discuss the question.

257

# Sequence

When events happen in a certain order, they happen in **sequence**. When you think about sequence, use:

- time order words, such as *first, next, then, finally*

- names of days, months, and seasons

Look at these pictures of Carmen and Rachel.

## Map and Talk

You can make a sequence chain to show the order of events. Here's how you make one.

Each event goes in a box in the sequence chain. The first event goes in the first box. The second event goes in the second box, and so on.

**Sequence Chain**

| First, Carmen and Rachel decide to paint a mural. | → | Next, Carmen and Rachel discuss their different ideas. | → | Then they negotiate an agreement. | → | Finally, they paint the mural. They are pleased with the results. |

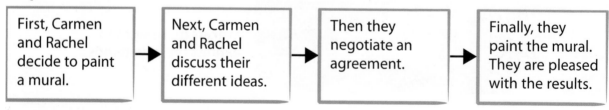

**Talk Together**

Use a sequence chain to tell about something you negotiated. Tell the events in time order while your partner makes a sequence chain.

# More Key Words

Use these words to talk about "Harvesting Hope: The Story of César Chávez" and "A Filmmaker for Justice."

## barrier
(**bar**-ē-ur) *noun*

A **barrier** prevents you from getting to something. The wall was a **barrier** to freedom.

## conflict
(**con**-flikt) *noun*

A **conflict** is a disagreement between people or groups.

## demonstrate
(**de**-mun-strāt) *verb*

When you **demonstrate** something, you show or express your feelings or knowledge about it.

## oppose
(u-**pōz**) *verb*

**Oppose** means to disagree with an idea or action. They protested to **oppose** the government's decision.

## require
(ri-**kwīr**) *verb*

**Require** means to need. A plant **requires** sunlight to survive.

### Talk Together

Work with a partner. Make an **Expanded Meaning Map** for each **Key Word**.

**Expanded Meaning Map**

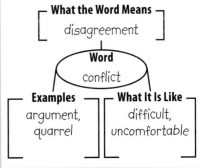

┌ **What the Word Means** ┐
disagreement

**Word**
conflict

┌ **Examples** ┐    ┌ **What It Is Like** ┐
argument,          difficult,
quarrel            uncomfortable

**Build Background:** Watch a video about justice.
NGReach.com

# Learn to Make Inferences

Look at the cartoon. The caption does not say why the women are demonstrating. You can use what you see and what you already know to figure out, or **make an inference** about, what the women are protesting.

**Protest in front of Atti's Movers.**

When you read, you can **make inferences**, too.

## How to Make Inferences

| | | |
|---|---|---|
|  | **1.** Look for details in the text. | I read _____ . |
| | **2.** Think about what you already know about the details and the topic. | I know _____ . |
|  | **3.** Put your ideas together. What else can you figure out about the text? | And *so* _____ . |

**Talk Together**

Read Carmen's editorial for the school newspaper. Read the sample. Then use **Language Frames** to make inferences. Tell a partner about them.

Editorial

## Peaceful Protest—It Works!

Today I learned that peaceful **protest** works. A week ago, I noticed a group of women workers marching outside Atti's Movers. They were protesting because they **opposed** the fact that they did not have the same rights as the men workers. They wanted to break the **barriers** between men and women on the job. They wanted equal pay for equal time. One of the signs they carried read, "We **Require** Equal Pay for Equal Work!"

This morning, I spotted an Atti's moving van across the street. New neighbors were moving in. I also noticed that the movers were both men and women. They seemed to be laughing and joking with each other. ◀

I could tell that the **conflict** was over. The **strike** had been a success. The women presented their demands, and Atti's Movers heard them.

This **demonstrates** that peaceful protest, or **nonviolence**, is a great way for getting results! We should remember that through peaceful negotiation, anything is possible. ◀

> "I read that the women wanted equal pay.
>
> I know that when people protest they want to change something.
>
> And so the women must be earning less than the men."

◀ = a good place to stop and make an inference

261

# Read a Biography

## Genre

A **biography** is the story of a person's life, written by another person. Dates and words such as *then*, *finally*, and *later* tell you when events happen.

## Point of View

Point of view describes how a story is told. In the third-person point of view, a narrator outside the story tells it. When the third-person point of view is *limited*, the narrator does not know everything. Instead, the narrator may know what only one character thinks and feels.

César Chávez thought the whole world belonged to his family.

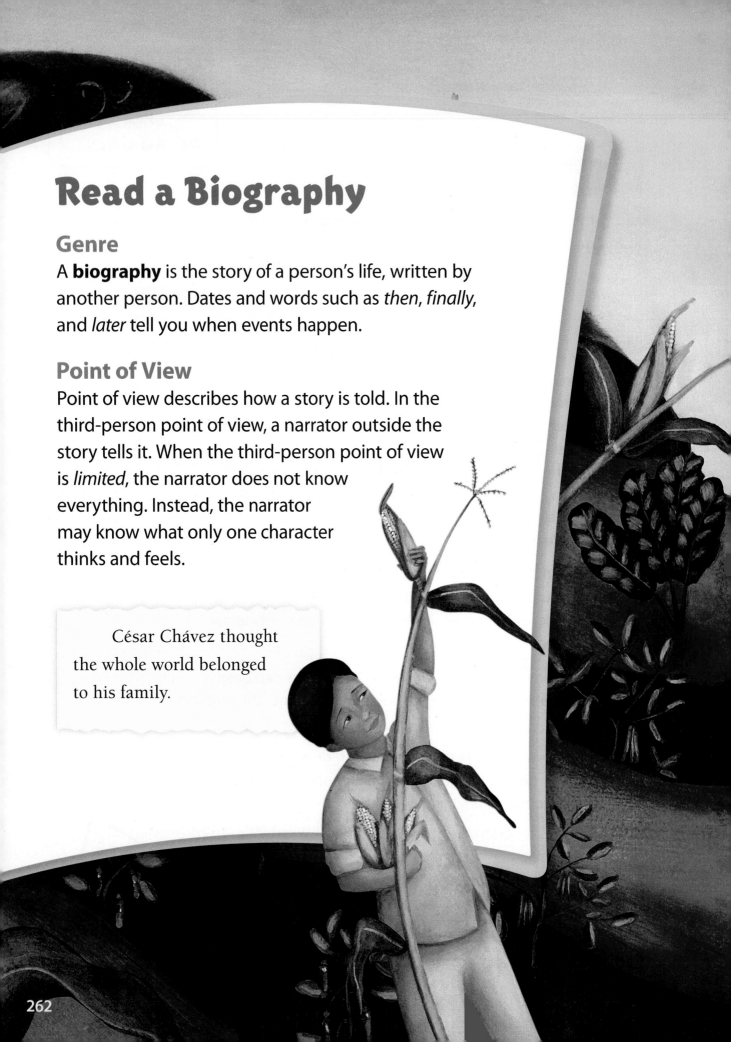

# Harvesting Hope

## The Story of César Chávez

by **Kathleen Krull**

illustrated by **Yuyi Morales**

▶ **Set a Purpose**
Find out how César Chávez's life
changed when he was ten.

Until César Chávez was ten, every summer night was like a *fiesta*. César and his brothers, sisters, and cousins settled down to sleep outside, under netting to keep mosquitoes out. But who could sleep, with uncles and aunts singing and telling tales of life back in Mexico?

César Chávez thought the whole world belonged to his family. The eighty acres of their **ranch** were an island in the **shimmering** Arizona desert, and the starry skies were all their own.

César's grandfather had built their large adobe house to last forever. A vegetable garden, cows, and chickens supplied all the food they could want. With hundreds of cousins on farms nearby, there was always someone to play with.

**In Other Words**
*fiesta* party (in Spanish)
**ranch** farm
**shimmering** shining

César was so happy at home that he was a little afraid
when school started. On his first day, he grabbed the seat next
to his older sister, Rita. The teacher moved him to another seat.
César flew out the door and ran home. It took three days of
**coaxing** for him to return to school and take his place with the
other first graders.

César **was stubborn**, but he was not a fighter. His mother
**cautioned** her children against fighting, **urging** them to use their
minds and mouths to work out **conflicts**.

**In Other Words**
**coaxing** gentle talking
**was stubborn** had strong beliefs
**cautioned** warned
**urging** telling

Then, in 1937, the summer César was ten, the trees around the ranch began to **wilt**. The sun baked the farm soil rock hard. A drought was **choking** the life out of Arizona. Without water for the crops, the Chávez family couldn't make money to pay its bills.

**In a daze**, César watched his father strap **their possessions** onto the roof of their old car. They had no choice but to join the hundreds of thousands of people fleeing to the green valleys of California to look for work.

**In Other Words**
**wilt** get very dry
**choking** taking
**In a daze** Shocked and confused
**their possessions** everything they owned

César's old life had **vanished**. Now he and his family were migrants, working on other people's farms. They **crisscrossed** California to pick whatever fruits and vegetables were ready to be picked.

Farm work was hard, painful work. Pulling beets out of the ground cut César's hands. Bug-killing chemicals made his eyes **sting** and his lungs **wheeze**. Farm chores on someone else's farm felt like a form of slavery.

The Chávez family talked constantly of saving enough money to buy back their ranch. But they made so little money. As time went on, they spoke of the ranch less and less.

**In Other Words**
**vanished** disappeared
**crisscrossed** traveled around
**sting** burn painfully
**wheeze** work hard for air

▶ **Before You Move On**

1. **Author's Style** What details of sight and touch show how César's life changed?
2. **Point of View** Does the narrator of this story know what all the characters think and feel? How do you know?

267

▶ **Predict**
How will César try to make
farmworkers' lives better?

As César worked, it **disturbed him** that landowners treated their workers more like farm tools than human beings. They **provided** no clean drinking water, rest periods, or access to bathrooms. Anyone who complained was **fired**, beaten up, or sometimes even murdered.

So, like other migrant workers, César was afraid and **suspicious** whenever outsiders showed up to try to help. How could they know about feeling so powerless?

**In Other Words**
**disturbed him** made him angry
**provided** gave
**fired** told to leave the job
**suspicious** not trusting

Yet César had never forgotten his old life in Arizona. Farm work did not have to be this **miserable**.

**Reluctantly**, he started paying attention to the outsiders. He began to think that maybe there was hope. And in his early twenties, César decided to **dedicate** the rest of his life to fighting for change.

Again he crisscrossed California. This time his goal was to talk people into joining his fight. At first, out of every hundred workers he talked to, perhaps one would agree with him. One by one, this was how he started.

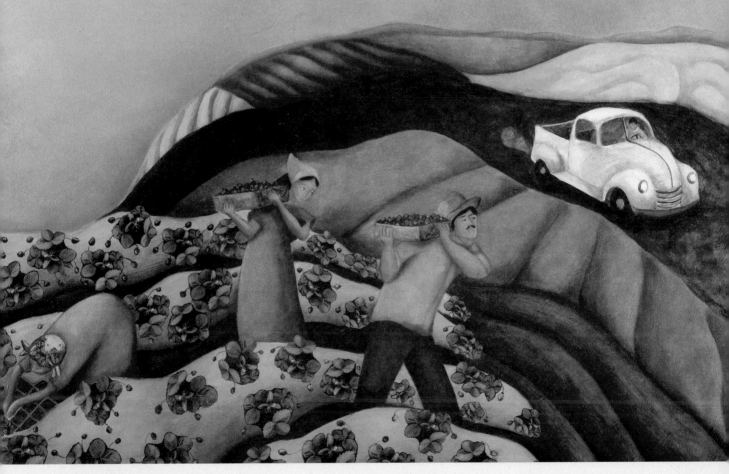

**In Other Words**
**miserable** hard; difficult
**Reluctantly** Slowly
**dedicate** give

At the first meeting César organized, a dozen women gathered. He sat quietly in a corner. After twenty minutes, everyone started wondering when the organizer would show up. César **thought he might die of embarrassment.**

"Well, I'm the organizer," he said, and he forced himself to keep talking.

But despite his shyness, César **showed a knack for** solving problems. People trusted him. With workers he was endlessly patient and **compassionate**. With landowners he was stubborn and demanding. He was learning to be a fighter.

**In Other Words**
**thought he might die of embarrassment** felt very shy
**showed a knack for** was good at
**compassionate** caring

In a fight for justice, he told everyone, truth was a better weapon than violence. "**Nonviolence**," he said, "takes more **guts**." It meant using imagination to find ways to **overcome powerlessness.**

More and more people listened.

One night, 150 people poured into an old abandoned theater in Fresno. At this first meeting of the National Farm Workers Association, César **unveiled** its flag. It was a bold black eagle, the sacred bird of **the Aztec Indians**.

*La Causa,* The Cause, was born.

**In Other Words**
**guts** bravery; spirit
**overcome powerlessness** get power
**unveiled** showed everyone
**the Aztec Indians** people who lived in
   what is now Mexico

▶ **Before You Move On**

1. **Confirm Prediction** How did César try to make life better for himself and others?

2. **Author's Style** How does the author use dramatic retelling to describe the first meeting of the farmworkers' organization?

I t was time to **rebel**, and the place was Delano. Here, in the heart of the lush San Joaquin Valley, brilliant green **vineyards** reached toward every horizon. Poorly paid workers hunched over grapevines for most of each year. Then, in 1965, the vineyard owners cut their pay even further.

César chose to fight just one of the forty landowners, hopeful that **others** would get the message. As plump grapes drooped, thousands of workers walked off that company's fields in a **strike**.

Grapes, when **ripe**, do not last long.

**In Other Words**
**rebel** fight back
**vineyards** grape farms
**others** the other 39 landowners
**ripe** ready for picking

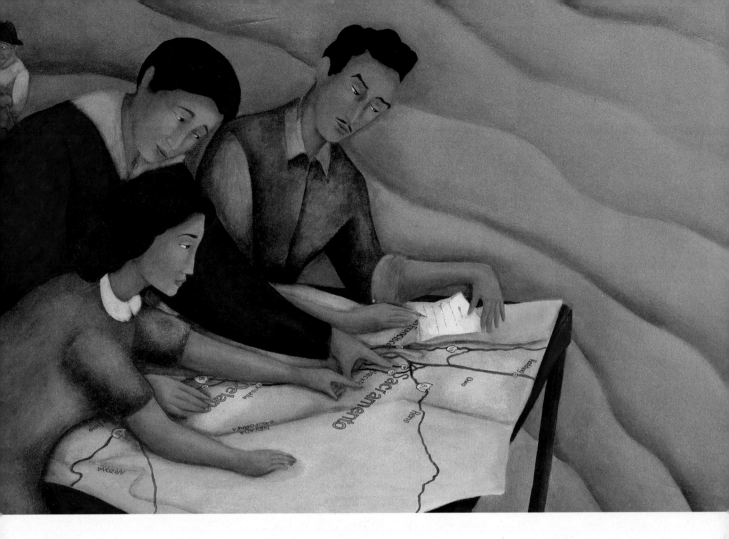

The company fought back with everything from punches to bullets. César refused to respond with violence. Violence would only hurt *La Causa*.

Instead, he organized a march of more than three hundred miles. He and his supporters would walk from Delano to the state capitol in Sacramento to ask for the government's help.

César and sixty-seven others started out one morning. Their **rallying cry** was *Sí Se Puede*, or "Yes, It Can Be Done."

**In Other Words**
**rallying cry** call for action

274

Single file they continued, covering an average of fifteen miles a day. They inched their way through the San Joaquin Valley, while unharvested grapes in Delano turned white with mold. César developed painful blisters right away. He and many others had blood seeping out of their shoes.

The **word** spread. Along the way, farmworkers offered food and drink as the marchers passed by. When the sun set, marchers lit candles and kept going.

The long, peaceful march was a **shock** to people unaware of how California farmworkers had to live. Now students, public officials, religious leaders, and citizens from everywhere offered help. For the grape company, the **publicity** was becoming **unbearable**.

One evening, César received a message. Officials from the grape company were ready to recognize the authority of the National Farm Workers Association. They promised to give workers a contract, more money, and better conditions.

**In Other Words**

**word** news of the **strike**
**shock** surprise
**publicity** attention
**unbearable** very uncomfortable

▶ **Before You Move On**

1. **Figurative Language** What sensory details help you understand what César did to help the farmworkers?

2. **Sequence** In what year did the **strike** take place?

▶ **Predict**
What will César's success mean
for farmworkers?

When the marchers arrived in Sacramento, the parade was ten-thousand people strong.

From the steps of the state capitol building, the joyous announcement was made to the public: César Chávez had just signed the first contract for farmworkers in American history.

The parade **erupted into** a giant *fiesta*. Crowds swarmed the steps, some people cheering, many **weeping**. Prancing horses carried men in ***mariachi*** outfits. Everyone sang and waved flowers or flags. They **made a place of honor** for the fifty-seven marchers who had walked the entire journey.

**In Other Words**
**erupted into** suddenly became
**weeping** crying
***mariachi*** traditional Mexican musician (in Spanish)
**made a place of honor** respectfully made room

Speaker after speaker, addressing the audience in Spanish and in English, took the microphone. "You cannot close your eyes and your ears to us any longer," cried one. "You cannot pretend that we do not exist."

The crowd celebrated until the sky was full of stars.

Much more work lay ahead, but the victory was **stunning**. Some of the wealthiest people in the country had been **forced to recognize** some of the poorest as human beings. César Chávez had won this fight, without violence, and he would never be powerless again. ❖

**In Other Words**
**stunning** amazing
**forced to recognize** made to respect

▶ **Before You Move On**

1. **Author's Style** What details make the author's description of the celebration more dramatic?

2. **Make Inferences** What do you think was the effect of César's success on farmworkers?

## Talk About It

1. What is the most important event in the **biography** of César Chávez? How does the author lead up to this event?

2. Imagine that you are César Chávez, talking with officials from the grape company. Use **Language Frames** to **negotiate** a contract for the National Farm Workers Association.

3. Compare life as a migrant farm worker to the life César and his family had when they owned their own ranch.

   On their own ranch, _____. As migrant farmers, _____.

Learn test-taking strategies.
🌐 **NGReach.com**

## Write About It

Imagine that the National Farm Workers Association has put a statue of César Chávez in your community. You have been asked to make a sign for the statue. Write three sentences to put on the sign. Use **Key Words** to tell why César Chávez is a hero.

César Chávez is a hero because _____.
He showed us that _____.

# Sequence

Use the sequence chain to show what happened in "Harvesting Hope."
In your own words, write the events in the order that they happened.

**Sequence Chain**

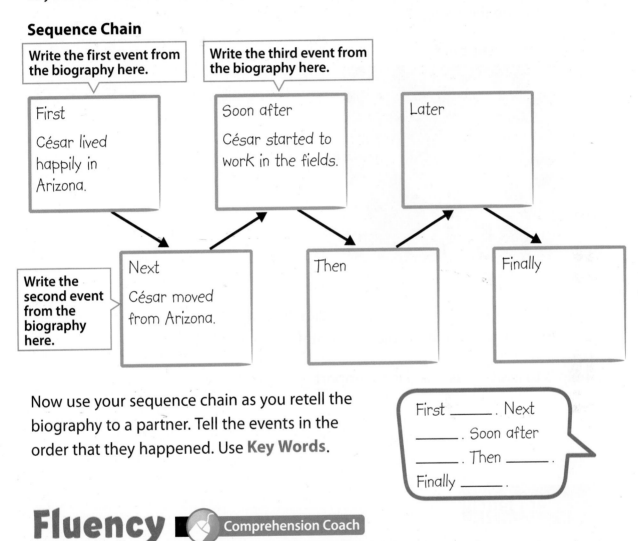

Now use your sequence chain as you retell the
biography to a partner. Tell the events in the
order that they happened. Use **Key Words**.

First _____. Next
_____. Soon after
_____. Then _____.
Finally _____.

# Fluency  Comprehension Coach

Use the Comprehension Coach to practice reading with phrasing.
Rate your reading.

**Talk Together**

How did César Chávez achieve justice? Draw a picture of people
today who are working for justice. Write a caption for your picture.
Use **Key Words**. Share your picture with the class.

# Synonyms

**Synonyms** are words that have the same, or nearly the same, meaning, such as *hard* and *difficult*. One word can have several synonyms. What words describe this picture?

**support**

**help**                                       **aid**

**assist**

Sometimes synonyms are used in analogies. Identifying synonyms can help you figure out analogies. Look at these analogies.

[ help is to assist ]  as  [ aid is to support ]

## Try It Together

Read each item. Choose the word that best completes the analogy.

1. **barrier is to obstacle as problem is to** _____

   A solution

   B dilemma

   C argue

   D procedure

2. **Quiet is to silent as noisy is to** _____

   A sound

   B loud

   C outrageous

   D easy

NATIONAL
GEOGRAPHIC
EXCLUSIVE

**Connect Across Texts** Read about a filmmaker who shows how women in different countries are working for justice.

**Genre** A **social studies article** gives facts about a real person, place, or event.

# A Filmmaker for Justice
## by **Nancy-Jo Hereford**

▲ Roshini Thinakaran makes movies about women around the world who are fighting for their rights.

## Shining a Light

Think about the difference between night and day. What can you see in the dark? What can you see in the light of day? It is harder to fight an injustice when the problem stays in the dark. **Shining a light on** unfair treatment makes it harder to ignore. Roshini Thinakaran (rō-**she**-nē **thin**-uh-ko-ren) is a young filmmaker. She uses a video camera like a light. She makes movies about women who are fighting for their rights in countries at war, such as Iraq and Afghanistan.

**In Other Words**

**Shining a light on** Making people see

▶ **Before You Move On**

1. **Figurative Language** How does Roshini use a video camera like a light?

2. **Make Inferences** What problem do you think Roshini is trying to solve? Support your answer with examples from the text.

281

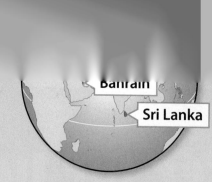
Bahrain
Sri Lanka

## Escaping War

Roshini knows something about war and how it affects people. She was born in Sri Lanka, an island country south of India. A **civil war there** made it difficult for her father to find work. So he left for an engineering job in Bahrain, a country in the Persian Gulf. When the violence in Sri Lanka got worse, the family joined him. In 1986, they moved to America. Roshini was eight years old.

Years later, when Roshini went to college, she studied **journalism**. She gained the skills she would need to tell stories of women's struggles in the world.

Photo by Safia Safi

▲ Roshini uses her journalism skills to interview this woman.

**In Other Words**

**civil war there** war between different groups within the country

**journalism** how to find and report news stories

282

▲ In her film, Roshini shines a light on the lives of Iraqi women.

Iraq

## Telling Stories in Iraq

In 2003, Roshini took a job in Iraq. It was after the war began, and she was working with members of the Iraqi **news media**. She saw what was happening to people in the country. And she paid special attention to what was happening to women.

Iraqi women were invited to join the new Iraqi police forces. "They were promised jobs that would help them take care of their families," says Roshini. "Many women also saw being a police officer as a way to help rebuild Iraq."

But the Iraqi female police officers were treated unfairly. For example, they were ordered to give up their guns for male officers to use. That meant the women could not protect themselves. To the women, it meant their lives were not important.

**In Other Words**

**news media** group of people who report the news through radio, TV, and the Internet

▶ **Before You Move On**

1. **Make Inferences** How do you think Roshini's childhood experiences affected her decision to become a filmmaker?

2. **Sequence** What happened after the Iraqi women joined the police force?

▲ Roshini talks with students in Afghanistan to learn about their problems.

## Documenting Injustice

For some of those women, talking to Roshini **on camera** was a way to **stand up for their rights**. Roshini creates a type of film called a documentary. It "documents," or explains, a problem through the experiences of real people. A documentary can be a powerful way to **spotlight** injustice. When people watch and don't like what they see, it can push them to work for change.

**In Other Words**
**on camera**  while she filmed them
**stand up for their rights**  speak against injustice
**spotlight**  make people see

Afghanistan

## Making a Better Future

Roshini finished her documentary about Iraq in 2008. She plans to make her next documentary about Afghanistan. She wants to feature Safia, a young woman studying to be **a photojournalist**. In Afghanistan, girls and women have been **attacked** for going to school.

Roshini also plans to film a documentary about women in Sri Lanka. The civil war that her family escaped from finally ended in 2009.

Roshini has given her documentaries a name: "Women at the Forefront." That's because in places where there is **conflict** , she sees women stepping forward to make a difference.

"Women try to create new roles for themselves," Roshini explains. "They try to make a better future for their families and their country."

Photo by Safia Safi

▲ Roshini keeps her ideas in a notebook. She will use her notes to plan her next documentary.

### In Other Words

**a photojournalist** someone who tells news stories through photographs

**attacked** hurt

### ▶ Before You Move On

1. **Make Inferences** Why do some women think that talking on camera is helpful?
2. **Make Comparisons** In your own words, explain how Roshini works for justice and how César Chávez worked for justice.

## Change Happens Slowly

Like others before her, Roshini understands that changing the way people think takes time. The fight for women's rights in United States history is one example.

Carrie Chapman Catt worked for thirty years to get women the right to vote. She and thousands of other women organized marches, parades, and other events to make their voices heard. The 19th Amendment to the Constitution, which guarantees women can vote, was passed in 1920. "The struggle for the vote," Catt said, "was an effort to bring men to **feel less superior** and women to **feel less inferior**."

▲ **These American women worked hard to get the right to vote. Here, they cast their ballots for the first time.**

**In Other Words**

**feel less superior** stop thinking of themselves as better than women

**feel less inferior** stop thinking that they are not as important as men

However, changing the way people think takes time. It took years for women to be able to vote. It took years to change laws that were unfair to African Americans.

The first step is always for someone to shine a light on a way of thinking or acting that is unfair. That's what Roshini Thinakaran's documentaries do for women working for change.

"Justice is a basic right," Roshini says. "Everyone has a right to be treated fairly. How do we **achieve** justice?" she asks. "With imagination, **determination**, and support!" ❖

▲ Roshini will continue to use her camera, and her determination, to fight injustice.

**In Other Words**

**achieve** get

**determination** the strength to keep trying

▶ **Before You Move On**

1. **Compare/Contrast** How is Roshini's work similar to Catt's work?

2. **Make Connections** Think of another example of injustice in U.S. history. How was determination used to overcome it?

**Key Words**

| barrier | nonviolence |
|---|---|
| conditions | oppose |
| conflict | protest |
| demands | require |
| demonstrate | strike |
| labor | |

# Compare Literary Language

Authors often use **literary language**, such as similes and metaphors, to compare things and to describe what they want you to see, hear, and feel. Authors also use **literary devices**, such as imagery and foreshadowing, to communicate with readers in a special way.

- **Imagery** helps readers imagine how people and things look, sound, smell, taste, or feel.

- **Foreshadowing** gives clues at the beginning of the text that gets readers interested to find out what will happen at the end.

Work with a partner to complete the chart. Look for literary language and literary devices in the selections.

**Comparison Chart**

| | "A Filmmaker for Justice" | "Harvesting Hope" |
|---|---|---|
| **Similes** | p. 281 _____ . | p. 264 every summer night was like <br><br> p. 264 _____ . |
| **Metaphors** | p. 284 _____ . | p. 264 _____ . |
| **Imagery** | p. 284 work for change | pp. 264–265 singing, happy, _____ . |
| **Foreshadowing** | p. 282 _____ . | p. 268 or p. 269. _____ . |

**Talk Together**

What helps us form our ideas about justice? How does each biography help you understand how childhood can affect a person's ideas about justice? Use **Key Words** to discuss your ideas.

## Grammar and Spelling

# Forms of *Be* and *Have*

The verbs *be* and ***have*** use special forms. Each verb must agree with its subject. You can write some subjects and verbs as contractions. A contraction is a short way of writing two words as one word.

| **Grammar Rules** Forms of *Be* and *Have* | Forms of *Be* | Forms of *Have* |
|---|---|---|
| • For **I**, use | I **am** or **I'm** | I **have** or **I've** |
| • For **you**, use | you **are** or **you're** | you **have** or **you've** |
| • For **he**, **she**, **it**, use | she **is** or **she's**<br>he **is** or **he's**<br>it **is** or **it's** | she **has** or **she's**<br>he **has** or **he's**<br>it **has** or **it's** |
| • For **we**, use | we **are** or **we're** | we **have** or **we've** |
| • For **they**, use | they **are** or **they're** | they **have** or **they've** |

## Read Forms of *Be* and *Have*

Read the passage about Roshini Thinakaran. What forms of *be* and ***have*** can you find? Tell a partner when are they used as helping verbs.

> Roshini has named her documentaries "Women at the Forefront." She often sees women who are stepping forward to make a difference. She's proud to show them as leaders in the fight for their rights.

## Write Forms of *Be* and *Have*

Look at the photo on page 284. Write two sentences about it. Use the verb *be* or ***have*** in each sentence. Be sure the subject and verb agree. Compare your sentences with a partner's.

# Write As a Researcher

## Write a Research Report ✏️

Write a report about an event in U.S. history when justice was achieved. Place your reports in a journal called *Justice in America*.

## Study a Model

For a research report, you gather information from several sources. You think about what you've learned and decide what it all means.

Read William's report about a famous fight for civil rights justice.

### A Bus Ride to Justice
William Brown

In 1955, an African-American woman named Rosa Parks refused to give up her seat on the bus to a Caucasian. She was arrested for this "crime." The event led to a famous protest: the Montgomery Bus Boycott. **The boycott showed that people could fight for justice without using violence**.

In the early 1950s, the bus system in Montgomery, Alabama, was segregated. African Americans had to sit at the back of the bus. They also had to give up their seats if the Caucasian section filled up. This is what Rosa Parks refused to do.

Rosa Parks' arrest angered African-American leaders They asked African American's to refuse to ride the city

The title and introduction capture the reader's interest.

A **statement of the main idea** tells what the writer will try to prove in his report.

Each paragraph has a topic sentence that supports the main idea. The writer supports each main idea with evidence.

The paper has a clear organization. Events are presented in the sequence in which they happened.

buses. A group was organized to handle the boycott. They asked a new young minister, Dr. Martin Luther King, Jr., to lead the group. He agreed.

King insisted that the boycott be kept peaceful. He said, **"We are not here advocating violence."** He showed people that they could fight back without breaking any laws.

Thousands of African Americans boycotted the buses for over a year. Eventually the protest was successful. In 1956, the United States Supreme Court ordered Montgomery to provide integrated seating on public buses.

Quotation marks show a **direct quotation**.

## Sources

Delano, Marfé Ferguson. *American Heroes*. Washington, D.C: National Geographic Society, 2005.

"King, Martin Luther, Jr." *World Book Encyclopedia*. 2009. Print.

Dove, Rita. "The Time 100: Rosa Parks." Time, Inc., 20 Nov. 2009. Web.15 Feb. 2010. http://www.time.com/time/ time100/heroes/profile/parks01.html

A final page lists the sources William used for the report.

## Prewrite

1. **Choose a Topic**  What is justice?  What examples can you find in America's past?  Work with a partner to brainstorm and discuss ideas. Narrow your topic to one that you can cover well in a short report.

2. **List Your Research Questions**  What do you already know about your topic? What do you want to find out? Write questions you could use to guide your research.

> ### Research Questions
> • Why did the Montgomery Bus Boycott happen?
> • Where did it take place?
> • Who participated in the boycott?
> • How were the buses segregated?
> • What did city officials do?

3. **Create a Research Plan**  A research report must contain information from several sources. Your research plan contains your topic and your ideas about the sources you can use to answer them. There are two main types of sources, **primary sources** and **secondary sources**.

> Topic: The Montgomery Bus Boycott
>
> | Primary Sources | Secondary Sources |
> |---|---|
> | * Rosa Parks' journal  or diary | * books about Montgomery Bus Boycott |
> | * letters written by people who participated in the boycott | * online articles about Rosa Parks and the bus boycott |
> | * arrest documents | * encyclopedia entry about Montgomery Bus Boycott |

**Primary sources, such as letters, diaries, and official documents, provide direct, firsthand knowledge from eyewitnesses to the event.**

**Secondary sources give information based on primary sources. They include nonfiction books, newspapers, and Web sites.**

# Gather Information

1. **Identify Sources**  Valid, or reliable, sources are up to date. They are written by a group or person who is an expert in the area. Skim the source to see if it has the information you need.

2. **Create source cards**  Use index cards to record important information about each source you use. Give each card a number.

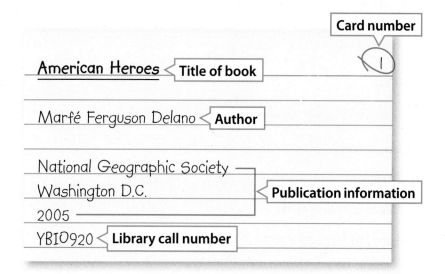

Card number

American Heroes — Title of book

Marfé Ferguson Delano — Author

National Geographic Society
Washington D.C.
2005 — Publication information
YBIO920 — Library call number

3. **Make Note Cards**  Record important ideas on note cards. **Paraphrase**, or put all of the information in your own words. Use quotation marks for anything you pick up word for word.

    Try to use some visuals in your report. Keep a separate file for any pictures, maps, or charts you may want to use.

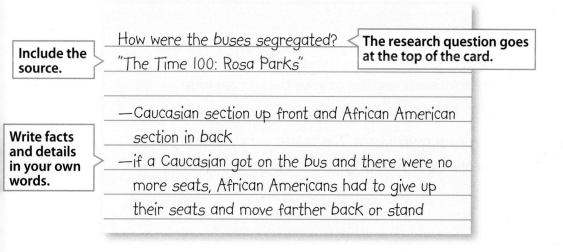

Include the source.

How were the buses segregated? — The research question goes at the top of the card.
"The Time 100: Rosa Parks"

Write facts and details in your own words.

—Caucasian section up front and African American section in back
—if a Caucasian got on the bus and there were no more seats, African Americans had to give up their seats and move farther back or stand

## Get Organized

1. **Sort Your Cards** Use the research questions at the top of your cards to put them into groups. Put the groups in an order that would make sense to your reader.

2. **Organize Your Details** Use an outline or other graphic organizer to help you. Each group, or category, from your cards becomes a main idea. The details from each card support the main ideas.

**Outline**

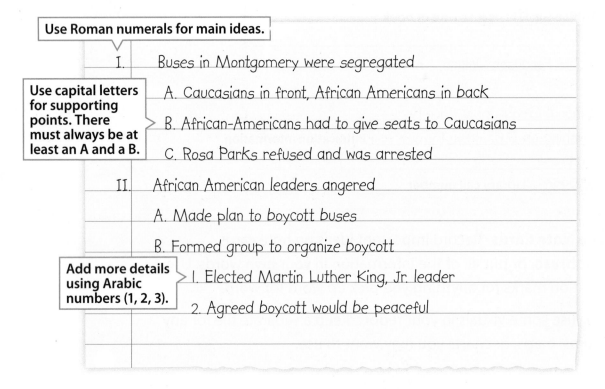

Use Roman numerals for main ideas.

I.  Buses in Montgomery were segregated

Use capital letters for supporting points. There must always be at least an A and a B.

A. Caucasians in front, African Americans in back

B. African-Americans had to give seats to Caucasians

C. Rosa Parks refused and was arrested

II. African American leaders angered

A. Made plan to boycott buses

B. Formed group to organize boycott

Add more details using Arabic numbers (1, 2, 3).

1. Elected Martin Luther King, Jr. leader

2. Agreed boycott would be peaceful

## Draft

- Write an interesting introduction that tells what the report is about. Then, write a paragraph from each section of your outline. Include maps, photos, or charts to help explain your ideas.

- Put all the information in your own words. Never use words directly from the source. This is called **plagiarizing**, and it's a type of stealing.

# Revise

1. **Read, Retell, Respond**  Read your draft aloud to a partner. Next, talk about ways to improve your writing.

2. **Make Changes**  Think about your draft and your partner's suggestions. Use the Revising Marks on page 629 to mark your changes.

   - Have you put everything in your own words? If not, think of a new way to present the information.

   > He showed people that they could fight back without breaking any laws. ~~Instead, he encouraged people to use legal protest as their main weapon.~~

   - Are your facts presented in a logical order that your readers can follow? Move any that seem out of place.

   > Eventually the protest was successful. ~~That was after~~ thousands of African Americans boycotted the buses for over a year.

# Edit and Proofread

Carefully check all your facts, as well as names, dates, and numbers. Make sure direct quotes are in quotation marks.

# Publish

1. **Make a Final Copy**  Make a final copy of your research report. Ask your teacher if there is a special format, or way of presenting your report, that you should use. Add a source list at the end.

2. **Share With Others**  Present your paper as an oral report or multimedia slideshow. Then, with your classmates, collect your reports and put them in a book called *Justice in America*.

## Talk Together

In this unit, you found lots of answers to the **Big Question**. Now use your concept map to discuss the **Big Question** with the class.

**Concept Map**

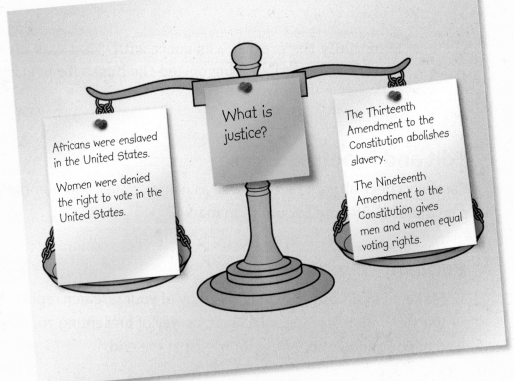

What is justice?

Africans were enslaved in the United States.

Women were denied the right to vote in the United States.

The Thirteenth Amendment to the Constitution abolishes slavery.

The Nineteenth Amendment to the Constitution gives men and women equal voting rights.

## Make a Poster

Make a poster about justice. Use your concept map to help you.

# Share Your Ideas

Choose one of these ways to share your ideas about the **Big Question**.

## Write It!

### Make a Collage

Make a collage of headlines that have to do with justice. Look in magazines and newspapers. Cut out the headlines and glue them on a sheet of paper. Cut out or draw a picture to go with the headlines.

## Talk About It!

### Hold a Debate

With a small group, hold a debate. Choose an issue people are talking about now in your school or community. Write arguments for and against the issue on index cards. Use the cards to help you make your points.

DON'T CLOSE OUR PARK!

## Do It!

### Research Protest Songs

Work in a group to research protest songs, or songs that shine a light on injustice. Collect several examples of protest songs, and put them together in a book. Write an introduction that tells about each song.

## Talk About It!

### Meet the Reporters

Role-play a press conference with the real people and the story characters in this unit. Have "reporters" ask questions about the fight for equal rights. The "freedom fighters" answer the questions by telling what they did to help people find freedom or win equal rights.

PRESS
No. 567

# Every
# DROP

**? BIG Question**

**Why is water so important?**

**Unit**
**5**

## Share What You Know

**Do It!**

❶ **Think** of the things you did today that required water.

❷ **Act** out one of the things for the class.

❸ **Say** one reason why you think water is so important to our lives.

**Build Background:** Watch a video about water.
 **NGReach.com**

# Define and Explain

Listen to Elena's song. Then use **Language Frames** to tell a partner what you think about the importance of water.

# The Drought *Song* (((MP3)))

Our farmland is dry and our soil is dust,

And there has been no rain.

This means there's a drought

And we are without

Fresh water for our grain.

For example, our wheat and corn

Have shriveled in the sun.

This happens because a drought has come,

Affecting everyone.

Tune: "Over the River and Through the Woods"

Key Words

atmosphere
condensation
evaporation
fresh water
precipitation
runoff
water cycle
watershed

# Key Words

A **watershed** is a group of habitats that surround a river or stream. Use **Key Words** and other words to talk about the **water cycle** within this watershed.

**The Water Cycle**

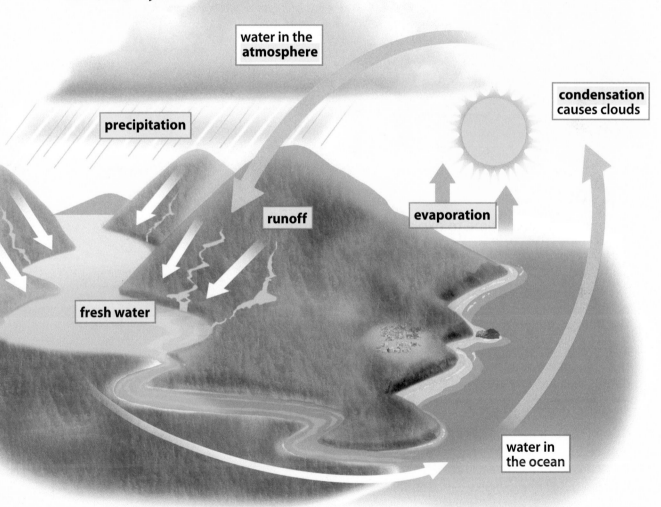

water in the
**atmosphere**

**precipitation**

**condensation**
causes clouds

**runoff**

**evaporation**

**fresh water**

water in
the ocean

**Talk Together**

How are we connected to the water cycle? In a group, use **Language Frames** from page 300 and **Key Words** to explain your answer.

# Main Idea and Details

When you want to explain something, start with the most important idea. This is called the **main idea**. Then give **details** to add more information. Details tell more about the main idea.

The pictures show how a drought affected Elena's farm.

## Map and Talk

You can make an outline to explain an event. Write the main idea about each picture. Add at least two details that support each main idea.

**Outline**

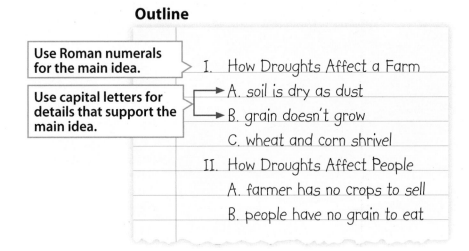

**Use Roman numerals for the main idea.**

**Use capital letters for details that support the main idea.**

I. How Droughts Affect a Farm
  A. soil is dry as dust
  B. grain doesn't grow
  C. wheat and corn shrivel
II. How Droughts Affect People
  A. farmer has no crops to sell
  B. people have no grain to eat

**Talk Together**

Talk with your partner about the main reasons why water is important to your life. Your partner can make an outline.

# More Key Words

Use these words to talk about "One Well" and "Picturing the Pantanal."

## access
(**ak**-ses) *noun*

When you have **access** to something, you can get or use it. A library offers access to many books.

## consequence
(**kahn**-su-kwens) *noun*

A **consequence** is the result of an action. A flood is a **consequence** of heavy rain.

## conservation
(kahn-sur-**va**-shun) *noun*

When you turn off lights, you are practicing **conservation**. You are using energy carefully.

## deplete
(di-**plēt**) *verb*

When you **deplete** something, you use it up. They **depleted** the forest of trees.

## shortage
(**shor**-tij) *noun*

**Shortage** is when you don't have enough. In a water **shortage**, the grass turns dry and brown.

### Talk Together

Make a Vocabulary Example Chart for the **Key Words**. Compare your chart with a partner's.

| Word | Definition | Example from My Life |
|------|-----------|----------------------|
| access | use of | I wish I had access to a swimming pool in my neighborhood. |

Add words to My Vocabulary Notebook.
NGReach.com

# Learn to Make Connections

Look at the photo. If it reminds you of something, then you have **made a connection**.

When you read, you **make connections**, too.

## How to Make Connections

| | | |
|---|---|---|
|  | **1.** Think about what the text is about. | The topic is _____ . |
|  | **2.** As you read, think about things in your life, or things you know, that relate. | _____ reminds me of _____ . |
|  | **3.** Decide how the connection helps you understand the text. | Now I understand _____ . |

**Talk Together**

Read Elena's personal narrative. Read the sample
connection. Then use **Language Frames** to tell
a partner about the connections you make.

Personal Narrative

# A Visit to the Desert

I visited my aunt and uncle in California last month. They live in
the desert. It's a beautiful place, with clear blue skies and tall
mountains, but there is hardly any **precipitation** there. They
always have a water **shortage**, so they are incredibly careful
about not wasting water. We had to take really fast showers
and never leave the tap running. We only used the washing
machine when we had a full load of clothes.

Instead of a lawn that needs watering, my aunt and uncle
have a rock garden. As a **consequence**, there are no flowers,
grasses, or fruit trees. Those plants would all die without water.
Except for cactuses, there is not a green plant in sight! ◄

The water **conservation** they practice is something I have
decided to do, too. If we don't use water with care, we could
**deplete** the supply we have. Then we won't have **access** to
enough **fresh water** to meet all our needs. I plan to continue
conserving water at home. I know it's the right thing to do. And I'm
going to get all my friends and neighbors to do the same! ◄

> "The topic is what to
> do in a water shortage.
>
> Fast showers reminds
> me of a water shortage
> we had in our town.
>
> Now I understand the
> problems Elena's aunt
> and uncle have."

◄ = a good place to stop and make a connection

# Read a Science Feature

## Genre

A **science feature** is a nonfiction text about the natural world. Science features often include tables and other text features that give information visually. Science features are often longer than science articles, and they may have broader topics.

## Text Feature

A **table** is made up of facts and numbers that are organized in rows and columns. Tables can help you quickly find and compare information.

### Where Is the Water on Earth?

| WATER LOCATION | PERCENTAGE OF ALL WATER |
|---|---|
| oceans | 97.32% |
| icecaps and glaciers | 2.14% |
| groundwater | 0.61% |
| freshwater lakes | 0.009% |
| inland saltwater seas | 0.008% |
| moisture underground | 0.005% |
| water in the atmosphere | 0.001% |
| rivers | 0.0001% |

column head

row

column

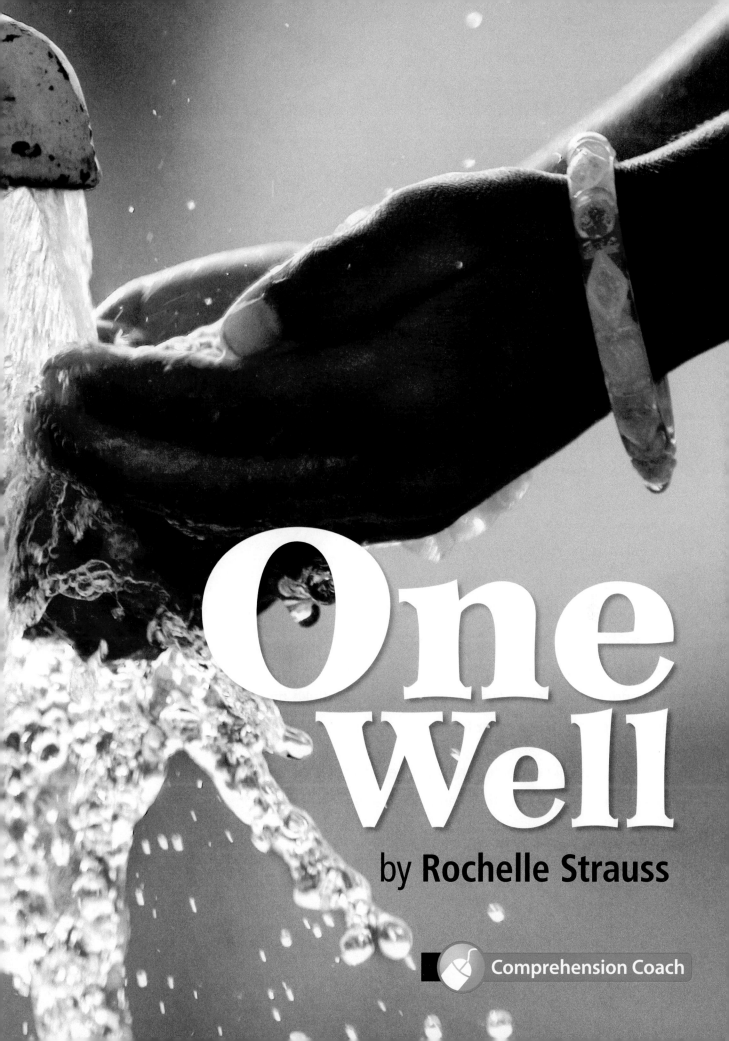

# One
# Well

by Rochelle Strauss

Antarctic polar icecap

▲ **If you look at Earth from space, most of what you see is water.**

# One Well

Imagine for a moment that all the water on Earth came from just one well. This isn't as strange as it sounds. All water on Earth is connected, so there really *is* just one source, one **global** well, from which we can **draw** all our water. Every ocean wave, every lake, stream, and underground river, every raindrop and snowflake and every bit of ice in **glaciers and polar icecaps** is a part of this global well.

Because it is all connected, how we treat the water in the well will affect every species on the planet, now and for years to come.

**In Other Words**
**global**  worldwide
**draw**  take
**glaciers and polar icecaps**  the large
  areas of ice on Earth

308

## Where Is the Water on Earth?

| WATER LOCATION | PERCENTAGE OF ALL WATER |
|---|---|
| oceans | 97.32% |
| icecaps and glaciers | 2.14% |
| groundwater | 0.61% |
| freshwater lakes | 0.009% |
| inland saltwater seas | 0.008% |
| moisture underground | 0.005% |
| water in the atmosphere | 0.001% |
| rivers | 0.0001% |

▲ This table shows the distribution of water on Earth.

We live on a watery planet. Around 70 percent of Earth's surface is covered with water. This surface water is found in oceans, lakes, rivers, streams, marshes, even in puddles and morning **dew**. There is so much water that if you look down on Earth from space, it appears blue.

There is also water we can't see, beneath Earth's surface. This "groundwater" can be found just about everywhere. It fills the spaces between rocks, grains of sand, and soil. Most groundwater is close to Earth's surface, but some of it is buried deep underground.

**In Other Words**

**dew** condensation

▶ **Before You Move On**

1. **Figurative Language** What metaphor does the author use to describe the source of all water on Earth?

2. **Use Text Features** How much of the water on Earth is found in the air?

# Recycling Water in the Well

Did you know that there is the same amount of water now as there was 100 million years ago when dinosaurs walked the Earth? The same water keeps going through a cycle. This constant movement of water is called the **water cycle**.

## The Water Cycle

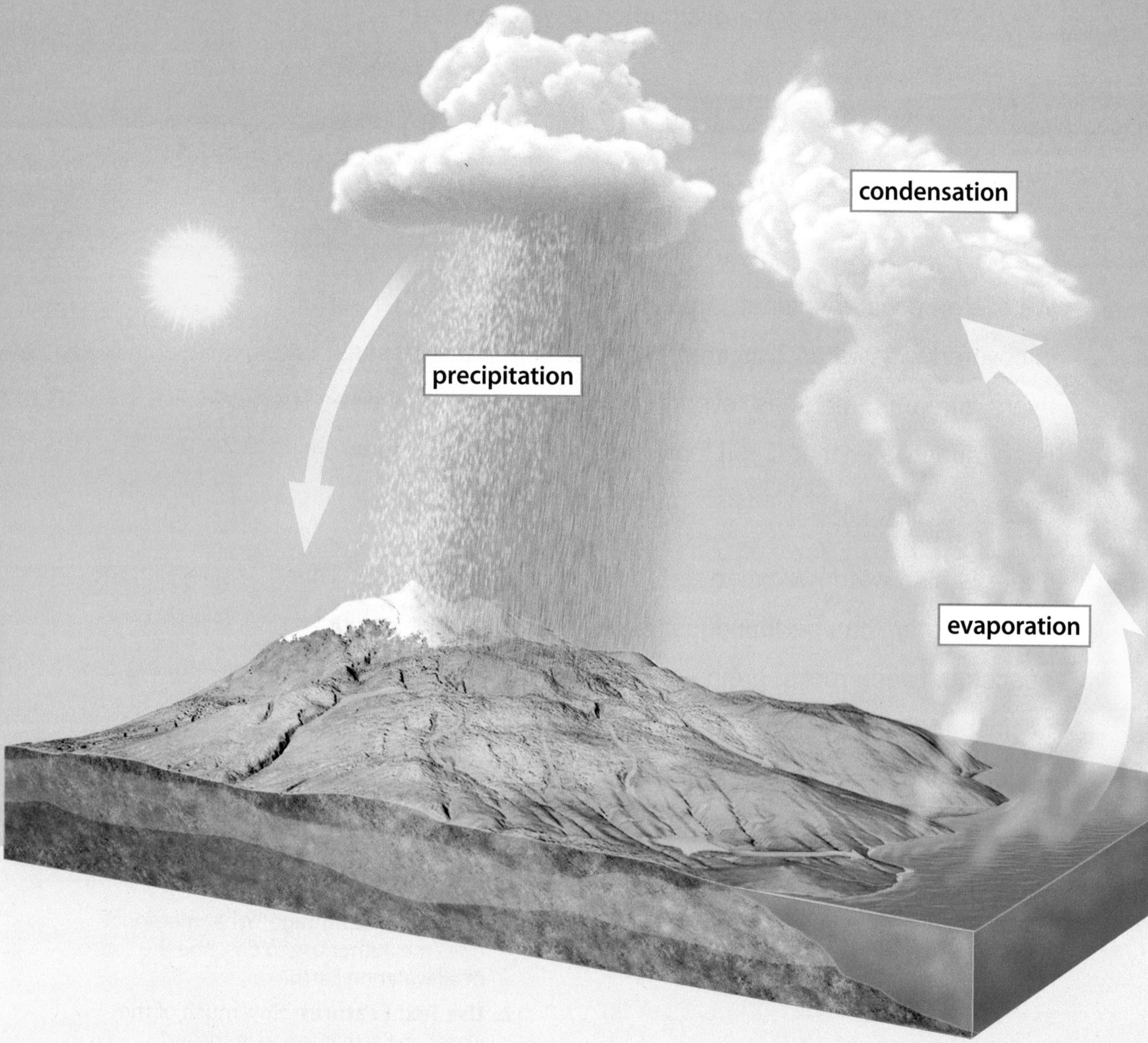

condensation

precipitation

evaporation

During the water cycle, water evaporates from oceans, rivers, and other water sources. When **evaporation** occurs, water turns from a liquid into a gas, or vapor.

As water vapor rises, it cools into tiny water droplets. This is called **condensation**. These droplets gather together to form clouds. Gradually, clouds collect more and more water droplets.

When water droplets get too heavy, they fall from the clouds as rain, **hail**, or snow. Rain, hail, and snow are called **precipitation**. The water that falls as precipitation returns to oceans, lakes, and rivers. Year after year, water constantly moves through the water cycle.

▲ Evaporation is usually invisible. In this photo, however, it can be seen.

▲ Condensation makes clouds of all shapes and sizes.

▲ Precipitation comes in the form of rain, hail, or snow.

**In Other Words**
**hail** frozen rain

▶ **Before You Move On**

1. **Use Text Features** Use the diagram on page 310 to explain how clouds form.
2. **Make Connections** Think about what happens when you boil water. Compare it to the part of the **water cycle** you see in the top photo.

# Plants at the Well

Plants depend on water from the well for survival, and the well depends on plants to help move water through its cycle. Without plants, the water cycle would be **disrupted**. Without water, plants could not survive.

In fact, plants are made up mostly of water. Water helps give plants their shape and form. Without it, they **droop**, **shrivel**, and even lose their leaves.

▲ This is an African baobab tree during the dry season.

▲ This is an African baobab tree during the rainy season.

**In Other Words**
**Plants at the Well** How Plants Use the Water on Earth
**disrupted** broken; interrupted
**droop, shrivel** lose their shape

## Transpiration

A plant's roots absorb water, which is carried to the stem and leaves. From the leaves, water, in the form of vapor, is **released** into the **atmosphere**. This is called transpiration.

Water transpires from the leaves into the air.

Rain falls to the earth. The soil absorbs it.

The roots absorb water in the soil. The stem carries water to the leaves.

## Photosynthesis

Water also helps plants make food for themselves. Plants use the sun's energy to change water and carbon dioxide into simple sugars that feed the plant. This process is called photosynthesis.

The leaves use sunlight to change water and carbon dioxide into sugars.

The leaves take in carbon dioxide from the air.

The leaves release oxygen into the air.

The roots absorb water in the soil. The stem carries water to the leaves.

**In Other Words**
**released** let go

▶ **Before You Move On**

1. **Use Text Features** Study the diagrams. Name three things a leaf does for a plant.
2. **Make Connections** What should you give to a plant that has lost its shape?

▲ When you sweat and breathe, you add water to the atmosphere.

# Animals at the Well

Like plants, animals (including you) are mostly made of water. Humans are about 70 percent water. Think of everything it does in your body. It carries nutrients, helps **digestion**, removes waste, controls body temperature, and even cleans eyes.

Animals need water to survive, and, like plants, they are also part of the water cycle. Animals add water to the **atmosphere** by breathing, sweating, and even drooling. Eventually, this water comes back to Earth. The water you brushed your teeth with today may have been the **spray of a beluga whale** ten years ago.

spray

beluga whale

**In Other Words**

**digestion**  break down and absorb food

◄ **spray of a beluga whale**
  the water from a beluga whale's blowhole

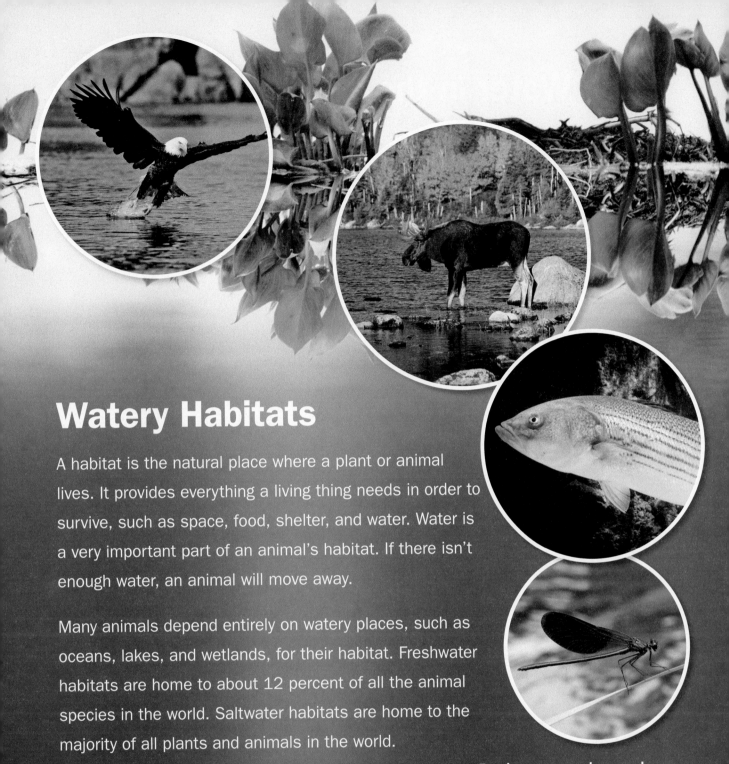

# Watery Habitats

A habitat is the natural place where a plant or animal lives. It provides everything a living thing needs in order to survive, such as space, food, shelter, and water. Water is a very important part of an animal's habitat. If there isn't enough water, an animal will move away.

Many animals depend entirely on watery places, such as oceans, lakes, and wetlands, for their habitat. Freshwater habitats are home to about 12 percent of all the animal species in the world. Saltwater habitats are home to the majority of all plants and animals in the world.

**Freshwater marshes are home to a wide variety of animals.**

▶ **Before You Move On**

1. **Make Connections**  In what way are you part of the **water cycle**?
2. **Details**  Give two examples of a water habitat.

315

# Fresh Water in the Well

Though we live on a watery planet, not all of that water can be used. That's because most of the water on Earth, about 97 percent, is salt water. Only 3 percent is **fresh water**. Many living things, including people, need fresh water for survival.

But most of the fresh water, over 99 percent, is not accessible to us. It is frozen in icecaps and glaciers, trapped too far underground to reach, or suspended in the **atmosphere**, so we can't use it. While there is a lot of water on the planet, we have **access** to less than 1 percent of it.

# Access to the Well

Some families are lucky. They can turn on the **tap** to get drinking water, to fill a bathtub, or to water the garden. Other families around the world are **less fortunate**.

While the amount of water on Earth is always the same, the distribution of water across the world isn't. Huge differences in rainfall can happen from country to country, and even within the same country. Less rainfall means less water is available in an area. Yet many people may live there.

Because water is not evenly distributed across the globe, nearly 20 percent of **the world's population does** not have access to enough water.

## Worldwide Water Use

| PLACE | AVERAGE DAILY WATER USE PER PERSON<br>One bucket = 10 liters (2.6 gallons) |
|-------|-------------------------------------------------------------------------|
| North America | 🪣🪣🪣🪣🪣 🪣🪣🪣🪣🪣 🪣🪣🪣🪣🪣 🪣🪣🪣🪣🪣 🪣🪣🪣🪣🪣 🪣🪣🪣🪣🪣<br>🪣🪣🪣🪣🪣 🪣🪣🪣🪣🪣 🪣🪣🪣🪣🪣 🪣🪣🪣🪣🪣 🪣🪣🪣🪣 |
| Russia | 🪣🪣🪣🪣🪣 🪣🪣🪣🪣🪣 🪣🪣🪣🪣🪣 🪣🪣🪣🪣🪣 🪣🪣🪣🪣🪣 🪣🪣 |
| Poland | 🪣🪣🪣🪣🪣 🪣🪣🪣🪣🪣 🪣🪣🪣🪣 |
| India | 🪣🪣🪣🪣🪣 🪣🪣 |
| Nepal | 🪣🪣🪣🪣 |
| Haiti | 🪣🪣 |
| Ethiopia | 🪣 |

▲ North Americans use more water than people in other parts of the world.

▶ **Before You Move On**

1. **Details** What are some reasons people do not have **access** to **fresh water**?

2. **Use Text Features** On average, how many more liters of water are used by a person in India than a person in Nepal each day?

# Use of Water in the Well

We use water in our homes, in **industry**, and in agriculture. At home we use water for cleaning, cooking, drinking, flushing toilets, and for bathing. Water also helps **generate** electricity. In industry, water heats and cools things, and washes away waste. Farms use the most water. They need huge amounts for **crops** and **livestock**.

Look around. Almost everything you see was made using water. Water was used to grow and make the food you eat. Water was even used to make the paper for this book and the ink used to print the words.

**How People Use Water**

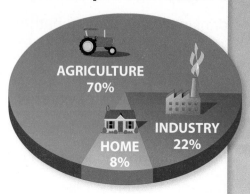

AGRICULTURE 70%

INDUSTRY 22%

HOME 8%

Crops like this one must be irrigated, or watered, in order to grow.

◄ **Making paper requires water.**

**In Other Words**

**industry** businesses that make things
**generate** make
**crops** plants used by people
**livestock** farm animals

318

# Demands on the Well

The number of people on Earth is growing. More people means a greater **demand** for water. We need to find a balance between our demand for water and the amount of water that is available to us.

A growing population also means we need more space. As towns and cities grow to **accommodate** all these people, they **gobble up** land. This affects nearby water. Houses, buildings, and roads sometimes take the place of wetland habitats. Pavement blocks rainwater from refilling underground water supplies. We are using more water than ever before, but all the water we have is all the water we ever will have.

## Human Population Growth

| YEAR | POPULATION<br>= 1 billion people |
|------|----------------------------------|
| 1804 | |
| 1927 | |
| 1960 | |
| 1974 | |
| 1987 | |
| 1999 | |
| 2013 | |
| 2028 | |
| 2054 | |

▲ The worldwide human population is likely to grow to 9 billion people by the year 2054.

**In Other Words**

**Demands on** Increasing Use of Water in
**demand** need
**accommodate** make room for
**gobble up** take over

▶ **Before You Move On**

1. **Paraphrase** In your own words, explain how people use water.
2. **Main Idea** Why is the demand for water growing?

# Pollution in the Well

The **water cycle** helps keep Earth's water clean. When water **evaporates**, minerals and **pollutants** in the water are left behind as the water vapor rises. Plants also help keep water clean. As water travels through plants, they can remove chemicals in it.

▲ **Pollution flows into the ocean from this city's inner harbor.**

But more and more waste from factories, farms, and homes is getting into the water. **Runoff** from backyards, city streets, and farms dumps dirt and harmful chemicals into lakes, rivers, streams, and ponds.

Pollution in the **atmosphere** from cars and factories mixes with water vapor in the air. When the water vapor forms droplets and falls as rain, it brings the pollutants back down to Earth. This can create "acid rain," which is so full of acids that it can kill the plants it falls on.

▼ **Acid rain killed many of the trees in this forest.**

**This tanker ship adds pollution to both the air and the water.** ▶

**In Other Words**

**pollutants** harmful chemicals and other polluting materials

Our actions may be **overloading** the water cycle's natural ability to create clean water. As more water becomes polluted, there is less clean water **available** in the world. Nearly 80 percent of all sicknesses in the developing world are caused by unsafe water.

Wildlife suffers, too. Water pollution threatens the health of many species and habitats across the planet.

Because of water's self-cleaning powers, the effects of pollution can be reduced. But we also need to reduce the amount of pollution that gets into the water in the first place.

▽ Trash pollutes this freshwater habitat.

**In Other Words**
**overloading** harming
**available** that can be used

▶ **Before You Move On**

1. **Details** What details support the idea that there is pollution in the well?
2. **Make Connections** Name one example of water pollution described in the text that can be found in your town or city.

# Saving the Water in the Well

Water has the power to change everything. A single splash can sprout a seed, **quench** a thirst, provide a habitat, generate energy, and **sustain life**. Water is the most basic and important need of all life on Earth.

Earth's one well is in trouble, though. There is simply not enough clean water to go around.

Taking actions to conserve water can help save the well. Conserving water means protecting both the **quantity** and quality of water on Earth. By becoming more aware of how you use water and by using less, you too can protect the water in Earth's one well. Remember, every drop **counts**! ❖

**In Other Words**
**quench** satisfy
**sustain life** make life possible
**quantity** amount
**counts** is important

▶ **Before You Move On**

1. **Main Idea** What does the author want readers to understand?
2. **Paraphrase** In your own words, explain why water is important to all life on Earth.

## Meet the Author
# Rochelle Strauss

Rochelle Strauss has a challenge for you. First, she would like you to list all the ways water is a part of your life. Do you live near water? What kind? Do you play in it, or use it in a special way? How many times a day do you wash your hands? Brush your teeth? Flush the toilet?

Are you ready for the challenge? Study your list. Think of one simple thing you can do to help conserve water. Then do it. Afterward, tell five people what you did, and why. Then challenge them to do the same thing. In this way, you will be passing along your new water awareness and helping to change the world for the better.

▲ **Rochelle Strauss lives in Canada.**

> " I hope to inspire kids to do something, even just one simple thing, to protect Earth's 'one well.' "

## Writer's Craft

In the first paragraph of "One Well," the author asks you to imagine something new about water. This strong beginning gets your attention and gives important information about the topic. Reread the beginning of "One Well." Then write a strong beginning to a report of your own.

# Talk About It

1. Why is this selection called a **science feature**?

   *It is called a science feature because _____ .*

2. **Explain** the **water cycle** to someone who has never heard of it. **Define** what it is and tell why it is important.

   *The water cycle is _____ . For example, _____ . It is important because _____ .*

3. The selection states that **fresh water** is not distributed evenly around the world. What fact supports this idea? What fact describes a **consequence** of it? Check with a partner to see if you find the same facts.

**Learn test-taking strategies.**
🔵 **NGReach.com**

# Write About It

What should people do to help with water **conservation**? Write a water conservation tip. Use **Key Words** to help get your points across.

> **Water Conservation Tip**
>
> When you _____ , remember to _____ .
> Try to _____ .
> Everybody can help conserve water!

# Main Idea and Details

Make an outline for "One Well." Write the main idea for each section. Then add details that support each main idea.

**Outline**

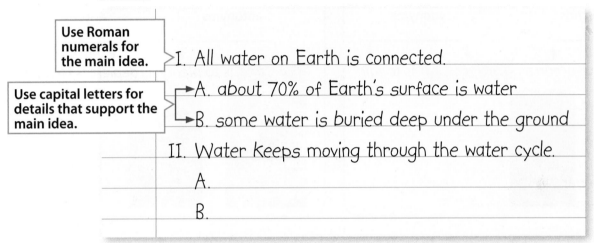

| Use Roman numerals for the main idea. | I. All water on Earth is connected. |
| Use capital letters for details that support the main idea. | A. about 70% of Earth's surface is water |
| | B. some water is buried deep under the ground |
| | II. Water keeps moving through the water cycle. |
| | A. |
| | B. |

Now use your outline to summarize each section of the selection for a partner. Tell the main idea of each section and use the details to tell more about it. Use **Key Words** in your retelling.

> This section is about _____.

# Fluency  **Comprehension Coach**

Use the Comprehension Coach to practice reading with phrasing. Rate your reading.

**Talk Together**

Why is water so important to living things? Write a poem about the importance of water. Think about the sounds that water makes as it drips, flows, and rushes through the world. Try to include those sounds as well as **Key Words** in your poem, and share the poem with the class.

# Analogies

An **analogy** has two word pairs that are related in the same way. Look at these examples of analogies.

| synonyms | synonyms |
| --- | --- |

*sea* is to *ocean* as **precipitation** is to *rain*

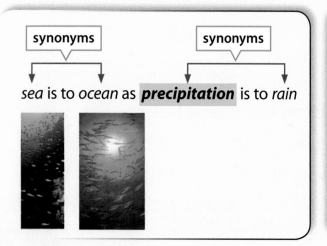

| antonyms | antonyms |
| --- | --- |

**shortage** is to *plenty* as *deplete* is to *replace*

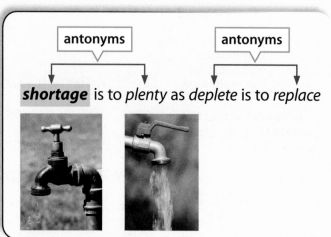

Often, analogies are written like this:

precipitation : rain as sea : ocean

stands for "is to"

### Try It Together

Read the analogies below. Then find the word that completes each one.

1. **day : night as conservation : _____**

   **A.** waste

   **B.** rain

   **C.** water

   **D.** honesty

2. **fast : quick as result : _____**

   **A.** pollution

   **B.** consequence

   **C.** aquifer

   **D.** evaporation

**Connect Across Texts** Read about a scientist who is studying one of the greatest wetlands on the planet.

**Genre** A **science article** is nonfiction. It gives facts about a topic related to the natural world.

# Picturing the
# PANTANAL

## by Lisa Berti

Imagine a place that is ruled by the rain. From October to April, it falls almost endlessly from the sky. It flows into rivers, which become large and fast moving. It **patters** and pours on hundreds of small lakes. It floods across the land, creating a giant water world.

Pantanal

**In Other Words**
**patters** splashes; falls

▶ **Before You Move On**

1. **Make Connections** Think of a time when it rained a lot. What was it like? How was it like the rain in the Pantanal?

2. **Figurative Language** Why does the author use the phrase "ruled by the rain"?

327

# A Watery Wonderland

This place may sound imaginary, but it is real. Welcome to the Pantanal, the largest **pristine** tropical wetland in the world. Located in the middle of South America, it extends across the countries of Brazil, Bolivia, and Paraguay. If you want to explore the Pantanal, you'll need some very good **galoshes**. That's because this wetland is as big as the state of Florida!

The Pantanal is huge, and it is constantly changing. Every year, it fills with water from overflowing rivers. Then, slowly, much of the water dries up. This cycle of flooding and drying brings **nutrient-rich sediments** into the ecosystem. These sediments help plants grow, and support a great diversity of life. Over 190 different kinds of mammals, 270 kinds of fish, and 650 kinds of birds call the Pantanal home.

▲ **These caimans and this capybara are supported by plants, which form the base of Pantanal food chains.**

**These red-capped cardinals are among the many birds living in the Pantanal.** ▶

**In Other Words**

**pristine** healthy and unspoiled

**galoshes** rain boots

**nutrient-rich sediments** soil that has a lot of food for plants and animals

◀ **Satellites like this one capture the sun's radiation as it hits Earth.**

Image courtesy of JAXA

# Studying Water from the Skies

Are the waters of the Pantanal changing? Many scientists want to know. Because water connects all living things in the Pantanal, any changes to it have far-reaching effects. One scientist who is looking for answers is Dr. Maycira Costa. Like most scientists, Maycira goes into **the field** to collect information. However, she also studies water in a different way.

Maycira studies images taken from satellites high above Earth. The images are created by special detectors inside the satellites. The detectors sense the sun's energy as it hits Earth. They capture that energy in an image. Then scientists **convert** the information in the image into colors that human eyes can see.

**In Other Words**
**the field** nature
**convert** change

▶ **Before You Move On**

1. **Make Connections** How might the waters of the Pantanal be changing like they are in other places you have read about?
2. **Explain** How does flooding help plants in the Pantanal?

This **modified satellite image** shows different water levels in the Pantanal at different times of the year. ▶

■ = rising water
■ = low water
■ = high water

©JAXA and METI. Research was conducted under the ALOS K&C initiative project of JAXA/EORC. Mosaic created by Teresa Evans and Maycira Costa

SOUTH AMERICA

Brazil

Bolivia

Paraguay

# Science Through Satellite Images

Studying satellite images shows Maycira many things. Different colors show her how large the flooded areas are. They also show where **the vegetation is**, and how much sediment is in the water. In addition, the images can give Maycira an idea of how much light is penetrating, or going down into the water.

The baseline, or basic information Maycira gathers in her work, is important. She and others can use it to compare unspoiled parts of the Pantanal with parts that are influenced by human activities, such as building **dams**, farming, logging, and mining. This way, she can see how changes in the water affect the plants, animals, and people who depend on it.

▲ This collared anteater is one of over 190 different mammals that live in the Pantanal.

**In Other Words**

**modified satellite image** satellite image that has been adjusted to lay across a flat surface

**the vegetation is** plants are

◀ **dams** walls to contain water

# Tracking a Changing Ecosystem

The information Maycira is gathering is important for another reason. By knowing what the wetlands are like today, she can watch for changes over time. She can see how changes in climate, or average weather over time, affect the Pantanal. In addition, her work will help answer questions about how changes in the pattern and amount of floodwater affect the plants, animals, and people that call the Pantanal home.

Through her work, Maycira is giving people a big "picture" of the Pantanal. She is showing how the area is, in fact, a single, interconnected ecosystem—one that is **worth protecting**. ❖

▲ **Dr. Maycira Costa's work helps people understand what the Pantanal is, and why it is important.**

**In Other Words**

**worth protecting** valuable and deserves to be saved

▶ **Before You Move On**

1. **Main Idea** Why is it important for Maycira to gather basic information about the Pantanal?

2. **Author's Purpose** What was the author's purpose in writing about Maycira's work?

# Respond and Extend

# Compare Texts

Look back at "Picturing the Pantanal" and "One Well." How are the two selections alike? How are they different? As you compare the two pieces, think about their genres, topics, main ideas, and text features.

**Comparison Chart**

| | "Picturing the Pantanal" | "One Well" |
|---|---|---|
| Genre | | |
| Topic | | |
| Main Idea | Through photos, Dr. Maycira Costa studies the Pantanal, and learns how life there is affected by changes to the area. | |
| Text Features | Photos: Yes<br><br>Tables:<br><br>Diagrams: | Photos: Yes<br><br>Tables:<br><br>Diagrams: |

**Talk Together**

Think about the demands on water in today's world. Why does this make water conservation so important? Use **Key Words** to talk about your ideas.

# Adjectives

**Adjectives** describe, or tell about, nouns.

## Grammar Rules **Adjectives**

| | |
|---|---|
| • Use a **capital letter** for adjectives that describe a country of origin. | **A**frican baobab tree |
| • Add **-er** to the adjective when you compare two things. | A lake is deep**er** than a pond. |
| • Add **-est** to the adjective when you compare three or more things. | Crater Lake is the deep**est** lake in the United States. |
| • Some adjectives have special forms for comparing things. These include **good**, **better**, **best**. | When you are thirsty, a sip of water is **good**. A cup of water is **better**. A whole bottle of water is **best**! |

## Read for Adjectives

Read this passage based on "One Well." What adjectives can you find?

Huge differences in rainfall happen around the world. People in places that get the smallest amounts of rain can suffer. An Ethiopian person, for example, might have access to only 10 liters of water a day.

## Write Adjectives

Think about three ways you can save water. Write three sentences using *good, better,* and *best* to describe your ideas. Compare your sentences with a partner's.

# Clarify

Listen to Bobby's dialogue with his father. Then use **Language Frames** to tell a partner why you think it is important to conserve water.

# *Water* in Our Lives *Dialogue* ((MP3))

**Dad:** Another day without rain! The aquifer is shrinking. That's a big problem for us.

**Bobby:** What does *aquifer* mean? Why is it a problem if it shrinks?

**Dad:** The aquifer is our underground water supply. If the aquifer shrinks, it means there won't be enough water for the pond, our wells—even this stream.

**Bobby:** What should we do?

**Dad:** We need to use less water. For example, we can wash the car on the lawn and water the grass at the same time.

**Bobby:** I can do that. And I think we should talk to our neighbors about doing the same thing!

# Key Words

| Key Words |
|---|
| aquifer |
| canal |
| channel |
| climate |
| course |
| gourd |
| region |

Look at the pictures. Use **Key Words** and other words to talk about how people around the world get and store water.

| **Storing Water** | **Moving Water** |
|---|---|

In some **regions**, people get their water from aquifers under the ground.

In dry, hot **climates**, some people might collect and store water in a gourd.

People sometimes build canals that **channel** water from a distant lake to a place where people live.

The natural **course** of a river carries water toward the ocean.

**Talk Together**

What do people in a **region** do when water is scarce? In a group, use **Language Frames** from page 334 and **Key Words** to discuss this question.

# Character

A **character** is a person, animal, or imaginary being in a story.
When you talk about characters, think about the

- role a character plays in the story

- function of the character, or what he or she does

- relationships between characters

Look at the picture of Bobby with his dad.
Think about the relationship that Bobby and his dad share.

## Map and Talk

You can use a chart to share information about Bobby and
his dad. First write the names of the characters. Next write
the characters' roles. Then write the main function of each
character. Finally describe their relationship to each other.

**Character Chart**

| Character | Role | Function | Relationship |
|-----------|------|----------|--------------|
| Bobby | son | listens<br>has ideas | loving<br>learns from<br>   father |
| Bobby's dad | father | teaches<br>sets an example | loving<br>teaches son |

**Talk Together**

Talk with your partner about the characters in a story you have read. Your partner
can make a chart to explore the characters' roles, functions, and relationships.

# More Key Words

Use these words to talk about "My Great-Grandmother's Gourd" and "Juan del Oso and the Water of Life."

## acquire
(u-**kwīr**) *verb*

When you **acquire** something, it becomes yours. She **acquired** a shirt from her mom.

## availability
(u-vā-lu-**bi**-lu-tē) *noun*

**Availability** means having access. The **availability** of books inspires us to read.

## capacity
(ku-**pa**-su-tē) *noun*

**Capacity** is how much something can hold. This bucket has a **capacity** of three gallons of water.

## distribution
(dis-tru-**byū**-shun) *noun*

**Distribution** is the way something is divided. This shows an equal **distribution** of pizza.

## scarcity
(**skair**-su-tē) *noun*

If there is a **scarcity** of something, there is not enough of it. There's a **scarcity** of water here.

## Talk Together

Make a Word Map for each **Key Word**. Then compare your maps with a partner's.

| Definition: *too little of something* | |
|---|---|
| **scarcity** | |
| Example: The birds had a scarcity of food. | Characteristics: limited, small, missing |

**Add words to My Vocabulary Notebook.**

NGReach.com

# Learn to Make Connections

Look at the poster. Does it remind you of something you've seen or read? You can **make connections** to something you've read before to understand something new.

Water
Don't deplete it. Save it.

When you read, think about how the story **connects** to something you've read before.

## How to Make Connections

| | |
|---|---|
| 🗨 | **1.** Think about what the text is about. |
| 👁 | **2.** As you read, think about other texts that relate. |
| 🧩 | **3.** Decide how the connection helps you understand the text. |

The topic is _____.

_____ reminds me of _____.

Now I understand _____.

**Talk Together**

Read Bobby's report. Read the sample connection.
Then use **Language Frames** to tell a partner about
the connections you make.

Report

# Bringing Water Home

There are many places in the world with a **scarcity** of water.
Some groups are working to help people **acquire** the water
they need. One great project took place in the village of
Cotzol, in Guatemala. There are about 500 people living there.
The nearest water was a spring five miles away. The project
workers had to figure out how the villagers could get access
to that water.

Workers built a large tank to hold the spring water. The tank
had a **capacity** of 4,900 liters (about 1,300 gallons). Then they
set up pipes to carry the water to the village. The pipes had to
be almost five miles long! ◄

The workers still had one more problem to solve. They had
to make **distribution** of the water easier. They installed many
faucets to help distribute the water to villagers. When the
water finally flowed into people's homes, it was the first time
for everyone. Now there is water **availability** all through
the village. ◄

"The topic is water
scarcity.

Water five miles away
reminds me of a story
I read. Settlers carried
water from a river.

Now I understand why
we need water nearby."

◄ = a good place to stop and make a connection

# Read a Story

## Genre

**Realistic fiction** is a story that sounds as if it could be true. The characters, plot, and setting all seem real.

## Setting

The setting of a story is *where* and *when* it takes place. This story takes place today, in a village in the country of Sudan, in eastern North Africa.

Sudan

▲ This boy lives in a region of Sudan that has a long dry season.

# My Great-Grandmother's Gourd

by **Cristina Kessler**

illustrated by **Walter Lyon Krudop**

▶ **Set a Purpose**
Find out how a new machine
changes life in a village.

I'll always remember the first day the blue pump worked. The men in their **turbans** and the women in their *towbs* laughed and chattered as the bright, shining pump was **fixed** on top of the old well.

"Imagine," said Ibrahim, the village chief, "no more camels pulling water for drinking and washing and cooking. No more filling of the old trees to get us through the dry season. Progress has come to our village."

Ahmed, the barber, called out, "Who shall take the first pump of this fancy new machine?"

Silence filled the air until Hanan, the neighbor, said, "Let it be a child, to show just how easy it will be. Fatima, you pump and we will watch the water flow. *Inshallah*."

**In Other Words**
◀ **turbans**  cloth hats
*towbs*  long, colorful clothing (in Arabic)
**fixed**  set in place
*Inshallah.*  God or Allah willing. (in Arabic)

I stepped to the long handle and pulled down. A soft creaking noise filled the silence. But not a drop fell.

I pulled again, and a second soft *creeeeak* was surrounded by stillness, something rare in our village. Out gushed a stream of clear water. A sudden cheer filled the air and drums began beating. Was it for me or the water? I wondered.

I looked for my grandmother, who always says she is so **proud of me**, but I didn't see her. As people pushed forward to try the pump, I pushed outward to find my grandmother.

There she stood all alone beneath her best friend, an old baobab tree.

"Grandmother, come see the new pump. The water is so easy to get now, our work will be less."

Grandmother looked at me, then patted the **gnarled** trunk of the giant baobab tree with her work-worn hand and said, "Go, child. Drink the fresh, cold water. And soon I'll be there too."

I ran back and danced with my friends, celebrating the new pump. But my grandmother did not come.

**In Other Words**
**proud of me** happy about what I do
**gnarled** twisted

Every morning I raced the girls of the village to the pump. The first one there got to pull down the long, **shimmering** handle for as long as she wanted, filling buckets and tins, head pans and **gourds**.

My grandmother spent more and more time with her friend the baobab. Leaning against its great trunk. Resting beneath its wide-reaching shadow. Watching and waiting for what, I didn't know.

Early one evening, after the food had been eaten and the sun's heat was only a whisper on my skin, I joined my grandmother beneath the tree.

**In Other Words**
**shimmering** shining

▶ **Before You Move On**
1. **Explain** What did the villagers do to get water before they had the pump?
2. **Make Connections** Think about the water sources described in "One Well." What water source is Fatima accessing?

Grandmother took my hand and placed it on the ancient bark. She didn't say a word, but her sadness was loud.

"Tell me, Grandmother, what makes you so sad?" I asked as I looked deep into her eyes. "Is it the pump? Don't you like it?"

With tired eyes she looked at me and said, "The rains are nearly here, and still no one works to prepare the trees. All the years of my life, drumbeats would fill the village, and voices would sing and chant as we all worked together. But now there's only the ***creeak, creeak* of metal**."

Gently patting the trunk, she said, "I always called this my great-grandmother's gourd. The name my grandmother called it. And her grandmother before her."

I smoothed the *towb* around her wrinkled face and said, "But, Grandmother, with the pump we don't need the trees. The days of **storing** water in trees are past."

She let go of my hand.

"Grandmother," I said, "that was then and this is now."

**In Other Words**
***creeak, creeak* of metal** sound of the pump
**storing** keeping; setting aside

I couldn't sleep that night, so I sat outside. I was thinking about my stubborn grandmother, when, silent as a shadow, she sat down beside me.

I **gazed upon** our family's only baobab and let my eyes wander up to the scrawny branches. Each branch looked small and separate in the light of the moon.

As if she **read my mind**, Grandmother said softly, "She gives us shade in the day. Shelter in the rain. And water in the dry season. She is the tree of life."

"No, Grandmother, the baobab will give us shade in the day and shelter in the rain. **Khalas**. And the pump will give us water in the dry season."

Shaking her head, she said, "Good-night, Granddaughter," and walked back to our hut.

I rose that next day with the first rays of the sun. Dressing quickly, I rushed to the well to pump away all the questions that my old-fashioned grandmother **stirred in me**.

I was first and I pumped till my shoulders ached. *Creeak, creeak* sang the pump.

**In Other Words**
**gazed upon** looked at
**read my mind** knew what I was thinking
*Khalas.* That is all. (in Arabic)
**stirred in me** made me think about

▶ **Before You Move On**
1. **Character** Why does Grandmother stay away from the new pump?
2. **Figurative Language** Why do you think Grandmother's family called the baobab tree a **gourd**?

The hut was empty when I returned. I looked toward our field to find Grandmother. Instead, I saw her bent over her hoe at the **base** of her baobab tree.

I ran to her and shouted, "Grandmother, people will laugh at you, preparing your tree."

She stood straight and said to me in a voice as hard as the dry earth, "Some may laugh. What do I care? I have work to do."

She worked in silence. *Creak, creak* sang the pump. *Hack, hack* went my grandmother's hoe.

"Can I help?" I asked.

"No," she said. She wiped the sweat dripping from her **brow** and bent back to her work.

**In Other Words**
**base** bottom
**brow** forehead

One day Ahmed, the **barber**, passed our tree and shouted with a laugh, "For some people new ideas are like puddles on the clay: they never **sink in**."

But Grandmother kept right on working. She was slowly digging out what looked like a large necklace around the base of the baobab's trunk.

Another day Nagla, the neighbor who never stops talking, passed. She said loudly, "Who but a fool makes extra work?" Then she laughed. And I realized she was laughing at my grandmother. Old-fashioned or not, *my* grandmother.

I grabbed my hoe and ran to the tree. Without a word, I started digging beside my grandmother.

**In Other Words**
**barber** haircutter
**sink in** are accepted

351

For days we dug, deepening the circle around the trunk. In peaceful silence, we shared the work of my grandmother's great-grandmother.

People passed us, but now no one said a word. We **worked on**.

*Creak, creak* went the blue pump.

One day as the sun **dipped below the earth's edge**, Grandmother put away her hoe. "Now," she said, "we must wait for the rains."

The first rain comes as **fiercely** as the first winds of the *haboob*. Grandmother and I stood in it, feeling the water dripping down our faces. We watched our necklace around the giant old tree's trunk slowly fill with water.

**In Other Words**
**worked on**  continued working
**dipped below the earth's edge**  went down
**fiercely**  strongly
*haboob*  windy season (in Arabic)

When the rain stopped, I climbed the tree and sat by a small hole at the top of the trunk. The hole that had been made by my grandmother's great-grandmother's great-grandmother.

I dropped the bucket tied to my waist down to Grandmother, who filled it to its **brim** from the baobab's necklace. Slowly I pulled the bucket up, then poured its contents into the tree. It took two breaths before we heard the splash of water hitting bottom, deep inside the tree. Grandmother's eyes sparkled at the old, **familiar** sound.

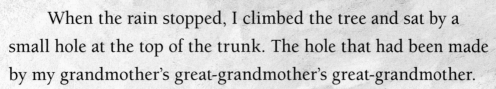

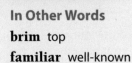

**In Other Words**
**brim** top
**familiar** well-known

▶ **Before You Move On**

1. **Character** Why does Fatima decide to work with Grandmother?
2. **Figurative Language** What sound image does the author use to describe the work of the pump? Why?

353

▶ **Predict**
Will the villagers stop making fun
of Fatima and Grandmother?

Ahmed, the barber, passed by, and said, "I guess some people like extra work." But we **took no notice of** him as the sweet splash of water rose higher and higher inside the old tree.

Day after day now, I climbed the tree, and Grandmother filled the bucket. We worked together, filling our tree. Finally, when the rains ended, the tree was full.

The **scorching** dry season came early. Each day the horizon danced where the shimmering blue sky met the earth's baking red clay. Lines formed at the well.

**In Other Words**
**took no notice of** did
 not pay attention to
**scorching** hot

354

From the first rays of light till the sun slipped away, people pumped. The steady *creeak*, *creeak* turned to *screech! screech!*

And then one day the pump stopped.

"We will fix it," said the chief, Ibrahim. Omar, the baker, and Musa, the butcher, brought out tools. People stood about in silence.

Musa pulled a large metal piece, sharp along one edge, from the pump's neck. "It has broken **clean**, from too much use. **Malesh**. I don't know what we shall do, for I have no **spare** part like this."

"I will make another piece," said Boubacar, the cart builder. "But it will take some days."

**In Other Words**
**clean** completely
**Malesh.** Sorry. (in Arabic)
**spare** extra

"How can we wait days?" cried Nagla. "What shall we do without water?"

"We go back to the old ways," said Ahmed. "We shall use the camels to pull the water out of the well." Then he looked straight at my grandmother and told Nagla, "And two smart villagers can use their tree."

"This year we will share our tree," said Grandmother, "Maybe it's **wise** to mix old with new."

Ahmed looked at her a moment, then **nodded**.

His son, Abu Bakar, called to his friends Ali, Salah, and Osman, "Get the buckets. We'll go to the tree."

With great **pride** I said, "Yes! To my great-grandmother's gourd."

**In Other Words**
**wise** smart
**nodded** moved his head to say yes
**pride** happiness and satisfaction

Before the next rainy season came, the village **throbbed with** drums and chants. The people worked together, preparing the trees for the rains, just in case the pump broke again.

I looked at Grandmother, whose smile shone brighter than the African sun, and said, "Remember last year? The silence and laughter as we worked alone?"

"Yes," she said. "But that was then and this is now."

And each day I pat the old baobab's trunk and say, "*Shukran*, my friend, for you give us shade in the day, shelter in the rain, and water in the dry season. One day you will be my great-granddaughter's gourd." ❖

**In Other Words**
**throbbed with** was full of the sounds of
*Shukran* Thank you (in Arabic)

▶ **Before You Move On**

1. **Character** How have the villagers changed?
2. **Make Connections** How does the **climate** affect the events in the last part of the story?

## Key Words

| | |
|---|---|
| acquire | climate |
| aquifer | course |
| availability | distribution |
| canal | gourd |
| capacity | region |
| channel | scarcity |

# Talk About It

1. What seems **realistic** about "My Great-Grandmother's Gourd?" Give at least two examples.

   *The story seems realistic because _____ .*

2. What does having the pump mean to the people who live in Fatima's village? Use **Language Frames** to **clarify** your answer.

   *_____ means _____ . For example, _____ .*

3. How did Fatima's relationship with her grandmother change by the end of the story?

   *At first, Fatima thought her grandmother was old-fashioned. But later, Fatima _____ .*

Learn test-taking strategies.
NGReach.com

# Write About It

The selection uses pictures and words to describe the old baobab tree. Write a poem to describe it. Use **Key Words** and metaphors in your poem. You might start your poem like this.

*Oh, beautiful baobab tree, you are the best water gourd.*
*Your trunk is the face of a wrinkled, wise woman.*

# Character

Use the chart to keep track of each character's role, function, and relationship in "My Great-Grandmother's Gourd."

| | Write the character's role here. | Write the character's function here. | Describe the character's relationship here. |
|---|---|---|---|

**Character Chart**

| Character | Role | Function | Relationship |
|---|---|---|---|
| Grandmother | grandmother | | |
| Fatima | | | |

Now use your chart as you retell the selection to a partner. Tell who the characters are, what their roles and functions are in the story, and what their relationship is. Use **Key Words** in your retelling.

> Fatima's role is _____.
> Her function is _____.
> Her relationship with _____ is _____.

# Fluency  Comprehension Coach

Use the Comprehension Coach to practice reading with expression. Rate your reading.

**Talk Together**

Why does Grandmother think that collecting water is so important? Write a song about the importance of water. Try to use **Key Words** in your song, and share the song with the class.

# Relate Words

**Synonyms** are words that have nearly the same meaning. **Antonyms** are words that have opposite meanings.

Look at the word webs for the antonyms *acquire* and *give*. Notice the synonyms for each word. Think about how the synonyms for *acquire* **relate** to the synonyms for *give*.

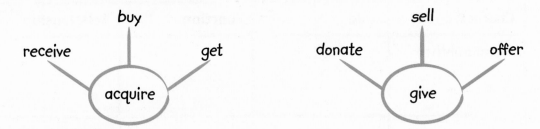

Knowing how words relate can help you choose the right word when you speak or write. They can help you with analogies, too. Look at these analogies. They are based on the words above.

acquire : give as receive : donate          get : offer as buy : sell

## Try It Together

Read the analogies below. Then find the word that completes each one. Use a word web to help you.

1. **many : plenty as scarcity : _____**

   **A.** acquire

   **B.** water

   **C.** pump

   **D.** shortage

2. **wet : dry as flood : _____**

   **A.** gourd

   **B.** drought

   **C.** rain

   **D.** capacity

**Connect Across Texts** You read how an African girl saved water for her village. Now read about a North American boy who moves water across mountains.

**Genre** Some of the most popular origin myths, or stories of how things came to be, are legends. A **legend** is a traditional tale about characters who bring about amazing events.

# Juan del Oso and the Water of Life

retold by **Enrique R. Lamadrid**
and **Juan Estevan Arellano**
illustrated by **Brandon Dorman**

In the early 1800s, a small group of **mestizo ranchers** did something very special. They built **canals**, or acequias, that made water flow backwards! The acequias brought water across a mountain and down to their dry village below. Their community **prospered**, and stories of their great achievement were passed from parents to children. But the stories changed over time. That is how this legend of Juan del Oso was born.

**In Other Words**

*del Oso* of the Bear (in Spanish)

*mestizo ranchers* ranchers from mixed Spanish and Native American backgrounds

*prospered* grew and was successful

▶ **Before You Move On**

1. **Main Idea** Where did this legend of Juan del Oso come from?

2. **Make Connections** How do you think this legend will be different from realistic fiction?

▶ **Set a Purpose**
Juan has two problems. Find out
what they are.

**E**n los tiempos de yupa, there lived a boy named Juan del Oso, who was as strong as a bear. Juan del Oso lived with his mother and father in their *fuertecito*, where the great forest meets the highest pastures of **the Mora Valley**.

Juan del Oso was much bigger than the other boys in his village, and they teased him without **mercy**. So Juan spent much of his time alone, walking in the forest.

In the valley below Juan's house, there was not enough water to grow what the villagers needed. There was only enough water for some fields of winter wheat and a few cattle. If they could not find more water, the villagers would soon have to move.

**In Other Words**
*En los tiempos de yupa*  A long time ago (in Spanish)
*fuertecito*  little log house (in Spanish)
◀ **the Mora Valley**  a dry valley in northern New Mexico
**mercy**  any kindness

One day, Juan del Oso was walking in the forest and saw two strange young men roasting meat. They were dancing around the fire and singing **an odd chant**, "*Ala run tun tún, ala run tun tún.*" Juan noticed that they were as big and strong as he was.

"***Soy*** Juan del Oso," he announced. "Who are you and what are you doing so far up in the mountains?"

**In Other Words**
**an odd chant**  a strange little song
***Soy***  I am (in Spanish)

▶ **Before You Move On**

1. **Character**  Why does Juan spend most of his time walking alone in the forest?
2. **Make Connections**  What problem is shared by Juan's village and the village in "My Great-Grandmother's **Gourd**"?

"**S**oy Mudacerros," one of them said, grabbing a huge oak shovel. "My job is to move hills." He pointed across the canyon to a huge mound of dirt.

"*Soy* Mudarríos," the other one said, holding a large iron bar. "My job is to change the course of rivers." He pointed toward the same area, where a muddy stream circled the mound.

The boys shared their stories with Juan. Mudacerros had gotten into trouble in his village for causing a **landslide**. Mudarríos had made a dam that caused a **flood**. Both events had been **accidents**. The boys were just too strong. Now they lived alone in the forest.

**In Other Words**
**landslide** hillside to crumble and fall
**flood** sudden, dangerous rise of the water level
**accidents** mistakes

To Juan, it seemed that the boys' work had no **purpose**. Then he had an idea. He told the boys about the dry valley near his village. He explained that the people did not have enough water for their crops.

"There is water for your people," said Mudacerros, "if we could only get it to the side of the mountain where they live."

Juan del Oso **could barely contain the hope in his heart**. That night, Juan told his father about the strong young men and their amazing **talents**.

"Mudacerros can move the earth itself. And Mudarríos can change the course of rivers. Maybe they can help us bring water to our valley!" Juan and his father got out a map, and they made a plan.

**In Other Words**

**purpose** reason or use

**could barely contain the hope in his heart** was very hopeful

**talents** skills

▶ **Before You Move On**

1. **Character** Describe the relationship between Juan, Mudacerros, and Mudarríos.
2. **Predict** What plan do you think Juan and his father will make?

365

▶ **Predict**
How will Juan and the others
help the villagers?

The next day, Juan, his father, Mudarríos, and Mudacerros
marched far up the rocky canyon to the source of the river.
After building a fire, dancing the "*Run tun tún*," and eating plenty
of ***esquite***, they made a ***presa*** high up in the rocky canyon.
It captured the flow of the river and made a deep pond.

Mudarríos carefully chose the route for the new *acequia*.
The canal would climb up along the **ridge**. It would carry water
over the mountain and down into the valley. They cleared a huge
path. Mudacerros removed the large rocks and lined the new
*acequia* with **cobbles**. Juan del Oso and his father pulled up the
trees that were in the way.

**In Other Words**
*esquite*  toasted corn (in Spanish)
*presa*  dam (in Spanish)
**ridge**  top part of the mountain
**cobbles**  small rocks

**366**

Soon water flowed from the deep pond along the ridge. Above the valley, the water **cascaded** down the mountains like a waterfall. It made a ruffling sound like a flock of **crows**.

The people in the village below joyfully shouted *"¡Allí viene el agua!"* They could not believe their eyes. They planted beans, corn, squashes, and even fruit trees, and their community prospered.

People still tell the story of Juan del Oso and his powerful young friends, and how rewarding hard work can be. Strength without purpose can lead to **destruction**. Strength channeled like the water in the *acequia* brings life to all. ❖

**In Other Words**

**cascaded** flowed beautifully

**crows** birds

*"¡Allí viene el agua!"* "There comes the water!" (in Spanish)

**destruction** damage; ruin

▶ **Before You Move On**

1. **Character** How is Juan able to use his size and strength to help others in the last part of the story?

2. **Figurative Language** What similes does the author use to describe the water as it travels down to the valley?

<table>
<tr><td colspan="2">Key Words</td></tr>
</table>

| Key Words | |
|---|---|
| acquire | climate |
| aquifer | course |
| availability | distribution |
| canal | gourd |
| capacity | region |
| channel | scarcity |

# Compare Themes

"My Great-Grandmother's Gourd" and "Juan del Oso" are stories from different cultures. Each has different **themes,** or messages. Which themes do both stories share? Which themes are special to one story? Compare and contrast the themes. Work with a partner to complete the chart below.

**Comparison Chart**

| | "Juan del Oso and the Water of Life" | "My Great-Grandmother's Gourd" |
|---|---|---|
| Many hands make light work. | Yes | |
| Work that has a purpose can benefit many. | | Yes |
| With hard work, anything is possible. | | |
| Don't give up old ways for new ways. | | |
| Water is important to our lives. | | |
| Teamwork works. | | |

**Talk Together**

Think about the selections and the chart above. How do the themes help you understand what people do when water is scarce? Use **Key Words** to discuss your ideas.

# Possessive Nouns and Adjectives

A **possessive noun** tells who owns something. **Possessive adjectives** do not use apostrophes.

| Grammar Rules | Possessive Nouns and Adjectives | |
|---|---|---|
| | **One Owner** | **More Than One Owner** |
| • Use an **apostrophe** (') with a possessive noun | **Grandmother's** baobab tree<br>**Juan del Oso's** strength | the **villagers'** pump<br>the **boys'** plan |
| • Use the correct possessive to tell about the number of owners | my<br>your<br>his, her, its | our<br>your<br>their |

## Read Possessive Nouns and Adjectives

Read these sentences from "Juan del Oso and the Water of Life."
What possessive nouns and adjectives can you find?

> To Juan, it seemed that the boys' work had no purpose.
> Then he had an idea. He told the boys about the dry
> valley near his village. He explained that the people did
> not have enough water for their crops.

## Write Possessive Nouns and Adjectives

Look at the picture on page 351. Write two sentences to describe what you
see. Use possessive nouns and possessive adjectives. Share your sentences
with a partner.

# Write As a Journalist

## Write a Magazine Article 🖊

Write a magazine article that explains something about the importance of water. Add it to a class magazine.

## Study a Model

A magazine article provides information in an engaging way. Read Sara's article about tips for saving water.

### Be Water Wise

#### by Sara Alvarez

Do you want to waste water? Probably not. If you let water run too long, you can waste thousands of gallons. **Here are some ways I conserved water**.

The toughest thing I did was to <u>stop taking long showers</u>! I set a timer for five minutes. **That way I saved almost 1,000 gallons a month**.

Also, I turned off the water while I was <u>brushing my teeth</u>. **I didn't want to be responsible for having four gallons a minute go down the drain**!

So, just by turning off the water I became water-wise. **How will you conserve water**?

An opening question gets the reader's attention. The **main idea** is in the opening paragraph.

**Supporting details** in each paragraph help develop the main idea.

Different **sentence types** keep the article interesting.

## Prewrite

1. **Choose a Topic**  Talk with a partner to find a topic that's interesting.

| Language Frames | |
|---|---|
| **Tell Your Ideas** | **Respond to Ideas** |
| • _____ is important because _____ . <br><br> • An interesting fact about _____ is _____ . <br><br> • If we don't _____ , then _____ . | • I don't understand what you mean by _____ . Can you say it in a different way? <br><br> • What else will you say about _____ ? <br><br> • Can you think of a more interesting idea than _____ ? |

2. **Gather Information**  Think about your main idea. What details can you use to develop it? Where can you find those details?

3. **Get Organized**  Use an outline like this one to help you organize your information.

   **Outline**

   I. Ways to Conserve Water
   
      A. stop taking long showers
   
      B. don't let water run while brushing your teeth

## Draft

Use your outline to write your draft. Use supporting details to develop your main idea. Vary your sentences to keep your writing interesting.

## Revise

1. **Read, Retell, Respond** Read your draft aloud to a partner. Your partner listens and retells what you said. Next, talk about ways to improve your writing.

| Language Frames | |
|---|---|
| **Retell** | **Make Suggestions** |
| • Your article is about _____ . | • Your main idea needs to be developed more. Add _____ . |
| • The important details are _____ . | • Your article would be more interesting if you _____ . |
| • The most interesting part is _____ . | • I'm not sure why you included _____ . |

2. **Make Changes** Think about your draft and your partner's suggestions. Then use the Revising Marks on page 629 to mark your changes.

   • Is your writing well-developed? Add details, if necessary, to make your ideas clear.

   > The toughest thing I did was to stop taking long showers! I set a timer for five minutes. ∧ That way I saved almost 1,000 gallons a month.

   • Is your article written in an engaging way? Vary your sentences to add interest.

   > Do you want to waste water?
   > ∧ It's important to conserve water and not waste it. ℯ

## Edit and Proofread

Work with a partner to edit and proofread your article. Check your use of apostrophes with possessive nouns. Remember that possessive adjectives do not use apostrophes.

## Publish

**On Your Own**  Make a final copy of your article. Read it to a group of your classmates.

| Presentation Tips | |
|---|---|
| **If you are the speaker...** | **If you are the listener...** |
| Pronounce your words. Make sure each one can be understood. | Listen for the main idea and supporting details. |
| Vary your volume and tone to keep your article interesting. | Afterwards, share your own ideas about the topic. |

**With a Group**  Combine your articles into a magazine. Design a cover and think of a great title. Format the articles in different ways. Vary the shape, colors, and fonts.

Water
**Works**
A Magazine About the Importance of Water

**Talk Together**

In this unit, you found lots of answers to the **Big Question**. Now use your concept map to discuss the **Big Question** with the class.

**Concept Map**

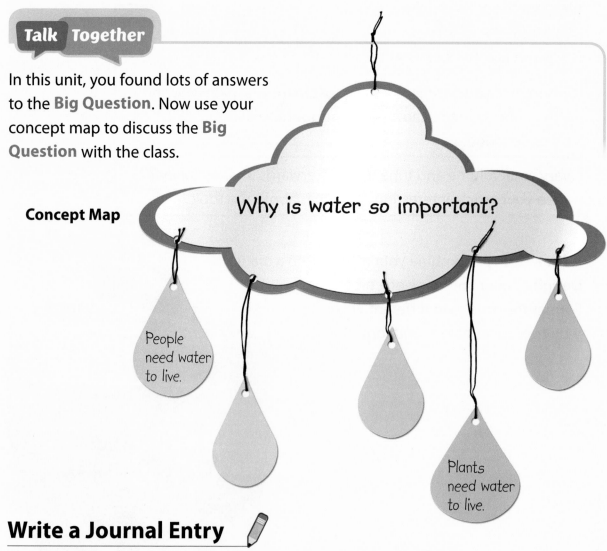

Why is water so important?

People need water to live.

Plants need water to live.

## Write a Journal Entry ✏️

Look at your concept map. Choose one reason that explains why water is important. Write a journal entry about it.

# Share Your Ideas

Choose one of these ways to share your ideas about the **Big Question**.

## Write It!

### Make a Poster

Create a poster that encourages people to conserve water. Include a picture or drawing, and write a catchy title.

Don't Let the Well Run Dry!

## Talk About It!

### Make a Presentation

Research one tropical wetland in the world. Then give a presentation to the class. Define what a wetland is and explain why wetlands are important. Include some pictures or drawings to make your presentation appealing.

## Do It!

### Choose the Best Way

What is the best way to get the message out about water conservation? Think about how TV shows, Web sites, blogs, and films give messages. Decide which one would be best. Work with a partner. Talk about the strengths of each type of media.

## Write It!

### Write a Legend

Write a short legend about how two or three characters use their strength and their brains to protect the water supply in your region. Read your "modern" legend to a partner.

# The WILD WEST

**BIG**
Question

What does it take to settle a new land?

**Unit at a Glance**
▶ **Language:** Describe Experiences, Express Opinions, Social Studies Words
▶ **Literacy:** Visualize
▶ **Content:** U.S. History

# Unit 6

## Share What You Know

**Do It!**

❶ **Think** about when you moved to a new place. What do you remember? Picture it in your mind.

❷ **Draw** the picture. How did you feel? Describe your feelings.

❸ **Describe** your drawing to the class. Read aloud the sentences.

I felt excited!

**Build Background:** Use this interactive resource to learn about settling the West.

NGReach.com

# Describe Experiences

Listen to Antoine's poem. Then use **Language Frames** to describe a place you visited that affected you.

## At South Pass   *Poem* ((MP3))

I stood at South Pass and imagined a time

When the bold pioneers had walked through.

It was lonely and cold in the mountains,

And they had faced great hardship, I knew.


The Rockies looked bleak, and I thought I could see

Marks from wagons of long ago.

The pass still seemed haunted by brave pioneers

Who had struggled in wind, rain, and snow.

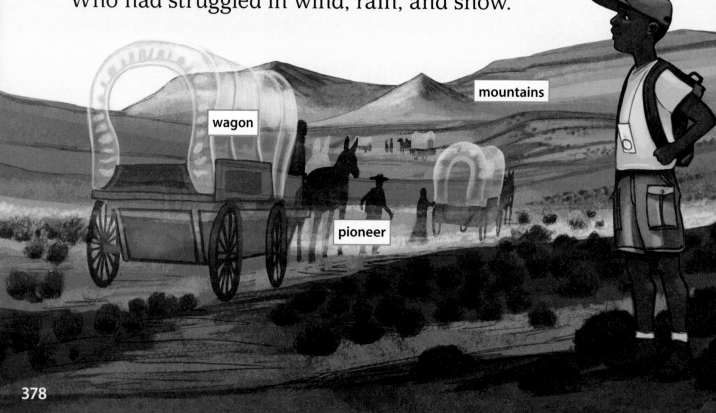

mountains

wagon

pioneer

**Key Words**

construction
gold rush
ranching
reservation
settler

# Key Words

Look at the pictures. Use **Key Words** and other words to talk about events that happened when **settlers** moved west.

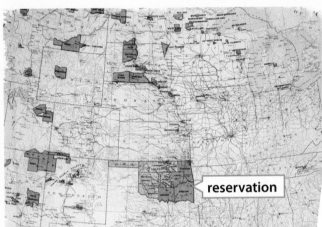

During the 1800s, Native Americans were moved onto **reservations**.

reservation

panning for gold

The **gold rush** began in the 1840s when people discovered gold in California. As a result, some **settlers** moved west to look for gold.

cattle

cowboy

Cowboys made a living by **ranching**. In this business, cattle are raised and sold for their meat.

**Construction** of railroads brought even more settlers to the West.

**Talk Together**

How would it feel to settle a new land? With a partner, use **Key Words** and **Language Frames** from page 378 to describe what settlers might have experienced.

# Cause and Effect

When you describe why something happens, you tell the **cause**. What happens as a result is the **effect**. Connecting causes and effects helps you understand what you read, hear, or see.

Look at the pictures. Think about what Antoine imagined.

## Map and Talk

You can make a cause-and-effect organizer to show what happened and why. Here's how you make one.

**Cause-and-Effect Organizer**

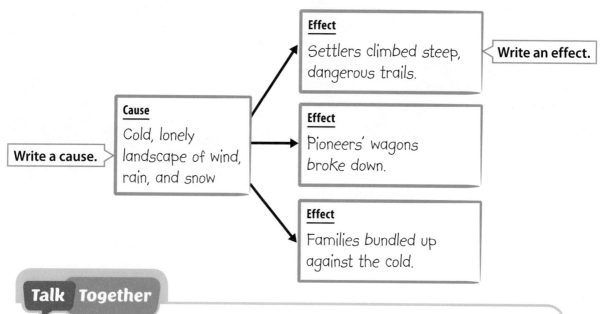

**Effect**
Settlers climbed steep, dangerous trails.
— Write an effect.

**Cause**
Cold, lonely landscape of wind, rain, and snow
Write a cause. ▷

**Effect**
Pioneers' wagons broke down.

**Effect**
Families bundled up against the cold.

**Talk Together**

Tell a partner about a place that affected you. Describe what happened and why it happened. Your partner can make a cause-and-effect organizer.

# More Key Words

Use these words to talk about "Westward Bound!" and "A Day in the Life of a *Vaquero*."

## establish
(i-**sta**-blish) *verb*

**Establish** means to put a person or thing in a successful position. The win **established** him as captain.

## expansion
(ik-**span**-shun) *noun*

**Expansion** is when something gets bigger. Blowing into a balloon causes its **expansion**.

## explore
(ik-**splawr**) *verb*

To **explore** means to look around a new place. They found a new park to **explore**.

## frontier
(frun-**tir**) *noun*

A **frontier** is a place where few or no people live. Space is a **frontier** for us to explore.

## individual
(in-du-**vij**-wul) *noun*

An **individual** is a person. Each **individual** at school is important.

## Talk Together

Work with a partner to complete an Expanded Meaning Map for each **Key Word**.

### Expanded Meaning Map

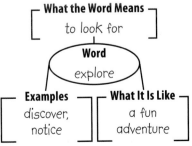

What the Word Means
to look for

Word
explore

Examples
discover, notice

What It Is Like
a fun adventure

**Add words to My Vocabulary Notebook.**
NGReach.com

# Learn to Visualize

Look at the cartoon of Antoine listening to a story about explorers. What pictures do you imagine, or **visualize**, when you think about the story?

"At last the pioneers stood high on a cliff and saw the sparkling waters of the Pacific Ocean."

When you read, you can **visualize**, too.

## How to Visualize

| | | |
|---|---|---|
|  | **1.** As you read, look for words that describe people, places, or events. | I read _____ . |
|  | **2.** Use the words to create pictures in your mind. | I picture _____ . |
| ✏ | **3.** To build your understanding, make a quick drawing to show what you visualize. | I draw _____ . |

**Talk Together**

Read the story about Antoine. Read the sample visualization. Then use **Language Frames** to tell a partner about the visualizations you make.

Science Fiction

# Back in Time

by Diane Zahler

It had worked! When Antoine opened the door of the time machine, he could hardly believe that everything was different. He was in a town in the western **frontier** . He was in the Wild West!

"What year is this?" Antoine asked a woman wearing a long skirt. She wore a hat with flowers.

"Why, it's 1866, of course!" the woman answered, smiling.

Antoine decided to **explore** the town. He walked down the wooden sidewalk. Cowboys rode horses down the unpaved street. Other **individuals** rode in wagons and carriages, raising clouds of dust. Shops and a hotel lined the street. Each building had a colorful painted sign.

Antoine looked into the distance. He could see people laying railroad tracks. It was so hot that the metal tracks shimmered.

"The railroad is coming!" a man in a furry hat said to him. "This **expansion** will be good for our town, lad. It will **establish** us as an important stop on the way to the Pacific Ocean!"

"I read that the woman wears a long skirt and a hat with flowers.

I picture a woman from long-ago, in old-fashioned clothes."

I draw

◀ = a good place to stop and visualize

383

# Read a History Article

## Genre

A **history article** is nonfiction. It can tell about people, places, and events in the past.

## Text Features

**Time lines** list events and dates to help you understand *when* things happened. **Maps** show place names and boundary lines to help you understand *where* they happened.

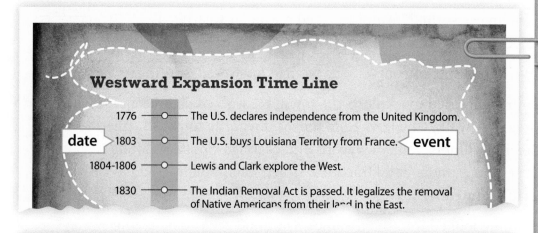

### Westward Expansion Time Line

- 1776 — The U.S. declares independence from the United Kingdom.
- **date** 1803 — The U.S. buys Louisiana Territory from France. **event**
- 1804-1806 — Lewis and Clark explore the West.
- 1830 — The Indian Removal Act is passed. It legalizes the removal of Native Americans from their land in the East.

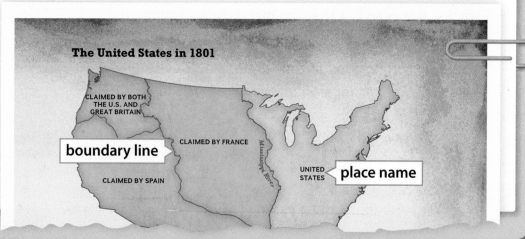

### The United States in 1801

CLAIMED BY BOTH THE U.S. AND GREAT BRITAIN

**boundary line** CLAIMED BY FRANCE

CLAIMED BY SPAIN

Mississippi River

UNITED STATES **place name**

# Westward Bound!

by **Michael J. Noble**

▶ **Set a Purpose**
Find out how the American
West was settled.

# The "Wild" West

If you ask anyone about the history of the West, they may tell you
about a wild, lawless time, when brave cowboys rode their horses
across wide, dusty plains. This is a popular vision of the Old West.
It is often shown on TV and in the movies. But it is not the
whole story.

The real history of the West is much more interesting. It is the story
of millions of different kinds of people, all with different ideas about
the land and their future on it. They came from many different
backgrounds, but they had one thing in common. They lived in a
time of great changes. It was the time of the westward **expansion**.

▲ **Many different kinds of people settled in the West.**

386

## The United States in 1801

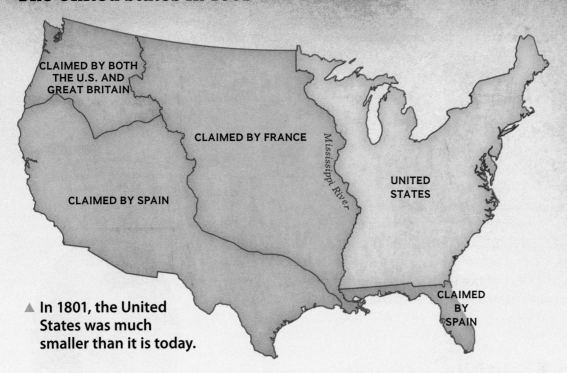

CLAIMED BY BOTH THE U.S. AND GREAT BRITAIN

CLAIMED BY FRANCE

CLAIMED BY SPAIN

Mississippi River

UNITED STATES

CLAIMED BY SPAIN

▲ In 1801, the United States was much smaller than it is today.

People from the East Coast of the United States began moving west in large numbers around 1790. These western **settlers** were mostly farmers, but they saw themselves as pioneers, the first people to settle the land.

They were wrong, though. Native Americans, the real pioneers, had been living on the land for thousands of years before them. Still, the American settlers took the land they wanted, often by force.

By 1801, settlers from the East **occupied** U.S. land all the way to the Mississippi River. Beyond it were large territories **claimed by** France, Spain, and Great Britain. At the time, it may have seemed that the western boundary of the U.S. had been reached.

**In Other Words**
**occupied** lived on
**claimed by** that were divided between

▶ **Before You Move On**

1. **Visualize** Can you picture the cowboys described in the first paragraph? What are they doing? What do they look like?

2. **Cause/Effect** Why didn't most **settlers** move beyond the Mississippi River in 1801?

▲ The shaded part of the map shows the territory bought by the United States in the Louisiana Purchase.

## The Louisiana Purchase

Then, in 1803, the western boundary of the United States changed **radically**. The United States bought the Louisiana Territory from France. For only $15 million, the size of the United States doubled.

Thomas Jefferson, the president at that time, was curious about all that land beyond the Mississippi River. Mainly, he wanted to find a river-based trade **route** to the Pacific Ocean. He also wanted to know how much of the land could be settled, what it looked like, and what kinds of plants and animals lived there. Finally, he wanted to **establish** friendships with Native Americans, and to build trade relationships with them.

▲ **Meriwether Lewis**

▲ **William Clark**

**In Other Words**
**radically** a lot
**route** way; trail

388

In the spring of 1804, Jefferson sent Captain Meriwether Lewis, Lieutenant William Clark, and a group of over forty men to **explore** the West. Their goal was to find a route to the Pacific Ocean, while recording as much information as they could along the way.

About halfway through their journey, a young **Shoshone woman** joined them. Her name was Sacajawea. She helped the group find food and communicate with other Native Americans.

Thanks in large part to Sacajawea's help, Lewis and Clark reached their goal. When they returned home, they were celebrated as national heroes. As a result, more people became interested in the mysterious land west of the Mississippi.

▲ **In his journal, Clark drew many of the things he saw along the way, like this sage grouse.**

**In Other Words**

**Shoshone woman** woman of the Shoshone, a Native American tribe

▶ **Before You Move On**

1. **Clarify** What was the main purpose of the Lewis and Clark expedition?
2. **Cause/Effect** How did Sacajawea affect Lewis and Clark's journey?

# Looking West

People went west for different reasons, and at different times. At first, English, Scottish, French, and U.S.-born fur traders went west to trade with Native Americans. Spanish settlers, soldiers, and **missionaries** went west to occupy the land claimed by their country.

Later, people went west to find gold or to work in the cattle or railroad industries. Still others went west for adventure, or to escape **religious persecution**.

Mostly, though, settlers went west to find land. Some were immigrants from faraway countries. Others came from different parts of the United States. Some had been set free from the plantation owners who had enslaved them. Others wanted to leave the industrial cities of the East, which were becoming overcrowded, dirty, and more dangerous. All were in search of better lives.

▲ **Poor living conditions in eastern cities prompted families like this one to go west.**

**In Other Words**

**missionaries** teachers of religion

**religious persecution** being attacked because of their religion

**prompted** caused

# Westward Expansion Time Line

| | |
|---|---|
| 1776 | The U.S. declares independence from Great Britain. |
| 1803 | The U.S. buys Louisiana Territory from France. |
| 1804-1806 | Lewis and Clark explore the West. |
| 1830 | The Indian Removal Act is passed. It legalizes the removal of Native Americans from their land in the East. |
| 1845 | Texas becomes a U.S. state. |
| 1846 | The Oregon Treaty is signed. Parts of Oregon Country become U.S. territory. |
| 1846-1848 | Mexico and the U.S. fight the Mexican War. |
| 1848 | The Treaty of Guadalupe Hidalgo is signed. Mexico gives up California and New Mexico territories to the U.S. Gold is discovered in California. |
| 1861-1865 | The American Civil War is fought. |
| 1862 | The Homestead Act is passed. Government offers free land to settlers. |
| 1869 | The Transcontinental Railroad is completed. |
| 1866-1886 | Cowboys drive cattle from Texas to railroads in the North. |
| 1890 | The U.S. Census announces that the western frontier is officially closed. |

▶ **Before You Move On**

1. **Cause/Effect** What were some things that caused people to move west?
2. **Use Text Features** Study the time line. What statement can you make about when westward **expansion** happened?

# Trails West

In 1837, the United States entered **an economic depression**. People lost their jobs and their savings. Many sold what they could and **headed** west, where they heard the land was fertile and free.

Many followed the Oregon Trail, a route that had been used by fur traders. The trail divided near Salt Lake City and headed north to Portland or south to Sacramento (**via** the California Trail).

Some settlers went even farther south into Mexican Territory. They followed trade routes called the Santa Fe and Old Spanish Trails. Others followed less popular routes, but they all headed west.

## Major U.S. Trails West, 1840s

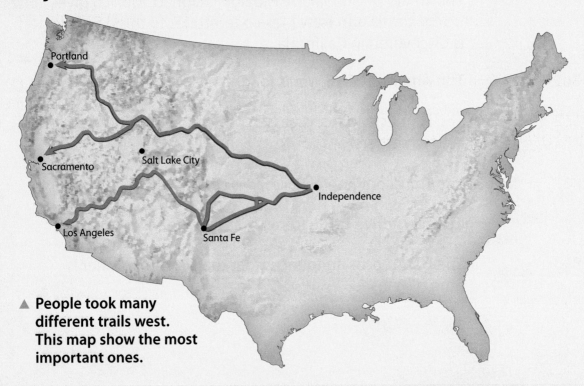

▲ **People took many different trails west. This map show the most important ones.**

**In Other Words**

**an economic depression** a period of time when businesses were losing money

**headed** went

**via** by way of

Usually, settlers didn't go it alone. That would be too dangerous. Instead, they gathered together in groups, called wagon trains. In a wagon train, each family or group shared a wooden wagon containing equipment and supplies. The wagons usually had **canvas** covers and were pulled by oxen or mules. Hundreds of people would gather together with their wagons and head for places like Oregon Country, California, and Texas.

Not everybody made it, though. Some people ran out of supplies before reaching their destination. Many died along the way. Cholera, a disease from the East, was a big killer. Another danger was the weather. Blizzards, **tornadoes**, and extreme temperatures were constant problems. Still, people kept heading west.

Then, in 1862, the Homestead Act was passed. The government offered free land to anyone who would live there for five years. Now there was another reason to pack up and take a trail west.

▲ Advertisements like this one encouraged people to go west.

**In Other Words**
**canvas** strong, heavy cloth
**tornadoes** powerful, twisting winds

▶ **Before You Move On**

1. **Visualize** Imagine you are part of a wagon train traveling across a flat prairie on a hot day. Describe what it looks and feels like.

2. **Explain** What does the idiom "go it alone" mean? How do you know?

# Native Americans in the West

While old movies about "the Wild West" often portrayed Native Americans as all the same, this was far from true. Many different Native American nations lived in the West at this time. Each of them had its own history, language, and customs.

Most Native Americans welcomed the settlers at first. They wanted to trade with the newcomers, and to learn about them.

The settlers kept coming, however. They brought diseases, weapons, and their desire for land. Conflicts increased. In 1830, Congress passed the Indian Removal Act. It was now legal to force tribes to move west. As a result, hundreds of thousands of Native Americans were forced to leave their homes and head to "Indian Territory."

## Native American Removal, 1825-1850

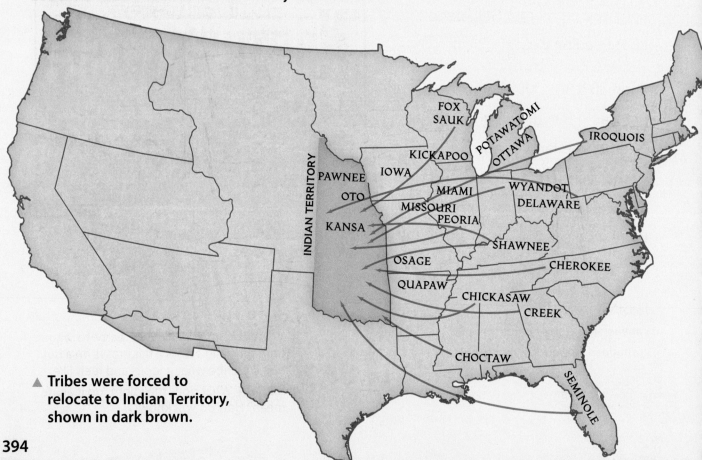

▲ Tribes were forced to relocate to Indian Territory, shown in dark brown.

That was just the beginning. Much more conflict and misunderstanding were to follow. As settlers poured into the land west of the Mississippi, they **claimed it** for themselves.

They began to kill large numbers of buffalo, which many Native American tribes depended on for survival. There were fierce battles, called "Indian Wars." Native Americans fought to save their land. But settlers and government soldiers usually won. By 1890, most Native Americans who had not died in conflicts were moved to **reservations**.

▲ Settlers shot buffalo for their skins and for sport. By the 1880s, only a few hundred bison were left in the United States.

**In Other Words**
**claimed it**  said it was

▶ **Before You Move On**

1. **Use Text Features** According to the map, where were eastern Native American tribes forced to go?
2. **Explain** Why did the relationship between Native Americans and **settlers** change?

# Pushing the Boundaries

In the 1840s, the boundaries of the United States changed again. First, in the Oregon Treaty of 1846, Britain gave up its claim to the Oregon Country, and the northern border of the U.S. was set.

Meanwhile, in the southern plains, settlers were crossing into Texas, which was then part of Mexico. The settlers fought for independence and, in 1837, Texas became independent from Mexico. (It joined the U.S. in 1845.)

Soon, the U.S. and Mexico were at war. When the Mexican War was over in 1848, the Treaty of Guadalupe Hidalgo set the border for Texas at the Rio Grande. The U.S. also got the land known as California and New Mexico. The country had grown once again.

## New Territories, 1783-1853

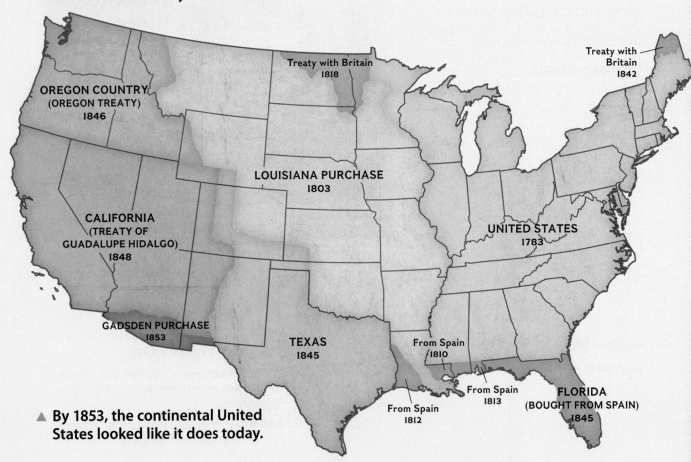

▲ By 1853, the continental United States looked like it does today.

▲ Prospectors look for gold in California.

▲ This photo shows what people believe to be the first piece of gold discovered in 1848. Its actual size is much smaller.

# The Gold Rush

Around the time the Treaty of Guadalupe Hidalgo was being signed, something **remarkable** happened in California. A **carpenter** noticed a shiny rock in a mountain stream. It was gold! Soon, thousands of people were headed to California, hoping to get lucky and "strike it rich."

The biggest **gold rush** was in California, but for many years there were smaller gold and silver rushes in other parts of the West. A few people did find gold and get rich. However, the ones who **benefited** the most from the gold rush were the shopkeepers who provided things the gold seekers needed. They were the lucky ones!

**In Other Words**
**remarkable** amazing; very interesting
**carpenter** woodworker
**benefited** got

▶ **Before You Move On**

1. **Main Idea** What two important events happened in the U.S. in 1848?
2. **Use Text Features** Study the map. When did the U.S. gain more territory, in 1803 or in the 1840s? Explain.

# Work . . .

Work in the West was often difficult. Farming and **ranching** were not easy, especially in the dry western deserts and prairies. Mining wasn't easy, either, and it was very dangerous. Miners were often hurt or killed trying to get gold and silver from deep in the earth.

Some people found work in railroad **construction**. That may have required the hardest work of all. In 1869, the Transcontinental Railroad was completed. It was 3,200 kilometers (2,000 miles) of track that had been laid almost entirely **by hand**. Thousands of workers played a part, including Chinese, Irish, and German immigrants, and people who had once been enslaved.

The farmers, railroad workers, and miners who helped build the West were tough and strong. They often risked their lives for the chance to **make a living**.

**The railroad workers in these photos laid miles of track every day.**

**In Other Words**

**by hand** without the help of complex machines

**make a living** make enough money to support themselves

# . . . and Play

Life was hard for farmers and ranchers, so they needed to find ways to have fun. Difficult tasks were often shared and turned into parties. Building barns, storing hay, and even **husking** corn were chances for people to connect with each other and also have a good time.

Dancing was popular, too. On special nights, people would dress in their best clothes, ride to the church hall, schoolhouse, or a neighbor's barn, and enjoy a community dance. They especially enjoyed a dance called the square dance. In it, four couples came together to form a square. At a square dance, everyone could join in, even the youngest and the oldest among the settlers.

**Settlers enjoyed every chance to gather and socialize.**

**In Other Words**
**husking** peeling

▶ **Before You Move On**

1. **Paraphrase** In your own words, explain why so many **settlers** were willing to risk their lives.
2. **Visualize** What descriptions help you imagine a homesteader party?

# Cowboys and Cattle Drives

Ranching in Texas began long before the settlers arrived. It wasn't until after the Civil War, however, that it really **boomed**. From 1866 to 1886, cowboys herded, or drove, more than 10 million cattle from Texas to the railroads in the North. It seemed that the growing country could not get enough beef.

The success of the cattle drives was the result of the hard work of thousands of cowboys. Most of them were in their late teens or twenties. Many of them were African Americans or Tejanos, Texans of Mexican descent. These brave young men lived exciting lives, and they soon became a symbol of the West.

▲ **A cowboy stops for a photo in 1887.**

▲ **Cowboys drive this herd of Texas cattle to a faraway market or train station.**

**In Other Words**
**boomed** expanded rapidly

## Population of Major U.S. Cities in 1890

▲ By 1890, the West had many large, growing cities.

**Key**
**City Population**

| | |
|---|---|
| ○ 1–10,000 | ● 200,000–500,000 |
| ○ 10,000–50,000 | ● 500,000–1,000,000 |
| ● 50,000–200,000 | ● More than 1,000,000 |

# The End of an Era

The days of the cattle drives didn't last long, however. Railroads now **transported** cattle. They transported people and goods, too.

From 1860 to 1890, the United States population grew from about 31 million people to about 63 million people. Many people living in the West lived in cities that now dotted the land.

In 1890, the **superintendent** of the **U.S. Census** declared the western **frontier** officially closed. The days of the westward movement were over. Still, they would never be forgotten. ❖

**In Other Words**

**transported** moved

**superintendent** president

**U.S. Census** organization that tracks population in the United States

▶ **Before You Move On**

1. **Visualize** How might a railroad transport cattle? Draw a picture showing how you imagine it might look.

2. **Use Text Features** Which western city had a population of more than 200,000 in 1890?

401

## Think and Respond

# Talk About It

**Key Words**

| | |
|---|---|
| construction | gold rush |
| establish | individual |
| expansion | ranching |
| explore | reservation |
| frontier | settler |

1. In the **history article**, what conditions caused people to move west? Why was it easier after 1803?

2. Imagine that you and your family rode across the **frontier** on a wagon train. **Describe** the experience.

   It was _____ . The frontier looked _____ .
   The _____ seemed _____ .

3. Why do you think Lewis and Clark were celebrated as heroes? What did their journey help **establish**?

Learn test-taking strategies.
⊘NGReach.com

# Write About It

You are a **settler** on the American **frontier**. Write a letter to your family back home. Tell them about the challenges you have faced so far. Use **Key Words** in your letter.

July 20, 1841

Dear _____ ,

I have settled in _____ . I am working as a _____ . So far, I have found _____ . The work is _____ .

    Love,

    _____

# Cause and Effect

Use a cause-and-effect organizer to show events that happen and the results of the events in each section of "Westward Bound!" First, read a section and look for a cause. Then think about the effects that happened as a result of the cause.

**Cause-and-Effect Organizer**

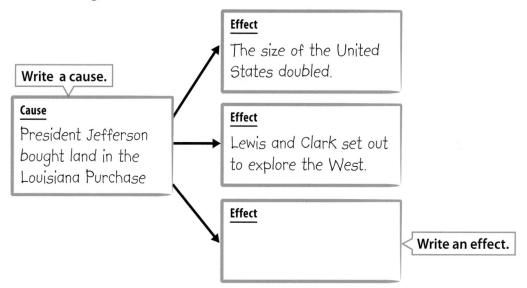

Write a cause.

**Cause**
President Jefferson bought land in the Louisiana Purchase

**Effect**
The size of the United States doubled.

**Effect**
Lewis and Clark set out to explore the West.

**Effect**

Write an effect.

Now tell a partner the causes and their effects in each section of "Westward Bound!" Use your cause-and-effect organizers as you retell the selection in an order that makes sense. Use **Key Words** and be sure that your retelling expresses the author's ideas.

_____ did _____ .
As a result _____ .

# Fluency 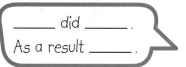 Comprehension Coach

Use the Comprehension Coach to practice reading with intonation. Rate your reading.

 **Talk** **Together**

How do you think **settlers** looked and felt after the long journey to the West? Write a description of one of the settlers. Include details that will help the reader form mental images. Try to use **Key Words** in your description, and share it with the class.

# Homographs

**Homographs** are words that are spelled the same but have different meanings.

Look at the dictionary entry for last .

¹**last** / last / *verb* **1**: to continue to happen *The tennis match lasted more than three hours.* **2**: stay in good shape *This coat will last for two years.* [Middle English, from Old English *læstan* to continue, follow, related, similar to Old English *lāst* footprint, track]

²**last** / last / *adverb* **1**: at the end *I won the race, but my friend came in last.* **2**: most recent *I saw her last in the third grade.*

You can use context, or the words around it, to figure out the correct meaning of a homograph.

**Example:**
The party **lasted** until nine o'clock.

> The words "until nine o'clock" helped me figure out that in this context, "lasted" means "continued to happen."

## Try It Together

Read the sentences. Then answer the questions.

> Some came from the eastern <u>part</u> of the United States. Others came from the South.

1. **What does part mean?**

   **A.** house

   **B.** region

   **C.** pioneer

   **D.** settler

2. **Which words help you figure out the meaning of part?**

   **A.** Others came

   **B.** Some came

   **C.** from the eastern

   **D.** of the United States

**Connect Across Texts** Find out what it's like to be a vaquero.

**Genre** An **essay** is a short piece of nonfiction that **explores** a single topic. Photos often provide information about the topic.

# A Day in the Life of a Vaquero

by **Phyllis Edwards**
photographs by **William Albert Allard**

▲ **William Albert Allard, photographer**

*Long before the era of westward movement began, there were already cowboys, called vaqueros, working in the West. These Native American and **mestizo cow-herders** worked on Spanish ranches throughout North America. When **settlers** with little or no experience began moving west in the 1800s, the vaqueros they met taught them valuable **ranching** skills.*

*Life for vaqueros has changed a lot since the 1800s. Still, some things remain the same. Learn how one young vaquero keeps the tradition alive.*

**In Other Words**

***mestizo* cow-herders** people from mixed Spanish and Native American backgrounds who worked with cows

▶ **Before You Move On**

1. **Cause/Effect** How did the vaqueros help the **settlers**?

2. **Author's Purpose** Based on the title and the introduction, what do you think is the author's reason for writing this essay?

A young vaquero opens his eyes to a wide Mexican sky. A chill breeze brings the smell of coffee to his nose. A crackling fire warms one side of his body. He stretches his legs under his thin **serape** and feels the pull of tired muscles. *What kind of a dream is this?* he wonders.

Then he remembers. This is not a dream. He is a real vaquero. He is living the life he always wanted, **herding *vacas*** and sleeping **under the stars**.

**In Other Words**
**serape** wool jacket
**herding *vacas*** moving around large groups of cows
**under the stars** outside

The young vaquero remembers the first time his **papá** put him on a horse. He was just five years old. He knew even then that he wanted to be just like his papá. The **open range** was his papá's idea of freedom. So it was for his papá's father and grandfather. No walls stood between them and the fresh air. No buildings kept them from moving freely across the land.

**In Other Words**
**papá** father (in Spanish)
**open range** grassy wild land

▶ **Before You Move On**

1. **Visualize** What sensory details does the author use? How do they help you understand a vaquero's daily life?

2. **Cause/Effect** Why does the young vaquero choose to work on the open range?

The horses begin to **stir** in the **corral** nearby. These horses mean more to vaqueros than transportation. They also provide companionship on long, lonely rides. Soon, there are several men moving toward the corral. Vaqueros often feed their horses before they eat their own breakfasts.

The young vaquero jumps to his feet. Today he will choose his own **string** of horses from the *remuda*. This is an important decision because only he will work with his horses. He will get to know them better and better each day in the months ahead.

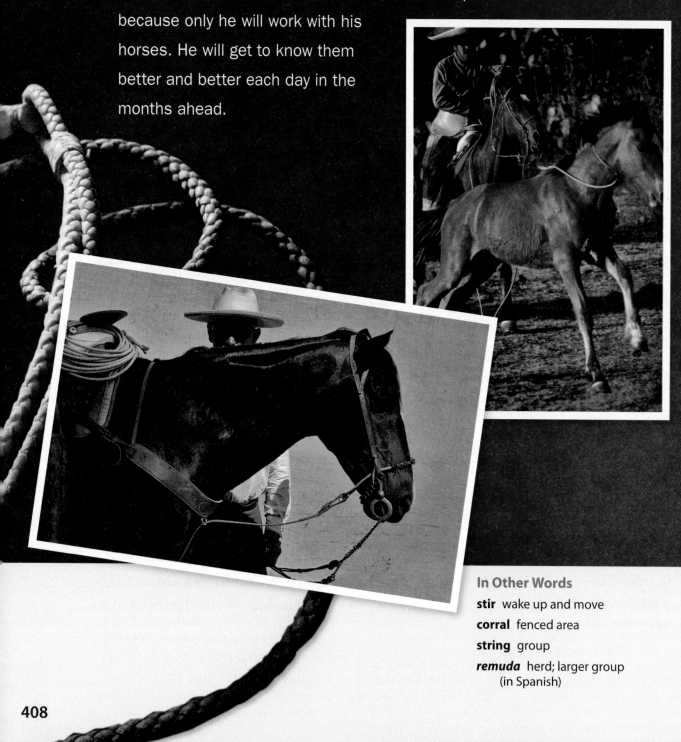

Now that the young vaquero has chosen his horses, he is ready for the spring *rodear*, or round-up. Cows from neighboring ranches have mixed together out on the open range. Many calves have been born, too. The vaqueros must figure out which animals belong to each ranch.

The young vaquero checks the equipment he needs to do his job. He pulls on his rope to test its strength. Some of his rope he made himself. For hours he cut stiff **cowhide** into long strips and **wove** them together, just as his papá taught him. Then he checks his **saddle**. It is **sturdy** and comfortable. So he and his horse will be able to work long hours.

**In Other Words**
**cowhide** dried cow skin
**wove** twisted; braided
**saddle** seat for riding on his horse
**sturdy** strong

▶ **Before You Move On**
1. **Main Idea** Why are horses important to vaqueros?
2. **Details** Why is a comfortable saddle important for the vaquero?

The young vaquero's job today is to help round up the cows. He uses his *lariat* to separate a calf from the herd so it can be marked with the ranch **brand**. The brand helps the ranchers keep track of how many cattle they own.

The vaquero's ***sombrero*** shades him from the sun. His bandanna protects his mouth and nose from dust. His serape keeps him warm in cold weather. His leather ***chaparajos*** and ***tapaderas*** protect his legs and feet from thorny plants.

**In Other Words**

***lariat*** lasso; rope (in Spanish)

**brand** mark that shows who owns the calf

***sombrero*** hat with a wide edge (in Spanish)

***chaparajos*** and ***tapaderas*** leg and foot coverings (in Spanish)

During the summer, the vaqueros will get the cattle ready for market. They will help the animals find good grass to eat. They will get cuts and bruises leading the animals out of dangerous bushes, and will ride for hours to find lost cows.

The young vaquero looks forward to the days ahead. But now, as **darkness falls** he thinks only of resting around the campfire with the other vaqueros. With their families far away, the camp is their home. Together, they sing songs, tell jokes, and share their love of the open range. ❖

◀ Small guitars like this one are easy to transport. They provide the vaqueros with music and cheer at the end of a long day on the range.

**In Other Words**
**darkness falls** the sunlight goes away

▶ **Before You Move On**

1. **Visualize** What details help you imagine a vaquero's life each night after work?
2. **Author's Purpose** How well does the author describe a day in the life of a vaquero? Give reasons for your answer.

**Key Words**

| | |
|---|---|
| construction | gold rush |
| establish | individual |
| expansion | ranching |
| explore | reservation |
| frontier | settler |

# Compare Author's Purpose

You read about people who settled the West, and about *vaqueros* who work in the West. Think about each author's main purpose, or reason, for writing each selection. Work with a partner to evaluate how well each author's purpose was achieved.

**Author's Purpose Chart**

| | "A Day in the Life of a *Vaquero*" | "Westward Bound!" |
|---|---|---|
| **What was the author's main purpose?** **Choose one:** <br> • give information or explain <br> • persuade readers <br> • entertain, describe, or express personal feelings <br> • tell how to do something | | |
| **How do you know?** Give examples. | | |

**Talk Together**

What does it take to settle a new land? Think about the selections and the chart above. How do they help you understand the role that **individuals** play in settling a new land? Use **Key Words** and your own words to discuss your ideas.

412

# Pronoun Agreement

When you replace nouns with pronouns, be sure they agree in gender and number. Gender means male or female.

## Grammar Rules Pronoun Agreement

| Gender | One | More Than One |
|---|---|---|
| • For **yourself** (boy or girl), use<br><br>• For **another person,** use | **I** or **me**<br><br>**you** | **we** or **us**<br><br>**you** |
| • For a **boy** or a **man,** use | **he** or **him** | **they** or **them** |
| • For a **girl** or a **woman,** use | **she** or **her** | **they** or **them** |
| • For a **thing,** use | **it** | **they** or **them** |
| • When you talk about a person twice in a sentence, use these pairs | **I, myself**<br>**you, yourself**<br>**he, himself**<br>**her, herself** | **we, ourselves,**<br>**you, yourselves,**<br>**they, themselves** |

## Read Pronouns

Read the passage about *vaqueros*. Talk to a partner about the pronouns you find. How do they agree in number and gender?

> The young *vaquero* remembers the first time his papá put him on a horse. It was huge, but he was not afraid. He was just five years old. He knew even then that he wanted to be just like his papá. They loved the open range.

## Write Pronouns That Agree

Write three sentences about one of the photos on pages 408–409. Use at least two pronouns. Be sure the pronouns agree. Compare your sentences with a partner's sentences.

413

# Express Opinions

Listen to Cristina and Mollie's dialogue. Then use **Language Frames** to express your own opinions.

# Saying Good-bye

**Dialogue** (((MP3)))

> Mollie, I have great news. My family has inherited some land in Alaska. We are going to move there!

> That is so far away. I feel sad to think of your moving.

> I think it will be an amazing place to live. But I will miss you and all my friends.

> In my opinion, it will be an adventure. I know! I'll throw you a going-away party!

**Key Words**

boomtown

claim

ghost town

investor

limited resources

mining

# Key Words

During the California gold rush, many towns grew quickly. Read on to find out why this happened. Use **Key Words** and other words to talk about gold rush towns.

**1.**

prospector

**Mining** is hard work, but a prospector is lucky! He finds gold on his **claim**, or the land he calls his own.

**2.**

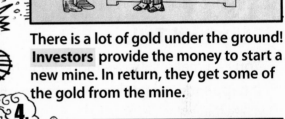

investor

There is a lot of gold under the ground! **Investors** provide the money to start a new mine. In return, they get some of the gold from the mine.

**3.**

People hear about the new gold mine, and a gold rush begins. Many people move to the town, and it quickly grows into a **boomtown**.

**4.**

The mine has **limited resources**. After a while, the gold runs out. People move away from the town. In time, the town becomes an old, empty **ghost town**.

**Talk Together**

How much money do you need to settle a new land? With a partner, use **Key Words** and **Language Frames** from page 414 to express your opinions.

# Cause and Effect

When you describe why something happens, you tell the **cause**. The cause can trigger an **effect**, or something to happen. That effect can then trigger another effect. Connecting causes and effects helps you understand what you read, see, and hear.

Look at the pictures. Think about the cause and the effects.

## Map and Talk

You can make a cause-and-effect chain to show what happened and why it happened. Here's how you make one.

**Cause-and-Effect Chain**

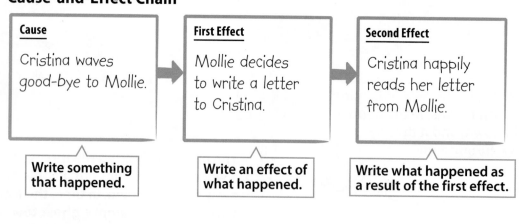

| **Cause** | **First Effect** | **Second Effect** |
|---|---|---|
| Cristina waves good-bye to Mollie. | Mollie decides to write a letter to Cristina. | Cristina happily reads her letter from Mollie. |
| Write something that happened. | Write an effect of what happened. | Write what happened as a result of the first effect. |

**Talk Together**

Tell a partner about a time when a friend or relative moved away. Your partner can make a cause-and-effect chain to show what happened because of the move.

416

# More Key Words

Use these words to talk about *The Road to Rhyolite* and "Rhyolite: The True Story of a Ghost Town."

### development
(di-**ve**-lup-munt) *noun*

**Development** is growth and progress. This is a new **development** in technology.

### discovery
(dis-**ku**-vu-rē) *noun*

A **discovery** is something new that someone finds. This leopard is a new **discovery**.

### economy
(i-**ko**-nu-mē) *noun*

A country's **economy** is its system of business. In a good **economy** people spend more.

### population
(po-**pyu**-lā-shun) *noun*

A **population** is the number of people living in an area. This city's **population** is large.

### speculate
(**spe**-kyu-lāt) *verb*

When you **speculate**, you make a guess. They **speculate** that people will buy lemonade.

## Talk Together

Make a Study Card for each **Key Word**. Then compare your cards with a partner's.

> discovery
>
> **What it Means:** finding something
>
> **Example:** finding gold in California
>
> **Not an example:** eating an apple

**Add words to My Vocabulary Notebook**

NGReach.com

# Learn to Visualize

Look at the photo. Visualize, or create pictures in your mind, about the people. How do you think they feel?

When you read, the words can help you **visualize**, too. Visualizing can help you identify your feelings, or emotional responses, to the text.

## How to Visualize

 **1.** Look for details. Find words that tell how people and places look, sound, smell, taste, and feel.

I read _____ .

 **2.** Use the details to picture the people and places in your mind.

I picture _____ .

 **3.** Tell how the picture makes you feel. How does it help you become more involved in the text?

I feel _____ .

**Talk Together**

Read Cristina's personal narrative. Read the sample visualization. Then use **Language Frames** to tell a partner about the visualizations you make.

Personal Narrative

# Alaska Adventure

My family's new home in Alaska was very different from the city where we lived before. There was a town nearby with a small **population**, but our land was quiet and peaceful. We moved there last summer. It had a big meadow full of flowers, and the air smelled clean and fresh. We could see tall mountains. My sister and I splashed in the cold stream and ran in the meadow. We loved it!

One day we woke up to hear a loud noise. It sounded like there was a highway outside our door! We made a terrible **discovery**. Builders were putting up several new houses right next to us! We could hardly believe it.

My parents **speculated** about how this new **development** would affect the town's population, given the growing **economy** in this town. The next night, it started to rain. It got colder and colder, and suddenly it was snowing!

"No more peace and quiet, and snow in August!" my father said. "That does it. We are going home!"

"I read that there is a meadow with flowers, the air smells fresh, and two girls are playing.

I picture a beautiful, clean place with nature and laughter.

I feel happy."

◀ = a good place to stop and visualize

**419**

# Read a Play

## Genre

A **play** is a story that is written for actors to perform.

## Elements of Drama

The parts of a play are called **acts** and **scenes**. They divide the play, and often have different settings. **Stage directions** can tell the characters how to talk, act, or move. The words characters say are called **dialogue**.

act and scene number >

**ACT I: SCENE I**

[**SETTING** *The play takes place in the Mojave (Mō-ha-vē) Desert in southern Nevada. Offstage:*

stage directions >

*a coyote howls. Enter* DUSTY COYOTE. *He looks like an ordinary person except for a bushy tail and ears. He walks to the front of the stage.*]

dialogue >

**COYOTE** [*to audience*]: My name is Dusty Coyote and I'm here to tell you the story of a town in the Mojave Desert of Nevada.

[COYOTE *walks slowly to a large rock and sits.*]

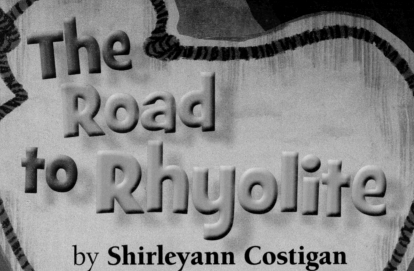

# The Road to Rhyolite

by **Shirleyann Costigan**
illustrated by **C.B. Canga**

## Characters

**DUSTY COYOTE**, narrator

**SHORTY HARRIS**, prospector

**EDDIE CROSS**, prospector

**JOHN DOYLE**, miner

**DYNAMITE MARY**, miner

**HARRY GISH**, miner

**TERRI YANG**, miner

**THIRSTY MINER**

**INVESTOR**

**TOWNSPEOPLE**

**MR. YOUNG**, barber

**MRS. YOUNG**, housewife

**WALTER**, son of Mr. and Mrs. Young

**KATE**, daughter of Mr. and Mrs. Young

**AGNES SEARS**, hotelkeeper

**NEWSBOY**

**TRAIN CONDUCTOR**

Comprehension Coach

## ACT I: SCENE I

[**SETTING** *The play takes place in the Mojave (Mō-ha-vē) Desert in southern Nevada. Offstage: a coyote howls. Enter DUSTY COYOTE. He looks like an ordinary person except for a bushy tail and ears. He walks to the front of the stage.*]

**COYOTE** [*to audience*]: My name is Dusty Coyote and I'm here to tell you the story of a town in the Mojave Desert of Nevada.

[COYOTE *walks slowly to a large rock and sits.*]

**COYOTE**: The Mojave has been here for thousands of years, and not much has changed. But in 1904, two **prospectors** came here. The desert began to change—for a while.

[*Curtain or lights go up on* SHORTY HARRIS *and* EDDIE CROSS. SHORTY *is kneeling. He is showing* EDDIE *a large lump of* **quartz veined with** *gold.*]

**SHORTY** [*in a* **stage whisper** *and looking around to make sure no one is listening*]: It's gold, Ed! It's the biggest **lode** I've ever seen and I found it here near Bullfrog Mountain!

**EDDIE** [*stage whisper*]: Wow! Look at that gold!

**In Other Words**
**prospectors** people searching for gold
*quartz veined with* rock with lines of
*stage whisper* whisper that the audience can hear
**lode** gold deposit

[*Miners* JOHN DOYLE, DYNAMITE MARY, HARRY GISH, *and* TERRI YANG *rush on stage.*]

**DOYLE** [*excited*]: Did someone say, "Gold"?

**MARY** [*pointing at the gold in* SHORTY'S *hands*]: Gold! Gold!
   **By golly**, there's gold!

**GISH** [*doing a little dance*]: Go-o-o-old!

**YANG** [*leaping*]: Follow those men. We're going to be rich!

[*The four miners run after* SHORTY *and* EDDIE. *All exit.*]

**COYOTE** [*to audience*]: And that's how it began.

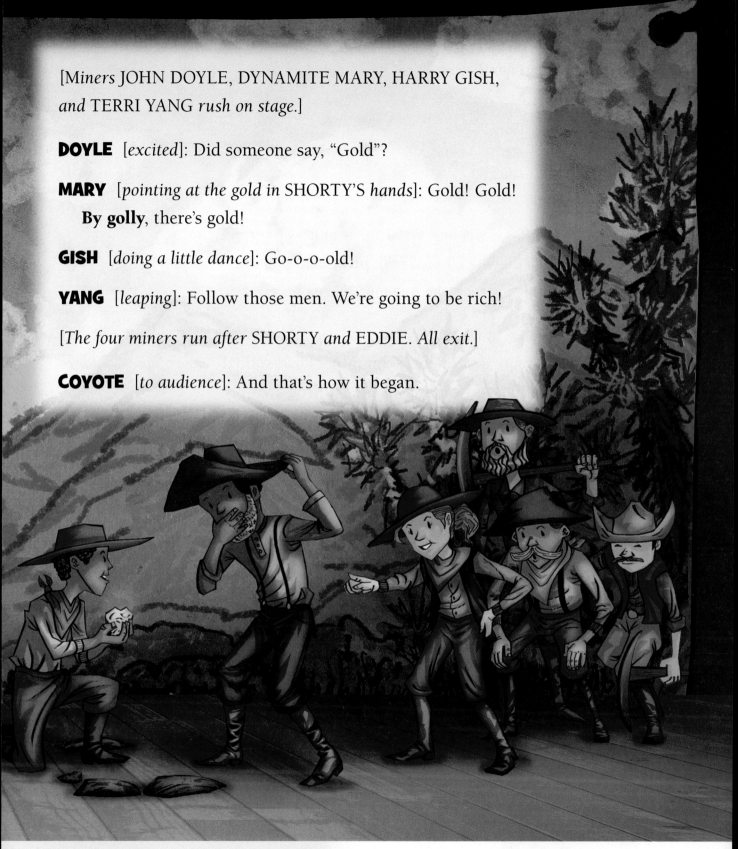

**In Other Words**
**By golly** For sure (slang)

► **Before You Move On**

1. **Drama** What **discovery** is made in Act 1: Scene 1?

2. **Visualize** What does each miner do to show excitement?

▶ **Predict**
What kinds of people do you think
will come to the desert next?

**ACT I: SCENE 2**

[*Enter* DOYLE, MARY, GISH *and* YANG. *The miners* **pantomime**
*setting dynamite and digging for gold with* **pickaxes**. *Offstage:*
*sounds of pickaxes hitting rock and dynamite blasts.*]

**COYOTE**: Before long, more miners came to dig and dynamite
the rock—then more, and more. Soon miners had staked
more than two thousand **claims** in the Bullfrog area,
even though the land was harsh, the nights were
freezing, the summers were **intolerably** hot . . .

**In Other Words**
◀ **mine shaft** opening to a mine
**pantomime** pretend they are
**pickaxes** sharp digging tools
**intolerably** much too

424

[*Enter* THIRSTY MINER, ***staggering and clutching*** *his throat.*
*The other miners ignore him.*]

**THIRSTY MINER** [*hoarsely*]: Water! . . .Water! . . .

**COYOTE**: . . . and very, very dry.

[*Exit* THIRSTY MINER.]

**COYOTE**: Well, in a year or so, the ground was covered with campsites and mining shafts, but the work was hard and slow.

**In Other Words**

***staggering and clutching***  walking unsteadily and holding

***hoarsely***  in a rough voice

**COYOTE**: Then came the rich **investors** who offered to **finance** the mines and share in the miner's **profits**.

[*Enter MARY and YANG. They begin setting up dynamite. Enter GISH and DOYLE, talking.*]

**GISH**: I tell you, Doyle, if we had a rock crusher we could dig twice as much **ore**.

**DOYLE**: We need someone rich to invest in our mine, but where would we find someone like that?

[*Enter INVESTOR carrying a long piece of paper.*]

**INVESTOR**: Right here, my friends. And here's **the deal**. I'll buy better equipment to help you dig and process more ore—and you give me 50 percent of all the gold you dig out of the ground.

**In Other Words**
**finance** pay for
**profits** money
**ore** rock that has gold in it
**the deal** how it will work

426

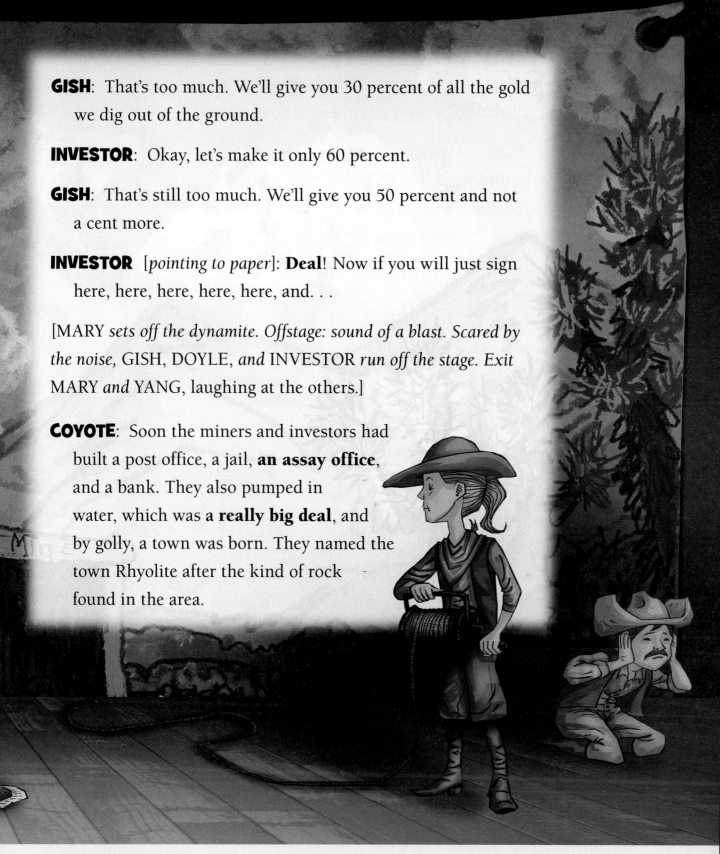

**GISH**: That's too much. We'll give you 30 percent of all the gold we dig out of the ground.

**INVESTOR**: Okay, let's make it only 60 percent.

**GISH**: That's still too much. We'll give you 50 percent and not a cent more.

**INVESTOR** [*pointing to paper*]: **Deal**! Now if you will just sign here, here, here, here, here, and. . .

[MARY *sets off the dynamite. Offstage: sound of a blast. Scared by the noise,* GISH, DOYLE, *and* INVESTOR *run off the stage. Exit* MARY *and* YANG, *laughing at the others.*]

**COYOTE**: Soon the miners and investors had built a post office, a jail, **an assay office**, and a bank. They also pumped in water, which was **a really big deal**, and by golly, a town was born. They named the town Rhyolite after the kind of rock found in the area.

**In Other Words**
**Deal!** I agree!
**an assay office** a place to test and weigh gold
**a really big deal** very important

**COYOTE**: During the following years, more people came to work in town and make money: doctors, bankers, schoolteachers, hotelkeepers . . .

[*Enter, in a line across the stage, TOWNSPEOPLE carrying suitcases and* **articles** *related to their* **occupations**. *As they walk, they talk excitedly about their new town. All exit.*]

**COYOTE**: . . . and whole families.

[*Enter YOUNG family: MR. YOUNG, his wife, MRS. YOUNG, and his two children KATE and WALTER. WALTER is holding a snake.*]

**MRS. YOUNG** [*to* WALTER]: Drop that snake, child. That's **no proper** pet!

**WALTER**: Ah, Ma-a-a!

**KATE** [*fussily*]: I'm hot! Are we there yet?

**MR. YOUNG** [*to* DUSTY COYOTE]: Hey! Is this the road to Rhyolite?

**COYOTE**: Yep, it's right around that hill.

**In Other Words**
***articles*** objects
***occupations*** jobs
**no proper** not a good
***fussily*** impatiently

**WALTER** [*pointing at* DUSTY COYOTE]: Ma, that person has a tail.

**MRS. YOUNG**: Don't point, Walter. It's not polite to point.

[*Exit* YOUNG *family.*]

**COYOTE**: People just kept coming **'cus** there was gold to find and money to be made in Rhyolite—and the town grew.

[*Offstage: sound of a dynamite blast. Exit* COYOTE.]

**In Other Words**
**'cus** because

▶ **Before You Move On**

1. **Drama** What do the stage directions help you understand about each member of the Young family?

2. **Visualize** What do you picture in this scene that makes you laugh?

▶ **Predict**
Will Rhyolite become
a **boomtown**?

## ACT 2: SCENE I

[*Enter* TOWNSPEOPLE. *Each uses an article representing his or her occupation to pantomime the occupation. Enter* AGNES SEARS.]

**AGNES** [*to audience*]: Hi, there! Welcome to Rhyolite, Nevada! I'm Agnes Sears, the keeper of that hotel right down the street.

**TOWNSPEOPLE** [*waving hello*]: Hi, Agnes!

[AGNES *turns and waves back.*]

**AGNES** [*to audience with* **enthusiasm**]: You are going to love Rhyolite. It is only three years old, but has everything a town needs, from **an opera house** to a swimming pool. It has lots of restaurants, a school, a hospital, a **telephone and telegraph** office, stores and shops, and three newspapers!

[*Enter* NEWSBOY.]

**NEWSBOY**: **Extra! Extra!** Earthquake destroys San Francisco!

[TOWNSPEOPLE *rush to buy the newspaper.*]

**In Other Words**
**enthusiasm** excitement
**an opera house** a theater for music shows
**telephone and telegraph** communications
**Extra! Extra!** Special news issue!

**AGNES** [*ignoring the news*]: And they also built two railroads that run right through the town!

[*Offstage: sound of a train whistle. Enter* TRAIN CONDUCTOR.]

**TRAIN CONDUCTOR**: All aboard for Las Vegas!

**AGNES**: Forget Las Vegas. That town will never **amount to anything**! But this town has gold! The miners find more every day. And they spend it all right here in Rhyolite! Here come some miners now!

[*Exit* NEWSBOY *and* **agitated** TOWNSPEOPLE.]

**In Other Words**
**amount to anything** be important
*agitated* worried; upset

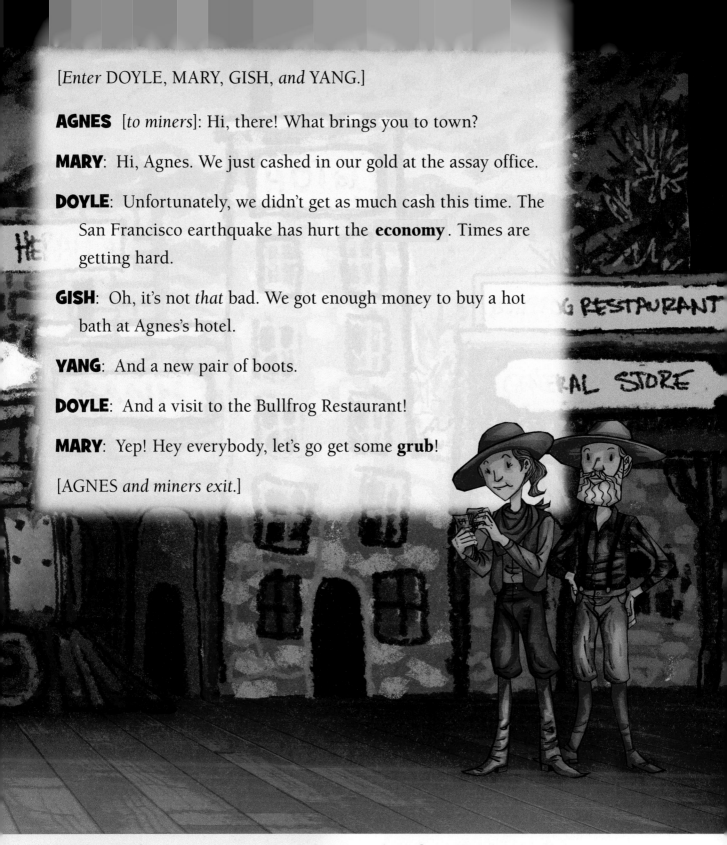

[*Enter* DOYLE, MARY, GISH, *and* YANG.]

**AGNES** [*to miners*]: Hi, there! What brings you to town?

**MARY**: Hi, Agnes. We just cashed in our gold at the assay office.

**DOYLE**: Unfortunately, we didn't get as much cash this time. The San Francisco earthquake has hurt the **economy**. Times are getting hard.

**GISH**: Oh, it's not *that* bad. We got enough money to buy a hot bath at Agnes's hotel.

**YANG**: And a new pair of boots.

**DOYLE**: And a visit to the Bullfrog Restaurant!

**MARY**: Yep! Hey everybody, let's go get some **grub**!

[AGNES *and miners exit.*]

**In Other Words**
**grub** food (slang)

▶ **Before You Move On**

1. **Summarize** In the first part of this scene, is Rhyolite a **boomtown** or a **ghost town**? How do you know?

2. **Cause/Effect** How does the San Francisco earthquake affect the price of gold?

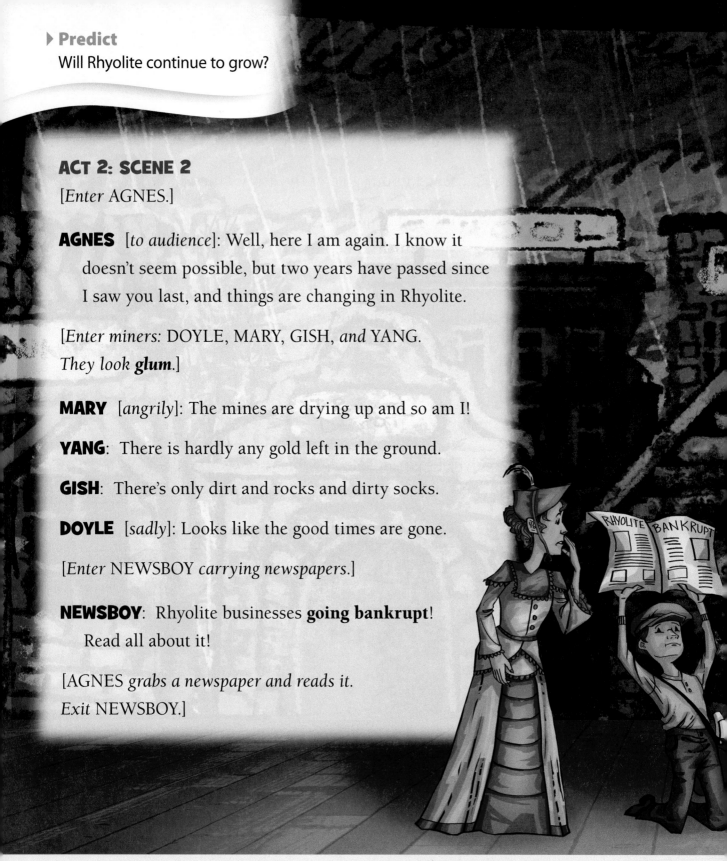

▶ **Predict**
Will Rhyolite continue to grow?

## ACT 2: SCENE 2

[*Enter* AGNES.]

**AGNES** [*to audience*]: Well, here I am again. I know it doesn't seem possible, but two years have passed since I saw you last, and things are changing in Rhyolite.

[*Enter miners:* DOYLE, MARY, GISH, *and* YANG. *They look* **glum**.]

**MARY** [*angrily*]: The mines are drying up and so am I!

**YANG**: There is hardly any gold left in the ground.

**GISH**: There's only dirt and rocks and dirty socks.

**DOYLE** [*sadly*]: Looks like the good times are gone.

[*Enter* NEWSBOY *carrying newspapers.*]

**NEWSBOY**: Rhyolite businesses **going bankrupt**! Read all about it!

[AGNES *grabs a newspaper and reads it. Exit* NEWSBOY.]

**In Other Words**
**glum** unhappy
**going bankrupt** running out of money

**AGNES** [*dismayed*]: This can't be happening!

[*Enter* INVESTOR.]

**INVESTOR**: Oh, it *is* happening, Agnes. The miners are leaving, and I can't invest in Rhyolite's industry anymore. Business is so bad the townspeople are leaving, and I am, too.

[*Exit* INVESTOR. *Enter, in a line across the stage,* TOWNSPEOPLE *carrying suitcases and articles related to their occupations. As they walk, they sigh, groan, and talk sadly about their lost town. All exit. Enter* SHORTY *and* EDDIE.]

**SHORTY and EDDIE** [*to* AGNES]: Are you coming?

**AGNES** [*hesitantly*]: I . . . I . . . well, I suppose I am.

[*Exit* AGNES, SHORTY, *and* EDDIE.]

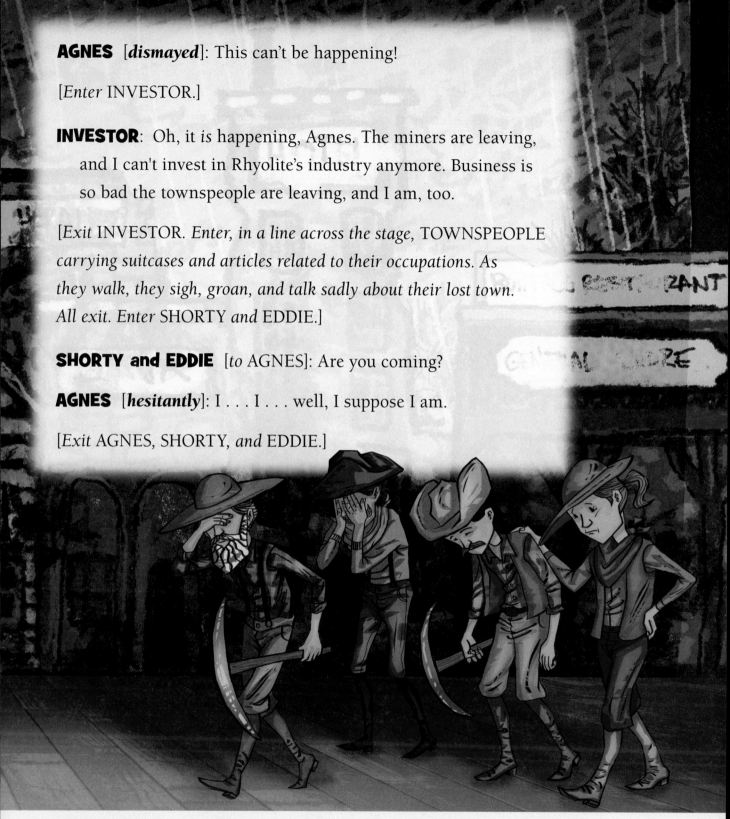

**In Other Words**
***dismayed***  very worried
***hesitantly***  in a slow, uncertain way

[*Enter* DUSTY COYOTE.]

**COYOTE** [*to audience*]: By 1919, the town of Rhyolite was no more. Oh yes, a few **tumbledown** buildings remained, but the people were gone. Since then, just tourists come to look, but they never stay. Only desert winds, like voices in the night, whisper among the ruins.

[*Exit* DUSTY COYOTE. *Offstage: sounds of far away, ghostly voices.* ***Voices overlap.***]

**SHORTY**: I tell you Ed, it's gold!

**YANG**: We're all going to be rich!

**MR. YOUNG**: Is this the road to Rhyolite?

**DOYLE**: It's gone now, all gone.

[*Offstage:* COYOTE *howls.*] ❖

**In Other Words**

**tumbledown** falling down

***Voices overlap.*** The characters speak at about the same time.

▶ **Before You Move On**

1. **Confirm Prediction** How does Rhyolite change, and why?

2. **Drama** Why do you think the author repeats dialogue from earlier in the play at the end of the play, in a ghostly voice?

## Meet the Author of the Original "Rhyolite"

# Diane Siebert

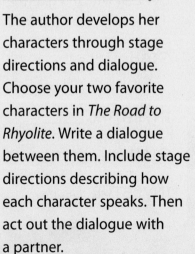

*The Road to Rhyolite* is based on a poem by Diane Siebert. The title of the poem is "Rhyolite: The True Story of a Ghost Town." That poem begins on page 441.

Diane Siebert got the idea for her poem when she took a motorcycle trip across the United States. The trip was supposed to take one summer. Instead, it lasted ten years! One of the places she visited was Rhyolite, which is now a famous Nevada ghost town.

**Diane Siebert visited the real Rhyolite, Nevada, which is now a ghost town.** ▼

## Writer's Craft ✏

The author develops her characters through stage directions and dialogue. Choose your two favorite characters in *The Road to Rhyolite*. Write a dialogue between them. Include stage directions describing how each character speaks. Then act out the dialogue with a partner.

# Talk About It

1. How does the **play** format affect the way the story of this **boomtown** is told?

2. Based on how Rhyolite and the Gold Rush are portrayed in the play, do you think people were smart to rush there? Why or why not?

   I think _____ . In my opinion, _____ .

3. Why do you think the author of *The Road to Rhyolite* chose a coyote as the narrator?

Learn test-taking strategies.
NGReach.com

# Write About It

Reread the conversation between the **investor** and **Gish** on pages 426–427. Rewrite their conversation so that **Gish** ends up getting the better deal.

INVESTOR: You give me 50 percent of all the gold.

GISH: That's too much. We'll give you _____ .

INVESTOR: _____ .

GISH: _____ .

INVESTOR: Deal!

# Cause and Effect

Use cause-and-effect chains to show what happened in Act 1 and Act 2 of *The Road to Rhyolite*.

**Cause-and-Effect Chain**

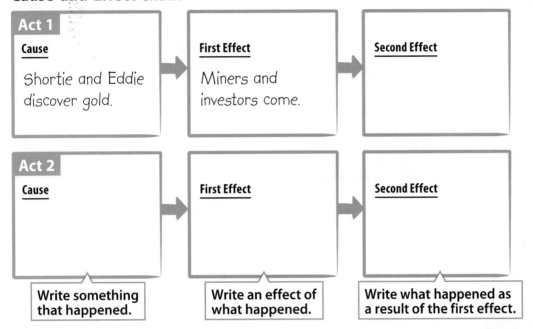

**Act 1**

**Cause**

Shortie and Eddie discover gold.

**First Effect**

Miners and investors come.

**Second Effect**

**Act 2**

**Cause**

**First Effect**

**Second Effect**

Write something that happened.

Write an effect of what happened.

Write what happened as a result of the first effect.

Talk to a partner. Use your cause-and-effect chains as you retell the selection in an order that makes sense. Use **Key Words** and your own words in your retelling. Be sure that it is correct and states the author's meaning.

_____ did _____ .
So _____ . As a result of this, _____ .

# Fluency 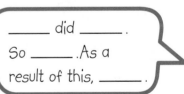 Comprehension Coach

Use the Comprehension Coach to practice reading with expression. Rate your reading.

**Talk Together**

Think about how you would feel if you found something valuable in your own backyard. Draw a picture to show how you would feel. Write a sentence about your feeling. Use **Key Words** as labels. Share your picture with the class.

# Compound Words

**Compound words** are made up of two or more smaller words. Look around your *classroom*. You'll probably see a *textbook* and a *keyboard*. There are three types of compound words: closed (*boomtown*) open (*gold rush*) and hyphenated (*brand-new*).

Here's how you can figure out the meaning of a compound word. Look for smaller words inside the long word. Think about the meaning of each part.

railroad  ➔  rail  +  road      rail + road = "road made of rails"

If you can't tell the meaning from the smaller words, then use your experience and context clues to figure out what the compound word means.

boomtown  ➔  boom + town  ≠  "a loud, noisy town"
boomtown  ➔  boom + town  =   "a town whose population and
                                      economy are growing quickly"

**Try It Together**

Break the following closed compound words into parts to figure out their meanings.

1. **farmhouse**
   A. a barn
   B. a type of farm
   C. a house on a farm
   D. a house that's a farm

2. **cowboy**
   A. a farmer
   B. a male cow
   C. a type of cow
   D. a man who takes care of cattle

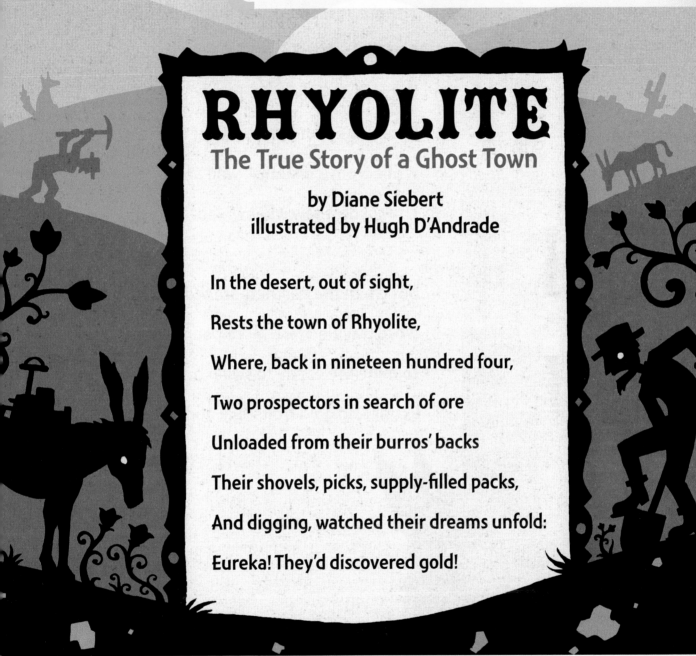

# RHYOLITE
## The True Story of a Ghost Town

### by Diane Siebert
### illustrated by Hugh D'Andrade

In the desert, out of sight,

Rests the town of Rhyolite,

Where, back in nineteen hundred four,

Two prospectors in search of ore

Unloaded from their burros' backs

Their shovels, picks, supply-filled packs,

And digging, watched their dreams unfold:

Eureka! They'd discovered gold!

**In Other Words**
**Eureka!** They found it!

▶ **Before You Move On**
1. **Poetry** How does the poet use rhyme in the last two lines on this page? What is its effect?
2. **Make Inferences** Why do you think the prospectors were travelling with burros?

They danced for joy, they laughed and yelled,

Amazed at what the desert held;

The ore, it seemed, was everywhere!

So, filled with hope, this lucky pair

Decided on a piece of ground

Where they could mine what they had found,

While from a distance, wild and free,

The coyotes saw what coyotes see.

But when the partners staked their claim,

Word traveled fast. More people came

To mine the earth, to sweat and toil,

Extracting gold from rock and soil....

**In Other Words**

**staked their claim**  announced
    this piece of ground was theirs
**toil**  work hard
**Extracting**  Taking the

442

Investors watched this booming town

And shrewdly laid their money down,

Financing projects, funding schemes

Of those whose hearts were heaped with dreams.

And oh! The people's dreams were grand!

For as they gazed upon the land

They mapped and measured, taking stock

Of wealth beneath volcanic rock.

The rock was known as "rhyolite."


So, with its future looking bright,

The town was named, and as it grew,

The people made their dreams come true. . . .

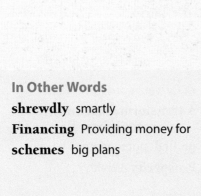

**In Other Words**

**shrewdly** smartly

**Financing** Providing money for

**schemes** big plans

▶ **Before You Move On**

1. **Analyze** What scene in the play *The Road to Rhyolite* does this part of the poem remind you of? Explain.

2. **Poetry** What word did the poet choose to rhyme with the word *rhyolite*? Why?

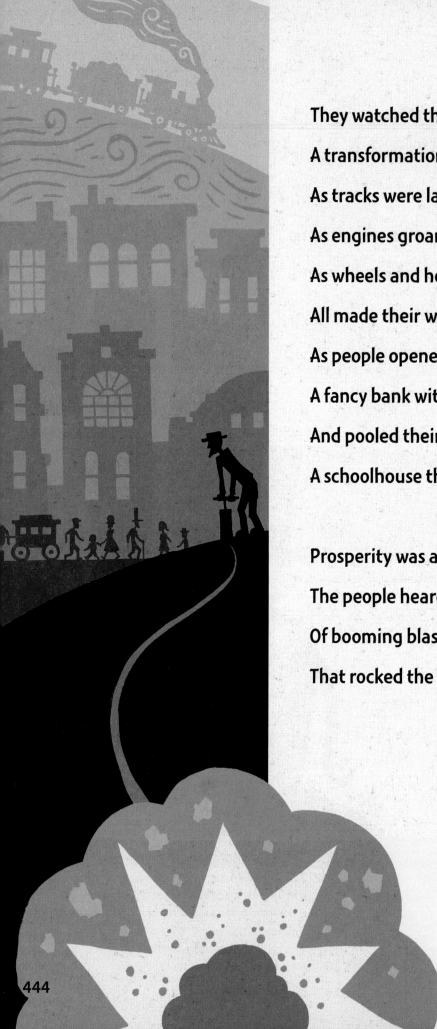

They watched the town expand each day,

A transformation under way

As tracks were laid and trains rolled through;

As engines groaned and whistles blew;

As wheels and hooves and human feet

All made their way down Golden Street;

As people opened shops and stores,

A fancy bank with marble floors,

And pooled their skills and funds to build

A schoolhouse that was quickly filled. . . .

Prosperity was all around;

The people heard it in the sound

Of booming blasts of dynamite

That rocked the town of Rhyolite. . . .

**In Other Words**
**A transformation under way**
    A change happening
**pooled**  put together
**Prosperity**  Wealth

Yes, times were as good as they could get.

The town was full of life, and yet

Financial woes that plagued the West

Soon put the boomtown to the test.

Investors, far away, backed out,

Their actions based on fear and doubt;

And, one by one, the mines shut down—

A costly blow that stunned the town.

The news was carried by the wind;

The ever clever coyotes grinned.

The streetlights dimmed in nineteen ten

To never come back on again. . . .

**In Other Words**

**Financial woes that plagued** Money problems
    that affected many towns in

**backed out** took their money away

▶ **Before You Move On**

1. **Cause/Effect** What caused Rhyolite's
   mines to shut down?

2. **Compare/Contrast** Compare how the
   townspeople are portrayed here with how
   they are portrayed in Act 2 of the play.

A town undone, its lifeblood drained,

For years a stubborn few remained,

Tenacious, hanging by a thread,

Their dreams, by nineteen nineteen, dead.


And when the air had finally cleared

And every soul had disappeared,

This mining town of boom and bust

Lay lifeless in the desert dust.


And where it stood, sunbaked and blown

Its walls of wood and brick and stone

Now crumble as the wind and sun

Keep doing what they've always done. . . .

**In Other Words**

**Tenacious, hanging by a thread,** They
stayed even though they were barely able
to support themselves,

But sometimes when the night is still

And shrouded in a desert chill . . .

The voices from long years ago

Begin to whisper, soft and low.

The shadows move, the music plays

While in their midst the coyotes raise

Sly, smiling faces to the sky

And laugh at human times gone by.


For in the darkness of the night,

They claim the town of Rhyolite—

A man-forsaken place that boasts

Of little more than graying ghosts.

**In Other Words**

**shrouded** covered

**Sly** Clever

**man-forsaken place** place that people
  have left

▶ **Before You Move On**

1. **Visualize** How do you feel about Rhyolite as you read the poem's ending?

2. **Figurative Language** What details related to sight, touch, and hearing does the poet use in this part of the poem? Why?

# Respond and Extend

**Key Words**

| | |
|---|---|
| boomtown | investor |
| claim | limited resources |
| development | |
| discovery | mining |
| economy | population |
| ghost town | speculate |

# Compare Genres

*The Road to Rhyolite* is a **play**. It was based on the **narrative poem** "Rhyolite: The True Story of a Ghost Town." How is the play like the poem? How is it different? Work with a partner to compare them. Use the comparison chart below.

**Comparison Chart**

| | Narrative Poem | Play |
|---|---|---|
| **Setting** | | |
| **Structure and Organization** <br> Use these words to tell about the organization and structure of the selections: <br> • acts and scenes <br> • dialogue <br> • plot <br> • rhyme <br> • verses | | |

**Talk Together**

Would it be exciting to settle a new land? Compare how the play and the poem tell the story of Rhyolite. Which one told a more powerful story about how a **boomtown** turned into a **ghost town**? Use the chart you completed above and **Key Words** to discuss your ideas.

# Different Kinds of Pronouns

**Possessive pronouns, demonstrative pronouns,** and **indefinite pronouns** are three different kinds of pronouns.

## Grammar Rules  Different Kinds of Pronouns

| | |
|---|---|
| • Use a **possessive pronoun** to tell who owns something: **mine, yours, his, hers, ours, theirs** | It is <u>my hotel</u>. It is **mine**.<br><br>It is <u>their gold</u>. It is **theirs**. |
| • Use a **demonstrative pronoun** to point to a specific noun without naming it. | "**This** is a gold nugget."<br><br>"**That** is a coyote." |
| • Use an **indefinite pronoun** when you're not naming a specific person or thing.<br><br>Examples: **all, both, many, nothing, anything, someone, somebody** | **Many** moved away.<br><br>**Somebody** asked for more time. |

## Read Different Kinds of Pronouns

Read the poem. Work with a partner to find different kinds of pronouns. Are they possessive, demonstrative, or indefinite pronouns?

> Where, back in nineteen hundred four, / Two prospectors in search of ore / Unloaded from their burros' backs / Their shovels, picks, supply-filled packs, / And digging, watched their dreams unfold: /Eureka! They'd discovered gold!

## Write Different Kinds of Pronouns

Look at the illustration on pages 424–425. Write three sentences about it. Try to use different kinds of pronouns. Compare your sentences with the sentences of a partner.

# Write Like a Poet

## Write a Narrative Poem

Write a poem that tells a story about the people or events in the Old West. You will share your writing during a poetry reading.

## Study a Model

A narrative poem is a poem that tells a story. Read what Eric wrote about a family making the journey to California.

### A New Life

by Eric Goode

We were heading out West to a new land
In a wagon with eight oxen strong.
Our new home would be California.
Our journey would last a year long.

"We'll have a good life," said our daddy.
"We can get us some land of our own.
We'll claim it and clear it and tame it.
We'll eat food that our family
    has grown."

So we traveled across plains
    and prairies,
Over mountains that reached to the sky.
Native people who lived there before us
Watched us quietly as we went by.

Now we have our own place in this
    new land
And we work it from morning 'til night.
It's hard and it's strange and it's lonely,
But somehow, it feels just right.

Like any good story, the poem **describes** events and **why** events are happening.

The poem is broken into stanzas.

The poet has a **clear voice** and style. A reader can hear a personality.

The poem has a regular pattern of **rhyme**.

## Prewrite

1. **Choose a Topic** What story will you tell in your poem? Talk with a partner to find a good idea.

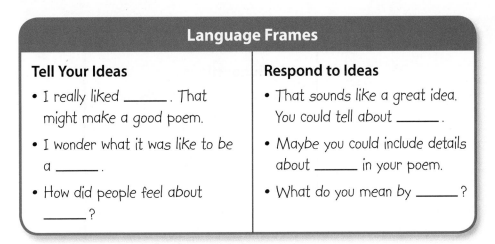

**Language Frames**

| Tell Your Ideas | Respond to Ideas |
| --- | --- |
| • I really liked _____. That might make a good poem. | • That sounds like a great idea. You could tell about _____. |
| • I wonder what it was like to be a _____. | • Maybe you could include details about _____ in your poem. |
| • How did people feel about _____? | • What do you mean by _____? |

2. **Gather Information** What event or problem will your story focus on? What details can you use to create characters and a realistic setting?

3. **Get Organized** Use a cause-and-effect chain to help you organize your details.

### Cause-and-Effect Chain

| Cause | First Effect | Second Effect | Third Effect | Fourth Effect |
| --- | --- | --- | --- | --- |
| wanted a new life | decide to move to California | start journey in covered wagon | | |

## Draft

Use your cause-and-effect chain and details to write your draft.

- Break your poem into stanzas.

- Make sure that both rhyme and rhythm follow a pattern.

- Think about your voice and writing style. Choose words that show your personality or the personality of your characters.

## Revise

1. **Read, Retell, Respond** Read your poem to a partner. Your partner listens and then summarizes the story. Next, discuss ways to improve your writing.

<table>
<tr><td colspan="2" align="center">**Language Frames**</td></tr>
<tr><td>**Retell**</td><td>**Make Suggestions**</td></tr>
<tr><td>

• Your poem was about _____ .

• The main events you described were _____ .

• Some good details you used were _____ .

</td><td>

• I had a little trouble following the story when _____ .

• Could you add details about _____ ?

• The voice and style didn't seem natural. One line where I noticed this was _____ .

</td></tr>
</table>

2. **Make Changes** Think about your draft and your partner's suggestions. Then use the Revising Marks on page 629 to mark your changes.

   • Does your writing have a clear voice and style? Replace words that don't fit you or your characters.

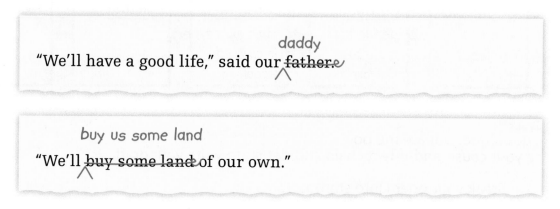

   "We'll have a good life," said our ~~father.~~ daddy

   "We'll ~~buy some land~~ buy us some land of our own."

   • Add details that tell about characters and setting.

   Do you want to waste water?
   ~~It's important to conserve water and not waste it.~~

## Edit and Proofread

Work with a partner to edit and proofread your narrative poem. Make sure you use adjectives and adverbs correctly. Use the marks on page 629 to show your changes.

## Publish

1. **On Your Own** Make a final copy of your narrative poem. Try to memorize it. Then present it as though you were telling a story.

**Grammar Tip**

✓ Be sure that your pronouns agree in gender:

For a **boy** or **man**, use **he** or **him**.

For a **girl** or **woman**, use **she** or **her**

| Presentation Tips | |
|---|---|
| **If you are the speaker...** | **If you are the listener...** |
| Look at your listeners as you read or say your poem. | Listen for word choice, rhyme, and rhythm. |
| Make sure the rhythm of your poem is clear, but be careful not to fall into a sing-song pattern. | Think about the best parts of the reader's presentation. Use them when you read your own poem. |

2. **In a Group** Collect all of the narrative poems from your class. Bind them into a book, and work together to think of a good title. Donate the poems to your school library. You may also want to post your poems on a Web site that features student writing.

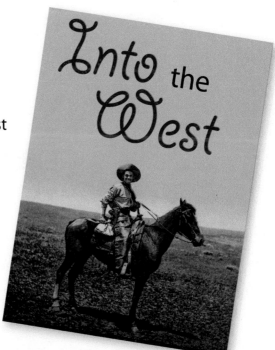

Into the West

## BIG Question

**What does it take to settle a new land?**

In this unit, you found lots of answers to the **Big Question**. Now, use your concept map to discuss the **Big Question** with the class.

courage and a sense of adventure

working hard for long hours

**Concept Map**

What does it take to settle a new land?

## Write a Description

Imagine that you visited Rhyolite or another boomtown when it was booming. Write a description of what you might have seen there. Use your concept map to help you.

# Share Your Ideas

Choose one of these ways to share your ideas about the **Big Question**.

## Write It!

### On the Road

Write a list of the things you would definitely take with you if you had to move to a new place. Explain why you would take each thing.

## Talk About It!

### Conduct an Interview

Choose people to represent characters from the play *The Road to Rhyolite*. Then prepare questions to ask these characters about their lives in the west.

## Do It!

### Put on a Comedy Show

Write three jokes about living in a new place. Then put on a comedy show to share them with the class. Use some props, too.

## Do It!

### Create a Photo-Essay

Find pictures that show what life was like for the settlers who went West. Then arrange the photos to make a photo-essay. Write one or two sentences to describe each photograph. Then share your essay with the class.

455

# Talking About
# TRASH

**?**
**BIG**
**Question**

Why should we care about garbage?

**Unit at a Glance**
► **Language:** Persuade, Make Comparisons, Science Words
► **Literacy:** Synthesize
► **Content:** Environmental Science

# Unit
# 7

## Share What You Know

**❶ Think** about an empty jelly jar.    *Do It!*

**❷ List** five ideas for reusing the empty jar. Then choose your favorite idea.

**❸ Share** your favorite with the class. Then write it on a classroom chart.

**Build Background:** Watch a video about reusing garbage.
 **NGReach.com**

# Persuade

Listen to Yannick's song. Then use **Language Frames** to try to persuade someone to reduce, reuse, or recycle.

## REDUCE, REUSE, RECYCLE

*Song*

We make too much garbage and throw too much away.
We have to recycle—it's the only way!
Our town is so dirty. It is a disgrace.
We should find a way to make our town a better place.

In the nearby town of Millbrook there's a rule:
"Reduce, reuse, recycle—at home and work and school!"
We should do the same. Our neighbors will approve.
Please join in this effort, and I know we can improve!

**Tune : "Sing a Song of Sixpence"**

# Science Vocabulary

## Key Words

| Key Words |
| --- |
| plastic |
| pollution |
| recycle |
| reduce |
| renewable |
| reuse |

# Key Words

Look at these photos. Use **Key Words** and other words to talk about **plastic** bottles and **pollution**.

**Plastic** is made of oil. Oil is not a **renewable** resource.

Why shouldn't bottles be made of **plastic**?

How does this cause **pollution**?

How can you **reduce** trash?

How can you **reuse** or **recycle** bottles?

**Talk Together**

Why is garbage an important topic? Use **Language Frames** from page 458 and **Key Words** to persuade a partner about your ideas.

459

# Author's Viewpoint

Your viewpoint is your opinion. You usually give examples, or evidence, to support your viewpoint. Authors have viewpoints, too. Identifying the **author's viewpoint** helps you think about what you see, hear, and read.

Look at these pictures of Yannick in his town.

Millbrook says:
REDUCE, REUSE, RECYCLE!

## Map and Talk

You can use a chart to show an **author's viewpoint** and the evidence that supports it. Here's how to make one.

Write the evidence that supports the viewpoint here.

Write the action that is needed here.

**Author's Viewpoint Chart**

Write the author's viewpoint here.

| Viewpoint | Evidence | Action Needed |
|---|---|---|
| There is too much garbage in town. We have to recycle. | Millbrook is much cleaner because they reduce, reuse, and recycle. | We need to start reducing, reusing, and recycling garbage. |

**Talk Together**

With a partner, discuss whether students should stay in from recess if their class does not recycle. Use an author's viewpoint chart to show your ideas.

# More Key Words

Use these words to talk about "The World of Waste" and "Message in a Bottle."

### argument
(**ar**-gyū-munt) *noun*

An **argument** is a reason for a viewpoint. There are **arguments** for keeping our streets safe and clean.

### balance
(**ba**-lunts) *noun*

You create **balance** by giving the right amount of importance to different things.

### debate
(di-**bāt**) *verb*

When you **debate** an idea, you talk about it with someone who has a different opinion.

### evidence
(**e**-vu-dunts) *noun*

You use **evidence** to prove an idea. The ball was **evidence** of how the window was broken.

### solution
(su-**lü**-shun) *noun*

A **solution** is something that solves a problem. Reading is a good **solution** for boredom.

## Talk Together

Make a Word Map for each **Key Word**. Then compare your maps with a partner's.

| Definition: | Characteristics: |
|---|---|
| end to a problem | gives an answer |
| *solution* | |
| Example: | Non-example: |
| studying with a friend | worrying about a test |

**Add words to My Vocabulary Notebook.**
NGReach.com

# Learn to Synthesize

When you synthesize, you combine information to come up with a new idea. One way to synthesize is to make general statements, or **form generalizations**, about people, things, or situations.

Look at the cartoon. What general statement can you make about the people?

When you read, you can **form generalizations**, too. Forming generalizations can help you better understand the ideas in the texts you read.

## How to Form Generalizations

| | | |
|---|---|---|
|  | **1.** Pay attention to what the text says about a person, thing, or situation. | I read _____ . |
|  | **2.** Think about similar people, things, or situations in your life. Are the ideas in the text true for your examples, too? | I know _____ . |
|  | **3.** Make a statement that seems true for what you read and applies to many people, things, or situations. | I think that most _____ . |

**Language Frames**

- 👁 I read _____ .
- 💭 I know _____ .
- 🧩 I think that most _____ .

**Talk Together**

Read the persuasive essay that John wrote about ways to save energy. Read the sample. Make your own generalizations. Then use **Language Frames** to tell a partner about them.

Persuasive Essay

# Saving Energy

We need to use less energy. Can little changes make a big difference? People continue to **debate** this topic. Some people say yes, and others say no. I say yes.

My **argument** is that personal action is a big part of the energy-saving **solution**. This doesn't mean you have to stop playing video games. It just means we have to create a **balance** in the amount of energy we use.

Here are some little things we can do:

- Change a light bulb. With a compact fluorescent bulb (CFL), you'll use 75 percent less energy.

- Put on a sweater. If you lower the heat in your house by just one degree in the winter, you will use up to 3 percent less energy.

- Unplug your computer. There is **evidence** that computers use energy even when they are turned off. ◄

- Recycle a can. A single recycled aluminum can saves enough energy to run a television for three hours.

These small changes save energy—and money too! ◄

> "I read that there is a debate over whether small changes help.
> I know people who are making small changes.
> I think that most people think small changes help."

◄ = a good place to stop and make a generalization

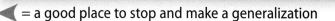

**463**

# Read a Persuasive Article

## Genre

In a **persuasive article**, a writer states an opinion, or viewpoint, about an issue and gives evidence to support it. The writer's evidence may come in the form of graphs and other visuals. He or she may also use comparisons.

## Text Feature

**Bar graphs** help you visualize information and make comparisons. The length of the bars shows different numbers or amounts. Look at the title, labels, and bars to help you understand the graph.

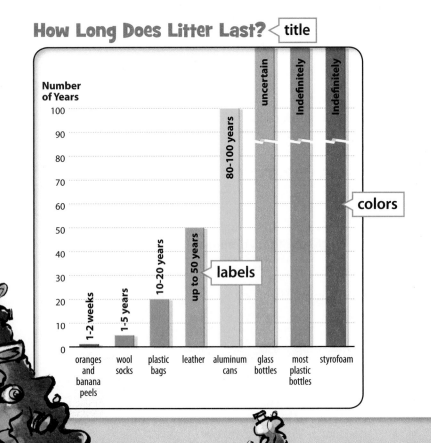

# The World of Waste

by Marybeth Lorbiecki

illustrated by Chris MacNeil

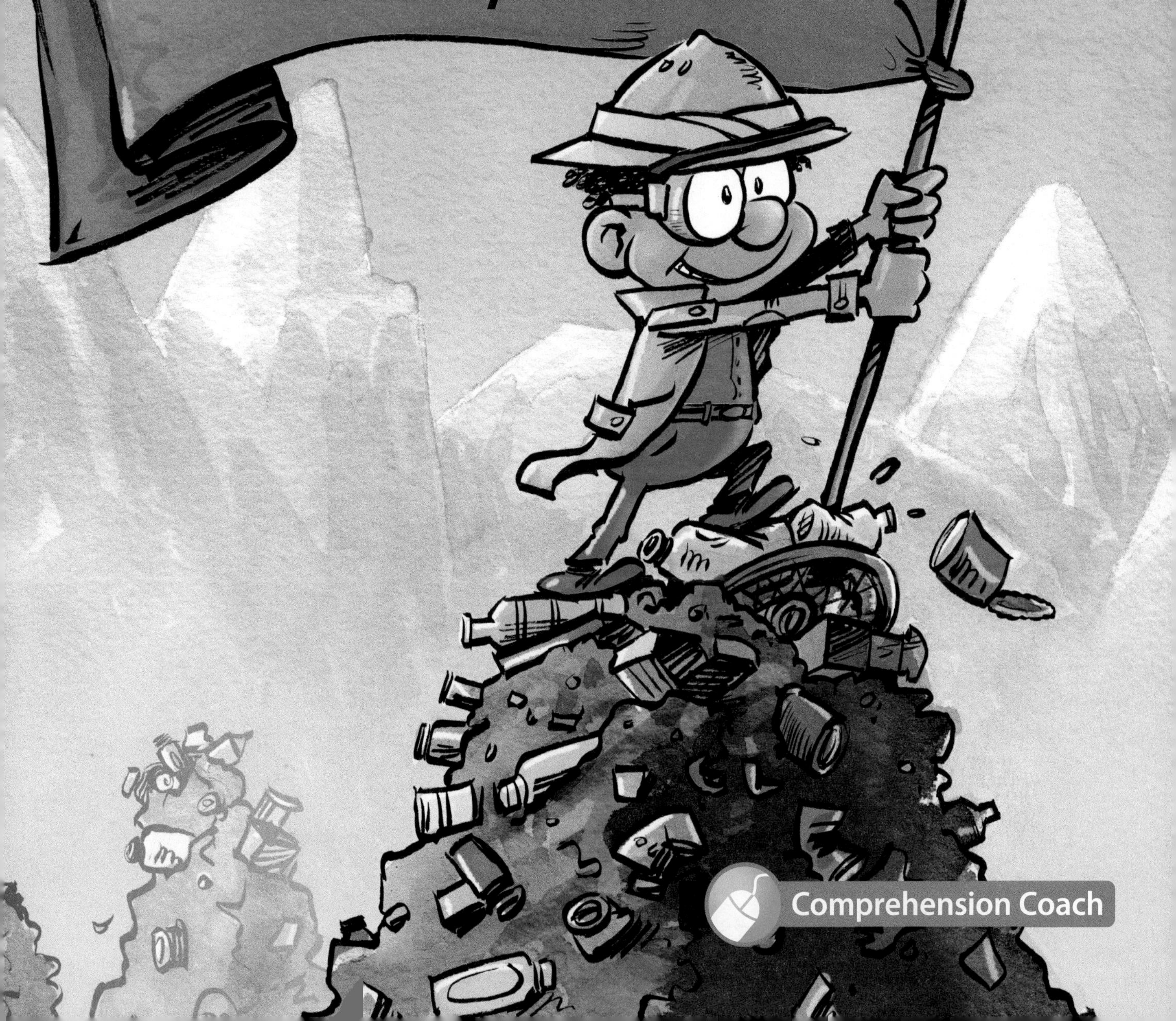

Comprehension Coach

▶ **Set a Purpose**
Find out about the complex
world of garbage and recycling.

# Garbage, Garbage Everywhere

Doesn't it seem like almost everything we do makes garbage? Food scraps, cans, bottles, packages, and wrappings are left after we eat. Paper piles up after we get the mail or do homework. There are broken games and toys, clothes we've outgrown, and books we no longer read.

People living in the United States throw away about 770 kilograms (1700 pounds) of solid **waste** per person, every year. How much do you weigh? Can you figure out how many times your own weight you create in garbage each year?

**In Other Words**
**waste** trash; garbage

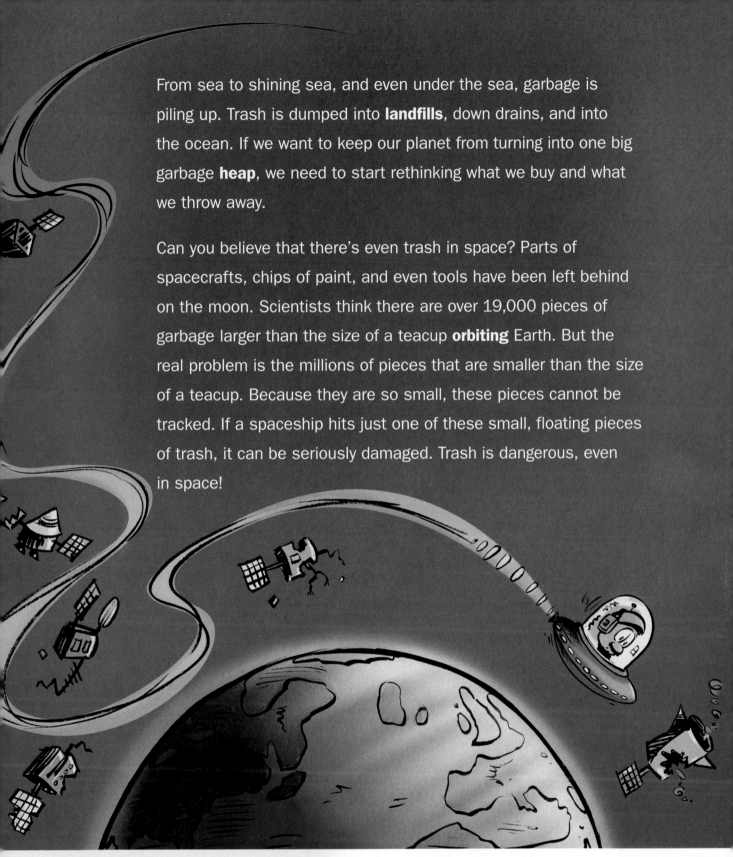

From sea to shining sea, and even under the sea, garbage is piling up. Trash is dumped into **landfills**, down drains, and into the ocean. If we want to keep our planet from turning into one big garbage **heap**, we need to start rethinking what we buy and what we throw away.

Can you believe that there's even trash in space? Parts of spacecrafts, chips of paint, and even tools have been left behind on the moon. Scientists think there are over 19,000 pieces of garbage larger than the size of a teacup **orbiting** Earth. But the real problem is the millions of pieces that are smaller than the size of a teacup. Because they are so small, these pieces cannot be tracked. If a spaceship hits just one of these small, floating pieces of trash, it can be seriously damaged. Trash is dangerous, even in space!

**In Other Words**
**landfills** huge garbage dumps
**heap** pile
**orbiting** circling

▶ **Before You Move On**

1. **Generalize** What statement can you make about the amount of trash in the world?
2. **Author's Viewpoint** What does the author want you to believe about trash? How do you know?

467

# Garbage Archaeology

What will **archaeologists** dig up **centuries** from now to learn about us? Probably they'll dig up trash from **our landfills**. There, garbage gets smashed so tightly that even things that are biodegradable, or able to rot and break down, don't have enough oxygen or water to do so quickly.

This bar graph shows how long certain types of trash take to biodegrade, even if they do have plenty of oxygen and water.

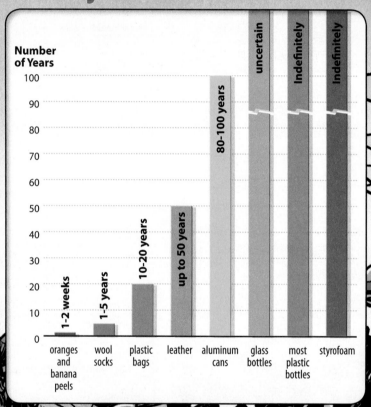

## How Long Does Litter Last?

Number of Years

|  |  |
|------|-------|
| oranges and banana peels | 1-2 weeks |
| wool socks | 1-5 years |
| plastic bags | 10-20 years |
| leather | up to 50 years |
| aluminum cans | 80-100 years |
| glass bottles | uncertain |
| most plastic bottles | Indefinitely |
| styrofoam | Indefinitely |

**In Other Words**

**archaeologists**  scientists who study past human cultures
**centuries**  hundreds of years
**our landfills**  the places where we dump it
**indefinitely**  do not know how long it stays, probably forever

# Why Plastic Lasts

When trash **biodegrades**, it is digested by decomposers, such as bacteria and fungi. Decomposers don't eat everything, however. Many types of **plastic**, for example, are completely **inedible**.

Instead of being digested by bacteria and fungi, most plastics break into smaller and smaller pieces over time. Sometimes it takes hundreds of years before the pieces disappear from sight. However, they may never completely go away.

The good news is that some plastics are being developed that won't last as long. Many new **environmentally friendly plastics** are even made of biodegradable materials.

## Biodegradable Plastics: The Break Down

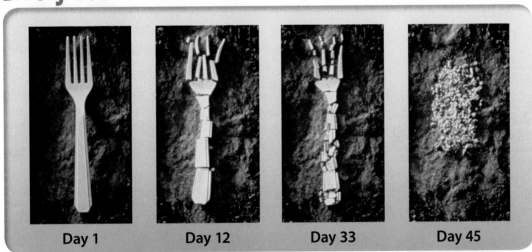

| Day 1 | Day 12 | Day 33 | Day 45 |

▲ Some plastics may require hundreds of years to break down, and they may never completely go away. In contrast, biodegradable plastics break down quickly, and can be digested by organisms in the soil.

**In Other Words**

**biodegrades** breaks down into small parts

**inedible** unable to be eaten

**environmentally friendly plastics**
　　**plastics** that won't harm the environment

▶ **Before You Move On**

1. **Problem/Solution** What problem and **solution** are described on this page?

2. **Use Text Features** Which item would biodegrade slowest: a leather jacket, a bottle of water, or a banana?

# Trash Around the World

Americans win first prize! We produce more garbage than any other country in the world. Look at the graphic at the right. It shows about how much trash each person produces in one day, in different countries. Compared with people in the United States, people in other countries produce less trash. How is this possible? They buy fewer things, and **reuse** and **recycle** more of them.

Some countries even **encourage** people to recycle. In Switzerland, for example, people have to pay for every bag of garbage they want taken away, but recyclable garbage is taken away for free. Now that's a good reason to recycle!

## Trash Per Person Per Day

**Ghana**
½ pound

**Sri Lanka**
¾ pound

**Egypt**
¾ pound

**Philippines**
1 pound

**Japan**
over 2 pounds

**Canada**
over 2 pounds

**Sweden**
over 3 pounds

**United States**
over 4½ pounds

**In Other Words**
**encourage** try to persuade

# Room for Improvement

People living in the United States are now recycling almost double what they did in 1990. Still, we could do better. Of all the trash we **generate**, about 60 percent of it could be recycled or **composted**. Only about 33 percent of it actually is! Another 13 percent is burned for energy, which leaves about 54 percent for the landfills.

## What Happens to Our Trash?

Goes to landfill 54%

Gets recycled 33%

13% Burned for energy

33% Gets recycled

60% Could be recycled

PLASTIC   GLASS

**In Other Words**

**generate** make

**composted** returned to the soil as nutrients

▶ **Before You Move On**

1. **Author's Viewpoint** What comparisons does the author make to support her view about the amount of garbage in the U.S.?

2. **Use Text Features** How do the circle graphs help you better understand the facts stated in the text?

# Garbage, the Great Resource

Did you know that much of the garbage we throw away can be reused? Some leftover food and lawn waste can be turned into **compost** for the garden. You can clean and **pass on** old clothes, or turn them into scarves or rags. Empty bottles and jars can be cleaned and refilled. **Worn** tires can be made into garden containers. You can decorate a cake or a gift with old toy figures. Plastic containers can be used for planting or for sorting and storing things.

▲ This bag was made by reusing a cardboard box, some newspaper, and a little string.

◄ There are many ways to **reuse** items you might otherwise throw away.

**In Other Words**
**compost** plant food
**pass on** give away
**Worn** Old and used
**otherwise** instead

If something can't be fixed or reused, it can probably be recycled and **transformed** into a new object. Factories melt glass bottles and jars into new glass containers, marbles, decorative tiles, and even **surfboards**! Metal objects are melted down and **molded** into car and bike parts, cookware, and yes, new cans. Plastic bottles are used in everything from park benches and playground equipment to ski jackets. Used paper and cardboard can be remixed into new paper and cardboard. As you can see, garbage is a great resource!

▼ Used plastic bottles were melted and shaped into plastic pellets, which were then melted and molded to create this play set.

plastic pellets

**In Other Words**
**transformed** changed
**surfboard** boards people use to ride waves
**molded** reshaped

▶ **Before You Move On**

1. **Generalize** What generalization can you make about the reuse of trash?

2. **Make Connections** What are some other things that we **reuse** or **recycle**?

# Kids Make a Difference

To earn money, kids around North America collect used bottles, cans, printer ink **cartridges**, and cell phones. They sell these items to recycling companies. This helps the environment and makes money for the kids' groups and schools. Everybody wins!

Some kids don't do it for the money. Jacob Komar started a **nonprofit**, Computers for Communities, when he was nine years old. It all began when his school decided to get rid of **a bunch of** old computers. Jacob had always been good at **programming**, so he decided to update all of the computers so they worked again. One by one, he fixed them and gave them away to local families who needed them.

computer circuit board

**In Other Words**
**cartridges** containers
**nonprofit** business to help people
**a bunch of** many
**programming** writing programs for computers

# Composting: How to Make a Soil Factory

Landfills get filled quickly with leaves, grass clippings, and food scraps. Why not turn this waste into soil? All you need is space for a compost pile or **bin**. Try this experiment to see how composting works outdoors.

1. **Find an old plastic container to use as your compost bin. Ask an adult to make holes in it for you.**

2. **Place the bin in a shady spot outdoors. Add "green" material, such as food scraps, "brown" material, such as dried leaves, and some soil.**

3. **Add water and stir. Add more yard waste and veggie scraps as you collect them. Keep everything moist. Wait a few months.**

4. **Your compost is ready when it is dark and soil-like. Spread it around your plants. It will help them grow larger and healthier.**

**In Other Words**

**bin** container

**veggie scraps** unused parts of vegetables and fruits

▶ **Before You Move On**

1. **Author's Viewpoint** What is the author's view about people who try to make money from recycling? Explain.

2. **Problem/Solution** What waste problem does composting solve?

# Smart Shopping

The best way to cut down on garbage and **pollution** is to be careful what you buy. Here are some tips. First, buy only the things you need or really want. If you have a temporary need for something, try borrowing it from someone. You will save yourself money and save the planet from too much stuff. Just remember the borrower's **motto**: Always return something in better **shape** than you received it!

Second, save money and packaging by buying **next-to-new** items. **Garage sales** and thrift shops are good places to go to find such items. And when you're done with them, you can return them, or just pass them on to someone else!

**In Other Words**
**motto** saying
**shape** condition
**next-to-new** slightly used
**Garage sales** Sales outside people's homes

Third, consider the packaging. Every month, Americans throw away their weight in packaging! Choose products that come in refillable or reusable containers. Some stores sell milk or soda in bottles that can be returned for **cash**. Next best are products in recyclable containers, such as glass bottles, recyclable plastics, and cans.

Finally, look for the products that are made in a safe and Earth-friendly way, using recycled materials, nontoxic (not poisonous) and **animal-friendly ingredients**. If you can't recycle the packaging, at least make sure that its contents are Earth-friendly!

## Juice Container Comparisons

▲ **Each example represents the same amount of juice.**

**In Other Words**

**cash** money

**animal-friendly ingredients** ingredients not tested on animals

▶ **Before You Move On**

1. **Analyze** How does buying items that are made to last help **reduce** waste?

2. **Use Text Features** Compare the graphics on this page. Which containers use the most packaging?

# Do You Need It or Do You Want It?

Commercials and **ads** are designed to make you think a product will make you better looking, more respected, happier, and healthier. But don't let yourself get tricked! Ask yourself: Do I need it? Or do I just want it?

Ads may also try to make you feel better about buying something by making you think it is Earth-friendly and **"green."** They may **exaggerate**, saying their product is better for the environment than it could possibly be. They may try to **mislead** you by suggesting something that isn't true. They may make contradictory statements, or give opposing information, about how the product affects the environment. Watch out for these tricks whenever you see an advertisement. They mean that the product is probably not as good as it seems. You should think again before you buy it!

**In Other Words**
**ads** advertisements
**"green."** will not harm the environment.
**exaggerate** expand the truth
**mislead** trick

The ads below are for similar cleaning products. The second ad has many problems, including exaggeration, misleading statements, and contradictory statements. Which of these two products would *you* buy?

**Ad #1**

# Clean Green *wipes*

Buy Clean Green Wipes! Each 3-pack of **durable** wipes comes with a bottle of non-toxic cleaning **solution**. Best of all, Clean Green Wipes are reusable. Made of 50 percent recycled plastic, they will last for more than 80 machine washes. Clean Green Wipes are perfect for the environmentally **conscious**!

**Ad #2**

# All-Natural wipes

Buy All Natural Wipes! These handmade, cotton cloths will last forever. They contain a non-toxic cleaning gel that smells like sunshine. When you're done with a Clean Green Wipe, just toss it in the trash. Clean Green Wipes are made from plastic, so they're good for the environment!

exaggeration

misleading statement

contradictory statement

**In Other Words**
**durable** long-lasting
**solution** liquid
**conscious** aware

▶ **Before You Move On**
1. **Summarize** How do ads try to make you want to buy their products?
2. **Make Judgments** Can you find another misleading statement in Ad #2? And another contradictory statement?

# Trash Is Treasure

Creating trash requires a lot of energy. Look at the book you are reading right now. How did all that paper get into your hands? First, trees were cut down to make **paper pulp**. Machines were used to turn the pulp into paper. Trucks brought the paper to a **printer**, where the book was put together. Finally, trucks were used to bring the paper to you. All of these steps required energy and special materials.

1. Trees are cut down for pulp.

2. Machines turn the pulp into paper.

3. Trucks deliver the paper to a printer, where the paper is made into a book.

4. Trucks bring the book to a store, where you can buy it.

**In Other Words**

**paper pulp** a thick mixture of water and small wood particles

**printer** business that prints books

Most of the energy we use today comes from **fossil fuels**, like oil. Oil is not a renewable resource. When it runs out, it will be gone forever. Non-renewable resources like oil are used to make many of the things that we throw away. Because of this, all trash should be treated like treasure.

Next time you buy something new, or use something once, think of the future. Try to reuse whatever you buy. When you're done with it, try to make sure it is reused, recycled, or returned to the earth. Don't throw it all away!

Instead of throwing your family's vegetable scraps in the trash, add them to a compost bin.

**In Other Words**
**fossil fuels** fuels that were made over millions of years

▶ **Before You Move On**

1. **Paraphrase** In you own words, explain the paper making process from start to finish.
2. **Make Inferences** If we don't follow the author's advice, what can happen?

481

# Talk About It

1.  What makes this a **persuasive article**? Give two examples.

2.  Imagine that you must **debate** that garbage is a problem with students who don't think garbage is a problem. You must persuade them to **recycle** more of what they throw away. Practice with a partner. Use evidence from the text to support your argument.

3.  Imagine that you are an archaeologist, digging in a landfill 100 years from now. What **evidence** of life today might you find there? What could this evidence tell you about the way people live today?

Learn test-taking strategies.
NGReach.com

# Write About It

Write an ad for a "green" product, for example, a **reusable** shopping bag. Tell how it **reduces** waste and **pollution**. Be persuasive, but don't exaggerate! Use **Key Words** and give details about how the product reduces waste and pollution.

Get _____ today.
It will _____ .
You can _____ , too.
We must _____ !

# Author's Viewpoint

Make an author's viewpoint chart about "The World of Waste."

**Author's Viewpoint Chart**

| Viewpoint | Evidence | Action Needed |
|---|---|---|
| Garbage can be good. | | |

Write the viewpoint here.

Write the evidence here.

Write the action needed here.

Retell the selection to a partner. Use the chart to tell the author's viewpoint and the evidence that supports it. Use **Key Words** and other words. Record your retelling.

> The author's viewpoint is _____. He believes this because _____. He thinks we must _____.

# Fluency ● Comprehension Coach

Use the Comprehension Coach to practice reading with intonation. Rate your reading.

**Talk Together**

Why does the author try to persuade us to care about trash? Make a poster to persuade classmates to reuse, reduce, and recycle trash. Include **Key Words** in your poster.

# Multiple-Meaning Words

Some words have more than one meaning. You can use **context**, or the words nearby, to get clues about a word's meaning.

**Scale** is a multiple-meaning word. Compare these examples.

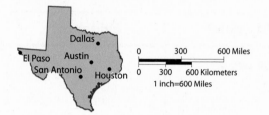

You can use a **scale** to weigh things.

**Meaning**: an instrument to measure weight

This map **scale** shows that one inch equals 600 miles.

**Meaning**: relationship between measurements on a map and real measurements

## Try It Together

Read the passage. Then answer the questions.

> In America, we produce 250 million tons of garbage a year. But all this trash that we create doesn't have to be the problem. It can be part of the solution, if you are willing to reduce, reuse, and recycle.

**1. What does produce mean?**

  A  make

  B  show

  C  grow

  D  are in charge of

**2. Which words give you a clue to the meaning of produce?**

  A  in America

  B  254 million tons

  C  trash we create

  D  reduce, reuse, recycle

**Connect Across Texts** You read about how garbage is a problem. Now read an essay by someone who has a **solution**.

**Genre** An **essay** is a short piece of nonfiction that focuses on a single topic.

# Message in a Bottle

## by David de Rothschild

When I decided to sail the *Plastiki*, a boat made out of **reclaimed** plastic soda bottles, across the Pacific Ocean, some people said I was crazy. It's too dangerous, they said. I think doing nothing is much more dangerous.

**I'm on a mission** to help Earth. Our planet is drowning in trash. We can do something to help Earth beat waste. More importantly, we must do something about it before it's too late.

David de Rothschild ›

**In Other Words**
**reclaimed** used
**I'm on a mission**
　　I'm going to do everything I can

▶ **Before You Move On**

1. **Author's Viewpoint** What problem does the author describe? How does he propose to solve it?

2. **Figurative Language** What does the author mean by "drowning in trash"?

# Turning Problems into Solutions

We need to make protecting the planet an adventure, not an **insurmountable** chore. What could be a bigger adventure than turning trash—12,500 tossed-away plastic bottles—into something useful and fun? Trash doesn't just have to be the problem. It can be part of the **solution**, too.

What does sailing a boat made out of plastic bottles have to do with saving the planet? I hope my adventure is like a neon sign—a giant, environmentally safe neon sign—that tells a **gripping** story about the problem and possible solutions.

Let's start with the problem. Sometimes it **boggles my mind** how big it is. I'm talking about trash. In the United States, we throw away 254 million tons of garbage every year. That yearly **rubbish heap** includes billions of empty plastic bottles.

◀ There is so much trash in the ocean that some animals eat it by mistake. All these items were found inside the stomachs of tiger sharks.

**In Other Words**
**insurmountable** impossible
**gripping** very interesting
**boggles my mind** amazes me
**rubbish heap** garbage pile

I think plastic bottles are a waste of our natural resources. Did you know it takes over 17 million barrels of oil a year to make the **plastic** for all these bottles? That's enough oil to power a million cars for a year. That doesn't count the water and energy needed to produce, **distribute**, and chill all these bottles of water.

There are places in the world that need bottled water. But in the United States, **we have access** to clean water. **Ultimately**, we're wasting a lot of Earth's natural resources for something that ends up trashed.

People throw away billions of plastic bottles every year. Some end up on the shores of oceans, rivers, and lakes like this one. ▶

**In Other Words**
**distribute** deliver
**we have access to** we can get
**Ultimately** In the end

▶ **Before You Move On**

1. **Author's Viewpoint** Why does the author think plastic bottles waste resources?

2. **Generalize** Based on what you read, how do you think most people feel about throwing away plastic bottles?

# Sailing Through a Sea of Plastic Soup

Here's what really shocks me. A lot of this plastic is ending up in our oceans. Where there are naturally forming gyres, places where **ocean currents** come together, you now find big swirling masses of trash. There are five of these large gyres in the world's oceans. Nearly 90 percent of the trash found in their waters is plastic.

The largest of these places is called the Great Eastern Pacific Garbage Patch. Located between California and Hawaii, the Garbage Patch covers an area twice the size of Texas! From the surface, the area looks like any other stretch of open ocean. But just below the surface, it's like a plastic soup. According to some reports, there are as many as six pieces of plastic for every one piece of **plankton** in the Garbage Patch. If you scoop that ocean water up and shake it, it looks like a **snow globe**.

Most people will never get to see this floating garbage first-hand. Out of sight should not mean **out of mind**.

This is a sample of water taken from the Great Eastern Pacific Garbage Patch. ▼

**In Other Words**

**ocean currents** moving ocean waters
**plankton** drifting plant or animal life
◄ **snow globe** toy that is full of small floating bits
**out of mind** we don't think about it

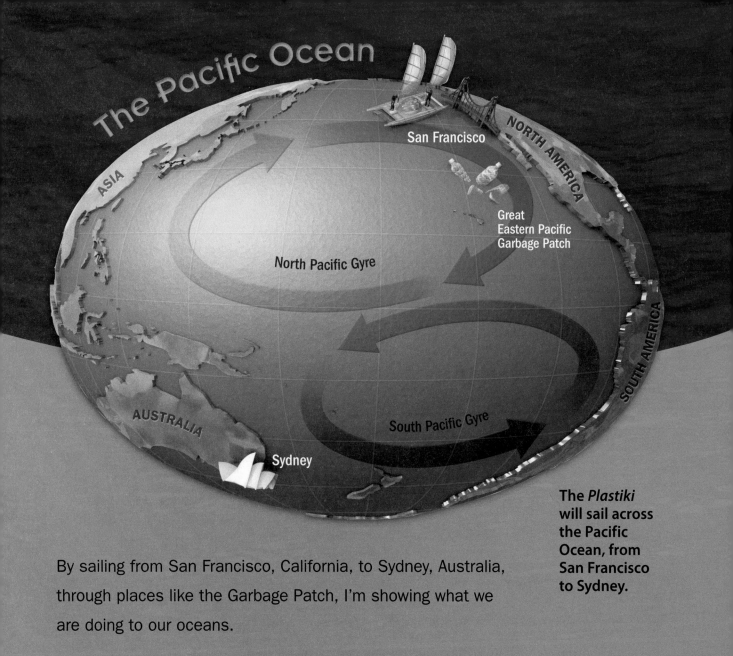

## The Pacific Ocean

ASIA

San Francisco

NORTH AMERICA

Great
Eastern Pacific
Garbage Patch

North Pacific Gyre

SOUTH AMERICA

AUSTRALIA

South Pacific Gyre

Sydney

The *Plastiki* will sail across the Pacific Ocean, from San Francisco to Sydney.

By sailing from San Francisco, California, to Sydney, Australia, through places like the Garbage Patch, I'm showing what we are doing to our oceans.

I believe we need to see what we are trying to protect. Not everyone has to, or can, sail the seas like me. But everyone can get out into nature. You should, too. Touch it. Feel it. Get mud under your fingernails. That way, we can create **a passion** for protecting nature. That's the first part of *Plastiki*'s message.

**In Other Words**
**a passion** strong enthusiasm

▶ **Before You Move On**

1. **Author's Viewpoint** What is the author trying to persuade the reader to do?

2. **Explain** What does the author mean by the saying "Out of sight, out of mind"?

Images by Peter Rubin

on-board garden

stationary bikes

72257

PLASTiKi

solar panels

# Turning Trash into Good

Here's the second part of *Plastiki's* message: We don't have to trash our trash. The *Plastiki* is proof. We made this 18-meter (60-foot) **catamaran** out of recycled bottles and a new kind of recycling plastic.

In the future, this special plastic could be used for making boats, surfboards, skateboards, and more. But that isn't its only **cool** feature. The *Plastiki* is packed with many other environmentally safe solutions.

**In Other Words**
**catamaran** sailboat
**cool** interesting (slang)

The glue that holds everything together is bio-based, made from natural materials like sugar and nuts. We grow food in an on-board garden. Energy comes from **wind turbines**, solar panels, stationary bikes, and even **methane** from our own human waste. Think about it: Cooking food with fuel made from our own waste. Now that's being resourceful!

Will my sailing the *Plastiki* halfway across the world solve the trash problem? No. But this great adventure story will get people thinking and hopefully saying, "Wow!", "What?!", or even "Eeewww!" When we create a reaction, we can come up with our best ideas to **tackle** the fourth "R" in solving the trash problem: recycle , reduce , reuse . . . and rethink.

You don't have to be a scientist or a politician to make a difference. You don't have to sail a plastic boat across the ocean. You just have to care. It just takes one stone to send a ripple across the pond. One stone, one person, one kid, can start that wave and push other people to make a difference. There's no telling what we can do to help the planet if we all work together. Saving the planet can be our greatest adventure! ❖

David de Rothschild—pictured here with plastic bottles—wants people to rethink the way they think about trash. ▽

▶ **Before You Move On**

1. **Generalize** Why is *Plastiki* good for the environment?
2. **Figurative Language** How does the author use the metaphor of a stone thrown into a pond to make his point?

## Key Words

| | |
|---|---|
| argument | recycle |
| balance | reduce |
| debate | renewable |
| evidence | reuse |
| plastic | solution |
| pollution | |

# Compare Author's Purpose

Authors generally have a main reason, or purpose, for writing. They write to inform, persuade, or entertain.

What is the **author's purpose** in each selection? Work with a partner. List the conclusions you can draw from each selection. Say how well each author's purpose was achieved.

**Author's Purpose Chart**

| | "The World of Waste" | "Message in a Bottle" |
|---|---|---|
| Tell the author's main purpose for each selection. | | |
| List three conclusions about each selection. | | |
| Say how well each author's purpose was achieved. | | |

### Talk Together

How can garbage be used for good? Think about the information in the article, the essay, and the chart. Use **Key Words** to talk about your ideas.

# Adverbs

**Adverbs** describe, or tell about, verbs, adjectives, or other adverbs.

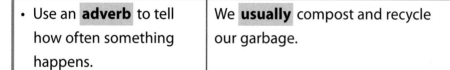

## Grammar Rules Adverbs

| | |
|---|---|
| • Use an **adverb** to describe a verb. | The *Plastiki* **sails slowly** across the Pacific Ocean. |
| • Use an **adverb** to tell how often something happens. | We **usually** compost and recycle our garbage. |
| • Use an **adverb** to describe another adverb. | Fruit biodegrades **somewhat** rapidly. |
| • Use an **adverb** to describe an **adjective**. | Some countries are **very** conscious about recycling. |

## Read Adverbs

Read the passage. What adverbs can you find? Tell what each describes.

> Jacob Komar started a nonprofit when he was nine years old. He updated very old computers so that they worked efficiently again. Jacob happily gave the computers to families that needed them.

## Write Adverbs

Write three sentences about the pictures on page 472 or page 473. Use at least two adverbs. Compare your sentences with a partner's.

493

# Make Comparisons

**Language Frames**

- _____ was _____ .
  _____ was _____ ,
  too.

- _____ was _____ .
  But _____ was
  _____ .

Listen to the song about twins who competed in a poster contest. Then use **Language Frames** to make comparisons of your own.

## The **Poster Contest**    *song* ((MP3))

Our town had a poster contest
To help kids clean up our school.
Paula's goal was win the contest;
Claire's goal was to win it, too.
So they both made their own posters.
They used different kinds of crafts.
Paula's was a lot of words
But Claire's was lots of photographs.
When they saw their separate posters,
They knew something must be done.
They combined their work together.
It was perfect—and it won!

Tune : "Reuben, Reuben"

# Science Vocabulary

**Key Words**

biodegradable

dispose

generate

landfill

transform

# Key Words

Actions have consequences, or results. Look at the photos. Use **Key Words** and other words to talk about the different consequences our actions can have.

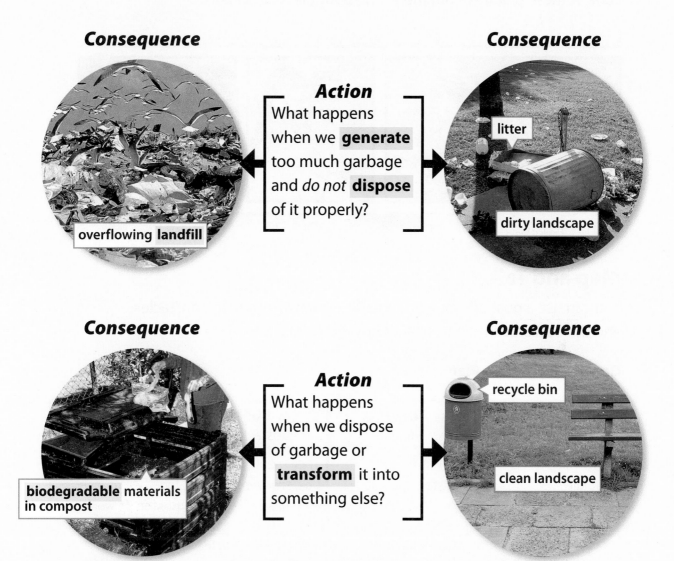

### Consequence

overflowing **landfill**

### *Action*
What happens when we **generate** too much garbage and *do not* **dispose** of it properly?

### Consequence

litter

dirty landscape

### Consequence

**biodegradable** materials in compost

### *Action*
What happens when we dispose of garbage or **transform** it into something else?

### Consequence

recycle bin

clean landscape

**Talk Together**

What are some consequences of too much garbage? With a partner, use **Language Frames** from page 494 and **Key Words** to discuss your ideas.

495

# Goal and Outcome

When you make a plan, or set a **goal**, you might encounter problems, or obstacles. These obstacles can change the **outcome**, or the results.

Look at these pictures from the song about Claire and Paula.

## Map and Talk

You can use a goal-and-outcome plan to show the goal, the obstacles, and the outcome in a story. Here's how you make one.

**Goal-and-Outcome Plan**

| SOMEBODY (Character(s)) | WANTED (Goal) | BUT (Obstacle(s)) | SO (Outcome) |
|---|---|---|---|
| Paula Claire | to win the poster contest | Their separate posters weren't very good. | They worked together on one poster. It won. |
| Write the characters here. | Write what the characters want here. | Write what got in the way here. | Write what happened here. |

**Talk Together**

Tell a partner about a story in which the character had a goal but encountered obstacles. Then tell the outcome. Your partner makes a goal-and-outcome plan.

# More Key Words

Use these words to talk about "Where I Live" and "Sarah Cynthia Sylvia Stout."

**affect**

(u-**fekt**) *verb*

If something **affects** you, it changes you or your situation. The snow can **affect** your plans.

**behavior**

(bi-**hā**-vyur) *noun*

**Behavior** is the way a person acts. Their bad **behavior** got them in trouble.

**benefit**

(**be**-nu-fit) *noun*

A **benefit** is something that helps. Fresh air and exercise are **benefits** of playing soccer.

**effect**

(i-**fekt**) *noun*

An **effect** is the result of something else. A runny nose is an **effect** of a cold.

**responsibility**

(ri-spahn-su-**bi**-lu-tē) *noun*

A **responsibility** is something you should do. It is my **responsibility** to walk my dog.

## Talk Together

Work with a partner. Write a question using at least one **Key Word**. Answer your partner's question using a different **Key Word**. Use each word twice.

**Questions**
What **effect** does hot weather have?
**Answers**
Hot weather **affects** your choice of clothes.

**Add words to My Vocabulary Notebook.**
NGReach.com

497

# Learn to Synthesize

When you synthesize, you combine information to come up with a new idea. You synthesize when you **draw conclusions**, or put details together to understand people, things, or situations.

Look at the cartoon. You can probably draw a conclusion about the kind of day Paula is having.

Paula

When you read, you can **draw conclusions**, too. Drawing conclusions can help you understand more about what you are reading.

## How to Draw Conclusions

| | | |
|---|---|---|
|  | **1.** Notice an important detail in the text. | I read _____ . |
|  | **2.** Look for another detail that you think is important. | I also read _____ . |
|  | **3.** Put the details together. Make a decision about what the details mean. | I conclude _____ . |

## Talk Together

Read the e-mail from Claire to her grandmother. Read the
sample. As you read, draw your own conclusions. Then
use **Language Frames** to tell a partner about them.

E-mail

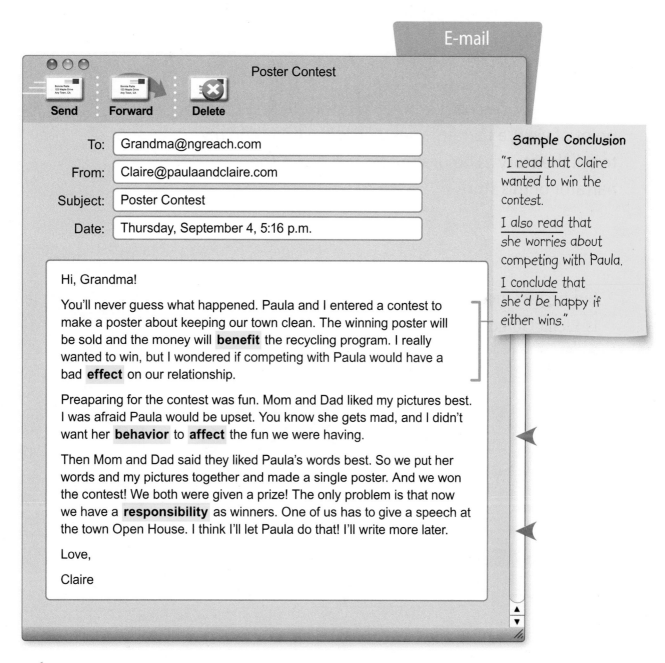

Poster Contest

**Send**    **Forward**    **Delete**

To: Grandma@ngreach.com

From: Claire@paulaandclaire.com

Subject: Poster Contest

Date: Thursday, September 4, 5:16 p.m.

Hi, Grandma!

You'll never guess what happened. Paula and I entered a contest to
make a poster about keeping our town clean. The winning poster will
be sold and the money will **benefit** the recycling program. I really
wanted to win, but I wondered if competing with Paula would have a
bad **effect** on our relationship.

Preaparing for the contest was fun. Mom and Dad liked my pictures best.
I was afraid Paula would be upset. You know she gets mad, and I didn't
want her **behavior** to **affect** the fun we were having.

Then Mom and Dad said they liked Paula's words best. So we put her
words and my pictures together and made a single poster. And we won
the contest! We both were given a prize! The only problem is that now
we have a **responsibility** as winners. One of us has to give a speech at
the town Open House. I think I'll let Paula do that! I'll write more later.

Love,

Claire

### Sample Conclusion

"I read that Claire
wanted to win the
contest.

I also read that
she worries about
competing with Paula.

I conclude that
she'd be happy if
either wins."

◀ = a good place to stop and draw a conclusion

499

# Read a Story

## Genre

A **short story** is a brief work of fiction. It usually focuses on a single problem that the main character tries to solve.

## Point of View

Point of view describes who tells a story. In first-person point of view, a narrator uses words like *I*, *me*, and *my* to tell the story as he or she sees it. Elena is the narrator of this story.

But first let me tell you about myself. My name is Elena Gomez. I live in a three-story apartment building. My bedroom faces the street, . . .

# Where I Live

## by Gary Soto
### illustrated by Chuck Gonzales

▶ **Set a Purpose**
Find out what Elena is thinking about as the story begins.

**W**hat if, instead of rain, big, ugly pieces of used gum fell from the sky? Wouldn't it be awful?

Or what if, instead of snow, the sky released aluminum cans? Aluminum cans are not soft like snow. You might get **clunked** on top of the head.

Or what if, instead of hail, you saw burger wrappers **swaying** slowly to the ground? It wouldn't be pretty, would it?

**In Other Words**
**clunked** hit
**swaying** moving back and forth

502

That's why I'm doing this report. But first let me tell you about myself. My name is Elena Gomez. I live in a three-story apartment building. My bedroom **faces** the street, and sometimes I open the window, **prop** my elbows on the sill, and look out. I'm doing that this very second. What do I see? I see Ricky Medina, my little neighbor, playing marbles with his cousin Pablo What's-His-Name.

"Ricky!" I holler.

Ricky looks up, startled. He can't see me because I've **ducked**, and the giggles inside me feel like burps trying to get out. When I finally stand up, Ricky smiles and waves. I wave back.

**In Other Words**
**faces** looks out onto
**prop** rest
**ducked** lowered my head

▶ **Before You Move On**

1. **Visualize** Describe the world Elena imagines. Then describe the world she actually sees.

2. **Goal/Outcome** Why do you think Elena is doing this report? What is her goal?

503

B̶ut I'm not here to talk about those boys playing
marbles. I'm here to tell you about a little market on
the corner. Outside the market, there are **stalls** with
fruits and vegetables, flowers for sale, and a stand for
newspapers in Spanish and English. If you wait long
enough, you'll see a kid my age come out of the store
eating potato chips. He'll look around and start walking.
When he finishes with his chips, he'll lick his fingers and
just **toss** the bag on the ground. *Trash!*

I want to scream, "Use a trash can, you big dummy!
You're messing up our street!" But does he care? Doesn't
he know about recycling?

**In Other Words**
**stalls** open containers
**toss** throw

504

I close the window, kind of hard because I'm mad. I go into the kitchen. My mom is peering into the refrigerator with sort of a lost look on her face. It's as if she had never seen all the food **stuff** before.

"What are you doing?" I ask.

"Oh," she **chirps**. "You scared me!"

*I* scared someone? I'm twelve years old and next to the shortest person in the fifth grade! The one thing that *is* big about me is **my ponytail**. My ponytail, I would guess, weighs at least a pound.

**In Other Words**
**stuff** items
**chirps** says
**my ponytail** the hair I tie behind me

"Sorry, Mom," I say, and hug her to make her feel better. "What are you doing?"

"We're out of eggs," she says, her hand stroking my ponytail. She **hands** me a five-dollar bill. "Go down to the store and get eggs and milk," she says as she hands me our shopping bag, the one that says *I am not a plastic bag!*

I race down the steps, one hand on the rail, and I'm suddenly standing in sunlight, blinking like a little chicken. I've been in my bedroom all morning doing my report, and I'm not used to the sunlight yet.

**In Other Words**
**hands** gives

"Hey," I call to Ricky, who is now by himself. Where did Pablo What's-His-Name go? Maybe his mother called him—mothers are always yelling from open windows, "*¡Venaca!* It's time to eat!"

Ricky, whose shoelaces are undone, joins me, the marbles clicking in his pocket with each step.

You're probably thinking, do I LIKE Ricky? No. He's smaller than me, only seven years old, and likes marbles and his army men. Also, if he were to show you his knees, you would see that they have **scabs** the color of bacon. I don't have scabs, and unlike Ricky, who always has *mocos* sliding out of his nostrils, I almost never catch colds. And if I do, I use tissue and **dispose** of it properly.

**In Other Words**

*¡Venaca!* Come in! (in Spanish)

**scabs** dried cuts

*mocos* mucus (in Spanish)

**dispose** of it properly throw it away in the right place

ICE CREAM SANDWICHES

At the market, I don't get the eggs and milk right away. We head down the aisle loaded with bread, crackers, and cookies, plus a large display of potato chips and **chicharrones**, plain and barbecue-flavored. We stop in front of the big noisy freezer, where the ice cream is. Neither of us has money to **treat ourselves**. Still, we can dream.

"Which one would you get?" I ask Ricky, who quickly aims a finger at the ice cream sandwich. "Good choice," I tell him, and then tell him I would **splurge** on an orange-flavored ice cream treat.

**In Other Words**
*chicharrones* fried pork rinds (in Spanish)
**treat ourselves** pay for a treat
**splurge** spend my money

The kind of ice-cream treat I want is the sort where you have to do some work. You lick a little, lick some more, maybe **chomp** if you're really hungry, and lick some more because the ice cream is starting to flow down the side of the cardboard tube it's in. Then you push from the bottom, and more ice cream **pops up**. You **make a face** when it's all gone, and even licking the sides no longer makes you happy.

**In Other Words**

***chomp*** bite

**pops up** comes up out of the tube

**make a face** look sad

▶ **Before You Move On**

1. **Confirm Prediction** What kinds of things does Elena notice about her family, friends, and neighbors?

2. **Draw Conclusions** Describe Elena's personality. What helps you understand her?

**B**ut let's not talk about ice cream. I'm here to buy eggs and
milk. I **hand over** the money to Mr. Asmara, and he hands me
back change, plus two small wrapped boxes of *chicle* because
he likes us. I like *him* because he keeps a recycle bin for soda
cans and water bottles right outside the door.

"Thank you," I say for both of us. I give one to Ricky.

As we leave, I unwrap my gum and toss the square pieces,
which are white as baby teeth, into my mouth. I **shove** the
wrapper in my front pocket. Ricky unwraps his gum. He
throws the wrapper onto the sidewalk.

**In Other Words**
**hand over**  give
*chicle*  gum (in Spanish)
**shove**  put

510

"Ricky!" I yell, **a frosty breath roaring between my lips**.

"What!" he asks.

"What am I going to do with you?" I grumble. I tell Ricky, "We shouldn't litter." Instead of asking him to pick it up, I bend down like **an ostrich** and do it for him. As I pocket the wrapper, my eyes spy the smallest bananas.

Bananas are generally a small fruit—not, for instance, like watermelons. But these bananas are really, *really* small, and are spotted like a leopard. I walk over to the fruit stall and lift up a tiny bunch of bananas. I say to Ricky, "Aren't they cute?"

"I could eat them all," Ricky says, and rubs his belly.

"And then throw the peels into the **gutter**, huh?" I'm still a little upset.

**In Other Words**

**a frosty breath roaring between my lips**
 in an angry voice

◀ **an ostrich**  a tall bird

**gutter**  place where the street meets the sidewalk

511

"No, I wouldn't," he says. "I would **compost the peels** . . . or eat them," he laughs.

"**Yeah, right**," I answer. "And close your mouth. I can see your gum!"

I know that bananas are **biodegradable**, another word that I recently learned. That means they will break down and disappear, not like things made of plastic. Plastic, I read on the Internet, is with us forever. Potato or apple peels, or watermelon rinds, or corn husks and eggshells, they're biodegradable. They slowly decompose, and can make excellent compost.

Ricky and I part. I walk up the steps but not before counting the pieces of gum right in front of our apartment building.

UNO, DOS, THREE...

**In Other Words**

**compost the peels** let the peels break down naturally in soil

**Yeah, right** I don't believe that

I point at each ugly gum **smear**, almost flat from all the people stepping on them. I count, 'One, two, three, four . . . eighteen, nineteen, twenty . . ."

But I stop counting when a teenage boy walks past me and tosses a greasy cardboard container that held french fries.

"Hey," I yell.

The boy turns, licking his greasy fingers.

"You littered," I tell him.

"Whatever," he says with a **snicker on his face**.

I'm upset that this boy seems to have no conscience, another word that I learned recently. It means that you are thoughtless, that you don't think about what you're doing, that you don't care. The dumb boy doesn't realize that litter will blow down the street and that someone else will eventually have to pick it up.

**In Other Words**
**smear** spot
**snicker on his face** quiet laugh

▶ **Before You Move On**

1. **Confirm Prediction** What does Elena say and do when she sees people litter?

2. **Goal/Outcome** How is the **behavior** of her neighbors an obstacle to Elena's goal?

513

▶ **Predict**
What will Elena write when she sits down to do her report?

I sigh. What can a fifth grader do? I climb the steps back to my apartment, go to my bedroom, and sit at my desk and continue writing my report. There are 11 apartment buildings on our street with **an average of** 24 plastered pieces of gum in front of each one of them. That means we have 264 pieces of gum pressed in the sidewalk just on our street—at least!

This is a horrible **statistic**. Now think of all the fast food wrappers being **flicked out** at this moment. Think of the ice cream sticks, the **expired** bus passes, candy wrappers, the broken glass, and the lottery tickets torn in half . . .

**In Other Words**
**an average of** about
**statistic** fact shown with numbers
**flicked out** littered
**expired** unusable

The list goes on and on, all the trash that piles up when so much of it could be recycled.

What do I want, you ask? A pretty place! I could show you the **scenes** from an old calendar. Each month has a pretty scene, like a frozen river in January or **daffodils** in April. I like August best because it shows a surfer riding a big wave. I used to wonder whether the surfer rode it all the way to the beach or if the wave pushed him over. *Now* I wonder if the ocean was polluted.

**In Other Words**
**scenes** pictures
**daffodils** flowers ▶

515

It's not asking too much, really. We can have a pretty environment. I'll have mine—a flower box **brimming** with flowers! I'll use the compost Mom and I have been making and plant flowers, lots of them. I bet you that the sunflowers will attract bees, hummingbirds, and even a high-flying butterfly.

Now *that* could be a scene in a calendar. ❖

**In Other Words**
**brimming** filled

▶ **Before You Move On**

1. **Draw Conclusions**  What will Elena write about in her report? Will she achieve her goal?

2. **Point of View**  How would the story be different if Ricky told it?

## Meet the Author
# Gary Soto

Gary Soto likes to make his characters interesting and imperfect, just like regular people. He says "As a writer, my duty is not to make people perfect. . . . I'm one who provides portraits of people in the rush of life."

Elena Gomez is just one of those characters. She lives "in the rush of life" in a busy, Spanish-speaking neighborhood, just like the one Gary Soto grew up in.

◄ **Like his character Elena, Gary enjoys planting flowers.**

## Writer's Craft

Throughout "Where I Live," the author's narrator, Elena, uses similes, or comparisons of unlike things. For example, she compares herself to a chicken and an ostrich, and describes how pieces of gum look like baby teeth. Think like Elena. Use at least two similes to describe your classroom.

517

# Talk About It

**Key Words**

| | |
|---|---|
| affect | effect |
| behavior | generate |
| benefit | landfill |
| biodegradable | responsibility |
| dispose | transform |

1. Who is the main character of the **short story** "Where I Live"? What problem does she try to solve?

2. How are Elena and Ricky alike? How are they different? **Make comparisons** between the two characters. Discuss your ideas with a partner.

3. Gary Soto's characters have both good traits and flaws, or weaknesses. What good traits does Elena have? How could Elena be a better person?

**Learn test-taking strategies.**
🔵 NGReach.com

# Write About It

Elena described how litter ruined her neighborhood. Write a paragraph explaining how litter **affects** the landscape. Tell whose **responsibility** it is to keep our world clean. Use **Key Words**.

> Litter is a big problem because
> _____ . No one wants to see _____ .
> I think _____ should _____ .

# Goal and Outcome

Make a goal-and-outcome plan to show whether Elena's plan for her neighborhood succeeds.

**Goal-and-Outcome Plan**

| SOMEBODY (Character(s)) | WANTED (Goal) | BUT (Obstacle(s)) | SO (Outcome) |
|---|---|---|---|
| Elena | | | |

Write the character's goal here.

Write the obstacles here.

Write the outcome here.

With your partner, use your goal-and-outcome plan to summarize "Where I Live." Use **Key Words** in your summary. Record your retelling.

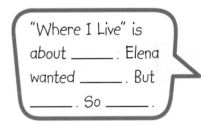

"Where I Live" is about _____. Elena wanted _____. But _____. So _____.

# Fluency  Comprehension Coach

Use the Comprehension Coach to practice reading with intonation. Rate your reading.

**Talk Together**

When is garbage gross in the story? Draw a picture that shows the terrible **effects** of littering. Use **Key Words** in your caption. Write at least three sentences.

# Context Clues

When you come across **unfamiliar words**, you can use context, or nearby words, to get clues to the meaning.

There are different kinds of context clues.

| Type of Clue | Example |
|---|---|
| **Restatement Clue:** gives the meaning in a different. way, usually after a comma. Look for the signal word: *or.* | Sarah **neglected**, **or** forgot, to take out the garbage. |
| **Example Clue:** gives an example of what the word. means. Look for the signal words: *for example, such as.* | There are many **benefits** of picking up litter. **For example**, it makes the environment pretty. |
| **Definition Clue:** explains the word directly in the text. Look for the signal words: *means, is.* | This boy has no **conscience**, which **means** he doesn't care if what he's doing is wrong. |

## Try It Together

Read the paragraph. Then answer the questions.

> Many poets use sound effects, such as rhyme. Using words in special ways affects, or causes a change in, how readers react to the poems.

1. **Which word is an example of a sound effect?**

   A poetry

   B special

   C rhyme

   D readers

2. **What does affect mean?**

   A writes poems

   B uses words

   C causes a change in

   D uses a sound effect

**Connect Across Texts** When is garbage gross? This poem uses humor and exaggeration to answer the question.

**Genre** A **poem** tells a story or expresses feelings. Poets use words to create sounds in their poems. These sound effects include **rhymes**, and words placed together that repeat the same sound.

# Sarah Cynthia Sylvia Stout Would Not Take the Garbage Out

written and illustrated
by **Shel Silverstein**

*Many people enjoy reading Shel Silverstein's poems aloud. Shel Silverstein himself did, too. He even made a recording of the book in which this poem appears. In it, he "**recited**, sung, and shouted" all of the poems! Silverstein liked his readers to discover his poems for themselves. He said, "Never explain what you do. It speaks for itself."*

▲ Shel Silverstein

**In Other Words**

**rhymes** words that sound alike, such as "Stout" and "out"

**recited** spoke

▶ **Before You Move On**

1. **Draw Conclusions** What kind of person do you think Shel Silverstein was?
2. **Make Inferences** Based on the title, what message do you think the poem might have?

**521**

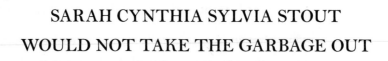

## SARAH CYNTHIA SYLVIA STOUT
## WOULD NOT TAKE THE GARBAGE OUT

Sarah Cynthia Sylvia Stout

Would not take the garbage out!

She'd scour the pots and scrape the pans,

Candy the yams and spice the hams,

And though her daddy would scream and shout,

She simply would not take the garbage out.

And so it piled up to the ceilings:

Coffee grounds, potato peelings,

Brown bananas, rotten peas,

Chunks of sour cottage cheese.

It filled the can, it covered the floor,

It cracked the window and blocked the door

With bacon rinds and chicken bones,

Drippy ends of ice cream cones,

Prune pits, peach pits, orange peel,

Gloppy glumps of cold oatmeal,

Pizza crusts and withered greens,

Soggy beans and tangerines,

Crusts of black burned buttered toast,

Gristly bits of beefy roasts . . .

The garbage rolled on down the hall,

It raised the roof, it broke the wall . . .

**In Other Words**
**scour** clean
**Candy the yams** Cook the yams in sugar
**withered greens** dry old vegetables
**Gristly** Tough

Greasy napkins, cookie crumbs,

Globs of gooey bubble gum,

Cellophane from green baloney,

Rubbery blubbery macaroni,

Peanut butter, caked and dry,

Curdled milk and crusts of pie,

Moldy melons, dried-up mustard,

Eggshells mixed with lemon custard,

Cold french fries and rancid meat,

Yellow lumps of Cream of Wheat.

At last the garbage reached so high

That finally it touched the sky.

And all the neighbors moved away,

And none of her friends would come to play.

And finally Sarah Cynthia Stout said,

"OK, I'll take the garbage out!"

But then, of course, it was too late . . .

The garbage reached across the state,

From New York to the Golden Gate.

And there, in the garbage she did hate,

Poor Sarah met an awful fate,

That I cannot right now relate

Because the hour is much too late.

But children, remember Sarah Stout

And always take the garbage out!

▶ **Before You Move On**

1. **Compare/Contrast** What lesson does this poem teach? Compare it to the theme of "Where I Live."

2. **Poetry** How does Silverstein use the sound of certain words and letters for effect in this poem?

# Compare Characters

Think about the characters Elena Gomez and Sarah Cynthia Sylvia Stout. How are the two characters alike? How are they different? With a partner, **compare and contrast** the characters.

**Venn Diagram**

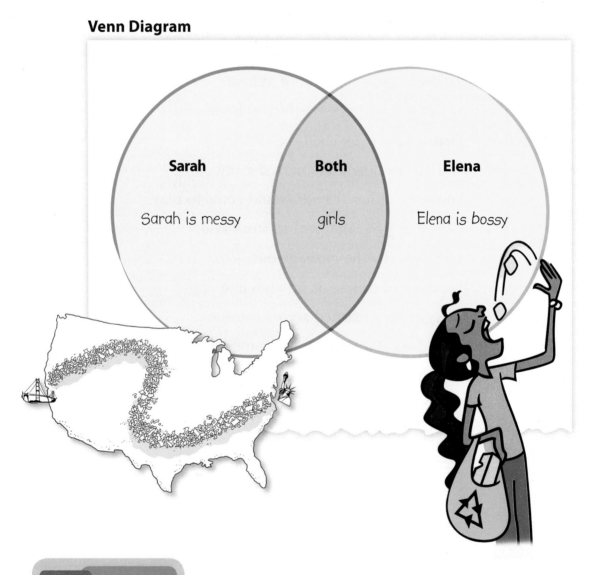

| Sarah | Both | Elena |
|---|---|---|
| Sarah is messy | girls | Elena is bossy |

**Talk Together**

Think about the short story, the poem, and the chart. What happens when people do not **dispose** of waste properly? What **effect** does it have on people and the landscape? Use **Key Words** when you give your answers.

# Prepositional Phrases

A **prepositional phrase** is a group of words that starts with a preposition and ends with a noun or pronoun.

| Grammar Rules Prepositional Phrases | |
| --- | --- |
| Use prepositional phrases to | |
| • show location. | Elena lives **in the city** |
| • show direction. | Mr. Asmara's shop is just **around the corner**. |
| • show time. | Shel Silverstein published many books **during his lifetime**. |
| • give details. | Silverstein's poems are well known **for their humor**. |

## Read Prepositional Phrases

Read the passage. Work with a partner to find the prepositional phrases.

> I go back to my apartment to write my report. There are 264 pieces of gum on the sidewalk. This is a horrible statistic. Everybody must try to keep litter off the streets.

## Write Prepositional Phrases

Look at the illustrations on pages 506 and 507. Write two sentences about them. Include at least two that tell time, location, direction, or interesting details. Read your sentences to a partner.

# Write As a Citizen

## Write a Persuasive Essay

What can you do about garbage? Write an essay that persuades people to reduce the amount of trash they produce. Post your essay in a "Taking Care of Trash" display.

## Study a Model

In a persuasive essay, you present your viewpoint, or opinion. You try to affect what your readers think or do. Read Jay's persuasive essay about something he'd like to make happen at his school.

### Good Garbage
by Jay Patel

What does our school need most? You might think gym equipment or computers. **What we need, though, is a compost bin**!

Compost bins are just big boxes used to break down biodegradeable garbage. We need them because our school makes more trash than we realize.

Every day, our school custodians collect 26 bags of garbage, just from the cafeteria! **That's 4,550 bags of lunchroom garbage a year**! It all piles up in our local landfill.

Compost bins would help solve that problem. They would turn trash into something useful. Once the garbage decomposes, it can be used as fertilizer.

Compost bins are a great way for us to reduce the trash we produce. They also put garbage to good use. Let's build some bins now!

The introduction captures the reader's attention. Jay clearly states his **opinion**.

Jay gives **reasons** for his opinion. He develops the reasons with specific **facts and details**.

The last paragraph tells what action Jay wants people to take.

# Prewrite

1. **Choose a Topic** What could you persuade people to do about trash? Talk with a partner to find an idea.

2. **Gather Information** What evidence, or reasons, will you give to support your viewpoint? What facts and details can you give to develop those ideas?

3. **Get Organized** Use an author's viewpoint chart to help you organize your ideas.

**Author's Viewpoint Chart**

| Viewpoint | Evidence | Action Needed |
|---|---|---|
| We need a compost bin at our school. | We produce 26 bags of lunch garbage each day. Trash ends up in our local landfill. | |

# Draft

Use your author's viewpoint chart and the evidence you collected to write your draft.

- Begin by stating your viewpoint.

- Support your viewpoint with reasons and details.

- End by telling your readers what you want them to do.

## Revise

1. **Read, Retell, Respond** Read your draft aloud to a partner. Your partner listens and then retells your main points. Next, talk about ways to improve your writing.

> ### Language Frames
>
> | **Retell** | **Make Suggestions** |
> |---|---|
> | • Your viewpoint is _____ . | • Your viewpoint isn't very clear. You could try saying _____ . |
> | • The reasons you gave included _____ . | • Could you add more details to support _____ ? |
> | • You want people to _____ . | • I'm not sure what you want people to think or do. Maybe you could _____ . |

2. **Make Changes** Think about your draft and your partner's suggestions. Then use the Revising Marks on page 629 to mark your changes.

   • Did you state each reason clearly? If not, try rewriting them.

   > our school makes more trash than we realize.
   > We need them because ~~they could help us with trash.~~ e

   • Make sure your facts and details are as specific as possible.

   > 26 bags of garbage, just
   > Every day, our school custodians collect ~~a lot of garbage~~ e from the cafeteria. That's 4,550 bags of lunchroom garbage a year!

## Edit and Proofread

Work with a partner to edit and proofread your persuasive essay. Pay special attention to adverbs and prepositional phrases. Use the marks on page 629 to show your changes.

Use the marks on page 629 to show your changes.

> **Grammar Tip**
>
> ✓ Use **adverbs** to make your adjectives and adverbs stronger, e.g. **extremely** creative, **very** rapidly.

## Publish

1.  **On Your Own** Make a final copy of your persuasive essay. Put the key points on note cards and present it to your class as a persuasive speech.

| Presentation Tips | |
|---|---|
| **If you are the speaker…** | **If you are the listener…** |
| Since you are persuading others, be sure to look listeners in the eye as you speak. | Make sure you understand all of the speaker's reasons. If you don't, ask questions. |
| Be ready to answer your listeners' questions or arguments with more details and examples. | Decide whether the speaker has supported his or her opinion with enough facts and details. |

2.  **In a Group** Collect all of the persuasive essays from your class. Post them on a bulletin board or in a wall display called "Taking Care of Trash." You can also publish one essay each week in a class blog.

## Talk Together

In this unit, you found lots of answers to the **Big Question**. Now, use your concept map to discuss the **Big Question** with the class.

**Concept Map**

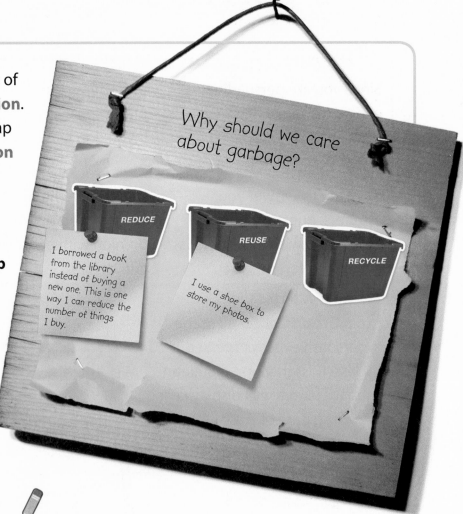

## Write an Editorial ✏

Write an editorial for a school newspaper persuading readers why we need to create less garbage and recycle. Include examples of items that are thrown away and their effect on the environment. Use your concept map to help you.

# Share Your Ideas

Choose one of these ways to share your ideas about the **Big Question**.

## Write It!

### Write a Poem

Write a gross garbage poem that uses sound effects, such as rhymes and words that repeat the same beginning sound. Practice your poem. Then recite it to the class.

## Talk About It!

### Give a Speech

Create a persuasive speech titled "What Kids Can Do to Rid the World of Litter!" Be creative, but also make sure your suggestions are doable. Practice your speech. Then present the speech to a group of your classmates.

## Do It!

### Perform a Skit

Perform a skit with some classmates about what might happen if Elena Gomez visits Sarah Cynthia Sylvia Stout's house. Use some props, too.

## Do It!

### Create a Piece of Art

Think of a way to use trash to create a piece of art, such as a sculpture or a collage. List the different items you would use. Then draw a picture of the work of art. Give your artwork a title. Share your art with the class.

531

**Unit at a Glance**
▶ **Language:** Express Ideas, Restate an Idea, Social Studies Words
▶ **Literacy:** Reading Strategies Review
▶ **Content:** Economics

**Unit 8**

# One Idea

**? BIG Question**

How can one idea change your future?

## Share What You Know

1. **Think** of all the things you have used today.

2. **List** three ways your life would have been different without these inventions.

3. **Share** your list with the class. Then place it on a bulletin board.

**Do It!**

Things I Used Today
1. cell phone
2. pencil
3. desk

**Build Background:** Watch a video about how businesses work.
**NGReach.com**

# Express Ideas

Listen to Diego and Sebastian's song. Then use **Language Frames** to express an idea of your own.

## A Dog-Gone Good Idea

*Song* ((MP3))

I know that people get
Lots of presents for their pets.
Why don't we make something dogs
   would like to eat?
We can sell fresh doggy treats.

I think that people do
Want treats to be healthy, too.
If we can invent a healthy doggy snack.
Ours will stand out from the pack.

Tune: "This Old Man"

# Key Words

**Key Words**

business

earnings

expenses

goods

income

profit

services

Look at the photos. Use **Key Words** and other words to talk about how a **business** works.

A **business** can offer. . .

goods

services

. . . **goods**, such as flowers.

. . . **services**, such as delivering flowers.

earnings, or income

expenses

profit

All businesses have **income**, or **earnings**.

All businesses have **expenses**, or bills.

A successful business makes a **profit**, or has money left over.

**Talk Together**

How can one business idea spark another idea? Use **Language Frames** from page 534 and **Key Words** to express your ideas to a partner.

535

# Steps in a Process

You can learn a new process or procedure more easily if you break it down into steps. Look at the pictures. They show the steps Diego and Sebastian used to start their business.

## Map and Talk

You can use a sequence chain to explain the steps in a process, or procedure. Here's how to make one.

First, write the goal of the procedure above the sequence chain. Then write the steps in an order that makes sense.

### How to Create a Healthy Dog Treats Business

| **First** | **Second** | **Third** |
|---|---|---|
| Make the treats. | Advertise the treats. | Sell healthy dog treats to dog owners. |

**Talk Together**

With a partner, think of an idea for a business. Use a sequence chain to explain the steps you would take to start the business.

# More Key Words

Use these words to talk about "Starting Your Own Business: Seven Steps to Success" and "Blind teen starts business."

### analyze
(a-nu-līz) *verb*

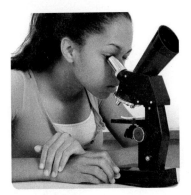

To **analyze** means to examine in detail. She **analyzed** the cell under a microscope.

### apply
(u-plī) *verb*

To **apply** means to ask for or to request something, usually in writing.

### cost
(kawst) *noun*

The **cost** of something is how much you pay to buy it. The **cost** of gas changes all the time.

### supply
(su-plī) *verb*

To **supply** means to provide things people need. Farms **supply** us with vegetables.

### value
(val-yū) *noun*

The **value** of something is its cost or how important it is. This jewelry has a high **value**.

## Talk Together

Work with a partner. Write a question using two **Key Words**. Have your partner answer, using a different **Key Word**. Take turns and keep going until you have used all of the words twice.

| Questions | Answers |
|---|---|
| Is the **cost** of this item too high for its **value**? | No; I **analyzed** the item and found that it was worth the price. |

**Add words to My Vocabulary Notebook.**
NGReach.com

# Strategic Reading

# Choose Reading Strategies

Good readers know that they need different strategies to understand the meaning of different texts. Often, you use more than one strategy. It is important to know which strategies to use and when to use them.

As you read:

- Think about the different strategies you have in your mental toolbox.

- Know what you are reading. Some strategies are better than others for different texts.

- Be flexible. Sometimes you need to drop one strategy and choose another. Switching or adding strategies gets easier the more you read. Even the best readers switch and add!

When you read, choose a reading strategy to help you understand.

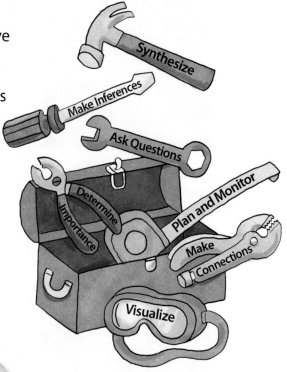

## **How to** Choose a Reading Strategy

| | | |
|---|---|---|
|  | **1.** Think about what you are trying to understand. | I want to know _____ . |
|  | **2.** Decide which strategy you can use to help you understand. | I can _____ . |
|  | **3.** Think about how the strategy helped you. | That strategy helped me _____ . |

Read the speech Sebastian gave at a school assembly. Tell a partner which reading strategies you used to help you understand the text.

Speech

# How We Succeeded in Business

Principal Hawes asked Diego and me to explain how we started and grew our **business**, Dog-Gone Healthy Treats. I love dogs, and Diego loves to bake. We wanted to **apply** our interests to our business. We also wanted to **supply** something that people needed.

Lots of pet owners worry that their dogs eat unhealthy foods. So we thought, "Why not make dog treats that are good for dogs?"

Diego was careful to put only natural ingredients in the treats. At first, they tasted so bad the dogs wouldn't touch them! He had to redo the recipe three times.

We **analyzed** what it would cost to make the treats. The **cost** of the ingredients was low, so our **profits** were high. We sold the snacks at the local farmers' market. The dog owners loved the treats. Most important, the dogs really loved them!

In closing, I have some advice for kids who want to start a business. Think about what people need. Provide **goods** or **services** that have real **value**. Think about what you like to do. Then work hard, and you will be successful!

# Read a Procedural Text

## Genre

A **procedural text** explains how to do something. Usually, procedural texts include steps to follow in a certain order.

## Text Feature

**Illustrations** are pictures that display information visually. In a procedural text, illustrations help show details related to each step of a process.

### Step 1 Plan Your Business

So you want to start you own business? First of all, you need to tell a parent or teacher. Then you need to make a plan. Successful entrepreneurs take time to plan their business before they start. They ask themselves questions. You can **keep track of** your questions and answers in a notebook or in a document on a computer.

What are your business goals? Do you want a short-term business that earns money for a specific item, like a new bike, musical instrument, or pet? Do you want a long-term business that **brings in steady money**? Or maybe you'd like to run your business only during school vacations.

Business goal:
To earn enough money to buy a big fish tank and some fish

Business type:
Short-term

illustration

# Starting Your Own Business:

## Seven Steps to Success

by Arlene Erlbach

illustrations by Gary LaCoste

Comprehension Coach

# Kids Are Business People, Too

Have you ever dreamed of having lots of money of your own? Then
you should think about starting a **business**. Every year, thousands
of kids start businesses. They earn extra money to spend or to
save. Some kids use their business **earnings** to pay for trips,
lessons, or for college later on. Kids do more than just **babysit** or
**mow lawns**. Many kids have found ways to make their businesses
different and special.

**In Other Words**

**babysit** take care of children for
parents

◀ **mow lawns** cut grass for people

542

People who start and **manage** their own businesses are *entrepreneurs*. Entrepreneurs are good planners and organizers. Before starting a business, an entrepreneur finds a need and thinks about how to fill it. Starting a business isn't always easy, but it's usually challenging and fun. Follow these steps to see how it's done.

**In Other Words**
**manage** run; control

▶ **Before You Move On**

1. **Ask Questions** What would you ask the author about becoming an entrepreneur?
2. **Use Text Features** Look at the section heading and the pictures. What do they tell you about the text?

# Step 1 Plan Your Business

So you want to start you own business? First of all, you need to tell a parent or teacher. Then you need to make a plan. Successful entrepreneurs take time to plan their business before they start. They ask themselves questions. You can **keep track of** your questions and answers in a notebook or in a document on a computer.

What are your business goals? Do you want a short-term business that earns money for a specific item, like a new bike, musical instrument, or pet? Do you want a long-term business that **brings in steady money**? Or maybe you'd like to run your business only during school vacations.

Business goal: To earn enough money to buy a big fish tank and some fish

Business type: Short-term

**In Other Words**
**keep track of**  collect
**brings in steady money**  earns money regularly

How much time can you **devote** to a business? Be realistic. If you spend a lot of time on homework, **chores**, or after-school activities, you won't have much time for a business. You'll need to choose a business that is easy to set up and manage.

What do you like to do and what are you good at? To help you decide what kind of business to try, make a chart like the one on this page. First list what you like to do and what you're good at. Then list business ideas related to your interests and talents.

| My Interests and Talents | Related Businesses |
| --- | --- |
| I'm good at baking. | cake-baking and decorating business |
| I like dogs. | dog-walking service |
| I like yard work. | |

**In Other Words**
**devote** give
**chores** everyday tasks at home

▶ **Before You Move On**

1. **Synthesize** Would a short-term or long-term **business** be best for a kid who needed to save money for college? Why?

2. **Use Text Features** What **business** could you add to the last row of the chart? Why?

# Step 2 Find Your Niche

Some businesses are service businesses. Service businesses do things for people. Walking dogs and mowing lawns are examples of service businesses. Other businesses sell **goods** , or things that are **manufactured**. Manufacturing businesses make products, such as jewelry, dog collars, or T-shirts. They also sell their products.

Before you start, you may want to think about what the people in your area need. Thinking carefully about **your market** can help you come up with business ideas and find your market **niche**.

Walking dogs is a
service business. ▶

◀ Making dog collars is a
manufacturing business.

**In Other Words**
**manufactured** made
**your market** the people you might
    sell to
**niche** specialty

These tips will help you find your own niche in the market.

- Think about items or **services** that might be needed in your neighborhood. Ask your family, neighbors, and friends for ideas.
- Think of businesses that already exist in the area. Maybe you could do a better job. Maybe you could do it for less money.
- Make a list of the results. Then ask yourself if you'd enjoy or be good at any of the businesses on your list.

| Businesses Needed in My Neighborhood | |
| --- | --- |
| Service Businesses | Manufacturing Businesses |
| taking care of pets | making and selling lemonade |
| party decorating | |
| **running errands** | making jewelry |
| shoveling snow | knitting clothes |
| **tutoring** | making greeting cards |
| | decorating T-Shirts |

◄ Shoveling snow is a good service business idea if you live in an area that gets snow.

**In Other Words**

**running errands** bringing things to people in their homes

**tutoring** helping other students with school work

► **Before You Move On**

1. **Plan and Monitor** What are the two main types of **businesses**? Describe them.
2. **Steps in a Process** What does the author want you to do in Step 2? Why is it an important step?

# Step 3 Get Started

The reason most people go into business is to make money, of course. But it usually takes at least a little money to start a business. That's something all entrepreneurs need to think about.

Start-up **costs** are what you pay to buy the materials you need to start your business. Your start-up costs may be small, or you may need to **invest in** a lot of **materials**.

▲ **If you are starting a gardening business, you may find some of your start-up materials at a hardware store.**

**In Other Words**
**invest in** buy
**materials** things

# Start-Up Materials

Let's say you're starting a gardening business. The first items on your list might be a shovel and gardening gloves. You might also find customers who will want you to water their houseplants. Then you may want to buy a watering can (unless they have one for you to use). A wagon might be useful for carrying your **equipment** and supplies from house to house.

# Start-Up Costs

How will you get some money for your start-up costs? Maybe you can do extra chores for your parents, or sell old toys and games. **Raising** your own start-up costs will make you look like a serious entrepreneur.

| MATERIALS | COST |
|---|---|
| shovel | $9.95 |
| gardening gloves | $3.95 |
| watering can | $10.95 |
| wagon (used) | $20.00 |
| advertising: 100 flyers at $.05 each | $5.00 |
| total start-up costs: | $49.85 (plus tax) |

| JOB | EARNINGS |
|---|---|
| extra chores | $29 |
| sold toys and games | $33 |
| total raised for start-up costs: | $62 |

**In Other Words**
**equipment** tools
**Raising** Making money to pay for

▶ **Before You Move On**

1. **Make Connections** Name one thing you would sell or do if you needed start-up money.

2. **Use Text Features** According to the charts above, did you earn enough money to pay for your start-up materials?

# Step 4 Plan the Pricing

People usually pay kids to do a job for two reasons: They like to help kids, and they like to save money. Adults know they won't be expected to pay a kid the same price they would pay an adult.

Still, you must charge enough for your goods and services to make money. You also need to keep your prices low enough to **attract** customers. How do you find the right price? For a while you may have to try different prices, and see what works.

**In Other Words**
**attract** get

550

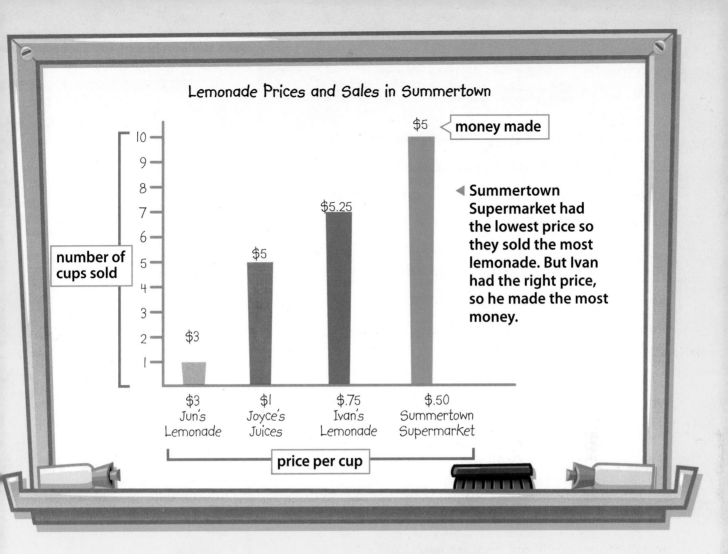

Lemonade Prices and Sales in Summertown

$5 — money made

number of cups sold

◄ Summertown Supermarket had the lowest price so they sold the most lemonade. But Ivan had the right price, so he made the most money.

| $3 | $5 | $5.25 | $5 |
| $3 | $1 | $.75 | $.50 |
| Jun's Lemonade | Joyce's Juices | Ivan's Lemonade | Summertown Supermarket |

price per cup

The best way to **figure** a fair price is by **checking out** the competition. Look at businesses similar to yours that are run by adults and by kids. Find out what price they charge. If you charge less, you'll **gain** customers. However, you need to charge enough to be able to pay for your materials and make money. If your competition is other kids, set your price a little lower than theirs. If kids with experience shoveling snow charge $10 to do a job, offer to do the same size job for $8. As you become more experienced, you can raise your price.

**In Other Words**
**figure** decide on
**checking out** examining; looking at
**gain** get more

▶ **Before You Move On**
1. **Synthesize** Study the picture on page 550. Why is Ivan smiling and Jun frowning?
2. **Use Text Features** How many cups of lemonade did the supermarket sell? Why didn't it make as much as Ivan?

# Step 5 Spread the Word

You may want to set aside some expense money for advertising. Advertising means **spreading the word** about your business. It can cost a little or a lot, depending on how creative you are.

One of the most **inexpensive** and **effective** ways to advertise is with flyers. Flyers are advertisements printed on sheets of paper. You can hand them out, mail them, or post them on bulletin boards.

When you advertise, be honest about your products or services. Don't make promises that are impossible to keep, or make yourself or your products seem better than what is considered normal. Such exaggerated and misleading statements make you appear dishonest, and customers will not contact you.

Also, be careful not to contradict, or go against, yourself in your advertisement. If you say you'll do something one way in one part of the advertisement, make sure you say the same thing in another part of the advertisement.

bulletin board

contact information

**In Other Words**

**spreading the word** making sure people know

**inexpensive** cheap

**effective** useful

flyer

### Car Wash and Wax Service

I will hand-wash and wax your car with care. Your car will look great in less than an hour. I live near Main Street in downtown Fairville, so you can go shopping while I work. $7 per wash, $5 per wax. Call 555-1234 to make an appointment.

CAR WASH 555-1234
CAR WASH 555-1234
CAR WASH 555-1234
CAR WASH 555-1234
CAR WASH 555-1234
CAR WASH 555-1234
CAR WASH 555-1234
CAR WASH 555-1234

▲ In this flyer, the person is honest about his or her abilities.

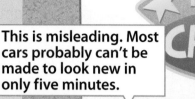

**This is misleading. Most cars probably can't be made to look new in only five minutes.**

Drop off your car with me, and it will look like a new car in just five minutes. No one in the world does a better job than I do. The lowest prices in town: $7 per wash, $5 per wax. Call 555-4321 to reserve your half-hour appointment.

**This contradicts the first part of the ad. If the job takes only five minutes, you wouldn't need a half-hour appointment.**

THE BEST CAR WASH 555-4321
THE BEST CAR WASH 555-4321
THE BEST CAR WASH 555-4321
THE BEST CAR WASH 555-4321
THE BEST CAR WASH 555-4321
THE BEST CAR WASH 555-4321

▲ In this flyer, the person is not honest about his or her abilities.

### ▶ Before You Move On

1. **Use Text Features** Which flyer gives the most information? Explain.
2. **Make Judgments** Find another misleading statement and another exaggeration in the second flyer.

# Step 6 Do the Math

Three very important words in business are **income**, **expenses**, and **profit**. Income is the money you **take in** from a business. Expenses are what it costs to run a business, such as the money you spend for supplies and equipment. Profit is what you have left after you subtract your expenses from the income.

## income-expenses=profit

**Income** Whenever you perform a service or sell **merchandise**, make a note of the amount of money you collected. You can write the amount in your notebook or type it in a document on a computer.

| | money taken in | | | money spent | | | money made |
|---|---|---|---|---|---|---|---|
| | Income | | – | Expenses | | = | Profit |
| Week 1 | Sandy | $4.00 | dog biscuits, 1 box | $5.00 | | | |
| | Chico | $6.00 | plastic bags | $1.00 | | | |
| | Molly | $4.00 | | | | | |
| | Thelma | $10.00 | | $6.00 | | | |
| | | $24.00 | | | | | $18.00 |

**In Other Words**
**take in** get; make
**merchandise** products

**Expenses** Whenever you buy something for your business, you'll receive a small piece of paper called a receipt. Save it. This is proof of the money you spent. Keep your receipts in an envelope inside your notebook. Label this envelope "Expenses."

**Profit** You should **figure** your profit weekly, and make sure your business is making a profit. If you are losing money, you will need to **adjust** your prices or reduce expenses.

To help you track your income, expenses, and profit, make a chart like the one on page 554. To make sure everything is correct, have an adult check your work.

proof of sale

# RECEIPT
## 9603

**Carla's Dog Store**
649 Main St.
Anytown, USA

Michele Ramirez ← name of buyer

1 Commercial St.

Anytown, TX 90043

| QUAN. | DESCRIPTION | PRICE | AMOUNT |
|-------|-------------|-------|--------|
| 1 | Dog Biscuits | $5.00 | $5.00 |
| 1 | Plastic Bags | $1.00 | $1.00 |
| | | goods bought | cost of each good |
| | | SUBTOTAL | $6.00 |
| | The government charges a tax for most sales. | TAX | $0.56 |
| | | TOTAL | $6.56 |

total amount spent

**In Other Words**

**figure** do the math to find out

**adjust** change

**a tax** an amount of money that goes to the public

▶ **Before You Move On**

1. **Use Text Features** Study the chart on page 554. What kind of **business** do you think it is used for?

2. **Analyze** In which part of the receipt would you find each item's cost?

555

# Step 7 Plan Your Steps

**Say** you are ready to start your own business. You have a great business idea that will work well in your neighborhood. You know exactly what tools you will need, the prices you will charge, and how you'll attract customers. You are so excited that you **hardly know** what to do next! Now is the time to plan your steps. A time line can help you stay organized and move forward, one step at time.

### Time Line for Samantha's Dog-Walking Service

| | |
|---|---|
| September 6th | Set up a business notebook. |
| September 12th | Explain business plan to Mom. Show her my notebook. |
| September 12th–26th | Do extra chores to earn money for start-up costs. |
| September 26th | Buy start-up materials: a leash, dog biscuits, plastic bags, paper, colorful markers. |
| September 27th–October 11th | Find out about other dog-walking businesses. What services do they offer? What prices do they charge? Decide on pricing. Tell Mom. |
| October 11th–14th | Make flyers. Post flyers at school. Announce my new business to my class and friends. |
| Weekly | Write my income and expenses in my notebook. Figure my profit. |

**In Other Words**
**Say** Imagine
**hardly know** can't even think of

556

# Go For It!

So go for it! Start a business. Make a list of things that you're good at or would enjoy doing. Then choose one idea. Good luck with your business! ❖

▶ **Before You Move On**

1. **Use Text Features** How much time does Samantha plan to spend on advertising? Do you think it is enough? Explain.

2. **Interpret** What steps are missing from the time line? Why aren't they shown?

557

# Think and Respond

## Talk About It

1. If you were starting a business, why would this **procedural text** be useful?

2. Imagine that your friend is going to start a **business**. **Express ideas** about the challenges your friend might face, based on what you have read.

   I think that _____ .
   I know that _____ .

3. Most people who start a business want to make a **profit**. How do you calculate profit?

   To calculate profit, you subtract _____ from _____ .

**Learn test-taking strategies.**
 NGReach.com

## Write About It

Imagine that you are starting a dog-walking **business**. Write an advertisement that convinces people that you have the best **service** in town. Use **Key Words**.

Wilma's Dog-Walking Service
I provide _____ and _____ dog-walking services. The cost to walk each dog is _____ . My customers say _____ .

558

# Steps in a Process

Make a sequence chain for each section of "Starting Your Own Business."

**Sequence Chain**

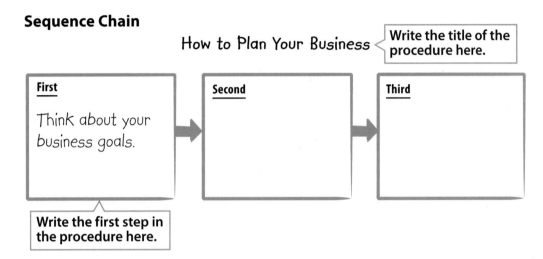

How to Plan Your Business — Write the title of the procedure here.

| First | Second | Third |
|-------|--------|-------|
| Think about your business goals. | | |

Write the first step in the procedure here.

Now use your sequence chains to explain the steps young people can use to succeed in business. Use the sentence frames and **Key Words**. Record your explanation.

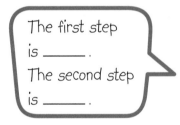

The first step is _____ .
The second step is _____ .

# Fluency  Comprehension Coach

Use the Comprehension Coach to practice reading with phrasing. Rate your reading.

**Talk Together**

How can a good business idea change your life? Think of a business that you've heard about. Use **Key Words** to tell a partner about the business.

# Idioms

An **idiom** is a colorful and fun way to say something. Usually, a few words combine to make an idiom. The words, when used together, mean something different from what the words mean by themselves.

Read this list of idioms and their meanings.

| Idiom | What it means | Example |
|---|---|---|
| at any cost | any way possible | I will make customers happy at any cost, even if it means I will have to work longer hours. |
| at face value | what something first seems to be | Because ads often exaggerate, you can't take them at face value. |
| deliver the goods | do what is expected or wanted | Our customers are happy because we always deliver the goods. |

## Try It Together

Read the paragraph. Then choose the best answer for each question.

My brother and I just started our T-shirt business two weeks ago, and already our shirts are selling like hotcakes. We can't make them fast enough. We're so happy! We feel like a million dollars!

1. **What does selling like hotcakes mean?**

   A look like pancakes

   B keeping customers warm

   C started our T-shirt business

   D can't make them fast enough

2. **Identify the other idiom above.**

   A we're happy

   B income is great

   C feel like a million dollars

   D business is a success

# Blind teen starts business creating Braille restaurant menus

## by Jane Rider of the *Missoulian*

**MISSOULA, MONTANA June 17, 2004**—Kayla Legare doesn't order chicken strips anymore when she goes to restaurants.

Legare, who attends high school in Helena, Montana, lost her vision at age 4. She has always tried to avoid the **hassle** of making someone else read her the choices off restaurant menus. That's why, until recently, she would only order chicken strips.

"I got **pretty sick of them**," she said.

▲ **Kayla Legare stands outside her high school in Helena, Montana.**

**In Other Words**
**hassle** discomfort
**pretty sick of them** very tired of eating just chicken strips

▶ **Before You Move On**
1. **Plan and Monitor** Why did Kayla order only chicken strips at restaurants?
2. **Use Text Features** Where and when was this article written? How do you know?

## Braille Menus Coming to Missoula

Today Legare can order any dish she wants. That's because a growing number of restaurants in the Helena area are customers of Legare's **business**, "Braille the World."

"Braille the World" creates Braille menus so that restaurants can better serve vision-impaired customers. Braille is a reading and writing system for the blind and visually impaired people.

Starting this week, Legare's business is bringing Braille menus to restaurants in Missoula, too.

## The Beginning of a Business

Legare's business was born less than a year ago, when she shared her idea with her uncle, Carl Schweitzer.

Schweitzer took Legare to visit his friend, Bob Keenan. Keenan owns a local hotel restaurant. The restaurant became the first to **pilot** Legare's idea of Braille menus.

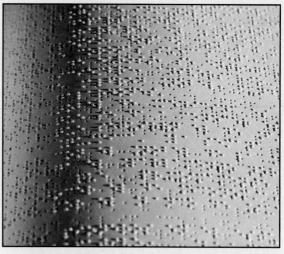

▲ The Braille alphabet uses raised dots. People read by touching them.

▲ Using her fingers, Legare reads a Braille menu she created.

**In Other Words**
**pilot** try out

▲ In the past, Braille was made by machines like this one. Now, people can use special computers to print Braille.

Then, using special computer software, Legare and Schweitzer created sample Braille menus for several restaurants in Helena. Last month, they gave a presentation at a meeting of the Montana Restaurant Association. Jeff Hainline, president of a major **restaurant chain**, heard it and was very interested.

"Everyone was impressed with the idea and the passion behind it," Hainline said.

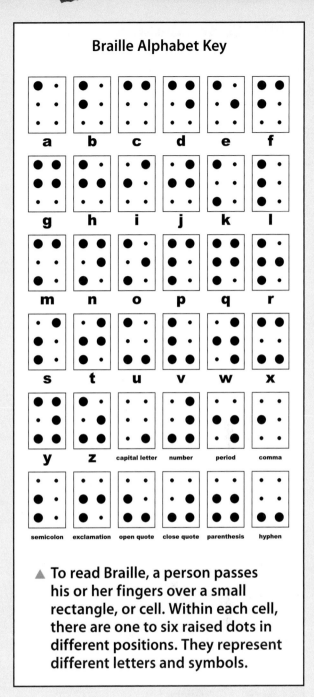

**Braille Alphabet Key**

a b c d e f
g h i j k l
m n o p q r
s t u v w x
y z capital letter number period comma
semicolon exclamation open quote close quote parenthesis hyphen

▲ To read Braille, a person passes his or her fingers over a small rectangle, or cell. Within each cell, there are one to six raised dots in different positions. They represent different letters and symbols.

**In Other Words**

**represent** show

**restaurant chain** group of restaurants with the same name

▶ **Before You Move On**

1. **Main Idea** What **goods** or **services** does Legare's **business** provide?
2. **Draw Conclusions** Use the key above to write your name. What can you conclude about the length of the Braille menus?

# Braille in Restaurants

Two days later, Hainline called Legare. He ordered twenty-six Braille menus, enough to place two copies in each of the restaurants. The twenty-three-page menus also include a Braille translation of the history of the restaurant chain.

Matt Castner is a "Braille the World" employee. He thinks Braille menus will make visually impaired diners feel more welcome.

"You think, 'Here is a restaurant that really cares about serving everybody,'" said Castner, who has been blind since birth. "A lot of places have ramps and special bathroom stalls for people who use wheelchairs, but where are the Braille menus?"

◄ Legare reads one of her Braille menus, which are now available in many Montana restaurants.

## Bringing Braille to the World

Legare is amazed at how quickly restaurant owners have **warmed up to** her idea. Now she wants to make her business grow even more. Her goal is to make the world **more accessible to** the visually impaired.

"I don't want to do just menus," she said. She envisions bank statements, bills, and educational materials in Braille. In fact, on Thursday, Legare is meeting with Montana Fish, Wildlife, and Parks. They will discuss the possibility of offering nature articles in Braille.

"I know it will be really hard, but I know we can do it if we put the energy into it," Legare said. ❖

▲ Seeing-eye dogs like Legare's help make the world more accessible to blind people. Legare hopes her menus will do the same.

▶ **Before You Move On**

1. **Generalize** What can a supermarket, for example, learn from Legare's **business**?

2. **Make Connections** According to "Starting Your Own Business," why is Legare's business successful?

# Respond and Extend

**Key Words**

| analyze | goods |
|---|---|
| apply | income |
| business | profit |
| cost | services |
| earnings | supply |
| expenses | value |

# Compare Procedures

The procedural text and the newspaper article both tell about starting a **business**. Work with a partner to interpret whether the steps listed in "Starting Your Own Business" were followed by Kayla Legare.

List the seven steps for starting a business in the first column. Then, in the second column, put a check mark next to the ones Kayla followed to start her Braille menu business.

**Comparison Chart**

| Steps in "Starting Your Own Business" | Steps Kayla Legare Used |
|---|---|
| 1. Plan your business | ✓ |
| 2. | |
| 3. | |
| 4. | |
| 5. | |
| 6. | |
| 7. | |

**Talk Together**

How do you think Kayla Legare's idea might change the future? How does this help you understand how one idea can be turned into a successful business? Use **Key Words** to talk about your ideas.

## Grammar and Spelling

# Past-Tense Verbs

**Regular** past-tense verbs end in *-ed*, but **irregular** past-tense verbs do not.

## Grammar Rules Past-Tense Verbs

| | Now | In the Past |
|---|---|---|
| • For most verbs, add **-ed**. | look | Leah **looked** around her neighborhood. |
| • For some verbs, change the base word before you add **-ed**. | analyze | She **analyzed** the need for a dog-washing business. |
| | plan | She **planned** where she would buy her supplies. |
| | worry (i) | She **worried** about all the expenses. |
| • Irregular verbs have special forms to show past tense. | be | She **was** soon busy washing dogs. |
| | give | She **gave** them some treats. |
| | go | The dogs **went** home, clean and content. |

## Read Past-Tense Verbs

Read the passage. Explain to a partner which words show the past tense.

Legare created "Braille the World." Her business was born less than a year ago, when she shared her idea with her uncle, Carl Schweitzer. Schweitzer took Legare to visit his friend.

## Write Past-Tense Verbs

Write one sentence describing the picture on page 550. Use one regular and one irregular past-tense verb. Compare your sentences with a partner's.

# Restate an Idea

Listen to Antonia's song. Then use **Language Frames** to restate an idea that you have heard or read about.

## Have a
# Warm Day

Song ((MP3))

I heard that some kids in our town are cold—

And that's not cool.

That's why I think we should collect some coats

Right here at our school.

I read that another town

Collected coats this way. So—

Let's start a coat drive to help everyone

Have a warm day.

Tune: "Pack Up Your Troubles in Your Old Kit Bag and Smile, Smile, Smile"

COATS FOR
KIDS
COAT
DRIVE

COA
DRIV

# Key Words

**Key Words**

borrow

credit

debt

entrepreneur

loan

Look at the illustrations. Use **Key Words** and other words to talk about how a business works.

Oscar needs to borrow money to start a business.

The banker agrees to extend Oscar the line of credit, or money, he needs.

Oscar takes out a loan.

Oscar opens his business. He is an entrepreneur.

Oscar has debt, or money he owes the bank.

Oscar pays back the bank little by little each month. He pays other bills, too.

**Talk Together**

How can borrowing money affect your life? Talk to a partner. Use **Language Frames** from page 568 and **Key Words** to restate how the idea changed Oscar's life.

569

# Elements of Fiction

When you think about a story, you usually think about the different story elements, such as the characters, the setting, and the plot. Then you think about the theme.

Look at the pictures. They tell the story of Antonia's coat drive.

## Map and Talk

You can use a story map to show the different elements of a story. Here's how you make one.

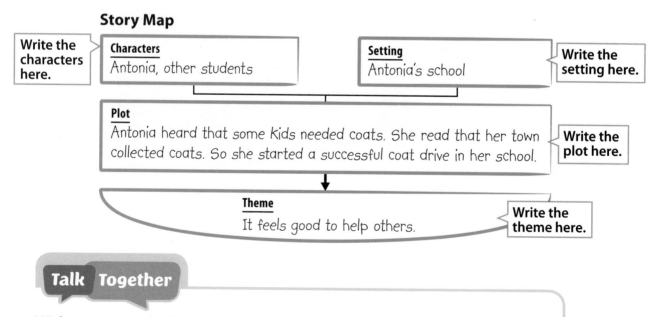

**Story Map**

Write the characters here. → | **Characters** Antonia, other students

**Setting** Antonia's school ← Write the setting here.

**Plot** Antonia heard that some kids needed coats. She read that her town collected coats. So she started a successful coat drive in her school. ← Write the plot here.

**Theme** It feels good to help others. ← Write the theme here.

**Talk Together**

With a partner, think of a story you both know. Use a story map to show the different parts of the story.

# More Key Words

Use these words to talk about "One Hen" and "Another Way of Doing Business."

### advantage
(ud-**van**-tij) *noun*

An **advantage** is something that helps you. Being fast is an **advantage** in tennis.

### determine
(di-**tur**-mun) *verb*

To **determine** is to decide something. The doctor **determined** that her patient had the flu.

### favorable
(fā-vu-ru-bul) *adjective*

Something that is **favorable** is good. They had **favorable** weather for the party.

### influence
(**in**-flü-uns) *verb*

If something **influences** you, it affects you. Her kindness **influenced** me to be kind.

### organization
(awr-gu-nu-**zā**-shun) *noun*

An **organization** is a business or other official group. This **organization** helps lost pets.

## Talk Together

Make a Vocabulary Example Chart for each **Key Word**. Then compare your chart with a partner's.

| Word | Definition | Example from My Life |
|------|-----------|----------------------|
| favorable | good | When the winds are **favorable**, I like to fly a kite. |

Add words to My Vocabulary Notebook.
NGReach.com

# Use Reading Strategies

**Reading Strategies**

- Plan and Monitor
- Ask Questions
- Determine Importance
- Make Inferences
- Make Connections
- Visualize
- Synthesize

Good readers use strategies all the time! Get in the habit of using reading strategies before, during, and after you read. Here's how to read actively.

- **Before you read**, look through the text quickly to get an idea of what it will be about. Decide on your purpose, or reason, for reading.

- **While you are reading**, stop now and then to ask yourself: Does this make sense? Use a reading strategy to help you understand better.

- **When you finish reading**, pause and reflect. Decide what you want to remember about the text.

## How to Use a Reading Strategy

| | | |
|---|---|---|
|  | **1.** Before you read a text, stop and think: What strategies can help me get ready to read? | Before I read, I will _____ . |
|  | **2.** During reading, think about which strategies can help you better understand what you are reading. | As I read, I can _____ . |
|  | **3.** After reading, ask yourself: What strategies can I use to help me think about what I read? | Now that I'm done, I think _____ . |

Antonia wrote a story based on something that happened at the coat drive. Read her story. Tell a partner which reading strategies you used to help you understand the text.

Story

# A Warm Welcome

Maddie lived with her father and her little brother Will in a house in the city. The **organization** her father worked for went out of business, so her father lost his job. The family had to be careful about spending money.

Winter was coming, and Will had grown too big for his winter coat. Maddie **determined** he needed a new coat. She had heard **favorable** things about a group called Coats for Kids. In fact, some volunteers from the group were working at her school. This gave her an **advantage**.

After school, she went to talk to Hector, the student in charge of Coats for Kids. He was busily folding coats, and Maddie started to help him.

"My brother could use a warm coat," Maddie said.

Hector smiled. "That's why we're here. What size is your brother?" Hector and Maddie found the perfect coat. It was green, Will's favorite color. As Maddie turned to leave, she paused and asked, "Do you need another volunteer?"

Hector knew the experience **influenced** her. "We can always use new volunteers," he said. "Welcome to our coat drive, Maddie!"

573

# Read a Story

## Genre

**Fiction** is writing about imaginary people, places, things, or events. Sometimes, however, parts of fictional stories can be real. This fictional story is based on the life of a real person.

## Point of View

Point of view describes how a story is told. In third-person point of view, a narrator outside the story tells the story. When the third-person point of view is *omniscient*, the narrator has unlimited knowledge of the story's events, including characters' hidden thoughts and feelings.

The banker sits back in his chair. This is not a story he hears every day.

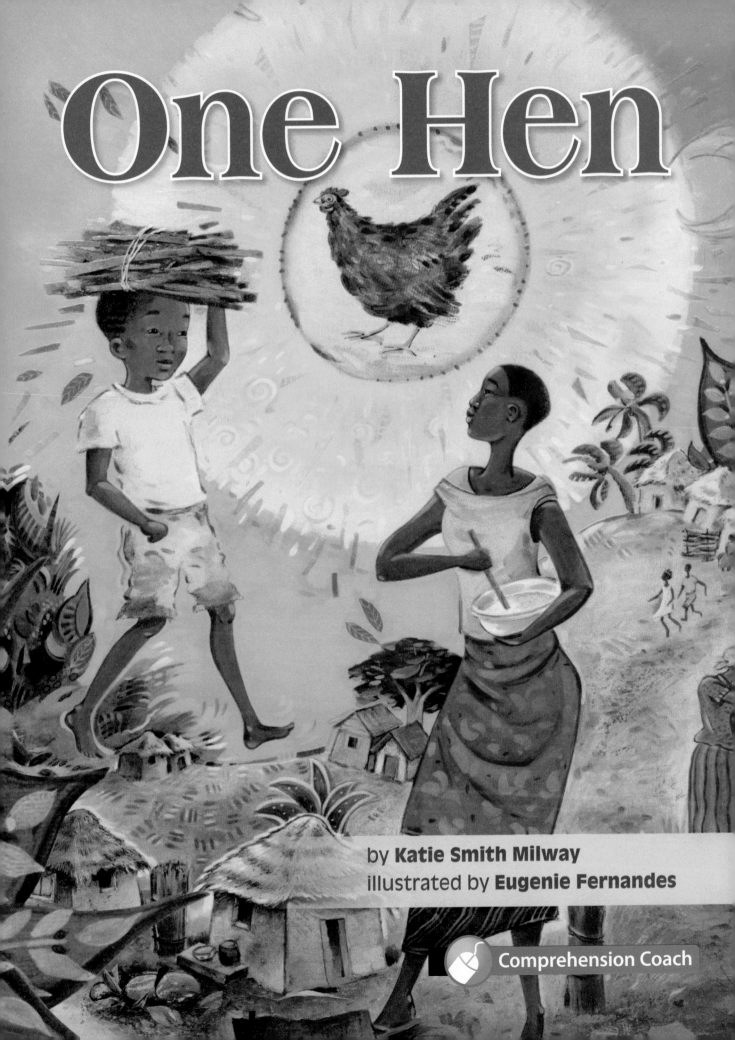

# One Hen

by **Katie Smith Milway**

illustrated by **Eugenie Fernandes**

Comprehension Coach

▶ **Set a Purpose**
Find out how villagers use **loans**
to improve their lives.

**K**ojo **hoists** a bundle of firewood onto his head. Since his father died, he has had to quit school and help his mother collect wood to sell at the market.

Kojo and his mother live in a village in the Ashanti region of **Ghana**. They live in a mud-walled house. Beside it is a garden where they grow their own food. They never have much money or much to eat.

None of the twenty families in the village have much money, but they do have a good idea. Each family promises to save a bit of money so that one family can **borrow** all the savings to buy something important.

Ghana

**In Other Words**
**hoists** lifts; puts
◀ **Ghana** a country in West Africa

The Achempong family is first to borrow the money. They use it to buy two cartloads of fruit, which they sell for a profit at the market. When they pay back the **loan** , the Duodu family borrows the money to buy a sewing machine. They will **turn** the cloth they **weave** into clothing to sell.

One day it is Kojo's mother's **turn**. She uses the loan to buy a cart to carry more firewood to market. She also hopes to rent the cart to people.

There are a few coins left over. Kojo asks if he can have them to buy something. He has a good idea, too.

**In Other Words**
**turn** change
**weave** make
**turn** chance; opportunity

Kojo's idea is to buy a hen. He and his mother will eat some of the eggs it lays and sell the rest. It takes Kojo two hours to walk to the chicken farm. He wonders how he will know which hen to choose.

When he arrives, Kojo tries to look over *all* the chickens. A white one pecks the ground near his foot. Should he choose this hen? A **speckled** one flaps her wings and clucks. Is she the one? Kojo **spies** a plump brown hen with a bright red comb. He **knows in his heart** that she is the one. He pays for the hen.

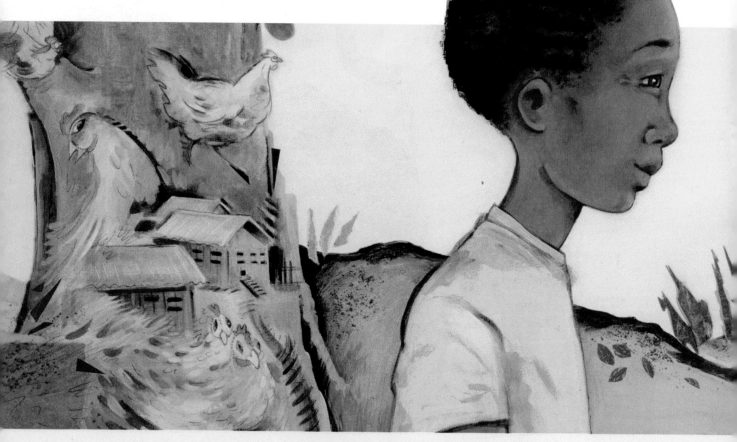

**In Other Words**
**speckled** spotted
**spies** sees
**knows in his heart** has a strong feeling

Kojo makes a nest for his hen and **checks it** for eggs every day. On the first day he finds . . . nothing. On the second, what is this? In the corner, under some straw, a smooth brown egg!

His hen lays five eggs the first week. Kojo and his mother eat one egg **apiece**, and he saves the other three for the market.

On market day, he finds a good place to set down his small basket and call out for customers. Kojo sells two eggs to Ma Achempong and one to Ma Duodu. He clutches his egg money tightly so he won't lose it.

**In Other Words**
**checks it** looks in it
**apiece** each

▶ **Before You Move On**

1. **Plot** How does Kojo use the **loan** to help his family?
2. **Make Connections** How is Kojo's process similar to the process described in "Starting Your Own Business"?

▶ **Predict**
    Will Kojo's plan succeed?

Slowly, Kojo's egg money grows. After two months he saves enough to pay his mother back. In four months he has enough to buy another hen. After six months he buys a third hen, and he and his mother **have an** egg a day. **Bit by bit**, one small hen is making a big difference.

One year later Kojo has built up his **flock** to twenty-five hens. Selling eggs has given Kojo savings. Maybe he can pay for something he's been dreaming of: **fees** and a uniform so that he can go back to school.

"Your eggs have made us stronger, Kojo," says his mother. "Now go to school and learn."

**In Other Words**
**have an**  eat one
**Bit by bit**  Slowly, over time
**flock**  group of hens
**fees**  money

In school Kojo works hard to **catch up with other students on** reading and spelling and arithmetic. He learns to write essays and solve math and science problems. He learns about his country's history and resources, and about other countries in Africa and around the world.

His dreams are growing bigger, but now he sees that he will need more education to make them come true. Kojo studies even harder and wins **a scholarship** to an agricultural college to learn more about farming. His mother will care for his chickens while he is away.

At college Kojo's dreams start to take shape, the shape of a farm of his own.

After Kojo finishes college, he decides to take a big **risk**. He will use all the money he and his mother have saved to start a real **poultry** farm. He buys a large plot of land and enough wood and wire to build **chicken coops**. Now he needs nine hundred hens to start the farm. He needs another **loan**, a big one.

This time Kojo goes to a bank in Kumasi, a nearby town. When the banker hears that Kojo wants to buy nine hundred hens, he shakes his head. He does not want to lend money to a young man from a poor family.

Kojo does not give up. He goes to the capital city, Accra, and visits the bank's **headquarters**. Kojo tells the bank president that he has schooling and will work hard. The banker has heard such stories before and frowns. Then Kojo tells him about the small loan and the brown hen and the egg money he has used to build his flock.

The banker sits back in his chair. This is not a story he hears every day. He smiles and nods. Kojo will get his loan.

Back home Kojo buys his hens. Soon there will be so many eggs that he will need helpers to collect them all.

**In Other Words**
**risk**  chance that he might lose money
**poultry**  chicken
◀ **chicken coops**  buildings for chickens
**headquarters**  most important office

Kojo's hens **are good layers**. There are more than enough eggs for his village, so he travels to Kumasi to sell to the shopkeepers there.

One shopkeeper is called Lumo. Kojo knows him well. This man grew up in the same village that Kojo's father did and was his good friend. Kojo always goes to Lumo's shop last and sometimes stays for **supper**. He likes to hear stories about his father. And he likes the peanut stew and palm oil soup that Lumo's daughter makes.

Her name is Lumusi, and she is a teacher. She has many stories about boys just like Kojo once was, boys who want to learn and who have big dreams. Kojo loves these stories, and he visits more and more often. One day he asks if Lumusi will be his wife.

Lumusi is **proud** to marry Kojo and join him on the farm. As the years go by, they have three boys and two girls. With the money from Kojo's eggs they build a bigger house. Kojo's mother comes to live with them and **tend** the garden. She will never have to sell firewood again.

**In Other Words**
**are good layers** lay a lot of eggs
**supper** dinner
**proud** happy and satisfied
**tend** take care of

▶ **Before You Move On**

1. **Plot** What steps does Kojo take to become a successful **entrepreneur**?
2. **Point of View** How would the story be different if it were in third-person *limited* point of view?

585

▶ **Predict**
How will Kojo improve the lives of other people in Ghana?

**B**efore long, many people are working on Kojo's farm. Men feed the chickens and clean the coops. Women collect the eggs and pack them in boxes. Other workers drive the eggs to markets.

The workers have families. One hundred and twenty people depend on the **wages** from Kojo's farm. Families like the Odonkors have enough food to eat and money for their children's school fees. Ma Odonkor can buy medicine when her daughter Adika **falls ill**. Pa Odonkor can rebuild the walls of their mud home with **cinderblocks**.

The workers on Kojo's farm can even afford **livestock** of their own. Some families buy a goat, others a sheep, and some start with one brown hen.

**In Other Words**
**wages** money paid to workers
**falls ill** gets sick
◀ **cinderblocks** strong blocks made of cement
**livestock** farm animals

Kojo's farm is now the largest in Ghana. One day, Kojo hears a knock at the door. Adika Odonkor, **all grown up**, is there. She greets Kojo and holds out a small sack of coins.

She tells Kojo that she has saved her wages. With just a bit more, she says, she could buy a **mechanical grain mill** and start a business helping families turn their grain into flour. Would it be possible to have a small **loan**?

Kojo likes this idea. He makes Adika promise that one day she will loan money to another family. Adika agrees and, bit by bit, as one person helps another, the lives of many families improve.

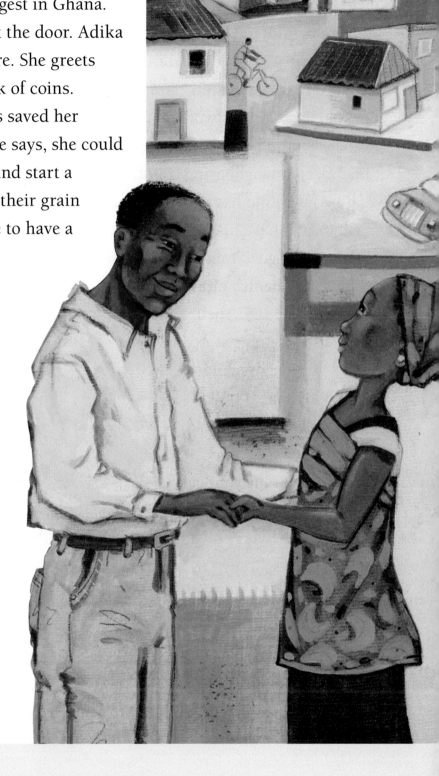

**In Other Words**

**all grown up** who is now an adult

**mechanical grain mill** machine that breaks grain

As the years pass, Kojo's poultry farm becomes the largest in all of West Africa. He is older now and a proud grandfather. His grandchildren visit often and help collect eggs. "Where will this one go?" they ask. "And that one?"

"To Bamako in Mali," Kojo replies, "or to Ouagadougou in Burkina Faso." Kojo's workers pack thousands of eggs a day, and Kojo feels proud each time an egg truck pulls away to take food to families in neighboring countries.

By now Kojo has paid **many taxes** to the government of Ghana. So have his workers and the shopkeepers who sell his eggs. The government uses the tax money to build roads, schools, and **health clinics** across the country. It uses the money to improve the port at Accra where ships from many countries come to trade.

One more egg truck drives away, and Kojo looks down at his youngest grandson. The next time the boy asks Kojo where an egg will go, Kojo will say "To your future, my child."

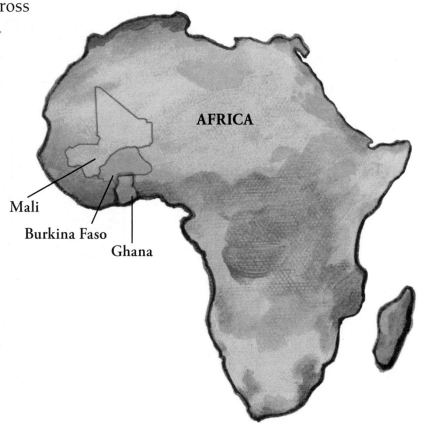

AFRICA

Mali

Burkina Faso

Ghana

**In Other Words**
**many taxes**  much money
**health clinics**  places that offer medical services

This is the way that one young boy named Kojo, with one small **loan** to buy one brown hen, **eventually** changed the lives of his family, his community, his town and his country. It all started with a good idea and one small loan that made it come true. It all started with one hen. ❖

**In Other Words**
**eventually** slowly, over time

▶ **Before You Move On**

1. **Theme** How do small loans continue to improve the lives of Kojo and others in Ghana?

2. **Make Inferences** Why do you think Kojo trusts Adika to pay back the loan?

## Meet the Author

# Katie Smith Milway

AWARD WINNER

Many books are fun to read and have beautiful art. Some books, like "One Hen," also have a purpose. Katie Smith Milway wrote "One Hen" so kids might think about the different ways they can help themselves and others.

Milway based her story on the life of Kwabena Darko. Like Kojo, Kwabena was a poor boy who grew up to be a successful poultry farmer in Ghana. Like Kojo, he gave loans to people who wanted to start their own businesses. You can find out more about Kwabena at Katie's website, which can be accessed at NGReach.com.

◄ Katie Smith Milway

◄ Kwabena Darko, the "real" Kojo

### Writer's Craft 🖊

In "One Hen," the author uses varied sentences, both short and long, to tell the story of Kojo's success. Retell one part of the story using a variety of sentence lengths. What impact does it have on your storytelling?

591

# Talk About It

1. "One Hen" is **fiction**, but it is based on some real events. What events do you think really happened? Tell which details you think the author made up.

2. Imagine that you are talking to Kwabena Darko, the man "One Hen" is based on. **Restate ideas** you learned in the story. Then ask Darko a question that will help you understand more about his life.

   I read that _____ . I heard that _____ .

3. "One Hen" is told from the third-person omniscient point of view. How would the story be different if Kojo narrated the story?

Learn test-taking strategies.
NGReach.com

# Write About It

Imagine that you are one of Kojo's grandchildren who is now grown up. Write a **favorable** essay about Kojo that you would want your children to read. Use **Key Words**.

Grandfather Kojo was _____ . The thing I remember most about him was _____ . One important lesson he taught me was _____ .

**Key Words**

| | |
|---|---|
| advantage | entrepreneur |
| borrow | favorable |
| credit | influence |
| debt | loan |
| determine | organization |

# Elements of Fiction

Fill in the elements of the story "One Hen" on this story map.

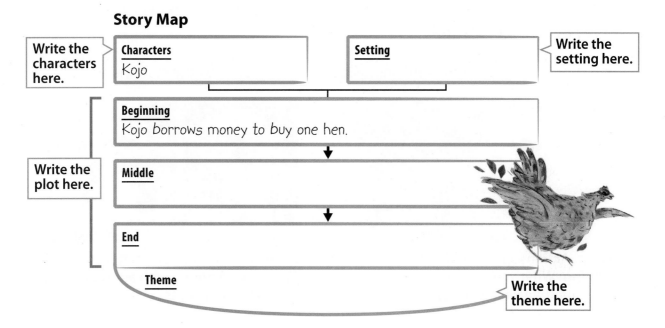

**Story Map**

Write the characters here. | **Characters**
Kojo

**Setting** | Write the setting here.

Write the plot here.

**Beginning**
Kojo borrows money to buy one hen.

**Middle**

**End**

**Theme**

Write the theme here.

Now use your story map to retell the story.
Use the sentence frames and **Key Words**.
Record your retelling.

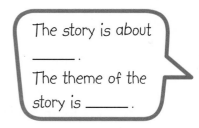

The story is about
_____ .
The theme of the
story is _____ .

# Fluency  Comprehension Coach

Use the Comprehension Coach to practice reading with expression.
Rate your reading.

**Talk  Together**

How can one person change many lives? Think about a business or an organization in your community that has changed the lives of others.
Use **Key Words** to tell a partner about it.

593

# Sayings

**Sayings** are well-known statements that usually tell something about life or people. Some sayings have been passed down over the centuries because people believe they are true.

Read these sayings and their meanings. Say if you agree with the statements.

**Saying:** Actions speak louder than words.
**Meaning:** What you do is more important than what you say.

**Saying:** Two heads are better than one.
**Meaning:** Working with another person brings better results.

## Try It Together

Read the passage. Then answer the questions.

> I asked my grandfather for money to buy a video game. "You know what they say," he said. "A penny saved is a penny earned."
>
> I smiled and said, " Grandpa, they are on sale this week. And you know what they say, "Strike while the iron is hot!" Grandpa smiled.

1. **A penny saved is a penny earned.**
   **What does this saying mean?**

   A Everyone should help other people.

   B Great things come from small actions.

   C Save your money, don't spend it.

   D It is hard to tell what people are like by the way they look.

2. **Identify another saying in the passage above.**

   A Grandpa smiled.

   B A penny saved is a penny earned.

   C Strike while the iron is hot.

   D I asked my grandfather for money to buy a video game.

**Connect Across Texts**  Find out how a small group of **entrepreneurs** learned to live in balance with the natural world.

**Genre**  A **magazine article** gives information about a topic. It often includes headings, facts, and pictures.

# Another Way of Doing Business  by Greta Gilbert

An elephant and her family walk through the wild grass in Zambia, Africa. They are looking for a snack. Soon, they arrive at a farmer's cornfield. The mother dips her trunk into the delicious-looking corn plants. As she prepares to **feast**, she notices some smaller plants beside her legs. They have tasty-looking red fruits. She quickly **stuffs** a few into her mouth. Then, just as quickly, she begins to sneeze.

Photo by John Antonelli

chili pepper plant

**In Other Words**
**feast** eat
**stuffs** puts

▶ **Before You Move On**
1. **Visualize**  How does the text help you to visualize what the elephant sees?
2. **Make Inferences**  Why do you think the elephant starts to sneeze?

In the distance, a farmer watches and laughs as the red-hot chili plants **take effect**. The elephant thrashes her head and sneezes wildly. Then she and her family run away, back into the wild grass. The farmer knows that the chilis will not harm the elephant. He also knows that she will never again try to eat his corn.

## Living Together in Peace

Here in Zambia's North Luangwa National Park, people and elephants have learned to live together in peace. It wasn't always this way, however. Not long ago, the elephants here were in danger of **extinction**. People were poaching, or illegally killing the animals, for their **tusks**.

North Luangwa
National Park

Photo by Hosea Jemba

North Luangwa elephants like these were once in danger of extinction.

**In Other Words**
**take effect** start to work
**extinction** disappearing forever
◀ **tusks** long, pointy teeth

# A Demand for Ivory

Beginning in the 1970s, more people around the world wanted to buy ivory, the material in elephant tusks. It was used to make everything from piano keys to statues to jewelry. People who killed elephants could make a lot of money by selling their tusks. Since there were **an estimated** 1.3 million elephants on the continent of Africa alone, the **supply** of ivory seemed endless.

By the 1990s, hundreds of thousands of elephants across Africa had been killed for their tusks. In many villages, including the villages outside North Luangwa National Park, many people had learned to **support themselves** by poaching elephants.

**Ivory is often used to make jewelry, such as this ivory bracelet** ▶

▲ **These officials process tusks taken illegally by poachers.**

▶ **Before You Move On**

1. **Make Inferences** Why won't the elephant return later to eat the farmer's corn?
2. **Cause/Effect** Why were so many elephants poached by the 1990s?

monkey orange

Photo by Hosea Jemba

▲ Hammer tells kids in one North Luangwa village how to dry monkey oranges and make them into items they can sell.

# A Man with an Idea

This way of life could not last. Because of poaching, the elephant population in North Luangwa National Park had gone from 17,000 to only 1,300 in 1994, and it was getting smaller every day. Soon, all the elephants would be gone. The villagers understood that selling tusks was not going to earn money for them for much longer. Still, it was the only business they knew.

One man, however, had another idea. His name was Hammerskjoeld Simwinga, or "Hammer," for short. He had studied **agronomy** in college, so he knew how villagers could make a living from the land without harming wildlife. Hammer started the North Luangwa Wildlife Conservation and Community Development Program. Slowly, one village at a time, he introduced a system through which the villagers could help each other succeed without poaching.

**In Other Words**
**agronomy** soil and plant sciences

# A System of Loans

Here is how Hammer's system worked: Each family in a village would put money into **a collection**. The amount of money would be small—only what each family could afford. Put together, however, the amount of money would be large—enough money for a **loan**.

That loan would help one family buy tools, supplies, seeds, or whatever they needed to start a business. The family would then pay the other families back over time, with their profits. There was only one rule: The business they started could not harm the elephants or other animals of North Luangwa National Park.

▼ **Hammer shows kids how to feed fish at a fish farm. The farm is one of many new businesses created with small loans.**

Photo by Hosea Jemba

**In Other Words**

**a collection** one place

▶ **Before You Move On**

1. **Make Inferences** Why do you think Hammer wanted to help the villagers find another way to make a living?

2. **Explain** How were the villagers able to make many **loans** to each other over time?

599

# New Ways to Make a Living

Slowly, villagers started new businesses with the money they gave to each other through **loans**. This led to a wide variety of new businesses, which required villagers to learn new skills. Some villagers learned how to keep bees. Others learned how to raise fish in fish ponds. Many learned skilled trades, and began to make some of the things they used to buy with poaching money.

One of the most popular businesses was sunflower **cultivation**. In the past, the villagers had spent much of their money on cooking oil. Hammer explained to them that they could make their own cooking oil. All they needed was a **sunflower press machine**, seeds for the first crop, some hard work, and a small loan.

**Hammer shows former poachers how to make "hay tents" to protect their young vegetables from the sun's heat.** ▶

**In Other Words**

**cultivation** growing

◀ **sunflower press machine** machine for getting the oil out of sunflower seeds

# One Idea, Many People

Today, the elephant population in North Luangwa National Park is increasing, and the elephants are **thriving**. Thanks to Hammer Simwinga, the people in the villages around the park are thriving, too. Under Hammer's **micro-lending** system, the villagers have started businesses ranging from vegetable cultivation to fish farming to bee-keeping.

Most importantly, the villagers are passing along what they have learned to people in other villages. Throughout Zambia, people are realizing that they do not have to rely on elephant poaching to survive. Slowly, through hard work and cooperation, they are improving their environment and **transforming** their own lives. They have found another way of doing business. ❖

Photo by Hosea Jemba

▲ Hammer examines some locally made items that are for sale at a nearby museum.

Photo by Hosea Jemba

**In Other Words**
**thriving** doing very well
**micro-lending** small **loan**
**transforming** changing

▶ **Before You Move On**

1. **Make Judgments** In what ways do you think the villagers' lives have improved?

2. **Visualize** What descriptions in the text help you picture what a North Luangwa village might look like today?

**Key Words**

| advantage | entrepreneur |
|---|---|
| borrow | favorable |
| credit | influence |
| debt | loan |
| determine | organization |

# Compare Ideas

"One Hen" and "Another Way of Doing Business" tell about how people started successful businesses. How are the businesses the same? How are they different? With a partner, complete the chart to compare the two selections.

**Comparison Chart**

| | "Another Way of Doing Business" | "One Hen" |
|---|---|---|
| Name the businesses. | | Hens and eggs |
| Who started it? | | Kojo |
| Where did the start-up costs come from? | A small-business loan | |
| Name the start-up materials. | | |
| Do you think it will continue to be successful? Why? | | |

---

**Talk Together**

How did one idea change the future of many Africans? Look back at the selections with your partner. Use **Key Words** to talk about your ideas.

# Future Tense

There are two ways to show the **future tense**.

## Grammar Rules  Future Tense

| | |
|---|---|
| • Use the helping verb *will* before a **main verb**. | Kojo **will go** on a trip tomorrow. |
| • Use *am going to, are going to,* or *is going to* before a **main verb**. | I **am going to borrow** some money.<br><br>She **is going to rent** a cart.<br><br>They **are going to care** for the chickens. |

## Read in the Future Tense

Read the passage. Then work with a partner to find examples of the future tense.

> Kojo is going to buy a hen. He and his mother will eat some of the eggs it lays. They are going to sell the rest. It will take Kojo two hours to walk to the chicken farm. He wonders how he is going to choose the best hen.

## Write in the Future Tense

Look at the illustrations on page 578 and 579. Write two sentences describing what will happen to Kojo. Use the future tense in each sentence. Compare your sentences with a partner's.

603

# Write As a Citizen

## Write a Procedure ✏️

Think of an idea that could change your life or the lives of others. Write a procedure telling about it. Publish it in a newsletter.

## Study a Model

A procedure explains how to do something. When you write this kind of text, you describe the steps in the order that they must be done.

Read Lisa's idea for making a difference one penny at a time.

---

### Penny Power!
#### by Lisa Han

You know those containers of spare change that everyone has at home? If you collect those coins, you can make amazing things happen! Our school can do that with a Penny Harvest.

A group called Common Cents helps people do Penny Harvests. **First**, we choose a group or project that the money will go to.

**Next**, students form teams. The teams begin collecting pennies and spare change from friends, neighbors, and local businesses.

The **last** part is the best. We see how much money we've raised. Then we give a check to our chosen group.

---

The writer uses words that sound like her. The writing has a clear **voice** and **style**.

The **beginning** tells what process is being explained.

Clear, **step-by-step** instructions tell the reader what to do. Words like *first*, *next*, and *last* make the order clear.

The ending tells what the outcome of the process is.

## Prewrite

1. **Choose a Topic** What idea will you share with others? Talk with a partner to choose one you think you could really make happen.

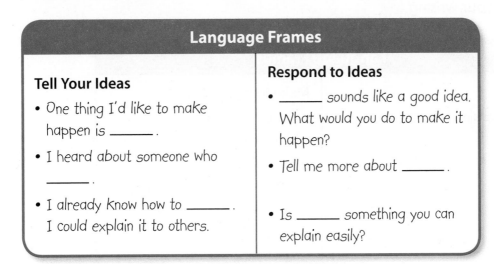

**Language Frames**

| Tell Your Ideas | Respond to Ideas |
| --- | --- |

**Tell Your Ideas**
- One thing I'd like to make happen is _____ .
- I heard about someone who _____ .
- I already know how to _____ . I could explain it to others.

**Respond to Ideas**
- _____ sounds like a good idea. What would you do to make it happen?
- Tell me more about _____ .
- Is _____ something you can explain easily?

2. **Gather Information** Decide exactly what steps your readers would have to follow. Collect details that explain each step clearly.

3. **Get Organized** Use a sequence chain to help you organize your details.

**Sequence Chain**

How to Organize a Penny Harvest

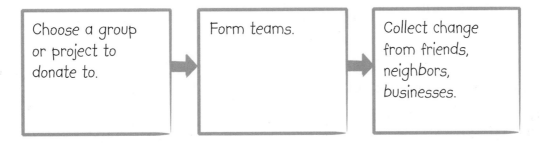

| Choose a group or project to donate to. | → | Form teams. | → | Collect change from friends, neighbors, businesses. |

## Draft

Use the steps in your sequence chain to write your draft. Begin by telling what process you are explaining. Then tell each step. Be sure to put the steps in the correct order. Add diagrams if it would make the process clearer.

## Revise

1. **Read, Retell, Respond** Read your draft aloud to a partner. Your partner listens and then retells the process. Next, talk about ways to improve your writing.

| Language Frames | |
|---|---|
| **Retell** | **Make Suggestions** |
| • You explained how to _____ . | • I didn't understand _____ . Could you say it differently? |
| • The goal or end result is _____ . | • The steps seemed out of order. Maybe you should move _____ . |
| • The main steps were _____ . | • The writing didn't sound like you. Change words like _____ . |

2. **Make Changes** Think about your draft and your partner's suggestions. Then use the Revising Marks on page 629 to mark your changes.

   • Are your steps presented in a clear order? Check to make sure.

   > Students form teams. We choose a group or project that we want to donate money to.

   • Make sure your writing sounds like you.

   > If you collect the coins, you can make amazing things happen! ~~People can collect coins and donate to good causes.~~

# Edit and Proofread

Work with a partner to edit and proofread your procedure. Pay special attention to verb tenses. Use the marks on page 629 to show your changes.

Use the marks on page 629 to show your changes.

# Publish

1. **On Your Own**  Make a final copy of your procedure. Share it with other students in your school. Encourage them to try it out.

| Presentation Tips | |
|---|---|
| **If you are the speaker…** | **If you are the listener…** |
| Try explaining the procedure from memory. Keep steps in the correct order. | Do you understand the steps of the process?  If not, ask questions! |
| If you explain your procedure to younger children, simplify your language. | Restate the steps in your own words. Then check with the speaker to see if you understood them. |

2. **In a Group**  Collect all of the ideas and procedures from your class. Present them in a newsletter or online. Think of a good title like "Great Ideas." Share the ideas both in and out of school.

## GREAT IDEAS
### NEWSLETTER

### Penny Power!
—by Lisa Han

You know those containers of spare change that everyone has at home? If you collect those coins, you can make amazing things happen! Our school can do that with a Penny Harvest.

A group called Common Cents helps people do Penny Harvests. First, we choose a group or project that the money will go to.

Next, students form teams. The teams begin collecting pennies and spare change from friends, neighbors, and local businesses.

The last part is the best. We see how much money we've raised. Then we give a check to our chosen group. What a simple way to make a big difference!

### Fun Fundraisers
—by Liam O'Niel

for kids are easy to do if  Some

best money-maker in the world but it i
easy and simple way to introduce kids
rity and raise some money for a g

## Talk Together

In this unit, you found lots of answers to the **Big Question**. Now make a concept map to discuss the **Big Question** with the class.

**Concept Map**

One idea can improve people's lives

How can one idea change your future?

## Write a Magazine Article ✏

Use your concept map. Write an article for a teen magazine explaining how one idea can change lives.

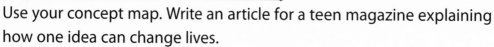

# Share Your Ideas

Choose one of these ways to share your ideas about the **Big Question**.

## Write It!

### Plan a Business

Choose a business that you would like to start. List the steps you need to take to get the business started. Be sure to write the steps in the order that you would do them. Share your list with the class.

## Talk About It!

### Make Up a Song

Think of something that you could not live without. Make up a funny or serious song about what the world would be like if someone hadn't thought of the idea. Choose a tune that people are familiar with. Perform your song for the class.

## Do It!

### Organize an Activity

Organize an activity that would help your school raise money, such as a bake sale or a clean-up day. Figure out all the things that need to be done and assign people to those tasks. Be sure people know when your activity is going to take place.

## Talk About It!

### Make a Presentation

Do research on the Internet to find a business that was started by a kid. Then give a presentation to your class, stating what you know and what you read. Also include some pictures or drawings to make your presentation come alive.

# Strategies for Learning Language

**These strategies can help you learn to use and understand the English language.**

**❶ Listen actively and try out language.**

| What to Do | Examples |
|---|---|
| Repeat what you hear. | **You hear:** Way to go, Joe! Fantastic catch! / **You say:** Way to go, Joe! Fantastic catch! |
| Recite songs and poems. | My Family Tree<br>Two grandmas, one brother,<br>Two grandpas, one mother,<br>One father, and then there's me.<br>Eight of us together<br>Make up my family tree. / Two grandmas, one brother,... |
| Listen to others and use their language. | **You hear:** "When did you know that something was missing?" / **You say:** "I knew that something was missing when I got to class." |

**❷ Ask for help.**

| What to Do | Examples |
|---|---|
| Ask questions about how to use language. | Did I say that right? / Did I use that word in the right way? / Which is correct, "bringed" or "brought"? |
| Use your native language or English to make sure that you understand. | **You say:** "Wait! Could you say that again more slowly, please?" / **Other options:** "Does 'violet' mean 'purple'?" "Is 'enormous' another way to say 'big'?" |

**3** **Use gestures and body language, and watch for them.**

| What to Do | Examples |
|---|---|
| Use gestures and movements to help others understand your ideas. | I will hold up five fingers to show that I need five more minutes. |
| Watch people as they speak. The way they look or move can help you understand the meaning of their words. | Let's give him a hand.  Everyone is clapping. "Give him a hand" must mean to clap for him. |

**4** **Think about what you are learning.**

| What to Do | Examples |
|---|---|
| Ask yourself: Are my language skills getting better? How can I improve? | Was it correct to use "they" when I talked about my grandparents?  Did I add 's to show ownership? |
| Keep notes about what you've learned. Use your notes to practice using English. | How to Ask Questions<br>• I can start a question with "is," "can," or "do": Do you have my math book?<br>• I can start a question with "who," "what," "where," "when," "how," or "why" to get more information: Where did you put my math book? |

# Vocabulary Strategies

When you read, you may find a word you don't know. But, don't worry! There are many things you can do to figure out the meaning of an unfamiliar word.

## Use What You Know

Ask yourself "Does this new word look like a word I know?" If it does, use what you know about the familiar word to figure out the meaning of the new word. Think about:

- **word families**, or words that look similar and have related meanings. The words *locate, location,* and *relocate* are in the same word family.

- **cognates**, or pairs of words that look the same in English and in another language. The English word *problem* and the Spanish word *problema* are cognates.

### On the Top of the World

Mount Everest is the highest mountain in the world. It is 29,028 feet (8,848 meters) high. This **magnificent** mountain is covered in permanently frozen snow and ice. But this doesn't stop **adventurous** climbers from trying to reach its peak.

This English word looks like **magnifico**. That means "beautiful" in Spanish. I think that meaning makes sense here, too.

I know that **adventure** means "an exciting event" and that an **adventurer** is "someone who takes risks." So, **adventurous** probably means "willing to be a part of risky activities."

# Use Context Clues

Sometimes you can figure out a word's meaning by looking at other words and phrases near the word. Those words and phrases are called **context clues.**

There are different kinds of context clues. Look for signal words such as *means, like, but,* or *unlike* to help you find the clues.

**Extremely cold temperatures are hazardous to mountain climbers.**

| Kind of Clue | Signal Words | Example |
|---|---|---|
| **Definition**<br>Gives the word's meaning. | *is, are, was, refers to, means* | Hazardous ***refers to*** something that causes harm or injury. |
| **Restatement**<br>Gives the word's meaning in a different way, usually after a comma. | *or* | Mountain climbing can be hazardous, ***or*** result in injuries to climbers. |
| **Synonym**<br>Gives a word or phrase that means almost the same thing. | *like, also* | Sudden drops in temperature can be hazardous. ***Also*** dangerous are very high altitudes that make it hard to breathe. |
| **Antonym**<br>Gives a word or phrase that means the opposite. | *but, unlike* | The subzero temperatures can be hazardous, ***but*** special gear keeps the climbers safe. |
| **Examples**<br>Gives examples of what the word means. | *such as, for example, including* | Climbers prepare for hazardous situations. ***For example***, they carry extra food, equipment for heavy snowfall, and first-aid kits. |

# Vocabulary Strategies, *continued*

## Use Word Parts

Many English words are made up of parts. You can use these parts as clues to a word's meaning.

When you don't know a word, look to see if you know any of its parts. Put the meaning of the word parts together to figure out the meaning of the whole word.

## Compound Words

A compound word is made up of two or more smaller words. To figure out the meaning of the whole word:

**1.** Break the long word into parts.

**2.** Put the meanings of the smaller words together to predict the meaning of the whole word.

keyboard = key + board

key = button
+
board = flat surface

keyboard = flat part of computer with buttons

**3.** If you can't predict the meaning from the parts, use what you know and the meaning of the other words to figure it out.

lap + top = laptop

*laptop* means "small portable computer," not "the top of your lap"

## Prefixes

A prefix comes at the beginning of a word. It changes the word's meaning. To figure out the meaning of an unfamiliar word, look to see if it has a prefix.

**1.** Break the word into parts. Think about the meaning of each part.

I need to **rearrange** the files on my computer.

re- + arrange

The prefix *re-* means "again." The word *arrange* means "to put in order."

**2.** Put the meanings of the word parts together.

The word *rearrange* means "to put in order again."

**Some Prefixes and Their Meanings**

| Prefix | Meaning |
|--------|---------|
| anti- | against |
| dis- | opposite of |
| In- | not |
| mis- | wrongly |
| pre- | before |
| re- | again, back |
| un- | not |

616

## Suffixes

A suffix comes at the end of a word. It changes the word's meaning and part of speech. To figure out the meaning of new word, look to see if it has a suffix.

**Some Suffixes and Their Meanings**

| Suffix | Meaning |
|--------|---------|
| -able | can be done |
| -al | having characteristics of |
| -ion | act, process |
| -er, -or | one who |
| -ful | full of |
| -less | without |
| -ly | in a certain way |

1. Break the word into parts. Think about the meaning of each part.

My **teacher** helps me find online articles.

teach + -er

The word *teach* means "to give lessons." The suffix *-er* means "one who."

2. Put the meanings of the word parts together.

A *teacher* is "a person who gives lessons."

noun

## Greek and Latin Roots

Many words in English have Greek and Latin roots. A root is a word part that has meaning, but it cannot stand on its own.

1. Break the unfamiliar word into parts.

I won't be done in time if there's one more **interruption**!

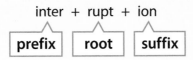

inter + rupt + ion

prefix | root | suffix

2. Focus on the root. Do you know other words with the same root?

"I've seen the root **rupt** in the words *erupt* and *rupture*.

'rupt' must have something to do with breaking or destroying something."

3. Put the meanings of all the word parts together.

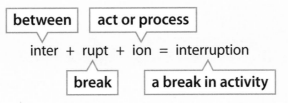

between | act or process

inter + rupt + ion = interruption

break | a break in activity

# Look Beyond the Literal Meaning

Writers use colorful language to keep their readers interested. They use words and phrases that mean something different from their usual definitions.  Figurative language and idioms are kinds of colorful language.

## Figurative Language: Similes

A simile compares two things that are alike in some way. It uses the words *like* or *as* to make the comparison.

| Simile | Things Compared | How They're Alike |
|---|---|---|
| Cory hiked across the desert **as sluggishly as a snail**. | Cory and a snail | They both move very slowly. |
| His skin was **like sheets of sandpaper.** | skin and sandpaper | They are both rough and very dry. |

## Figurative Language: Metaphors

A metaphor compares two things without using the words *like* or *as*.

| Metaphor | Things Compared | Meaning |
|---|---|---|
| The **sun's rays were a thousand bee stings** on his face. | sun's rays and bee stings | The sun's rays blistered his face. |
| His only **companion was thirst.** | friend and thirst | His thirst was always there with him. |

## Figurative Language: Personification

When writers use personification they give human qualities to nonhuman things.

| Personification | Object | Human Quality |
|---|---|---|
| The **angry sun** kept punishing him. | sun | has feelings |
| A **cactus reached out to** him. | cactus | is able to be friendly |

## Idioms

An idiom is a special kind of phrase that means something different from what the words mean by themselves.

| **What you say:** | **What you mean:** |
|---|---|
| If the topic is Mars, **I'm all ears.** | If the topic is Mars, **I'll listen very carefully**. |
| **Break a leg!** | **Good luck!** |
| Rachel had **to eat her words.** | Rachel had **to say she was wrong.** |
| **Give me a break!** | **That's ridiculous!** |
| **Hang on.** | **Wait.** |
| I'm **in a jam.** | I'm **in trouble.** |
| The joke was so funny, Lisa **laughed her head off.** | The joke was so funny, Lisa **laughed very hard.** |
| Juan was **steamed** when I lost his video game. | Juan was **very angry** when I lost his video game. |
| Let's **surf the Net** for ideas for report ideas. | Let's **look around the contents of the Internet** for report ideas. |
| I'm so tired, I just want to **veg out**. | I'm so tired, I just want to **relax and not think about anything.** |
| Rob and Zak are together **24-seven**. | Rob and Zak are together **all the time.** |
| **You can say that again.** | **I totally agree with you.** |
| **Zip your lips!** | **Be quiet!** |

# Reading Strategies

Good readers use a set of strategies before, during, and after reading. Knowing which strategy to use and when will help you understand and enjoy all kinds of text.

## Plan and Monitor

Good readers have clear plans for reading. Remember to:

- **Set a purpose** for reading. Ask yourself: Why am I reading this? What do I hope to get from it?

- **Preview** what you are about to read. Look at the title. Scan the text, pictures, and other visuals.

- **Make predictions**, or thoughtful guesses, about what comes next. Check your predictions as you read. Change them as you learn new information.

Monitor, or keep track of, your reading. Remember to:

- **Clarify ideas and vocabulary** to make sure you understand what the words and passages mean. Stop and ask yourself: Does that make sense?

- **Reread, read on,** or **change your reading speed** if you are confused.

## Determine Importance

How can you keep track of all the facts and details as you read? Do what good readers do and focus on the most important ideas.

- Identify the **main idea**. Connect details to the main idea.

- **Summarize** as you read and after you read.

## Ask Questions

Asking yourself questions as you read keeps your mind active. You'll ask different types of questions, so you'll need to find the answers in different ways.

- Some questions are connected to answers **right there** in the text.

- Others cover more than one part of the text. So, you'll have to **think and search** to find the answers.

Not all answers are found in the book.

- **On your own** questions can focus on your experiences or on the big ideas of the text.

- **Author and you** questions may be about the author's purpose or point of view.

## Visualize

Good readers use the text and their own experiences to picture a writer's words. When you **visualize**, use all your senses to see, hear, smell, feel, and taste what the writer describes.

## Make Connections

When you make connections, you put together information from the text with what you know from outside the text. As you read, think about:

- **your own ideas and experiences**
- what you know about the **world** from TV, songs, school, and so on
- **other texts** you've read by the same author, about the same topic, or in the same genre.

## Make Inferences

Sometimes an author doesn't tell a reader everything. To figure out what is left unsaid:

- Look for what the author emphasizes.
- Think about what you already know.
- Combine what you read with what you know to figure out what the author means.

## Synthesize

When you **synthesize**, you put together information from different places and come up with new understandings. You might:

- **Draw conclusions**, or combine what you know with what you read to decide what to think about a topic.
- **Form generalizations**, or combine ideas from the text with what you know to form an idea that is true in many situations.

# Writing and Research

Writing is one of the best ways to express yourself. Sometimes you'll write to share a personal experience. Other times, you'll write to give information about a research topic. Whenever you write, use the following steps to help you say want you want clearly, correctly, and in your own special way.

## Prewrite

When you prewrite, you choose a topic and collect all the details and information you need for writing.

**1** **Choose a Topic and Make a Plan** Think about your writing prompt assignment or what you want to write about.

- Make a list. Then choose the best idea to use for your topic.

- Think about your writing role, audience, and form. Add those to a RAFT chart.

- Jot down any research questions, too. Those will help you look for the information you need.

**RAFT Chart**

**Role:** scientist

**Audience:** my teacher and classmates

**Form:** report

**Topic:** honeybees

**2** **Gather Information** Think about your topic and your plan. Jot down ideas. Or, use resources like those on pages 579–582 to find information that answers your questions. Take notes.

# Use Information Resources

## Books

**A book is a good source of information.**

**Notecard**

Where do honeybees live? — **research question**

The Honey Makers, by Gail Gibbons, page 6 — **name of source**

—Many honeybees live in dark places like hollow trees. — **notes in your own words**

—"Honeybees cared for by today's beekeepers live in box-shaped wooden hives." — **author's exact words in quotation marks**

**Read the pages to find information you need. Take notes.**

WILD HONEYBEE HIVE

WOODEN BEEHIVE

Many honeybees like to make their homes in dark, enclosed places. Often a colony of wild honeybees builds its hive in a hollow tree. Honeybees cared for by today's beekeepers live in box-shaped wooden hives.

## Encyclopedias

Each encyclopedia volume has facts about different topics.

**guide words**

●Rain forest

# Rain forest

**Tropical rain forests** have more kinds of trees than anywhere else in the world.

Rain forests are thick forests of tall trees. They are found where the weather is warm the year around, and there is plenty of rain. Most rain forests grow near the equator, a make-believe line around Earth's middle. Africa, Asia, and Central and South America have large rain forests. Smaller rain forests are found in Australia and islands in the Pacific.

Tropical rain forests have more kinds of trees than anywhere else in the world. More than half of all the kinds of plants and animals on Earth live in tropical rain forests.

The tallest rain forest trees are as tall as 165 feet (50 meters). The treetops form a leafy covering called the canopy

**article**

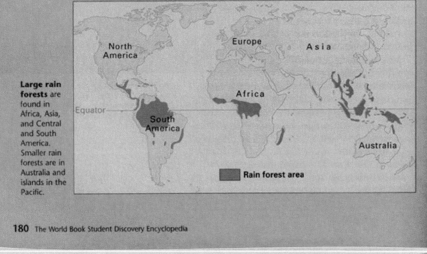

**Large rain forests** are found in Africa, Asia, and Central and South America. Smaller rain forests are in Australia and islands in the Pacific.

North America
Europe
Asia
Africa
Equator
South America
Australia
■ Rain forest area

**180** The World Book Student Discovery Encyclopedia

1. Look up your topic in the correct encyclopedia **volume** or on the **CD-ROM**.

2. Read the **guide words**. Keep turning the pages until you find the article you want. Use alphabetical order.

3. Read the **article** and take notes.

## Magazines

This is the **title of** the magazine.

The **date** tells when the **issue** was published.

PATHFINDER EDITION   NATIONALGEOGRAPHIC.COM/NGEXPLORER   MAY 2008

# NATIONAL GEOGRAPHIC
## Explorer!

## Rain Forest

Wall of Wonder 10   Animal Armor 18

This is the **main topic** of the issue.

These are some of the **topics** in the issue.

## . . . and Experts

Arrange a time to talk to an **expert,** or someone who knows a lot about your topic.

- Prepare questions you want to ask about the topic.

- Conduct the interview. Write down the person's answers.

- Choose the notes you'll use for your writing

625

## Internet

The Internet is a connection of computers that share information through the World Wide Web. It is like a giant library. Check with your teacher for how to access the Internet from your school.

1. **Go to a search page.** Type in your key words. Click Search.

2. **Read the list of Web sites, or pages, that have your key words.** The underlined words are links to the Web sites.

3. **Click on a link to go directly to the site, or Web page.** Read the article online. Or print it if it is helpful for your research. Later on, you can use the article to take notes.

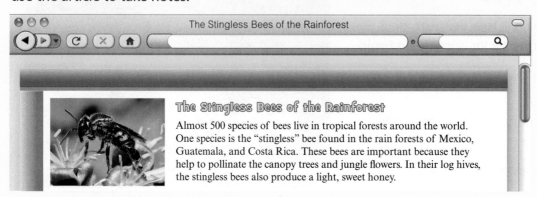

4. **Get Organized** Think about all the details you've gathered about your topic. Use a list, a chart, or other graphic organizer to show what you'll include in your writing. Use the organizer to show the order of your ideas, too.

**Cluster**

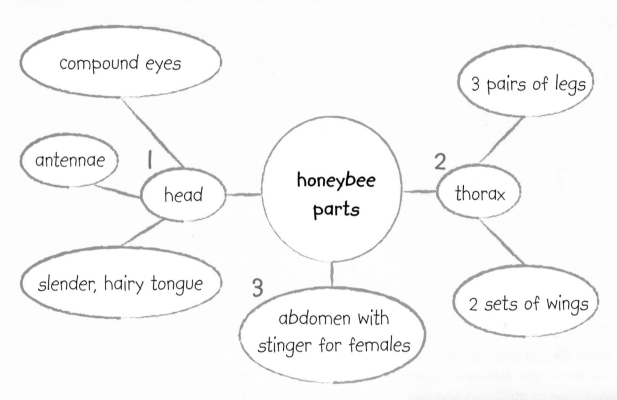

compound eyes

3 pairs of legs

antennae

1 head

honeybee parts

2 thorax

slender, hairy tongue

3 abdomen with stinger for females

2 sets of wings

**Outline**

The Helpful, Sweet Honeybee

I. Important insects

  A. help pollinate plants

    1. flowers and trees

    2. fruits

  B. turn nectar into honey

II. Honeybee homes

  A. around the world

  B. hives

## Draft

When you write your first draft, you turn all your ideas into sentences. You write quickly just to get all your ideas down. You can correct mistakes later.

### Cluster

Turn your main idea into a topic sentence. Then add the details.

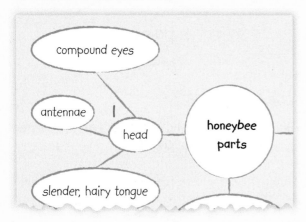

### Beginning of a Description

One main part of a honeybee is the head. The *bee's* head seems to be mostly eyes! They are called compound eyes and have a lot of tiny lenses in them.

### Outline

Turn the main idea after each Roman numeral into a topic sentence. Then turn the words next to the letters and numbers into detail sentences that tell more about the main idea.

The Helpful, Sweet Honeybee

I. Important insects
   A. help pollinate plants
      1. flowers and trees
      2. fruits

### Beginning of a Report

The Helpful, Sweet Honeybee

You may think that all the honeybee does is make honey. But, believe it or not, this insect is always busy with another important job.

A honeybee helps keep plants growing. It helps to spread the pollen flowers and trees need to start new plants.

# Revise

When you revise, you make changes to your writing to make it better and clearer.

**❶ Read, Retell, Respond** Read your draft aloud to a partner. Your partner listens and then retells your main points.

> You are describing a honeybee's hive. Isn't a bee's nest the same as a hive?

> Yes, it is. I don't need the word "nest," so I'll take it out.

Your partner can help you discover what is unclear or what you need to add. Use your partner's suggestions to decide what you can to do to make your writing better.

**❷ Make Changes** Think about your draft and what you and your partner discussed. What changes will you make? Use Revising Marks to mark your changes.

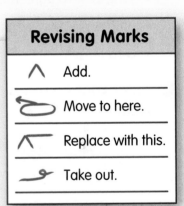

| Revising Marks | |
|---|---|
| ∧ | Add. |
| ∾ | Move to here. |
| ⋏ | Replace with this. |
| ⸎ | Take out. |

In the wild, honeybee scouts look for places to make hives ~~and nests.~~ The opening needs to be high off the ground. (They look for openings in hollow tree trunks.) That way the hive will be

predators
safe from ~~harmful animals~~. A hive needs to

the nectar and pollen
hold thousands of bees and all ∧ they gather.

The best bee's nest will also face south so it stays warm.

## Edit and Proofread

**When you edit and proofread, you look for mistakes in capitalization, grammar, and punctuation.**

**1 Check Your Sentences** Check that your sentences are clear, complete, and correct. Add any missing subjects or predicates

**2 Check Your Spelling** Look for any misspelled words. Check their spelling in a dictionary or a glossary.

**3 Check for Capital Letters, Punctuation, and Grammar** Look especially for correct use of

- capital letters in proper nouns
- apostrophes and quotation marks
- subject-verb agreement
- pronouns
- verb tenses

**4 Mark Your Changes** Use the Editing and Proofreading Marks to show your changes.

**5 Make a Final Copy** Make all the corrections you've marked to make a final, clean copy of your writing. If you are using a computer, print out your corrected version.

It is crowded and busy inside a honeybee hive. A hive can have more than 50,000 honeybees. Most of them are worker bees. The worker bees create wax from their bodies to build combs. The combs are layers of cells, or holes. The cells hold nectar, pollen, or larvae.

| Editing and Proofreading Marks | |
|---|---|
| ∧ | Add. |
| ✐ | Take out. |
| ∧ | Replace with this. |
| ◯ | Check spelling. |
| ≡ | Capitalize. |
| / | Make lowercase. |
| ¶ | Make new paragraph. |

# Publish

**When you publish your writing, you share it with others.**

**1 Add Visuals** Visuals can make your writing more interesting and easier to understand. Maybe you will

- import photographs or illustrations
- insert computer clip art
- add graphs, charts, or diagrams

**2 Present Your Writing** There are a lot of ways to share your finished work. Here are just a few ideas.

- E-mail it to a friend or family member.
- Send it to your favorite magazine or publication.
- Turn it into a chapter for a group book about the topic.
- Make a video clip of you reading it to add to a group presentation.

## A Home for the Honeybee

In the wild, honeybee scouts look for places to make hives. They look for openings in hollow tree trunks. The opening needs to be high off the ground. That way the hive will be safe from predators. A hive also needs to be big enough for thousands of bees and all the nectar and pollen they gather. The best hive will also face south so it stays warm.

# Writing Traits

Good writing is clear, interesting, and easy to follow. To make your writing as good as it can be, check your writing to be sure it has the characteristics, or traits, of good writing.

## Ideas

Writing is well-developed when the message is clear and interesting to the reader. It is supported by details that show the writer knows the topic well.

| | Is the message clear and interesting? | Do the details show the writer knows the topic? |
|---|---|---|
| **4** | ❑ All of the writing is clear and focused.<br>❑ The writing is very interesting. | ❑ All the details tell about the topic. The writer knows the topic well. |
| **3** | ❑ Most of the writing is clear and focused.<br>❑ Most of the writing is interesting. | ❑ Most of the details are about the topic. The writer knows the topic fairly well. |
| **2** | ❑ Some of the writing is not clear. The writing lacks some focus.<br>❑ Some of the writing is confusing. | ❑ Some details are about the topic. The writer doesn't know the topic well. |
| **1** | ❑ The writing is not clear or focused.<br>❑ The writing is confusing. | ❑ Many details are not about the topic. The writer does not know the topic. |

# Organization

Writing is organized when it is easy to follow. All the ideas make sense together and flow from one idea to the next in an order that fits the writer's audience and purpose.

| | Is the writing organized? Does it fit the audience and purpose? | Does the writing flow? |
|---|---|---|
| **4** | ❑ The writing is very well-organized.<br>❑ It clearly fits both the writer's audience and purpose. | ❑ The writing is smooth and logical. Each sentence flows into the next one. |
| **3** | ❑ Most of the writing is organized.<br>❑ It mostly fits the writer's audience and purpose. | ❑ Most of the writing is smooth. There are only a few sentences that do not flow logically. |
| **2** | ❑ The writing is not well-organized.<br>❑ It fits the writer's audience or the writer's purpose, but not both. | ❑ Some of the writing is smooth. Many sentences do not flow smoothly. |
| **1** | ❑ The writing is not organized at all.<br>❑ It does not fit the writer's audience or purpose. | ❑ The sentences do not flow smoothly or logically. |

**Organized**

**Not organized**

## Voice

Every writer has a special way of saying things, or a voice. The voice should sound genuine, or real, and be unique to that writer.

| | Does the writing sound genuine and unique ? | Does the tone fit the audience and purpose? |
|---|---|---|
| **4** | ❏ The writing is genuine and unique. It shows who the writer is. | ❏ The writer's tone, formal or informal, fits the audience and purpose. |
| **3** | ❏ Most of the writing sounds genuine and unique. | ❏ The writer's tone mostly fits the audience and purpose. |
| **2** | ❏ Some of the writing sounds genuine and unique. | ❏ Some of the writing fits the audience and purpose. |
| **1** | ❏ The writing does not sound genuine or unique. | ❏ The writer's tone does not fit the audience or purpose. |

## Word Choice

Readers can always tell who the writer is by the words the writer uses.

| | Do the writer's words fit the message? | Does the language fit the audience? Is it interesting? |
|---|---|---|
| **4** | ❏ The writer chose words that really fit the message. | ❏ The words and sentences fit the audience and are interesting. |
| **3** | ❏ Most of the words really fit the writer's message. | ❏ Most of the words and sentences fit the audience and are interesting. |
| **2** | ❏ Some of the words fit the writer's message. | ❏ Some of the words and sentences fit the audience and are interesting. |
| **1** | ❏ Few or no words fit the writer's message. | ❏ The language does not fit the audience and lose the readers' attention. |

# Fluency

Good writers use a variety of sentence types. They also use transitions, or signal words.

| | Is there sentence variety? Are there transitions? | Does the writing sound natural and rhythmic? |
|---|---|---|
| **4** | ❏ The writer uses lots of different types of sentences. <br> ❏ The writer uses useful transitions. | ❏ When I read the writing aloud, it sounds natural and rhythmic. |
| **3** | ❏ The writer uses many different types of sentences. <br> ❏ Most transition words are useful. | ❏ When I read the writing aloud, most of it sounds natural and rhythmic. |
| **2** | ❏ The writer uses some different kinds of sentences. <br> ❏ Some transition words are useful. | ❏ When I read the writing aloud, some of it sounds natural and rhythmic. |
| **1** | ❏ The writer does not vary sentences. <br> ❏ The writer does not use transitions. | ❏ When I read the writing aloud, it sounds unnatural. |

# Conventions

Good writers always follow the rules of grammar, punctuation, and spelling.

| | Is the writing correct? | Are the sentences complete? |
|---|---|---|
| **4** | ❏ All the punctuation, capitalization, and spelling is correct. | ❏ Every sentence has a subject and a predicate. |
| **3** | ❏ Most of the punctuation, spelling, and capitalization is correct. | ❏ Most of the sentences have a subject and a predicate. |
| **2** | ❏ Some of the punctuation, spelling, and capitalization is correct. | ❏ Some of the sentences are missing subjects or predicates. |
| **1** | ❏ There are many punctuation, spelling, and capitalization errors. | ❏ Several sentences are missing subjects or predicates. |

# Grammar, Usage, Mechanics, and Spelling

## Sentences

A sentence expresses a complete thought.

### Kinds of Sentences

**There are four kinds of sentences.**

| | |
|---|---|
| A **statement** tells something. It ends with a **period**. | Ned is at the mall now**.**<br>He needs a new shirt**.** |
| A **question** asks for information. It ends with a **question mark**. | Where can I find the shirts **?** |

#### Kinds of Questions

| | |
|---|---|
| Some questions ask for "Yes" or "No" answers. They start with words such as **Is**, **Do**, **Can**, **Are**, and **Will**. | **Do** you have a size 10**?**<br>    **Answer:** Yes.<br>**Are** these shirts on sale?<br>    **Answer:** No. |
| Other questions ask for more information. They start with words such as **Who**, **What**, **Where**, **When**, and **Why**. | **What** colors do you have?<br>    **Answer:** We have red and blue.<br>**Where** can I try this on?<br>    **Answer:** You can use this room. |

| | |
|---|---|
| An **exclamation** shows strong feeling. It ends with an **exclamation mark**. | This is such a cool shirt**!**<br>I love it **!** |
| A **command** tells you what to do or what not to do. It usually begins with a **verb** and ends with a period.<br><br>If a command shows strong emotion, it ends with an exclamation mark. | **Please** bring me a size 10.<br>**Don't open** the door yet.<br><br><br>Wait until I come out! |

636

## Negative Sentences

**A negative sentence means "no."**

| | |
|---|---|
| A **negative sentence** uses a **negative word** to say "no." | That is **not** a good color for me.<br>I **can't** find the right size. |

## Complete Sentences

**A complete sentence has two parts.**

| | |
|---|---|
| The **subject** tells whom or what the sentence is about. | My friends buy clothes here.<br>The other store has nicer shirts. |
| The **predicate** tells what the subject is, has, or does. | My friends buy clothes here.<br>The other store has nicer shirts. |

## Subjects

| | |
|---|---|
| All the words that tell about a subject is the **complete subject**. | My younger sister loves the toy store. |
| The **simple subject** is the most important word in the complete subject. | My younger sister loves the toy store. |
| A **compound subject** has two nouns joined together by the words **and** or **or**. | Terry **and** Brittany never shop at this store.<br>My mom **or** my dad always comes with me. |

## Predicates

| | |
|---|---|
| All the words in the predicate is the **complete predicate**. | The stores open today at nine. |
| The **simple predicate** is the **verb**. It is the most important word in the predicate. | The stores open today at nine. |
| A **compound predicate** has two or more verbs that tell about the same subject. The verbs are joined by **and** or **or**. | We eat **and** shop at the mall.<br>Sometimes we see a movie **or** just talk with our friends. |

## Sentences (continued)

### Compound Sentences

**When you join two sentences together, you can make a compound sentence.**

| | |
|---|---|
| Use a comma and the conjunction **and** to combine two similar ideas. | My friends walk to the mall. I go with them.<br>My friends walk to the mall**, and** I go with them. |
| Use a comma and the conjunction **but** to combine two different ideas. | My friends walk to the mall. I ride my bike.<br>My friends walk to the mall**, but** I ride my bike. |
| Use a comma and the conjunction **or** to show a choice of ideas. | You can walk to the mall with me. You can ride with Dad.<br>You can walk to the mall with me**, or** you can ride with Dad. |

### Complex Sentences

**When you join independent and dependent clauses, you can make a complex sentence.**

| | |
|---|---|
| An **independent clause** expresses a complete thought. It can stand alone as a sentence. | Mom and her friends walk around the mall for exercise.<br>They walk around the mall. |
| A **dependent clause** does not express a complete thought. It is not a sentence. | before it gets busy<br>because they want to exercise |
| To make a **complex sentence**, join an **independent clause** with one or more **dependent clauses**.<br><br>If the dependent clause comes first, put a **comma** after it. | **Before it gets busy , Mom and her friends walk around the mall for exercise.**<br>**They walk around the mall because they want to exercise.** |

### Condensing Clauses

**Condense clauses to create precise and detailed sentences.**

| | |
|---|---|
| **Condense clauses** by combining ideas and using complex sentences. | It's a plant. It's green and red. It's found in the tropical rainforest. → It's a green and red plant that is found in the tropical rainforest. |

# Nouns

Nouns name people, animals, places, or things.

## Common Nouns and Proper Nouns

**There are two kinds of nouns.**

| | |
|---|---|
| A **common noun** names any person, animal, place, or thing of a certain type. | I know that **girl**.<br><br>She rides a **horse**.<br><br>I sometimes see her at the **park**.<br><br>She walks her **dog** there. |
| A **proper noun** names a particular person, animal, place, or thing.<br><br>• Start all the important words with a capital letter.<br><br><br><br>• Start the names of streets, cities, and states with a capital letter.<br><br>• Also use capital letters when you abbreviate state names. | I know **Marissa**.<br><br>I sometimes see her at **Hilltop Park**.<br><br>She walks her dog **Chase** there.<br><br>Her family is from **Dallas, Texas**.<br><br>They live on **Crockett Lane**. |

### Abbreviations for State Names in Mailing Addresses

| | | | | | | | | | |
|---|---|---|---|---|---|---|---|---|---|
| Alabama | AL | Hawaii | HI | Massachusetts | MA | New Mexico | NM | South Dakota | SD |
| Alaska | AK | Idaho | ID | Michigan | MI | New York | NY | Tennessee | TN |
| Arizona | AZ | Illinois | IL | Minnesota | MN | North Carolina | NC | Texas | TX |
| Arkansas | AR | Indiana | IN | Mississippi | MS | North Dakota | ND | Utah | UT |
| California | CA | Iowa | IA | Missouri | MO | Ohio | OH | Vermont | VT |
| Colorado | CO | Kansas | KS | Montana | MT | Oklahoma | OK | Virginia | VA |
| Connecticut | CT | Kentucky | KY | Nebraska | NE | Oregon | OR | Washington | WA |
| Delaware | DE | Louisiana | LA | Nevada | NV | Pennsylvania | PA | West Virginia | WV |
| Florida | FL | Maine | ME | New Hampshire | NH | Rhode Island | RI | Wisconsin | WI |
| Georgea | GA | Maryland | MD | New Jersey | NJ | South Carolina | SC | Wyoming | WY |

## Nouns (continued)

### Singular and Plural Count Nouns

**Count nouns name things that you can count. A singular count noun shows "one." A plural count noun shows "more than one."**

| | | | |
|---|---|---|---|
| Add **-s** to most singular count nouns to form the plural count noun. | bicycle<br>club | →<br>→ | bicycle**s**<br>club**s**  |
| Add **-es** to count nouns that end in **x**, **ch**, **sh**, **ss**, **z**, and sometimes **o**. | tax<br>bench<br>wish<br>loss<br>potato | →<br>→<br>→<br>→<br>→ | tax**es**<br>bench**es**<br>wish**es**<br>loss**es**<br>potato**es** |
| For count nouns that end in a consonant plus **y**, change the **y** to **i** and then add **-es**. For nouns that end in a vowel plus **y**, just add **-s**. | berry/i<br>family/i<br>boy<br>day | →<br>→<br>→<br>→ | berri**es**<br>famili**es**<br>boy**s**<br>day**s** |
| For a few count nouns, use special forms to show the plural. | man<br>woman<br>foot<br>tooth<br>child | →<br>→<br>→<br>→<br>→ | men<br>women<br>feet<br>teeth<br>children |

## Noncount Nouns

Noncount nouns name things that you cannot count.
Noncount nouns have one form for "one" and "more than one."

| | |
|---|---|
| **Weather Words** | fog  heat  lightning  thunder  rain<br><br>**YES:** **Thunder** and **lightning** scare my dog.<br><br>**NO:** Thunders and lightnings scare my dog. |
| **Food Words**<br>Some food items can be counted by using a measurement word such as **cup, slice, glass**, or **head** plus the word **of**. To show the plural form, make the measurement word plural. | bread  corn  milk  rice  soup<br><br>**YES:** I'm thirsty for **milk.**<br>I want **two glasses of milk.**<br><br>**NO:** I'm thirsty for milks.<br>I want milks. |
| **Ideas and Feelings** | fun  help  honesty  luck  work<br><br>**YES:** I need **help** to finish my homework.<br><br>**NO:** I need helps to finish my homework. |
| **Category Nouns** | clothing  equipment  mail  money  time<br><br>**YES:** My football **equipment** is in the car.<br><br>**NO:** My football equipments is in the car. |
| **Materials** | air  gold  paper  water  wood<br><br>**YES:** Is the **water** in this river clean?<br><br>**NO:** Is the waters in this river clean? |
| **Activities and Sports** | baseball  dancing  golf  singing  soccer<br><br>**YES:** I played **soccer** three times this week.<br><br>**NO:** I played soccers three times this week. |

## Nouns (continued)

### Words That Signal Nouns

**The articles *a*, *an*, *some*, and *the* help identify a noun. They often appear before count nouns.**

| | |
|---|---|
| Use **a**, **an**, or **some** before a noun to talk about something in general. | **Some jokes** are funny. <br> Do you have **a favorite joke**? <br> I have **an uncle** who knows a lot of jokes. |
| Use **an** instead of **a** before a word that begins with a vowel sound. | It is **an event** when my uncle comes to visit. <br> He lives about **an hour** away from us. |
| Do <u>not</u> use **a** or **an** before a noncount noun. | He drives in ~~a~~ snow, ~~a~~ fog, or ~~an~~ ice to get here. |

| | |
|---|---|
| Use **the** to talk about something specific. | Uncle Raul is **the** uncle I told you about. <br> **The** jokes he tells make me laugh! |
| Do <u>not</u> use **the** before the name of: | |
| • a city or state | Uncle Raul lives in **Dallas**. That's a city in **Texas**. |
| • most countries | He used to live in **Brazil**. |
| • a language | He speaks **English** and **Spanish**. |
| • a day, month, or most holidays | Uncle Raul often visits on **Saturday**. In **February**, he comes up for **President's Day**. |
| • a sport or activity | Sometimes he'll play **soccer** with me. |
| • most businesses | Then we go to **Sal's Café** to eat. |
| • a person's name | He likes to talk to **Sal**, too. |

**The words *this*, *that*, *these*, and *those* point out nouns. Like other adjectives, they answer the question "Which one?"**

| | |
|---|---|
| Use **this** or **these** to talk about things that are near you. | **This** book has a lot of photographs. |
| Use **that** or **those** to talk about things that are far from you. | **Those** books on the shelf are all fiction. |

| | Near | Far |
|---|---|---|
| **One thing** | this | that |
| **More than one thing** | these | those |

## Possessive Nouns

**A possessive noun is the name of an owner. An apostrophe (') is used to show ownership.**

| For one owner, add **'s** to the **singular noun**. | This is Raul**'s** cap.<br>The cap**'s** color is a bright red. |
|---|---|
| For more than one owner, add just the apostrophe (') to the **plural noun**. | The boys**'** T-shirts are the same.<br>The players**'** equipment is ready. |
| For plural nouns that have special forms, add **'s** to the **plural noun**. | Do you like the **children's** uniforms?<br>The **men's** scores are the highest. |

## Pronouns

**A pronoun takes the place of a noun or refers to a noun.**

### Pronoun Agreement

**When you use a pronoun, be sure you are talking about the right person.**

| Use a capital **I** to talk about yourself. | I am Jack. I want to find out about Mars.     Are **you** interested in Mars, too? |
|---|---|
| Use **you** to speak to another person. | |
| Use **she** for a girl or a woman. | Julia thinks Mars is a good topic.<br>**She** will help write a report about the planet. |
| Use **he** for a boy or a man. | Jack downloaded some photos.<br>**He** added the pictures to the report. |
| Use **it** for a thing. | The report is almost done.<br>**It** will be interesting to read. |

## Pronouns *(continued)*

### Pronoun Agreement

**Be sure you are talking about the right number of people or things.**

Use **you** to talk to two or more people.

Use **we** for yourself and one or more other people.

Use **they** for other people or things.

Are **you** prepared for tomorrow?

Yes. Sam and I are ready. **We** give a report tomorrow.

Scott and Tyrone set up the video camera.
**They** will record each presentation.

### Subject Pronouns

**Subject pronouns take the place of the subject in the sentence.**

**Subject pronouns** tell who or what does the action.

**Julia** is a good speaker.
**She** tells the class about Mars.

**The photos** show the surface of Mars.
**They** are images from NASA.

| Subject Pronouns | |
|---|---|
| **Singular** | **Plural** |
| I | we |
| you | you |
| he, she, it | they |

## Object Pronouns

**Object pronouns replace a noun that comes after a verb or a preposition.**

| | |
|---|---|
| An **object pronoun** answers the question "What" or "Whom." | The class asked **Jack and Julia** about Mars. |
| Object pronouns come after a verb or a preposition such as **to**, **for**, **at**, **of**, or **with**. | The class asked **them** about Mars. |

**Object Pronouns**

| Singular | Plural |
|---|---|
| me | us |
| you | you |
| him, her, it | them |

Jack put **the report** online.

Jack put **it** online.

## Reciprocal Pronouns

**Reciprocal pronouns replace objects that refer back to the subject.**

| | |
|---|---|
| The subject must be plural. It can be a compound subject. | **Jack and Julia** helped **each other** on the report. |
| The subject can also be a plural noun. | **The students** followed **one another** outside. |

**Reciprocal Pronouns**

| Plural |
|---|
| each other |
| one another |

## Possessive Pronouns

**Like a possessive noun, a possessive pronoun tells who or what owns something.**

| | |
|---|---|
| To show that you own something, use **mine**. | **I** wrote a report about the sun. The report about the sun is **mine**. |
| Use **ours** to show that you and one or more people own something. | **Meg, Bob, and I** drew diagrams. The diagrams are **ours**. |
| Use **yours** to show that something belongs to one or more people you are talking to. | Have you seen my report, Matt? Yes, that report is **yours**. |

**Possessive Pronouns**

| Singular | Plural |
|---|---|
| mine | ours |
| yours | yours |
| his, hers | theirs |

| | |
|---|---|
| Use **his** for one boy or man. Use **hers** for one girl or woman. | Here is **Carole's** desk. The desk is **hers**. |
| For two or more people, places, or things, use **theirs**. | **Ross and Clare** made posters. The posters are **theirs**. |

## Adjectives

**An adjective describes, or tells about, a noun.**

### How Adjectives Work

| | |
|---|---|
| Usually, an **adjective** comes <u>before</u> the noun it tells about. | You can buy **delicious** fruits at the market. |
| But, an **adjective** can also appear after verbs such as *is, are, look, feel, smell,* and *taste*. | All the fruit looks **fresh**.<br>The shoppers are **happy**. |
| **Adjectives** describe<br><br>• what something is like<br><br>• the size, color, and shape of something<br><br>• what something looks, feels, sounds, or smells like | The market is a **busy** place.<br><br>The **round, brown** baskets are filled with fruits and vegetables.<br><br>The **shiny** peppers are in one basket.<br>Another basket has **crunchy** cucumbers.<br>The pineapples are **sweet** and **juicy**. |
| Some **adjectives** tell "how many" or "in what order."<br><br><br><br><br>When you don't know the exact number of things, use the adjectives in the chart.<br><br>Possessive adjectives tell who owns something. | The sellers have **two** baskets of beans.<br><br>The **first** basket is near the limes.<br><br>When there's **a lot of** sun, the sellers sit in the shade.<br><br>**I** pick out some oranges.<br>**My** oranges are in the bag.<br><br>That basket is **Ryan's**.<br>**His** basket is full of apples.<br><br>**The sellers'** chairs are in the shade.<br>**Their** chairs are under umbrellas. |

| If you can count what you see, use: | | If you can't count what you see, use: | |
|---|---|---|---|
| many | several | much | not much |
| a lot of | only a few | a lot of | only a little |
| few | not any | a little | not any |
| some | no | some | no |

## Adjectives That Compare

**Adjectives can help you make a comparison, or show how things are alike or different.**

| | |
|---|---|
| To compare two things, add **-er** to the adjective. You will often use the word **than** in your sentence, too. | This is a **small** pineapple. <br> The guava is **smaller than** the pineapple. |
| To compare three or more things, add **-est** to the adjective. Always use **the** before the adjective. | The lime is **the smallest** fruit of them all. |

| | | |
|---|---|---|
| For some adjectives, change the spelling before you add **-er** or **-est**. | | |
| • If the adjective ends in silent **e**, drop the final **e** and add **-er** or **-est**. | larg~~e~~ <br> larg**er** <br> larg**est** | nic~~e~~ <br> nic**er** <br> nic**est** |
| • If the adjective ends in **y**, change the **y** to **i** and add **-er** or **-est**. | prett~~y~~**i** <br> prett**ier** <br> prett**iest** | craz~~y~~**i** <br> craz**ier** <br> craz**iest** |
| • If the adjective has one syllable and ends in one vowel plus one consonant, double the final consonant and add **-er** or **-est**. | big **g** <br> bigg**er** <br> bigg**est** | sad **d** <br> sadd**er** <br> sadd**est** |

| | | | |
|---|---|---|---|
| A few adjectives have special forms for comparing things. | good <br> better <br> best | bad <br> worse <br> worst | little <br> less <br> least |

| | |
|---|---|
| For adjectives with three or more syllables, do not use **-er** or **-est** to compare. Use **more**, **most**, **less**, or **least**. | **YES:** Of all the fruit, the guavas are the **most colorful**. <br> **NO:** Of all the fruit, the guavas are the colorfulest. <br> **YES:** The oranges are **more delicious** than the pears. <br> **NO:** The oranges are deliciouser than the pears. |
| When you make a comparison, use either **-er** or **more**; or **-est** or **most**. Do <u>not</u> use both. | The oranges are the ~~most~~ juiciest of all the fruits. |

# Grammar, Usage, Mechanics, and Spelling *continued*

## Verbs

**Verbs tell what the subject of a sentence is, has, or does. They show if something happened in the past, is happening now, or will happen in the future.**

### Action Verbs

| | |
|---|---|
| An **action verb** tells what someone or something does. | The children **ride** bikes. |
| | They **wear** helmets for safety. |
| | They **pedal** as fast as they can. |

### The Verbs *Have* and *Be*

| | | Forms of the Verb *have* |
|---|---|---|
| The verb **to have** tells what the subject of a sentence has. | I **have** a bicycle. | have |
| | It **has** twelve gears. | has |
| | My friend Pedro **has** a bicycle, too. | had |
| | Sometimes we **have** races. | |

| | | Forms of the Verb *be* |
|---|---|---|
| The verb **to be** does not show action. It tells what the subject of a sentence is (a noun) or what it is like (an adjective). | I **am** a fan of bicycle races. | am     was |
| | Pedro **is** excited about our next race. | are    were |
| | | is |

### Linking Verbs

| | |
|---|---|
| A few other verbs work like the verb **to be**. They do not show action. They just connect, or link, the subject to a word in the predicate. Some of these verbs are **look**, **seem**, **feel**, **smell**, and **taste**. | My bicycle **looks** fantastic! |
| | Pedro and I **feel** ready for the race. |

## Helping Verbs

A **helping verb** works together with an action verb. A helping verb comes before a **main verb**. Some helping verbs have special meanings.

- Use **can** to tell that someone is able to do something.
- Use **could**, **may,** or **might** to tell that something is possible.
- Use **must** to tell that somebody has to do something.
- Use **should** to give an opinion or advice.

Pedro and I **are racing** today.
We **will do** our best.

We **can work** as a team.

We **may reach** the finish line first.

We **must pedal** hard to win!

You **should practice** more.

## Contractions with Verbs

You can put a subject and verb together to make a **contraction**. In a contraction, an apostrophe (') shows where one or more letters have been left out.

**They are** riding fast.
**They are** riding fast.
**They're** riding fast.

You can make a contraction with the verbs **am**, **are**, and **is**.

| Contractions with *Be* | | | |
|---|---|---|---|
| I + am = | **I'm** | she + is = | **she's** |
| you + are = | **you're** | where + is = | **where's** |
| we + are = | **we're** | what + is = | **what's** |

You can make a contraction with the helping verbs **have**, **has**, and **will**.

| Contractions with *Have* and *Will* | | | |
|---|---|---|---|
| I + have = | **I've** | he + has = | **he's** |
| you + have = | **you've** | I + will = | **I'll** |
| they + have = | **they've** | it + will = | **it'll** |

In contractions with a verb and **not**, the word **not** is shortened to **n't**.

| Contractions with *Not* | | | |
|---|---|---|---|
| do + not = | **don't** | have + not = | **haven't** |
| did + not = | **didn't** | has + not = | **hasn't** |
| are + not = | **aren't** | could + not = | **couldn't** |
| was + not = | **wasn't** | should + not = | **shouldn't** |

The contraction of the verb **can** plus **not** has a special spelling.

can + not = **can't**

## Verbs, *(continued)*

### Actions in the Present

| | |
|---|---|
| All action verbs show when the action happens.<br><br>Verbs in the **present tense** show<br><br>• that the action happens now.<br><br>• that the action happens often. | Pedro **eats** his breakfast.<br>Then he **takes** his bike out of the garage.<br>Pedro and I **love** to ride our bikes on weekends. |
| To show the present tense for the subjects **he, she,** or **it**, add -**s** to the end of most action verbs.<br><br>• For verbs that end in **x, ch, sh, ss,** or **z**, add -**es.**<br><br>• For verbs that end in a consonant plus **y**, change the **y** to **i** and then add -**es.** For verbs that end in a vowel plus **y**, just add -**s.**<br><br>• For the subjects **I, you, we,** or **they**, do not add -**s** or -**es.** | **Pedro checks** the tires on his bike.<br>**He finds** a flat tire!<br><br>Pedro **fixes** the tire.<br>A pump **pushes** air into it.<br><br>"That should do it," he **says** to himself.<br>He **carries** the pump back into the garage.<br><br>I **arrive** at Pedro's house.<br>We **coast** down the driveway on our bikes. |
| The **present progressive** form of a verb tells about an action as it is happening. It uses **am, is,** or **are** and a main verb. The main verb ends in -**ing**. | We **are pedaling** faster.<br>I **am passing** Pedro!<br>He **is following** right behind me. |

## Actions in the Past

| | |
|---|---|
| Verbs in the **past tense** show that the action happened in the past. | Yesterday, I **looked** for sports on TV. |
| The past tense form of a **regular verb** ends with -**ed**.<br><br>• For most verbs, just add -**ed**.<br><br>• For verbs that end in silent **e**, drop the final **e** before you add -**ed**.<br><br>• For one-syllable verbs that end in one vowel plus one consonant, double the final consonant before you add -**ed**.<br><br>• For verbs that end in **y**, change the **y** to **i** before you add -**ed**. For verbs that end in a vowel plus **y**, just add -**ed**. | I **watched** the race on TV.<br>The bikers **arrived** from all different countries.<br>They **raced** for several hours.<br><br>People **grabbed** their cameras.<br>They **snapped** pictures of their favorite racer.<br><br>I **studied** the racer from Italy.<br>I **stayed** close to the TV. |
| **Irregular verbs** do not add -**ed** to show the past tense. They have special forms. | The Italian racer **was** fast.<br>He **broke** the speed record! |

### Some Irregular Verbs

| Present Tense | Past Tense |
|---|---|
| begin | began |
| do | did |
| have | had |
| make | made |
| take | took |
| ride | rode |
| win | won |

## Verbs, *(continued)*

### Actions in the Future

| | |
|---|---|
| Verbs in the **future tense** tell what will happen later, or in the future. | Tomorrow, Shelley **will clean** her bike. |
| To show the future tense, you can<br><br>• add the helping verb **will** before the **main verb**.<br><br>• use **am going to**, **are going to**, or **is going to** before the **main verb**. | She **will remove** all the dirt.<br><br>She **is going to remove** all the dirt.<br>I **am going to help** her. |
| If the **main verb** is a form of the verb **to be**, use **be** to form the future tense. | The bike **will be** spotless.<br>Shelley **is going to be** pleased! |
| To make negative sentences in the future tense, put the word **not** just after **will**, **am**, **is**, or **are**. | We are **not** going to stop until the bike shines.<br>Pedro is **not** going to believe it.<br>Her bike will **not** be a mess any longer. |

# Adverbs

**An adverb tells more about a verb, an adjective, or another adverb.**

## How Adverbs Work

| | |
|---|---|
| An **adverb** can come before or after a **verb** to tell "how," "where," "when," or "how often." | Josh **walks quickly** to the bus stop. (how) <br><br> He **will travel downtown** on the bus. (where) <br><br> He **will arrive** at school **soon**. (when) <br><br> Josh **never misses** a day of school. (how often) |
| An **adverb** can make an **adjective** or another adverb stronger. | Josh is **really good** at baseball. <br><br> He plays **very well**. |
| Some **adverbs** compare actions. Add **-er** to compare two actions. Add **-est** to compare three or more actions. | Josh **runs fast**. <br><br> Josh runs **faster** than his best friend. <br><br> Josh runs the **fastest** of all the players. |
| A few adverbs have special forms for comparing things. | well $\rightarrow$ better $\rightarrow$ best <br><br> badly $\rightarrow$ worse $\rightarrow$ worst |
| If the adverb ends in **-ly**, use **more**, **most**, **less**, or **least** to compare the actions. | less <br> Josh drops a ball frequently than the other players. |
| When you use **adverbs** to make a comparison with **-er**, **-est**, or with a special form, do not also use **more** or **most**. | Josh jumps ~~more~~ higher than I do. <br><br> He is ~~more~~ better than I am at catching the ball. |
| Make sure to use an **adverb** (not an adjective) to tell about a verb. | well <br> I do not catch ~~good~~ at all. |

## Prepositions

A preposition links a noun or pronoun to other words in a sentence. A preposition is the first word in a prepositional phrase.

### Prepositions

| | |
|---|---|
| Some prepositions tell **where** something is. | above over · under below beneath · beside next to by near · in front of · in back of behind · between · in · out · inside · outside · on · off |
| Some prepositions show **direction**. | up · down · through · across · around · into |
| Some prepositions tell **when something happens**. | **before** lunch · **in** 2003 · **on** September 16 · **during** lunch · **in** September · **at** four o'clock · **after** lunch · **in** the afternoon · **from** noon **to** 3:30 |
| Other prepositions have many uses. | about · among · for · to · against · at · from · with · along · except · of · without |

### Prepositional Phrases

| | |
|---|---|
| A **prepositional phrase** starts with a **preposition** and ends with a **noun** or a **pronoun**. Use prepositional phrases to add information or details to your writing. | At our school, we did many activities for Earth Day. We picked up the trash **along the fence**. Then we planted some flowers **next to it**. |

# Capital Letters

**A word that begins with a capital letter is special in some way.**

## How to Use Capital Letters

**A word that begins with a capital letter is special in some way.**

| | |
|---|---|
| Use a **capital letter** at the beginning of a sentence. | **O**ur class is taking an exciting field trip. **W**e are going to an airplane museum. |
| Always use a capital letter for the pronoun **I**. | My friends and **I** can't wait! |
| Use a capital letter for a person's<br>• first and last name<br>• initials<br>• title | **Matt J**. **K**elly and **Matt R**oss will ride with **D**r. **B**ye. **M**agdalena and I are going with **M**rs. **L**iu. |
| Use a capital letter for the names of<br>• the days of the week and their abbreviations<br>• the twelve months of the year and their abbreviations | We're going the first **S**aturday in **J**anuary. |

**Days of the Week**

| | |
|---|---|
| **S**unday | **S**un. |
| **M**onday | **M**on. |
| **T**uesday | **T**ue. |
| **W**ednesday | **W**ed. |
| **T**hursday | **T**hurs. |
| **F**riday | **F**ri. |
| **S**aturday | **S**at. |

**Months of the Year**

| | |
|---|---|
| **J**anuary | **J**an. |
| **F**ebruary | **F**eb. |
| **M**arch | **M**ar. |
| **A**pril | **A**pr. |
| **M**ay | |
| **J**une | |
| **J**uly | |
| **A**ugust | **A**ug. |
| **S**eptember | **S**ep. |
| **O**ctober | **O**ct. |
| **N**ovember | **N**ov. |
| **D**ecember | **D**ec. |

> These months are not abbreviated.

| | |
|---|---|
| Use a capital letter for each important word in the names of special days and holidays. | That will be after **C**hristmas, **K**wanzaa, and **N**ew **Y**ear's **D**ay.<br><br>**E**arth **D**ay   **F**ourth of **J**uly   **H**anukkah<br>**T**hanksgiving |

# Grammar, Usage, Mechanics, and Spelling *continued*

## Capital Letters, *(continued)*

### More Ways to Use Capital Letters

| Use a capital letter for each important word in the names of | |
|---|---|
| • public places, buildings, and organizations | The **W**ilson **A**irplane **M**useum is in the **V**eterans **M**emorial **H**all. It's in the middle of **V**eterans **P**ark, right next to the **P**iney **W**oods **Z**oo. |
| • streets, cities, and states | The museum is on **F**light **A**venue. It is the biggest airplane museum in **F**lorida. It's the biggest in the whole **U**nited **S**tates! |
| • landforms and bodies of water, continents, and planets and stars | |

| **Landforms and Bodies of Water** | **Continents** | **Planets and Stars** |
|---|---|---|
| **R**ocky **M**ountains | **A**frica | **E**arth |
| **S**ahara **D**esert | **A**ntarctica | **M**ars |
| **G**rand **C**anyon | **A**sia | the **B**ig **D**ipper |
| **P**acific **O**cean | **A**ustralia | the **M**ilky **W**ay |
| **C**olorado **R**iver | **E**urope | |
| **L**ake **E**rie | **S**outh **A**merica | |
| | **N**orth **A**merica | |

| Use a capital letter for the names of countries and adjectives formed from the names of countries. | My friend Magdalena is **C**hilean. She says they don't have a museum like that in **C**hile. |
|---|---|
| Use a capital letter for each important word in the title of a book, a story, a poem, or a movie. | We are reading *First Flight* about the Wright brothers. Magdalena wrote a poem about Amelia Earhart. She called it "**V**anished from the **S**ky." What a great title! |

656

# Punctuation Marks

**Punctuation marks make words and sentences easier to understand.**

 period     question mark     exclamation point     comma     quotation marks     apostrophe

## Period

| | |
|---|---|
| Use a **period** at the end of a statement or a command. | I don't know if I should get a dog or a cat. <br><br> Please help me decide. |
| Also use a **period** when you write a decimal, or to separate dollars from cents. | I saw a cute little dog last week. <br><br> It only weighed 1.3 pounds. <br><br> But it costs $349.99! |
| Use a **period** after an initial in somebody's name, and after most abbreviations. But, don't use a period after state abbreviations. | The salesperson gave me this business card: <br><br> Kitty B. Perry <br><br> **Downtown Pet Sales** <br> **2456 N. Yale Ave.** <br> **Houston, TX 77074** <br><br> **TX is the abbreviation for the state of Texas.** |

## Question Mark

| | |
|---|---|
| Use a **question mark** <br> • at the end of a question <br> • after a question that comes at the end of a statement. | Do you want to go to the pet store with me? <br><br> You can go right now, can't you? |

## Exclamation Point

| | |
|---|---|
| Use an **exclamation point** at the end of a sentence to show strong feelings. | I'm glad you decided to come! <br><br> This is going to be fun! |

## Punctuation, _(continued)_

### Commas  9

| Use a **comma** | |
|---|---|
| • when you write large numbers | There are more than 1,300 pets at this store. |
| • to separate three or more things in the same sentence | Should I get a dog, a cat, or a parrot? |
| • before the words **and**, **but**, or **or** in a compound sentence. | I came to the store last week, and the salesperson showed me some dogs. |
| | She was very helpful, but I couldn't make a decision. |

| Use a **comma** to set off | |
|---|---|
| • short words like **Oh**, **Yes**, and **Well** that begin a sentence | Oh, what a hard decision! |
| | Well, I'd better choose something. |
| • someone's exact words | The salesperson said, "This little dog wants to go with you." |
| | I said, "I like it, but I like those cats, too!" |

| Use a **comma** between two or more adjectives that tell about the same noun. | Do I get a big, furry puppy? |
|---|---|
| | Or do I get a cute, tiny kitten? |

| Use a **comma** in letters | |
|---|---|
| • between the city and state | 177 North Avenue |
| • between the date and the year | New York, NY 10033 |
| • after the greeting in a friendly letter | October 3, 2010 |
| • after the closing | Dear Aunt Mia, |
| | Can you help me? I want a pet, but don't know which is easier to care for, a cat or a dog? I need your advice. |
| | Your niece, |
| | Becca |

## Quotation Marks 66 99

| Use quotation marks | |
|---|---|
| • to show a speaker's exact words | "Ms. Perry, this is the dog for me!" Becca said. |
| • to show the exact words from a book or other printed material | The ad said "friendly puppies" for sale. |
| • the title of a magazine or newspaper article | I saw the idea in the article "Keeping Your Pet Happy." |
| • the title of a chapter from a book. | Now I'm on the chapter "Working Dogs" in my book. |
| Use periods and commas inside quotation marks. | "Many dogs are good with people," Ms. Perry said. "You just have to decide if you want to big dog or a little one." |

> Ms. Perry, this is the dog for me!

## Apostrophes ,

| Use an **apostrophe** when you write a **possessive noun**. | My **neighbor's** dog is huge. The **Smith s'** yard is just big enough for him. |
|---|---|
| Use an **apostrophe** to replace the letter or letters left out in a **contraction.** | **Let's** go back to the pet store. **I'll** look some more for the best pet for me. |

# Picture Dictionary

The definitions are for the words as they are introduced in the selections of this book.

## Pronunciation Key

Say the sample word out loud to hear how to say, or pronounce, the symbol.

### Symbols for Consonant Sounds

| | | | | |
|---|---|---|---|---|
| b | b<u>o</u>x | p | p<u>a</u>n | |
| ch | <u>ch</u>ick | r | <u>r</u>ing | |
| d | <u>d</u>og | s | bu<u>s</u> | |
| f | <u>f</u>ish | sh | fi<u>sh</u> | |
| g | <u>g</u>irl | t | ha<u>t</u> | |
| h | <u>h</u>at | th | Ear<u>th</u> | |
| j | <u>j</u>ar | <u>th</u> | <u>th</u>er | |
| k | ca<u>k</u>e | v | <u>v</u>ase | |
| ks | bo<u>x</u> | w | <u>w</u>indow | |
| kw | <u>qu</u>een | hw | <u>wh</u>ale | |
| l | be<u>ll</u> | y | <u>y</u>arn | |
| m | <u>m</u>ouse | z | <u>z</u>ipper | |
| n | pa<u>n</u> | zh | trea<u>s</u>ure | |
| ng | ri<u>ng</u> | | | |

### Symbols for Short Vowel Sounds

| | |
|---|---|
| a | h<u>a</u>t |
| e | b<u>e</u>ll |
| i | ch<u>i</u>ck |
| o | b<u>o</u>x |
| u | b<u>u</u>s |

### Symbols for Long Vowel Sounds

| | |
|---|---|
| ā | c<u>a</u>ke |
| ē | k<u>ey</u> |
| ī | b<u>i</u>ke |
| ō | g<u>oa</u>t |
| yū | m<u>u</u>le |

### Symbols for R-controlled Sounds

| | |
|---|---|
| ar | b<u>ar</u>n |
| air | ch<u>air</u> |
| ear | <u>ear</u> |
| īr | f<u>ir</u>e |
| or | c<u>or</u>n |
| ur | g<u>ir</u>l |

### Symbols for Variant Vowel Sounds

| | |
|---|---|
| ah | f<u>a</u>ther |
| aw | b<u>a</u>ll |
| oi | b<u>oy</u> |
| oo | b<u>oo</u>k |
| ow | c<u>ow</u> |
| ü | fr<u>ui</u>t |

### Miscellaneous Symbols

| | | |
|---|---|---|
| shun | frac<u>tion</u> | $\frac{1}{2}$ |
| chun | ques<u>tion</u> | ? |
| zhun | divi<u>sion</u> | $2\overline{)100}^{\,50}$ |

## Parts of an Entry

The **entry** shows how the word is spelled.

The **pronunciation** shows you how to say the word and how to break it into syllables.

The **picture** helps you understand more about the meaning of the word.

part of speech

The **definition** gives the meaning of the word.

The **sample sentence** uses the word in a way that shows its meaning.

**magnify**

(mag-nu-fī) *verb*
When you **magnify** something you make it appear larger.

*The butterfly wings are easier to see when you **magnify** them.*

# A

## abolish
(u-**bah**-lish) *verb*
When you officially end something, you **abolish** it.

*The scientist works to **abolish** disease.*

## absorb
(ub-**zorb**) *noun*
When you take something in and hold it, you **absorb** it.

*The sponge **absorbs** the water.*

## access
(**ak**-ses) *noun*
When you have **access** to something, you can get or use it.

*At a library you have **access** to many books.*

## acquire
(u-**kwir**) *verb*
When you **acquire** something, it becomes yours.

*She **acquired** a shirt from her mom.*

## adapt
(u-**dapt**) *verb*
If you **adapt**, you change.

*Visitors to Japan must **adapt** to a new way of eating.*

## advantage
(ud-**van**-tij) *noun*
An **advantage** is something that helps you.

*Being fast is an **advantage** in tennis.*

## affect
(u-**fekt**) *verb*
If something **affects** you, it changes you or your situation.

*The snow can **affect** your plans.*

## alternate
(**awl**-tur-nut) *adjective*
**Alternate** means different.

*They must find an **alternate** location.*

## analyze
(**a**-nu-līz) *verb*
To **analyze** means to examine in detail.

*She **analyzed** the cell under a microscope.*

a
b
c
d
e
f
g
h
i
j
k
l
m
n
o
p
q
r
s
t
u
v
w
x
y
z

# apply

(u-**plī**) *verb*

To **apply** means to ask for or to request something, usually in writing.

*The boy will **apply** for a job.*

# aquifer

(**a**-kwu-fur) *noun*

An **aquifer** is an area of water under the ground.

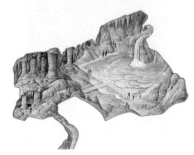

*This **aquifer** holds a lot of water.*

# argument

(**ar**-gyü-munt) *noun*

An **argument** is a reason for a viewpoint.

*There are **arguments** for keeping our streets clean.*

# assume

(u-**süm**) *verb*

When you **assume** something, you think it is true without checking the facts.

*Don't **assume** you know the way. Check your map!*

# atmosphere

(**at**-mu-sfear) *noun*

The **atmosphere** is a mixture of gasses that are all around a planet.

*The sky divers made a circle in the **atmosphere**.*

# availability

(u-vā-lu-**bi**-lu-tē) *noun*

**Availability** means having access.

*The **availability** of books inspired him to read.*

# B

# balance

(**ba**-luns) *noun*

You create **balance** by giving the right amount of importance to different things.

*It is good to have a **balance** of work and play time.*

# barrier

(**ber**-ē-ur) *noun*

A **barrier** prevents you from getting to something.

*The wall was a **barrier** to freedom.*

662

## behavior

(bi-**hā**-vyur) *noun*

**Behavior** is the way a person acts.

*Their bad **behavior** got them in trouble.*

## benefit

(**be**-nu-fit) *noun*

A **benefit** is something that helps.

*Fresh air and exercise are **benefits** of playing soccer.*

## biodegradable

(bī-ō-di-**grād**-du-bul) *adjective*

When things are **biodegradable**, they break down.

*Banana peels are **biodegradable**.*

## boomtown

(**büm**-town) *noun*

A **boomtown** is an area that gets a large increase in money or people.

*When people find gold in an area, a small village can turn into a **boomtown**.*

## borrow

(**bar**-ō) *verb*

When you **borrow** something, you get to use it because someone gives you permission.

*It is fun to **borrow** books from the library.*

## business

(**biz**-nus) *noun*

A **business** is a place that makes, buys, or sells things.

*She sells lotion in her makeup **business**.*

## canal

(ku-**nal**) *noun*

A **canal** is a narrow ditch that is used so water can travel from one area to another.

*Boats use **canals** to travel to the ocean.*

## capacity

(ku-**pa**-su-tē) *noun*

**Capacity** is how much something can hold.

*This bucket has a **capacity** for one gallon of water.*

a
b
c
d
e
f
g
h
i
j
k
l
m
n
o
p
q
r
s
t
u
v
w
x
y
z

a
b
c
d
e
f
g
h
i
j
k
l
m
n
o
p
q
r
s
t
u
v
w
x
y
z

# carnivore
(**kar**-nu-vor) *noun*
A **carnivore** is an animal that eats other animals.

*A lion is a **carnivore**.*

# challenge
(**cha**-lunj) *noun*
A **challenge** is a difficult task or situation.

*Carrying all the books at once is a **challenge**.*

# channel
(**cha**-nul) *verb*
When you **channel** something, you move it from one area to another.

*Farmers use pipes to **channel** water to the field.*

# chlorophyll
(**klor**-u-fil) *noun*
**Chlorophyll** is the green part of plants that lets them use sunlight to help make their food.

***Chlorophyll** is what makes plants look green.*

# circuit
(**sur**-kut) *noun*
A **circuit** is the path that electrical current will flow through.

*When electricity goes through the **circuit**, the light bulb turns on.*

# citizenship
(**si**-tu-zun-ship) *noun*
**Citizenship** is belonging to a country. Citizenship also gives you the rights and duties of that country.

*Her **citizenship** makes her proud and happy.*

# claim
(**klām**) *noun*
A **claim** is something that a person has a legal right to. An area of land was often called a claim.

*Many prospectors found gold on their **claims**.*

# classify
(**kla**-su-fī) *verb*
When you **classify** things, you put them into groups based on their similarities.

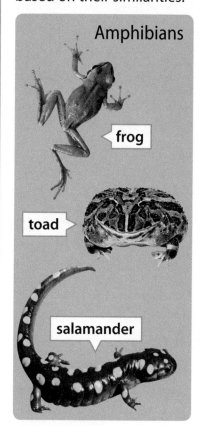

Amphibians

frog

toad

salamander

*You can classify frogs, toads, and salamanders as **amphibians**.*

## climate

(**klī**-mut) *noun*

**Climate** is the type of weather that usually happens in an area.

*Penguins live in a cold* **climate**.

## condensation

(kon-dun-**sā**-shun) *noun*

When water in the air cools down and forms drops, it is called **condensation**.

**Condensation** *will form on windows when it is cold outside.*

## conditions

(kun-**di**-shuns) *noun*

All of the details of a situation are its **conditions**.

*Some people want better working* **conditions**.

## conduct

(kon-**dukt**) *verb*

An object **conducts** sound, heat, or electricity if it lets any of them pass through it.

*Copper wire is used to* **conduct** *electricity.*

## conflict

(**kon**-flikt) *noun*

A **conflict** is a disagreement between people or groups.

*They had a* **conflict** *about responsibilities at home.*

## consequence

(**kon**-su-kwens) *noun*

A **consequence** is the result of an action.

*A flood is a* **consequence** *of heavy rain.*

## conservation

(kon-sur-**vā**-shun) *noun*

When you turn off lights, you are practicing **conservation**. You are using energy carefully.

**Conservation** *is good for the planet.*

## construction

(kun-**struk**-shun) *noun*

**Construction** is the process of building something.

*The house is under* **construction**.

## consumer

(kun-**sü**-mur) *noun*

A **consumer** eats plants or animals. All animals are consumers.

*A horse is a* **consumer** *of grass.*

a
b
c
d
e
f
g
h
i
j
k
l
m
n
o
p
q
r
s
t
u
v
w
x
y
z

a
b
c
d
e
f
g
h
i
j
k
l
m
n
o
p
q
r
s
t
u
v
w
x
y
z

## cooperate

(kō-**ah**-pu-rāt) *verb*

When you **cooperate**, you work together.

*We **cooperated** to clean up the messy room.*

## cost

(**kawst**) *noun*

The **cost** of something is how much you pay to buy it.

*The **cost** of gas changes all the time.*

## country

(**kun**-trē) *noun*

A **country** is an area that has its own laws and government.

*People can travel from one **country** to another.*

## course

(**kors**) *noun*

**A course** is the direction or route something goes in.

*The river's **course** takes it all the way to the ocean.*

## credit

(**kre**-dit) *noun*

If someone uses **credit** to pay for something, it means they will pay for it later.

*She buys the flowers on **credit**.*

## culture

(**kul**-chur) *noun*

**Culture** is the way a group of people live: their ideas, their customs, and their traditions.

*It's part of their culture to **celebrate** Cinco de Mayo.*

## current

(**kur**-unt) *noun*

The **current** is the movement of electricity through a wire.

*If the electric **current** does not reach my TV, I can't turn it on.*

## custom

(**kus**-tum) *noun*

**A custom** is a tradition in a culture or a society.

*It is their **custom** to go see the parade on the 4th of July.*

# D

## debate
(di-**bāt**) *verb*
When you **debate** an idea, you talk about it with someone who has a different opinion.

*The boys **debated** which sport is best.*

## debt
(**det**) *noun*
A **debt** is something you have to pay back.

*She borrowed a dollar, and will pay back the **debt** next week.*

## decrease
(di-**krēs**) *verb*
To **decrease** means to become less or smaller.

*When I spend money, my savings **decrease**.*

## demands
(di-**mands**) *noun*
**Demands** are things people ask for strongly.

*Respect for one and all are her **demands**.*

## demonstrate
(**de**-mun-strāt) *verb*
When you **demonstrate** something, you show or express your feelings or knowledge about it.

*He **demonstrates** his science fair project to the judges.*

## deplete
(di-**plēt**) *verb*
When you **deplete** something, you use it up.

*They **depleted** the forest of trees.*

## determine
(di-**tur**-mun) *verb*
To **determine** is to decide something.

*The doctor **determined** that her patient had the flu.*

## development
(di-**ve**-lup-munt) *noun*
**Development** is growth and progress.

*This is a new **development** in technology.*

a
b
c
d
e
f
g
h
i
j
k
l
m
n
o
p
q
r
s
t
u
v
w
x
y
z

a
b
c
**d**
**e**
f
g
h
i
j
k
l
m
n
o
p
q
r
s
t
u
v
w
x
y
z

## discovery

(dis-**ku**-vu-rē) *noun*

A **discovery** is something new that someone finds.

*This leopard is a new* ***discovery***.

## dispose

(di-**spōz**) *verb*

When you **dispose** of something, you are throwing it away.

*His chore is to* ***dispose*** *of the trash.*

## distinguish

(di-**sting**-gwish) *verb*

**Distinguish** means to tell the difference between two things.

*It's hard to* ***distinguish*** *Chris from his twin Joe.*

## distribution

(dis-tru-**byü**-shun) *noun*

**Distribution** is the way something is divided.

*This shows an equal* ***distribution*** *of pizza.*

## diversity

(du-**vur**-su-tē) *noun*

The **diversity** of a group is how different the members of the group are.

*There is a* ***diversity*** *of students in my class.*

## earnings

(**ur**-nings) *noun*

**Earnings** are the payment someone receives for work.

*She put all her* ***earnings*** *into her piggy bank.*

## economy

(i-**kah**-nu-mē) *noun*

A country's **economy** is its system of business.

*In a good* ***economy***, *people spend more.*

**E**

## education

(e-ju-**kā**-shun) *noun*

An **education** is all the knowledge and skills someone has learned.

*She is proud of her college* ***education***.

## effect

(i-**fekt**) *noun*

An **effect** is the result of something else.

*A runny nose is an* ***effect*** *of a cold.*

## electrical
(i-**lek**-tri-kul) *adjective*
**Electrical** power comes from an electricity source, such as a wall outlet or a battery.

*The toaster will not work if it's not plugged into an **electrical** outlet.*

## emancipation
(i-mɑnt-su-**pā**-shun) *noun*
**Emancipation** is the act of setting a group of people free.

*After their **emancipation**, many enslaved people started new lives.*

## employment
(im-**ploi**-munt) *noun*
**Employment** is work someone does to earn money.

*His **employment** brings in extra money.*

## energy
(**e**-nur-jē) *noun*
**Energy** is the power to do work.

*It takes a lot of **energy** to run a marathon.*

## entrepreneur
(on-tru-pru-**nur**) *noun*
An **entrepreneur** is someone who starts new businesses and is good at making money.

*These **entrepreneurs** started a car-washing service.*

## equality
(i-**kwah**-lu-tē) *noun*
When people have **equality**, they all have the same rights.

***Equality** in sports makes it possible for both men and women to play.*

## escape
(is-**kāp**) *verb*
To **escape** means to get away from a bad situation.

*This dog **escapes** from his bath!*

a
b
c
d
**e**
f
g
h
i
j
k
l
m
n
o
p
q
r
s
t
u
v
w
x
y
z

## essential
(i-**sent**-shul) *adjective*
**Essential** means important or necessary.

*Water is **essential** for our survival.*

## establish
(i-**sta**-blish) *verb*
**Establish** means to put a person or thing in a successful position.

*The win **established** him as captain.*

## ethnic
(**eth**-nik) *adjective*
An **ethnic** group is people who share the same culture or race, or are from the same country.

*The United States is made up of many **ethnic** groups.*

## evaporation
(i-**va**-pu-rā-shun) *noun*
**Evaporation** is when a liquid changes into a gas or steam.

*Evaporation happens when mom makes tea.*

## event
(i-**vent**) *noun*
An **event** is something that happens.

*The street fair is a big **event**.*

## evidence
(**e**-vu-duns) *noun*
You use **evidence** to prove an idea.

*The ball was **evidence** of how the window was broken.*

## expansion
(ik-**span**-shun) *noun*
**Expansion** is when something gets bigger.

*Blowing into a balloon causes its **expansion**.*

## expenses
(ik-**spens**-ez) *noun*
**Expenses** are the money spent on something.

*Her medical **expenses** cost less than she expected.*

## explanation
(ek-splu-**nā**-shun) *noun*
An **explanation** gives a reason or makes something easy to understand.

*The teacher's **explanation** of DNA was helpful.*

670

## explore

(ik-**splor**) *verb*

To **explore** means to look around a new place.

*They found a new river to **explore**.*

**F**

## favorable

(**fā**-vu-ru-bul) *adjective*

Something that is **favorable** is good.

*They had **favorable** weather for the party.*

## food chain

(**füd**-chān) *noun*

A **food chain** is a sequence of plants and animals in which each feeds on the one below it.

*Cats and mice are part of a **food chain**.*

## foreign

(**for**-en) *adjective*

If something is **foreign** to you, it is something you have not seen before or is from another country.

*You can identify some **foreign** money by the images on it.*

## freedom

(**frē**-dum) *noun*

**Freedom** is being able to say, think, and do what you want.

*A bird has the **freedom** to fly.*

## fresh water

(fresh **wah**-tur) *noun*

**Fresh water** is found in lakes and rivers. It contains almost no salt.

*The Great Lakes, which border the U.S. and Canada, are full of **fresh water**.*

## frontier

(frun-**tear**) *noun*

A **frontier** is a new place where few, or no, people live.

*Space is a **frontier** for us to explore.*

## generate

(**je**-nu-rāt) *verb*

When you **generate** something, you make it.

*This family **generates** a lot of trash.*

**G**

## ghost town

(gōst town) *noun*

A **ghost town** is a place no one lives anymore.

*Many places in the West became **ghost towns** after all the gold and silver was gone.*

a
b
c
d
e
f
g
h
i
j
k
l
m
n
o
p
q
r
s
t
u
v
w
x
y
z

671

a b c d e f **g h i** j k l m n o p q r s t u v w x y z

## gold rush
(gōld rush) *noun*
A **gold rush** is when many people hurry to a place that has gold in the soil.

*In 1849 California had a gold rush. People came from all over the world to find gold.*

## goods
(goods) *noun*
**Goods** are things that are bought and sold.

*This market sells many types of goods.*

## gourd
(gord) *noun*
A **gourd** is a fruit with a hard shell that you can use as a container after the fruit is gone.

*He drinks water from a gourd.*

**H**

## heat
(hēt) *noun*
**Heat** is warmth from something that is hot.

*Our cat likes the heat from the fireplace.*

## herbivore
(hur-bu-vor) *noun*
An **herbivore** is an animal that only eats plants.

*A rabbit is an herbivore.*

**I**

## identity
(ī-den-tu-tē) *noun*
Your **identity** makes you who you are.

*Playing music is part of this boy's identity.*

## immigration
(i-mu-grā-shun) *noun*
**Immigration** is when you come to live in a country that is not where you were born.

*The early 1900s was a time of great immigration from Europe to the U.S.*

## income
(in-kum) *noun*
**Income** is money that someone receives on a regular basis.

*Her paycheck shows her weekly income.*

## individual
(in-du-**vi**-ju-wul) *noun*
An **individual** is a person.

*Each **individual** at school is important.*

## influence
(**in**-flü-uns) *verb*
If something **influences** you, it affects you.

*Her kindness **influenced** me to be kind.*

## insulate
(**in**-su-lāt) *verb*
To **insulate** something is to wrap or cover it so that heat, cold, or electricity will not get in or out.

*If you **insulate** your pipes, they won't freeze when it gets cold.*

## investigate
(in-**ves**-tu-gāt) *verb*
When you **investigate** something, you try to find out more about it.

*She **investigates** the insects on the leaf.*

## investor
(in-**ves**-tur) *noun*
An **investor** buys something hoping it will make money.

*She helps people become **investors** in start-up businesses.*

**L**

## labor
(**lā**-bur) *noun*
**Labor** is the hard work someone does.

*A lot of time and **labor** goes into making a chair.*

## landfill
(**land**-fil) *noun*
A **landfill** is a large area where garbage is stacked and then covered over with soil.

*Bulldozers are used to move the garbage around in **landfills**.*

## law
(law) *noun*
A **law** is a government's official rule.

*The police remind people to follow the **law**.*

a
b
c
d
e
f
g
h
i
j
k
**l**
**m**
**n**
o
p
q
r
s
t
u
v
w
x
y
z

## limited resources
(lĭ-mu-tud rē-**sors**-ez) *noun*
**Limited resources** are things people need and use that are in very short supply.

*Clean drinking water is a **limited resource**.*

## loan
(lōn) *noun*
A **loan** is money that you borrow from someone else, or from a bank, and that you must repay.

*Because of his good credit score, he got a **loan**.*

### M

## magnify
(**mag**-nu-fī) *verb*
When you **magnify** something you make it appear larger.

*The butterfly wings are easier to see when you **magnify** them.*

## microscope
(**mī**-kru-skōp) *noun*
A **microscope** is something that lets you see very small things by magnifying them, or making them look larger.

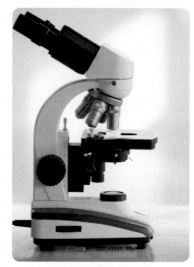

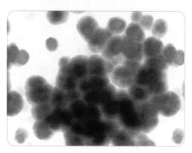

*You can see red blood cells with a **microscope**.*

## mining
(**mī**-ning) *noun*
**Mining** is digging for coal, or other precious things such as diamonds, silver, or gold.

*Coal **mining** is hard and dangerous work.*

### N

## nonviolence
(non-**vī**-u-luns) *noun*
**Nonviolence** is to not use force.

*These people believe in **nonviolence**. Their protest is peaceful.*

## nutrients
(nü-**trē**-untz) *noun*
**Nutrients** are things found in food that help plants, animals, and people to survive.

*The **nutrients** in fruit and vegetables help people stay healthy.*

## observe
(ub-**zurv**) *verb*
**Observe** means to watch someone or something closely.

*He **observes** birds in the trees.*

## obstacle
(**ob**-sti-kul) *noun*
An **obstacle** is something that stops you from succeeding.

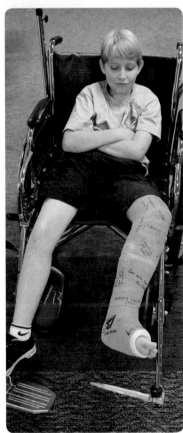

*A broken leg is an **obstacle** to playing soccer.*

## omnivore
(**om**-ni-vor) *noun*
An **omnivore** is an animal that eats both plants and meat.

*Bears are **omnivores**.*

## opportunity
(ah-pur-**tü**-nu-tē) *noun*
An **opportunity** is a good chance to do something.

*There is a job **opportunity** here.*

## oppose
(u-**pōz**) *verb*
**Oppose** means to disagree with an idea or action.

*They protested to **oppose** the government's decision.*

## organization
(or-gu-nu-**zā**-shun) *noun*
An **organization** is a business or other official group.

*This **organization** helps lost pets.*

## origin
(**or**-u-jun) *noun*
An **origin** is the beginning of something or where something came from.

*The **origin** of chocolate is the cacao bean.*

a b c d e f g h i j k l m n o p q r s t u v w x y z

# P

## partnership
(part-nur-ship) *noun*
Individuals in a **partnership** work together and share the results of their work.

*The kids formed a **partnership** to sell cookies and lemonade.*

## photosynthesis
(fō-tō-**sin**-thu-sus) *noun*
**Photosynthesis** is the process that plants use to make their food.

*A scientist grows plants to study **photosynthesis**.*

## plantation
(plan-**tā**-shun) *noun*
A **plantation** is a large farm, usually in a hot place, which grows crops such as coffee, cotton, or sugar.

*This tea **plantation** is in Japan.*

## plastic
(**plas**-tik) *noun*
**Plastic** is a synthetic, or human-made material, which is light weight. It is used for making many things.

*The toy duck is made of **plastic**.*

## pollution
(pu-**lü**-shun) *noun*
**Pollution** is harmful substances that hurt the air, water, and soil.

*Car exhaust causes air **pollution**.*

## population
(pah-pyü-**lā**-shun) *noun*
A **population** is the number of people living in an area.

*This city's **population** is large.*

## power
(**pow**-ur) *noun*
**Power** is strength and energy.

*This machine has the **power** to lift heavy things.*

676

## precipitation
(pri-si-pu-**tā**-shun) *noun*
**Precipitation** is rain, sleet, snow, or hail.

*When there is **precipitation**, it's good to take an umbrella.*

## producer
(pru-**dü**-sur) *noun*
A **producer** makes things.

*This bush is a **producer** of blueberries.*

## profit
(**prah**-fut) *noun*
**Profit** is when someone sells something for more than it cost to buy or make.

*Our house sold for a large **profit**.*

## propose
(pru-**pōz**) *verb*
**Propose** means to suggest something, such as an action.

*He **proposes** that his mom buy the blue shirt.*

## protest
(prō-**test**) *verb*
When you **protest,** you show that you do not like or agree with something.

*She **protests** that the paper was due the day before.*

**R**

## ranching
(**ranch**-ing) *noun*
**Ranching** is the business of raising animals on a ranch to be sold for their meat.

***Ranching** is hard work.*

## recycle
(rē-**sī**-kul) *verb*
When something is **recycled** it goes through a process that breaks it down into parts that can be used again.

*These cans were made from **recycled** aluminum.*

## reduce
(ri-**düs**) *verb*
**Reduce** means to make something smaller or to use less of something.

*Our family tries to **reduce** the amount of trash we make.*

a b c d e f g h i j k l m n o p q r s t u v w x y z

a
b
c
d
e
f
g
h
i
j
k
l
m
n
o
p
q
**r**
s
t
u
v
w
x
y
z

## reflect

(ri-**flekt**) *verb*

When light hits a mirror, it **reflects** the image, so you can see it.

*When a mirror **reflects** an image, the image is reversed.*

## refuge

(**re**-fyüj) *noun*

A **refuge** is a place where people go to be safe or to find shelter.

*These people found **refuge** from the rain.*

## region

(**rē**-jun) *noun*

A **region** is a large area or part of a place.

*Oregon is in the Northwest **region** of the United States.*

## rely

(ri-**lī**) *verb*

If you **rely** on something, you need it.

*We **rely** on electricity in our home.*

## renewable

(ri-**nü**-u-bul) *adjective*

Something is **renewable** when you can't use up all of it.

*Wind is a **renewable** resource.*

## require

(ri-**kwīr**) *verb*

**Require** means to need.

*A plant **requires** sunlight to survive.*

# reservation
(re-zur-**vā**-shun) *noun*
**Reservations** are places Native Americans were moved to in the 1800s.

*These Minionjou Sioux Native Americans are camping in tipis on a reservation in South Dakota.*

# responsibility
(ri-spon-su-**bi**-lu-tē) *noun*
A **responsibility** is something you should do.

*It is my responsibility to walk the dog.*

# reuse
(rē-**yüz**) *verb*
When you **reuse** something you use it again instead of throwing it into the trash.

*We reused this egg carton to sprout seeds.*

# risk
(**risk**) *verb*
When you **risk** something, you are in danger of losing or harming it.

*If she does not wear a helmet, she risks hurting herself.*

# route
(**rüt**) *noun*
A **route** is a path to go someplace.

*Do you take the shortest route to school?*

# runoff
(**run**-of) *noun*
**Runoff** is water that starts as rain or snow on land, and ends up going into the ocean.

*When ice melts, the runoff flows into the sea.*

**S**

# scarcity
(**skair**-su-tē) *noun*
If there is a **scarcity** of something, there is not enough of it.

*There's a scarcity of water here.*

# services
(**sur**-vu-sez) *noun*
A **service** is work someone does for money, such as delivering mail.

*Delivering the mail is a service.*

a b c d e f g h i j k l m n o p q r s t u v w x y z

a
b
c
d
e
f
g
h
i
j
k
l
m
n
o
p
q
r
**s**
t
u
v
w
x
y
z

# settler
(**set**-lur) *noun*
A **settler** is someone who moves to a new area to live.

*These pioneers were* **settlers** *in the western United States.*

# shortage
(**shor**-tij) *noun*
**Shortage** is when you don't have enough.

*In a water* **shortage**, *the grass turns dry and brown.*

# slavery
(**slā**-vu-rē) *noun*
**Slavery** is when one person owns another person.

*Slavery was abolished in the United States by an amendment to our Constitution.*

# society
(su-**sī**-u-tē) *noun*
A **society** is a group of people who share rules and customs.

*Our* **society** *has safety rules.*

# solar
(**sō**-lur) *adjective*
**Solar** is something that comes from the sun.

solar panels

*Solar power heats and cools this home.*

# solution
(su-**lü**-shun) *noun*
A **solution** is something that solves a problem.

*Reading is a good* **solution** *for boredom.*

# specialize
(**spe**-shu-līz) *verb*
To **specialize** is to learn or know a lot about one thing.

*He* **specializes** *in fixing bicycles.*

## speculate
(**spe**-kyu-lāt) *verb*
When you **speculate**, you make a guess.

*They **speculate** that people will buy lemonade.*

## store
(**stor**) *verb*
When you **store** something, you keep it somewhere until it is needed.

*They **store** their stuffed bunny with the towels.*

## strike
(**strīk**) *noun*
When people **strike,** they don't work because they do not agree with the boss or the company they work for.

*These people are on **strike**.*

## supply
(su-**plī**) *verb*
To **supply** means to provide things people need.

*Farms **supply** us with vegetables, such as lettuce.*

## symbol
(**sim**-bul) *noun*
A **symbol** is something that stands for something else.

*A heart shape is a **symbol** for love.*

## theory
(**thear**-ē) *noun*
A **theory** is an idea that explains something.

*Her **theory** is that the dog did it.*

## thermal
(**thur**-mul) *adjective*
Something is called **thermal** when it is hot.

*The water sprays out of this geyser because of the **thermal** energy in Earth. The water is very hot!*

a
b
c
d
e
f
g
h
i
j
k
l
m
n
o
p
q
r
s
t
u
v
w
x
y
z

**681**

# transfer

(trans-**fur**) *verb*
**Transfer** means to move from one place to another.

*She **transfers** the food to the plate.*

# transform

(**trans**-form) *verb*
To **transform** something means to change it.

*The old cans were **transformed** into new cans.*

# transition

(tran-**si**-shun) *noun*
A **transition** is a change from one situation to another.

*Moving to a new home is a big **transition**.*

# translate

(trans-**lāt**) *verb*
When you **translate**, you change words and ideas from one language to another.

*Do you speak sign language, or do you need someone to **translate** for you?*

# transmit

(tranz-**mit**) *verb*
To **transmit** something means to move it from one place or person to another.

*When we use the phone, my voice **transmits** to my friend's ear.*

v

# value

(**val**-yü) *noun*
The **value** of something is its cost or how important it is.

*This jewelry has a high **value**.*

# volt

(vōlt) *noun*

**Volts** are used to measure the force of electrical currents, and the amount of power stored in a battery.

*This battery stores 9 **volts** of power.*

## water cycle

(waw-tur sī-kul) *noun*

The **water cycle** is the process by which Earth's water changes form and is reused again and again.

*You can study one part of the **water cycle**, by watching a puddle dry up on a sunny day.*

# watershed

(waw-tur **shed**) *noun*

A **watershed** is a region of land where the precipitation drains into a lake or river.

*This beautiful waterfall is part of a **watershed** that will drain into a larger river.*

## watt

(**wot**) *noun*

A **watt** is a unit for measuring electrical power.

*A light bulb with more **watts** has more power, so it shines brighter.*

# Handwriting

It's important to use your best **penmanship**, or handwriting.
That way your audience will be able to read what you write.

## Handwriting Hints

You can **print** your words or write in **cursive**.

## Cursive

Cursive is good to use for longer pieces, such as letters or stories,
because you can write faster. You don't have to lift your pencil
between letters. Also, cursive writing gives your finished pieces a
polished look. When you write in cursive, hold the pencil and paper
this way.

Left-handed                          Right-handed

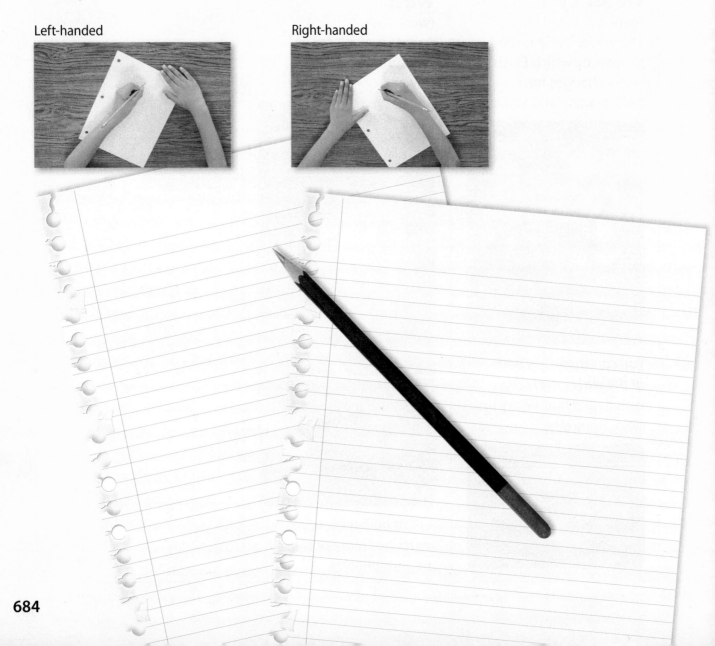

# Cursive Alphabet

## Capital Letters

## Lowercase Letters

## Writing Cursive Letters

Be careful not to make these common mistakes when you write in **cursive**.

| MISTAKE | NOT OK | OK | IN A WORD |
|---|---|---|---|
| The **a** looks like a **u**. | *u* | *a* | *again* |
| The **d** looks like a **c** and an **l**. | *d* | *d* | *dad* |
| The **e** is too narrow. | *e* | *e* | *eagle* |
| The **h** looks like an **l** and an **i**. | *h* | *h* | *high* |
| The **i** has no dot. | *ı* | *i* | *inside* |
| The **n** looks like a **w**. | *w* | *n* | *none* |
| The **o** looks like an **a**. | *a* | *o* | *onion* |
| The **r** looks like an **i** with no dot. | *ı* | *r* | *roar* |
| The **t** is not crossed. | *l* | *t* | *title* |
| The **t** is crossed too high. | *T* | *t* | *that* |

# Writing Words and Sentences

- Slant your letters all the same way.

NOT OK

*My Chinese-language class today was interesting.*

OK

*My Chinese-language class today was interesting.*

- Put the right amount of space between words.

NOT OK

*I learned how togreet    adults.*

OK

*I learned how to greet adults.*

- Write smoothly. Do not press too hard or too lightly.

NOT OK

*I practiced on my teacher. He was impressed.*

OK

*I practiced on my teacher. He was impressed.*

# Index

# E

**Earth science**
  saving energy  463
  waste  465–491
  recycling  465–491, 485–491
**Economics**
  entrepreneurs  561–565,
    595–601
  starting a business  541–557
**Ecosystems and their food chains**
  desert  177–181
  ocean  191–205, 209–213
**Explain**  17, 29, 133, 171, 251,
  329, 345, 393, 395, 489, 599
  *see also Speaking*

# F

**Facts**
  identifying  324
  interpreting from
    graphics  125, 129, 181,
    201, 211, 213, 311, 313
  verifying  **112**, 134
**Fiction**, elements of  **570**, **593**
**Figurative language**
  *see Imagery*
**Fluency**  27, **61**, **101**, **135**, **175**,
  **207**, **247**, **279**, **325**, **359**, **403**,
  **439**, **483**, **519**, **559**, **593**
**Foreshadowing  288**

# G

**Generalizations**
  *see Synthesize*
**Genres**
  advertisement  482, 558
  article  137, 249, 281, 327,
    370, 384, 402, 464, 482,
    492, 561, 566
  autobiography  **44**, 60
  blog  9, 116, 117, **118**, 134
  biography  **262**, 278, 279
  cartoon  260, 498
  description  99, 517

diary  25, 26, 36
documentary  **63**, 75
editorial  261, 530
e-mail  499
essay  148, **405**, **485**, 492,
  592
friendly letter  402
history article  **249**, **384**, 402
how-to article  **137**
interview  43, 189, **190**, 206,
  214, **216**
journal  25, 26, 74, 374
legend  **361**
magazine article  370, **595**
myth  70, **84**, 98, 100, 102,
  103, 110, **144**
narrative poem  **441**, 448,
  **450**
newspaper article  **561**, 566
oral history  **29**, 36
personal narrative  **70**, 157,
  229, 305, 419
persuasive article  **464**, 482
persuasive essay  463, **526**
play  **420**, 437, 438, 448
poetry  358, 441, 443, **521**,
  523
procedural text  **540**, 558,
  566, 604
realistic fiction  **158**, 174,
  **340**, 358
report  323, 339
research report  **290**
science article  **209**, 214, **327**
science feature  **306**, 324
science fiction  83, 383
short story  **500**, 518
story  **10**, **152**, 245, 573
social studies article  **281**
speech  539
tale  **230**, 246
thank-you letter  246
**Glossary** *(picture dictionary)*  660–691
**Goal and outcome  114, 121,**
  131, 133, **135, 496,** 503, 513,
  **519,** 604

**Grammar**
  adjectives  **333, 369,** *646, 647*
  adverbs  **493,** *653*
  articles  *642*
  capitalization  *655, 656*
  clauses
    condensing  *638*
    dependent  *638*
    independent  *638*
  compound subject  **69**
  conjunctions  73, 143, *638*
  nouns  37, **69,** 73, **183, 215,**
    **369,** *639, 640, 641, 643*
  prepositions  **525,** *654*
  pronouns  **413, 449,** *643,*
    *644, 645*
  punctuation
    apostrophes  369, *643, 659*
    commas  147, *638, 658*
    end-of-sentence marks  37
    exclamation point  *657*
    periods  *657*
    question marks  *657*
    quotation marks  *659*
  sentences  **37, 111, 143,** *636,*
    *637, 638*
  verbs  **69, 255, 289, 567,**
    **603,** *648, 649, 650, 651,*
    *652*
**Graphic organizers**
  author's purpose chart  **412,**
    **492**
  author's viewpoint
    chart  **460, 483,** 527
  cause-and-effect chain  **416,**
    **439**
  cause-and-effect
    organizer  **380, 403,** 451
  character chart  **6, 27, 80,**
    101, 145, 336, **359**
  cluster  *627*
  comparison chart  68, 110,
    142, 214, 254, 288, **332,**
    368, **448,** 566, 602
  concept map  74, 220, 296,
    374, 454, 530, 608
  diagram  113, 153, 185, 301

ask questions 7, 81, 497, 537

expanded meaning map 115, 259, 381

role-play 227

study cards 417

use what you know *614*

vocabulary example chart 155, 303, 571

word families *614*

word map 337, 461

word webs 41, 360

**Water**

Earth's water supply 307–322

water shortages 305, 339

wetlands 327–331

**Word origins**

*see Roots*

**Writing**

paragraphs 60, 75, 100, 174, 206, 220, 247, 518

sentences 6, 26, 37, 69, 81, 83, 111, 116, 134, 143, 146, 147, 183, 215, 255, 278, 279, 289, 323, 324, 333, 356, 369, 377, 413, 449, 455, 482, 493, 497, 519, 525, 558, 567, 591, 602

*see also Writing forms*

**Writing forms**

advertisement 482, 558

autobiography 60

biography 278

blog 134

caption 75, 221, 279, 519

chant 27, 149

description 99, 403, 454, 517

dialogue 437, 438

diary entry 25, 74

e-mail 75

editorial 530

essay 148, 592

friendly letter 75, 149, 402

interview **216**

introduction 297

jokes 455

journal 374

labels 439

legend 375

letter 75, 149, 246, 402

list 75, 77, 455, 457, 533

magazine article **370**, 608

myth **100**, **144**

narrative poem **450**

ode 221

personal narrative **70**, 419

persuasive article 482

persuasive essay **526**

play 437, 438

poem 61, 207, 221, 325, 358, 531

poster 296, 375, 483

procedural text 558, **604**, 609

realistic fiction 174

report 323

research report **290–291**

science feature 324

song 27, 149, 359

story 245

thank-you letter 246

tip 324

*see also Research report*

**Writing process**

drafting **71**, **145**, **217**, **294**, **371**, **451**, **527**, **605**, *628*

editing **73**, **147**, **219**, **295**, **373**, **453**, **529**, **607**, *630*

revising **72**, **146**, **217**, **295**, **372**, **452**, **528**, **606**, *629*

prewrite

planning **71**, **145**, **217**, **292**, **294**, **371**, **451**, **527**, **605**, *622*

organizing **71**, **145**, **217**, **294**, **371**, **451**, **527**, **605**, *622*

publishing **73**, **147**, **219**, **295**, **373**, **453**, **529**, **607**, *631*

**Writing traits**

conventions *635*

*see also Conventions, in writing*

fluency *635*

ideas *632*

organization *633*

voice *634*

word choice *634*

## Index of Authors

## Index of Illustrators

## Index of Photographers

# Acknowledgments, continued

## Text Credits

### Unit One

**Children's Book Press:** Excerpt from *My Diary from Here to There.* Copyright © 2002 by Amada Irma Perez. Illustrations © 2002 by Maya Christina Gonzales. Reprinted with permission of the publisher, Children's Book Press, San Francisco, Calif., www.childrensbookpress.org.

**Penguin Group (USA) Inc.:** Excerpt from *I Was Dreaming to Come to America* by Veronica Lawlor, copyright © 1995 by Veronica Lawlor. Used by permission of Viking Penguin, a division of Penguin Young Readers Group, a member of Penguin Group (USA) Inc., 345 Hudson Street, New York, NY 10014. All Rights reserved.

**Castle Works, Inc.:** Excerpt from "Teen Immigrants: 5 Stories," episode 430. Copyright © 1999 by Castle Works, Inc. For more information, to see video clips, or access a free discussion guide and resources see www. inthemix.org. Episodes are available in VHS and DVD with performance rights. Reprinted by permission of Castle Works, Inc.

**National Geographic Books:** "A Refugee Remembers: The Autobiography of John Bul Dau" from *God Grew Tired of Us* by John Bul Dau with Mike Sweeney. Copyright © 2007 John Bul Dau. Reprinted by permission of the National Geographic Society. All rights reserved.

### Unit Two

**Holiday House, Inc.:** Excerpt from *Ten Suns: A Chinese Legend* by Eric A. Kimmel. Copyright © 1998 by Eric A. Kimmel. Reprinted by permission of Holiday House, Inc.

### Unit Three

**Boyd Mills Press:** Excerpt from *Coyote and Badger: Desert Hunters of the Southwest* by Bruce Hiscock. Text and photographs copyright © 2001 by Bruce Hiscock. Published by Caroline House, an imprint of Boyd Mills Press, Inc. Reprinted with the permission of Boyd Mills Press, Inc.

**Tilbury House Publishers:** "Phyto-power!" from *Sea Soup: Phytoplankton* by Mary M. Cerullo. Copyright © 1999 by Mary M. Cerullo. Reprinted by permission of Tilbury House, Publishers.

### Unit Four

**Cinco Puntos Press:** Excerpt from *Crossing Bok Chitto* by Tim Tingle. Copyright © 2006 by Tim Tingle. Illustrations © 2006 by Jeanne Rorex Bridges. Used with permission of Cinco Puntos Press, www. cincopuntos.com. All rights reserved.

**Houghton Mifflin Harcourt:** Excerpt from *Harvesting Hope: The Story of Cesar Chavez* by Kathleen Krull, illustrated by Yuri Morales. Text copyright © 2003 by Kathleen Krull. Illustrations © 2003 by Yuri Morales. Used by permission of Houghton Mifflin Harcourt Publishing Company. All rights reserved.

### Unit Five

**Kids Can Press:** Excerpt from *One Well: The Story of Water on Earth* by Rochelle Strauss. Text copyright © 2007 by Rochelle Strauss. Reprinted by permission of Kids Can Press Ltd., Toronto.

**Curtis Brown, Ltd. and Walter Lyon Krudop:** "My Great Grandmother's Gourd" by Christina Kessler, illustrated by Walter Lyon Krudop. Text copyright © 2000 by Christina Kessler. Illustrations © 2000 by Walter Lyon Krudop. Reprinted by permission. All rights reserved.

**University of New Mexico Press:** Excerpt from *Juan the Bear and the Water of Life/La Acequia de Juan del Oso* by Enrique R. Lamadrid and Juan Estevan Arellano. Copyright © 2008 by the University of New Mexico Press. Used by permission of University of New Mexico Press. All rights reserved.

### Unit Six

**Houghton Mifflin Harcourt:** Excerpted from *Rhyolite: The True Story of a Ghost Town* by Diane Siebert. Text copyright © 2003 by Diane Siebert. Used by permission of Clarion Books, an imprint of Houghton Mifflin Harcourt Publishing Company. All rights reserved.

### Unit Seven

**Cooper Square Publishing:** "The World of Waste" adapted from *Planet Patrol: A Kids Action Guide to Earth Care* by Marybeth Lorbiecki. Copyright © 2005 by Two Can Publishing. Used by permission of Cooper Square Publishing, Lanham, Maryland.

**HarperCollins Publishers:** "Sarah Cynthia Silvia Stout Would Not Take the Garbage Out," from *Where the Sidewalk Ends: the poems and drawings of Shel Silverstein* by Shel Silverstein. Copyright © 1974, renewed 2002 by EVIL EYE, LLC. Reprinted with permission from the Estate of Shel Silverstein and HarperCollins Children's Books. Used by permission of HarperCollins Publishers.

### Unit Eight

**Lerner Publishing Group, Inc.:** Excerpt from *The Kids' Business Book* by Arlene Erlbach. Copyright © 1998 by Arlene Erlbach. Reprinted with the permission of Lerner Publications Company, a division of Lerner Publishing Group, Inc. All rights reserved. No part of this excerpt may be used or reproduced in any manner whatsoever without the prior written permission of Lerner Publishing Group, Inc.

**The Missoulian:** "Braille Menus" adapted from "Blind Teen Starts Creating Braille Menus" by Jane Rider from the *Missoulian*, June 16, 2009. Copyright © 2004 by the Missoulian (www.missoulian.com), Missoula, Montana. Reprinted by permission.

**Kids Can Press:** Material from *One Hen: How One Small Loan Made a Big Difference* by Katie Smith Millway. Text © 2008 Katie Smith Millway. Illustrations © 2008 by Eugenie Fernandes. Reprinted by permission of Kids Can Press Ltd., Toronto.

☐ **NATIONAL GEOGRAPHIC SCHOOL PUBLISHING**

National Geographic School Publishing gratefully acknowledges the contributions of the following National Geographic Explorers to our program and to our planet:

John Bul Dau, 2007 National Geographic Emerging Explorer
Thomas Culhane, 2009 National Geographic Emerging Explorer
Tierny Thys, 2004 National Geographic Emerging Explorer
Roshini Thinkaran, 2007 National Geographic Emerging Explorer
Maycira Costa, National Geographic grantee
William Allard, National Geographic Contributing Photographer
David de Rothschild, 2007 National Geographic Emerging Explorer
Hammerskjoeld Simwinga, 2008 National Geographic Emerging Explorer

## Photographic Credits

iv (tl) Malcolm Linton/Getty Images. v (tc) Michael Melford/National Geographic Image Collection. vi (tl) Paul Zahl/National Geographic Image Collection. vii (tl) Prints & Photographs Division, Library of Congress, LC-USZ62-75334 DLC. viii (tc) Nat Photos/White/Photolibrary. ix (tl) William Albert Allard/National Geographic Image Collection. x (tc) Emma Peios/Alamy Images. xi (tc) Hosea Jemba/Mill Valley Film Group. 2-3 Joel Sartore/National Geographic Image Collection. 5 (bl) Alejandro Rivera/iStockphoto. (br) Comstock/Jupiterimages. (t) Tom Bible/Alamy Images. (tl) Volina/Shutterstock. (tr) Eric Fowke/PhotoEdit. 7 (bl) Kablonk! RF/Golden Pixels LLC/Alamy Images. (br) Robin Sachs/PhotoEdit. (tc) G. Palmer/Alamy Images. (tl) Lars Klove/Getty Images. (tr) ckaeseberg/Shutterstock. 9 (l, r) sunnyfrog/Shutterstock. 13 (b) Thomas Culhane. 18 luchschen/Shutterstock. 19 (l) Kevin Atkinson/Alamy Images. (r) Andrea Skjold/Shutterstock. 25 Children's Book Press. 30 LL/Roger-Viollet/The Image Works, Inc. 39 (bc) Nir Darom/Shutterstock. (bl) Artville. (br) Quang Ho/Shutterstock. (tl) Alessandro Oliva/iStockphoto. (tr) Jeff Greenberg/PhotoEdit. 41 (bl) Thomas Northcut/Getty Images. (br) David Muscroft/Alamy Images. (tc) Relaximages/Alamy Images. (tl) Robert Harding Picture Library/SuperStock. (tr) Yellow Dog Productions/Getty Images. 42 20th Century Fox Film Corp. All rights reserved/courtesy Everett Collection. 45 Malcolm Linton/Getty Images. 46 Eli Reed/Magnum Photos. 47 John Bul Dau. 48 Helene Rogers/Alamy Images. 49 Sarah El Deeb/AP Images. 50 Wendy Stone/Corbis. 51 Derek Hudson/Sygma/Corbis. 52 Joachim Ladefoged/VII Photo Agency. 53 Eli Reed/Magnum Photos. 54 John Bul Dau. 55 (bg) Jorn Stjerneklar/Impact/HIP/The Image Works, Inc. (inset) Judith Collins/Alamy Images. 56 (l) edfuentesg/iStockphoto. (r) Comstock Images/Jupiterimages. 57 Joachim Ladefoged/VII Photo Agency. 58 (l, r) John Bul Dau. 59 Becky Hale/Hampton-Brown/National Geographic School Publishing. 60 Joachim Ladefoged/VII Photo Agency. 63 (l, r, cl, cr) CastleWorks Inc. 64 CastleWorks Inc. 65 CastleWorks Inc. 66 CastleWorks Inc. 67 (b) Distinctive Images/Shutterstock. (t) CastleWorks Inc. 69 CastleWorks Inc. 70 (b) mediablitzimages (uk) Limited/Alamy Images. (t) Heather Lewis/Shutterstock. 73 Keren Su/Danita Delimont Stock Photography. 74 (bl) pockygallery/Shutterstock. (br) PhotosIndia.com LLC/Alamy Images. (t) Joel Sartore/National Geographic Image Collection. 75 (bc) DigitalStock/Corbis. (br) PhotoDisc/Getty Images. (cr) Regisser/Shutterstock. (tl) Susan Law Cain/Shutterstock. (tr) Knorre/Shutterstock. 76-77 Bill Brooks/Alamy Images. 77 Liz Garza Williams/Hampton-Brown/National Geographic School Publishing. 81 (bl) Creatas/Photolibrary. (br) Radius Images/Alamy Images. (tc) Don Tran/Shutterstock. (tl) STOCK4B/Getty Images. (tr) Banana Stock/Photolibrary. 84 (t)(ct)(cb) Bruce Hiscock. 96 Ingram Publishing/Alamy Images. 99 Michael Wilhelm/Eric Kimmel. 102 Albachiaraa/Shutterstock. 104 Wolf Avni/National Geographic Image Collection. 115 (bl) David L. Moore - Healthcare/Alamy Images. (br) laughingmango/iStockphoto. (tc) White Packert/Getty Images. (tl) neal and molly jansen/Alamy Images. (tr) rixxo/Shutterstock. 118-119 (bg) Michael Melford/National Geographic Image Collection. 120 (b) Thomas Culhane. (t) efiplus/Shutterstock. 121 Thomas Culhane. 123 (b) Tatiana Popova/Shutterstock. (t) Serg64/Shutterstock. 124 acilo/iStockphoto. 126 (b) Thomas Culhane. (t) Robert Harbison / © 2001 The Christian Science Monitor (www.CSMonitor.com)/Christian Science Monitor Publishing Society. 131 (t, c, b) Thomas Culhane. 132 (t, b) Thomas Culhane. 133 (c, t) Thomas Culhane. 134 Thomas Culhane. 136 Albachiaraa/Shutterstock. 137 (b) Randy Montoya/Sandia National Laboratories. (t) Mark Thiessen/Hampton-Brown/National Geographic School Publishing. 138 Mark Thiessen/Hampton-Brown/National Geographic School Publishing. 139 (tl, tr, bl, br) Mark Thiessen/Hampton-Brown/National Geographic School Publishing. 140 (bl, br, tr) Mark Thiessen/Hampton-Brown/National Geographic School Publishing. 141 (b, tl, tr) Mark Thiessen/Hampton-Brown/National Geographic School Publishing. 148 (bl, br, inset) Dino O./Shutterstock. (t) Bill Brooks/Alamy Images. 149 (l) Hampton-Brown/National Geographic School Publishing. (r) Pavel K/Shutterstock. 150-151 fotoIE/iStockphoto. 153 (b) Creatas/Jupiterimages. (cb) FloridaStock/Shutterstock. (ct) Frank Leung/iStockphoto. (t) DigitalStock/Corbis. 155 (bl) Summer Jones/Alamy Images. (br) Michael Newman/PhotoEdit. (tc) Elena Elisseeva/Shutterstock. (tl) Oote Boe Photography 3/Alamy Images. (tr) Richard Hutchings/PhotoEdit. 157 Hannamariah/Shutterstock. 172 (l) Norbert Rosing/National Geographic Image Collection. (r) Konrad Wothe/Minden Pictures. 173 (b, r) Bruce Hiscock. 177 (bg) Stephen Sharnoff/National Geographic Image Collection. (c) Wolfgang Bayer/Photoshot. (l) Bill Florence/Shutterstock.

**69**

## Illustrator Credits